LINCOLN
and the
JEWS

ABRAHAM LINCOLN

WITH MALICE TOWARD NONE WITH CHARITY FOR ALL

LINCOLN
and the
JEWS

A HISTORY

JONATHAN D. SARNA
and BENJAMIN SHAPELL

THOMAS DUNNE BOOKS
ST. MARTIN'S PRESS ❦ NEW YORK

FRONTISPIECE: *On October 3, 1861, Abraham Lincoln asked his Secretary of State to see Polish-born Jewish lithographer Max Rosenthal. In 1908, Rosenthal etched this portrait of Lincoln based on an 1860 photograph of Lincoln.*

THOMAS DUNNE BOOKS.
An imprint of St. Martin's Press.

www.thomasdunnebooks.com
www.stmartins.com

Book design by Jason Snyder
"Lincoln's Jewish Connections" infographic by Pure+Applied

Library of Congress Cataloging-in-Publication Data

Sarna, Jonathan D.
  Lincoln and the Jews : a history / by Jonathan D. Sarna and Benjamin Shapell. — First edition.
      pages cm
  Includes bibliographical references and index.
  ISBN 978-1-250-05953-6 (hardcover)
  ISBN 978-1-4668-6461-0 (e-book)
  1. Lincoln, Abraham, 1809-1865—Relations with Jews. 2. Jews—United States—History—19th century.
  3. United States—History—Civil War, 1861-1865—Jews. I. Shapell, Benjamin. II. Title.
  E457.2.S327 2015
  973.70892'4--dc23

                              2014033453

Thomas Dunne books may be purchased for educational, business, or promotional use.
For information on bulk purchases, please contact the Macmillan Corporate and Premium Sales Department
at 1-800-221-7945, extension 5442, or write to specialmarkets@macmillan.com.

First Edition: March 2015

10 9 8 7 6 5 4 3 2 1

To my wonderful parents, David and Fela Shapell,
who made this book possible.

Benjamin Shapell

CONTENTS

Urbana, Oct. 21. 1856

A. Jonas, Esq
    My dear Sir:

      I am here at court, and find myself so "hobbled" with a particular case, that I can not leave, & consequently, can not be with you on the 23rd. I regret this exceedingly, but there is no help for it. Please make the best apology for me, in your power—

        Your friend as ever

          A. Lincoln—

FOREWORD

In the field of manuscript collecting, documents are traditionally prized for statements of grand historical fact. While I deeply appreciate those historic letters, I have always, however, been fascinated by the "other" letters of U.S. presidents; letters with an interesting turn of phrase; letters that express humanity, compassion, modesty, fragility, and irony. Letters one seldom comes across or reads about, such as presidents referring to the White House as a prison, or excoriating other presidents, or lamenting their failure to get reelected, or one, Benjamin Harrison, anxiously looking forward to "my discharge" and getting "out of this House." And then, too, there are ironically prophetic letters, such as President-elect James Garfield, writing, "Assassination can no more be guarded against than death by lightning." He would die at the hands of an assassin after only six months in office.

But in the thirty-five years I have been collecting, it is Lincoln, more than anyone else, who has most intently absorbed my interest. He was a self-made man, unschooled but not uneducated, who, with determination, persistence, and firmness of purpose, demonstrated that anyone could rise to, meet, and overcome the challenges of life. Despite the war's heavy toll on him and the country for four long years, the presidency to Lincoln was, as historian Stefen Lorant once wrote, a "glorious burden." Lincoln loved the presidency, finding humor where he could amid military and personal setbacks.

In reading through Lincoln's vast canon of collected writings, I find myself using the same word—*fascinating*—over and over again. His letters and writings are interwoven with jewels, full of wisdom, poetic flair, and marvelous turns of phrase. And while some of these letters are more recognizable than others—the first and second inaugurals, the Gettysburg Address, or his letter to Grace Bedell about growing a beard, it is still those "other" letters—the ones most Americans do not know about—that truly impress me. "'And this too shall pass away'—Never fear," Lincoln writes to comfort his campaign manager after losing his 1858 Senate race against Stephen A. Douglas. Or, on the eve of his assured election to the presidency, humbly expressing, "I am not a man of great knowledge or learning." Later, Lincoln, sticking to his principles, uses a coarse but effective phrase: "Broken eggs can not be mended. I have issued the Emancipation Proclamation and can not retract it."

Many of Lincoln's finest words were reserved for the generals who consistently disappointed him: to Major General George Meade, for allowing Robert E. Lee's defeated army to escape from Gettysburg ("I do not believe you appreciate the magnitude of the misfortune involved in Lee's escape. He was within your easy grasp, and to have closed upon him would, in collection with our other late successes, have ended the war"); about General of the Army of the Potomac George McClellan's slowness to engage the enemy ("If General McClellan does not want to use the army, I would

OPPOSITE

ABRAHAM LINCOLN TO ABRAHAM JONAS, OCTOBER 21, 1856

(see page 29).

like to borrow it for a time"). But in "other" letters to lesser-known generals, an even more complex relationship emerges between the commander in chief and his highest-serving men. Lincoln, regretting the pain he has caused a general by dismissing him, writes: "I bear you no ill will; and I regret that I could not have the example without wounding you personally." Or, in a poetic outburst to General Robert Milroy: "I would be glad to see Gen. Milroy were it not that I know he wishes to ask for what I have not to give."

Robert Louis Stevenson said: "To be wholly devoted to some intellectual exercise is to have succeeded in life." Collecting for me is the passion that constantly infuses my thoughts. It is the tireless, daily adventure of constructing something piece by piece, of drawing strength from history; it is the focus on building something unique and complementary and anchored to themes. I have been privileged to have acquired over the years—and include in this volume—some truly remarkable examples from Lincoln's pen, many formerly held in some of the greatest private collections ever assembled, including those of Oliver Barrett, Phillip Sang, and Malcolm Forbes, as well as new and great discoveries that have emerged from hidden estates or obscure auctions far beyond the beaten path, where their importance was often overlooked.

It is, in fact, those "overlooked" letters that have formed the genesis of a particular thread in my collection of "other" Lincoln documents: the barely known relationship between Lincoln and the Jews. One day, thirty years ago, I discovered something amazing: Lincoln knew Jews. Despite the minuscule number of Jews who lived in the "Western frontier," as Illinois was then considered, Lincoln still managed to run into Jews and they into him.

I first discovered the Lincoln-and-Jews relationship in an auction catalog when I acquired the "hobbled" letter (chapter 2), where Lincoln revealingly expresses his frustration, and no doubt embarrassment—at having to defend a wayward nephew accused of thievery. The recipient of the letter was one Abraham Jonas, who, I would come to learn, was a lifelong Jewish friend who supported, campaigned for, and helped engineer Lincoln's successful run for the presidency. It is the only known letter from Lincoln to Jonas in private hands, and a great favorite of mine.

As I came across letter after letter in which Lincoln expresses humility, biblical imagery, compassion, and respect for a people and a religion, I was transformed as a collector. Lincoln never wrote, "You are one of my most valued friends" to anyone, except to his friend and confidant Abe Jonas. And when the latter lay dying in 1864, it was Lincoln who immediately took pen to paper and ordered Jonas's son, Charles, a Confederate officer and prisoner of war, paroled for three weeks "to visit his dying father."

I am fortunate to include many examples of Lincoln and the Jews in my collection, most of which are included in this book. In my research over the years, I have found dozens more, housed in major public institutions, and all revealing the inescapable truth of the depth and breadth of this relationship and Lincoln's interest in the causes important to Jews. It was not during the war that Lincoln met and interacted with Jews for the first time but rather as a young man in Illinois, thirty years before. And over the course of his tragically foreshortened life, as this book shows, he represented Jews, befriended Jews, admired Jews, commissioned Jews, defended Jews, pardoned Jews, consulted with Jews, and extended rights to Jews. His relationships with Jews were not exploitative but warm and genuine, and went further and deeper than those of any previous American president.

We meet Issachar Zacharie, Lincoln's foot doctor, for whom Lincoln wrote three testimonials attesting to Zacharie's skill; amazingly, two of the handwritten cards were written during Lincoln's most historic week as president—the week he issued the preliminary Emancipation Proclamation—and one on the actual day itself, September 22, 1862. Lincoln almost always found time for Zacharie, who, the *New York World* wrote, "enjoyed Mr. Lincoln's confidence more than any other private individual" and even sent him on peace missions to the South during the war.

It was Lincoln who, for the first time, appointed Jewish military chaplains to serve the thousands of Jewish soldiers fighting for the Union, attended Jewish-themed plays, some multiple times, and, in the midst of his greatest trial, the secession of the Southern states, found parallels in the Old Testament with a line from Daniel, referring to the "troub'lous times" as Civil War loomed and the lions that were also surrounding him.

When Jews faced their own troublous times during the war, Lincoln acted with characteristic tolerance and inclusion. With anti-Semitism swirling through the military and the War Department, Lincoln did not flinch, whether in reversing an edict by his most successful general—Grant's General Orders No. 11—or deflecting offensive and odious comments from other generals, including the immensely successful William Tecumseh Sherman. Through all this, Lincoln was the Jews' most stalwart protector. In that respect, interestingly enough, he very much resembled Harry Truman, as both presidents desperately tried to find an end to a terrible war while at the same time trying to give the Jews, as Lincoln famously said, a "leg up" when it came to returning to their Promised Land. Perhaps it is not a coincidence, then, that both men had close Jewish friendships starting at a young age.

With more than 16,000 Abraham Lincoln books published and with hundreds more appearing every year, the question is constantly asked by historians: Is there anything new to say about Lincoln? This book is my obvious answer, being only the third or fourth work of its kind in over a hundred years. The subject of Lincoln and the Jews is still unknown to most. In 1961, a major exhibition in New York on Jews during the Civil War, including Lincoln's relationships with Jews, opened to mark the occasion of the hundredth anniversary of the beginning of the war. Now, on the occasion

of the hundred and fiftieth anniversary marking the end of the war and Lincoln's assassination, this book reveals fresh discoveries and revelations of Lincoln's profound and unusual relationship with Jews to a new generation of readers. So I take the liberty of borrowing a single line from a letter Lincoln wrote in response to a compliment on his second inaugural speech which best expresses my inspiration for this project: "it is a truth which I thought needed to be told."

In order to illustrate the full depth of the story of Lincoln and the Jews—when Lincoln first learned about Jews, respected them as individuals and considered them, as a group, entitled to full equality—we have chosen to introduce, by visual evidence, high-quality images of the documents, letters, photographs, lithographs, ephemera, and artifacts that catch the eye, enhance the story, and capture history, something never before accomplished for this subject.

On the last day of his life, Lincoln, according to his wife Mary's later recollections, turned his thoughts to Jerusalem, telling her, ironically, of his wish to see Jerusalem before he died. As a young man, Lincoln had seen the moral failings and indignations of slavery but now wondered, with right seemingly on the side of the North, why the bloody Civil War had lasted four long years. "Both read the same Bible, both pray to the same God," he intoned in his second inaugural, and yet, both the North and South had tolerated the institution and its cruelties for years before the war. In the end, Lincoln had no answers for the suffering and God's hidden purposes, yielding to a half verse from Psalms (part of the Jewish Shabbat liturgy), "The judgments of the Lord are true and righteous altogether," which immediately precedes his more famous conclusion "With malice toward none, with charity for all." Perhaps Lincoln thought the answers could be found in Jerusalem, where God dwells, as do his "righteous judgments." Sadly, he would never find out.

Benjamin Shapell

INTRODUCTION

In central Jerusalem, close by streets named for the medieval Jewish luminary Moses Maimonides and the modern Hebrew writer Peretz Smolenskin, and abutting the American consulate, lies a crooked street named for Abraham Lincoln. When questioned about what he did for the Jewish people to merit a street named for him in Jerusalem, even those Jerusalemites familiar with Lincoln's biography shake their heads and shrug.

Lincoln and the Jews provides the first full-scale answer to that question, based on newly discovered documents and years of painstaking research. It shows that Lincoln consorted with a wide range of Jewish friends and acquaintances, some of whom, like Abraham Jonas and Issachar Zacharie, he came to know well. It is impossible to point to any previous American president about whom like claims might have been pressed.

The fact that Abraham Lincoln was intimately acquainted with Jews mattered. Robert Putnam, a political scientist at Harvard, observes that "having a religiously diverse social network leads to a more positive assessment of specific religious groups, particularly those with low thermometer scores." "When birds of different feathers flock together," he concludes, "they come to trust one another."[1] Precisely because Lincoln, for fully half his life, had Jewish friends and acquaintances, he repeatedly intervened on Jews' behalf—most famously in 1862, when he overturned Ulysses S. Grant's order expelling "Jews as a class" from his war zone. "I do not like to hear a class or nationality condemned on account of a few sinners," Lincoln explained.[2] Experience had taught him to trust Jews, even when those around him displayed ugly prejudices against them.

Lincoln's life coincided with the emergence of Jews on the national scene. When he was born, in 1809, scarcely 3,000 Jews lived in the entire United States, most of them concentrated in half a dozen East Coast port cities. Growing up in Kentucky and Indiana, he probably encountered no living Jews; the only Jews he knew at that time were in the Bible. By the time of his assassination in 1865, by contrast, large-scale immigration, principally from central Europe, had brought the Jewish population of the United States up to more than 150,000. Jews, by then, had spread from coast to coast, and Lincoln encountered them frequently; many other Americans did, too.[3]

Lincoln's interactions with Jews thus form part of a much larger history. It is, in microcosm, the story of how America as a whole began to come to terms with its growing Jewish population and how Americans and Jews were both changed by that encounter. Lincoln, we shall see, was personally broadened by his encounters with Jews and also worked to broaden America so that Jews might gain greater acceptance as equals nationwide. Thanks to his personal intervention, for example, the military chaplaincy was widened to embrace non-Christians. He himself appointed the first Jewish chaplains to the armed forces, and he placed many other Jews into positions of authority as well. Remarkably, he justified one such appointment with the statement, "We have not yet appointed a Hebrew,"[4] a sign that he had made the inclusion of Jews a priority.

Lincoln also subtly changed his personal rhetoric in response to Jewish sensitivities. Early on, and as late as 1862, he reflexively described America in Christian terms and characterized Americans as a "Christian people."[5]

Later in his presidency, however, he increasingly took note of the presence of non-Christians in the United States. His Gettysburg Address and deeply religious second inaugural bespoke a conscious effort to redefine America through phrases like "this nation under God" that embraced Jews and other non-Christians as insiders.

Lincoln's willingness to embrace Jewish Americans as insiders paralleled his far better known efforts to abolish slavery and grant legal equality to black Americans. In the mid-nineteenth-century, persecution of Jews and persecution of blacks were frequently linked in the popular mind. A Canadian religious enthusiast named Henry Wentworth Monk, for example, specifically urged Lincoln to "follow the emancipation of the Negro by a still more urgent step—the emancipation of the Jew."[6] Sir Moses Montefiore of England similarly linked Lincoln's efforts to liberate slaves to his own efforts to liberate Jews from oppression. Two plays in Washington that the Lincolns are known to have attended, *Gamea* and *Leah*, likewise employed the theme of anti-Jewish persecution in ways that contemporaries considered highly relevant to the situation of blacks. To Lincoln, the connection between eradicating the persecution of blacks and ending the persecution of Jews must have seemed obvious. Underlying both, to his mind, was a common philosophy: a passionate belief that "all men are created equal."

Lincoln's interactions with Jews, we shall see, developed and changed over the course of his lifetime. That is why this book, unlike any previous study of Lincoln and the Jews, proceeds chronologically. Chapter 1 examines Lincoln's upbringing, his church's uncompromising opposition to missionizing Jews, and some of what he learned about Jews from the Bible, schoolbooks, and current events. Chapters 2 and 3 trace his earliest Jewish friends and acquaintances in Illinois, particularly his close and important relationship with Abraham Jonas, and recount the role Jews played in advancing Lincoln to the White House. Chapters 4 to 7 detail Lincoln's interactions with Jews during his presidency, beginning with a controversy over his first inaugural address and continuing with episodes such as his leadership in the battle to open the chaplaincy up to non-Christians, the countermanding of Ulysses S. Grant's General Orders No. 11, and other lesser-known episodes that reveal much about his character. For the first time, this book recounts in full the mysterious story of Lincoln's chiropodist, Issachar Zacharie, and the grisly story of Beverly Ford, where General George Meade ordered a Jew, two Catholics, and two Protestants shot for desertion while a rabbi, priest, and minister looked on. Chapter 7 concludes with the memorable Passover of 1865, which began joyfully amid news of General Lee's surrender at Appomattox Court House and ended tragically following Lincoln's assassination by John Wilkes Booth. Finally, the epilogue traces Jewish involvement in Lincoln's funeral and in the subsequent memorialization of Lincoln continuing down to contemporary times.

As part of her memorialization, Mary Lincoln recounted in 1866 that her husband had hoped to visit Palestine after his second term as president came to an end. The introduction of steamships, which made long-distance travel safer and more pleasurable, inspired many Americans of that time to make the trip. Herman Melville and Mark Twain published celebrated books based on their travels to the Holy Land, and Civil War figures like Ulysses S. Grant and William Seward toured there as well. Lincoln, had he lived, could easily have joined them.[7]

Perhaps the naming of a Jerusalem street in Lincoln's memory aimed to compensate for this thwarted presidential desire to visit Palestine. If so, that would have been highly appropriate. But Lincoln Street also memorializes the fact that so many American Jews considered Abraham Lincoln to be their friend. As this book demonstrates, he promoted the inclusion of Jews into the fabric of American life and helped to transform Jews from outsiders in America to insiders.

Jonathan D. Sarna

Lion Silverman

Louis (Lewis) Leon

Moses Strauss

Edgar M. Johnson

Julius Silversmith

Morris Leon

Benjamin Szold

Annie Elizabeth Jonas

Marcus M. Spiegel

Arnold Levy

Richard Wallach

George B. Jonas

Moritz Pinner

Benjamin Levy

Isaac Mayer Wise

Julian J. Jonas

Morris J. Raphall

Moses Waldauer

C. M. Levy

Lucia Jonas

Julius
Hammerslough
1832–1908

Meyer Wallach

Simon Wolf

Rosalie Jonas

Louis Salzenstein

Ferdinand Levy

Betty Wollman

Philip Wallach

Uriah Phillips Levy

Jonas Wollman

Sidney (Samuel)
Alroy Jonas

APPOINTMENTS & PARDONS (48)

ACQUAINTANCES (55)

**ASSOCIATES &
SUPPORTERS (14)**

FRIENDS (5)

Theodore Lowenthal

Julian Allen

Alfred T. Jones

Samuel G. Alschuler

Abraham Jonas
1801–1864

Leopold Markbreit

Michael (Meir) Allen

Isidor Bush

Cesar J. Kaskel

August Belmont

Emanuel Bamberger

William Mayer

Herman Koppel

Martin Bijur

**Lewis Naphtali
Dembitz**

Simon Bamberger

Nehemiah H. Miller

Jacob G. Cohen

Isaac Leeser

**Abram J.
Dittenhoefer**

Charles L. Bernays

Septima Maria
(Levy) Collis

Alfred Mordecai Jr.

Samuel A. Lewis

Lazarus J. Lieberman

Bernhard Felsenthal

Goodman L. Mordecai

Leopold Blumenberg

**Charles H.
Liebermann**

Arnold Fischel

Rudolph Blumenberg

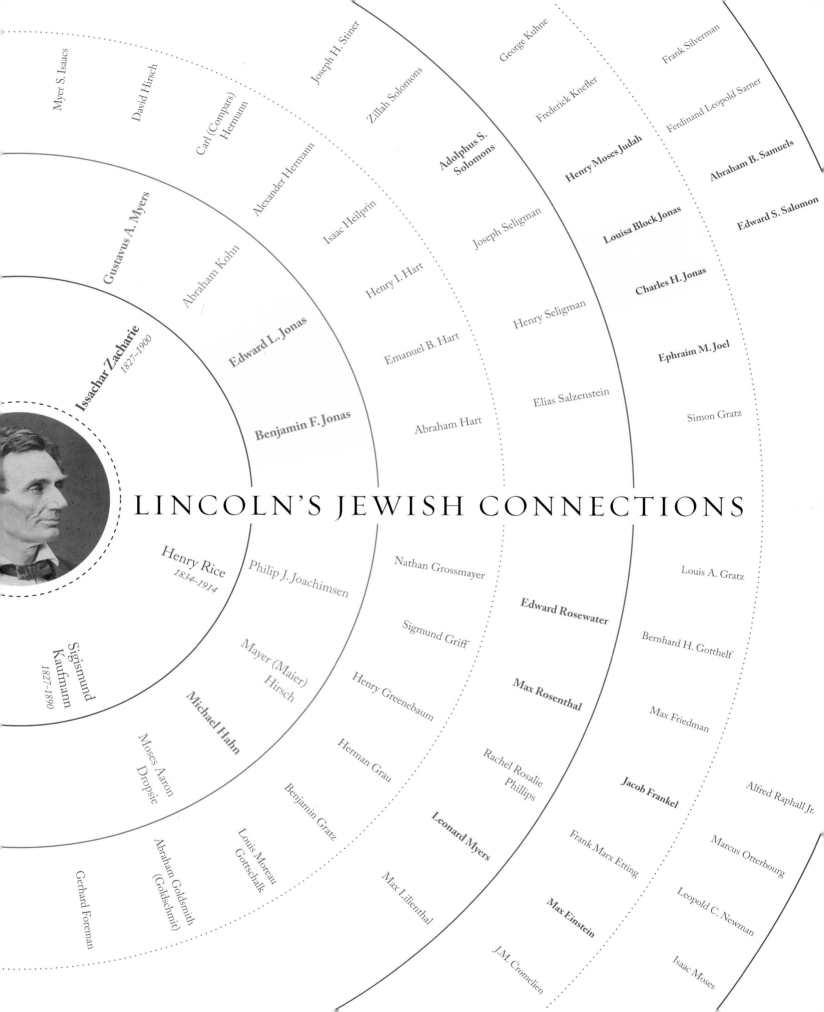

LINCOLN'S JEWISH CONNECTIONS

Myer S. Isaacs
David Hirsch
Carl (Compars) Hermann
Joseph H. Stiner
Zillah Solomons
George Kuhne
Frank Silverman
Ferdinand Leopold Sarner

Gustavus A. Myers
Alexander Hermann
Isaac Heilprin
Adolphus S. Solomons
Frederick Knefler
Henry Moses Judah
Abraham B. Samuels

Abraham Kohn
Henry I. Hart
Joseph Seligman
Louisa Block Jonas
Edward S. Salomon

Issachar Zacharie
1827–1900

Edward L. Jonas
Emanuel B. Hart
Henry Seligman
Charles H. Jonas

Benjamin F. Jonas
Abraham Hart
Elias Salzenstein
Ephraim M. Joel

Simon Gratz

Henry Rice
1834–1914
Philip J. Joachimsen
Nathan Grossmayer
Louis A. Gratz

Edward Rosewater
Bernhard H. Gotthelf

Sigmund Griff

Sigismund Kaufmann
1827–1890
Mayer (Maier) Hirsch
Henry Greenebaum
Max Rosenthal
Max Friedman

Michael Hahn
Herman Grau
Rachel Rosalie Phillips
Jacob Frankel
Alfred Raphall Jr.

Moses Aaron Dropsie
Benjamin Gratz
Leonard Myers
Frank Marx Etting
Marcus Otterbourg

Abraham Goldsmith (Goldschmit)
Louis Moreau Gottschalk
Max Lilienthal
Max Einstein
Leopold C. Newman

Gerhard Foreman
J.M. Cromelien
Isaac Moses

$11:11$

$5 - 1 - 3$

$12 \quad 13 \quad 2$

$22 \quad 13 - 17 - 2$
$2 \quad 35 \quad 19 \quad 10$
$19 \quad 17 \quad 17 \quad 9$
$22 \quad 23 - 17 - 7$

$21 - 2 - 3\frac{1}{2}$
$2 - 12 - 6\frac{3}{4}$
$9 - 9 \quad 4\frac{3}{4}$
$21 \quad 2 - 3\frac{1}{2}$

Ulm

Bildon

80 12

80 80

Abraham Lincoln his hand and pen he will be good

but God knows when Time what an empty vapor

ter and days how swift they are swift as an indian

fly on like a shooting star the present moment Just

then slides away in that we cannot say they

CHAPTER ONE

THE PROMISED LAND...
WHOSE STONES ARE IRON
AND OUT OF WHOSE HILLS
THOU MAYEST DIG BRASS

1809–1830

In all likelihood, Abraham Lincoln never met a Jew while he was growing up. No Jews lived in Hardin County, Kentucky, where he was born in 1809. Nor is there any record of a Jew living in the wilds of Spencer County, Indiana, where the Lincolns moved in late 1816. The entire Jewish population of the United States at that time did not exceed 3,000, with the vast majority of those Jews living in a small number of East Coast port cities.[1]

A few intrepid Jews, to be sure, had cast their eyes to the west. By 1812, Simon and Hyman Gratz owned Mammoth Cave in Kentucky, just fifty miles from where Lincoln was born. In 1819 Benjamin Gratz settled in Lexington, Kentucky. Samuel Judah, the first Jewish graduate of Rutgers and a respected attorney, moved to Vincennes, Indiana, at about that same time and became active politically. Within a few years, Cincinnati, Ohio, would become the fastest-growing Jewish community in the United States. But no Jewish community or formal Jewish organization existed anywhere in Kentucky or Indiana while the Lincolns lived there, and the family's poverty and isolation probably discouraged any wayfaring Jewish peddlers from stopping at their door. It is most likely, therefore, that Abraham Lincoln only heard stories about Jews during his first two decades of life.[2]

The first Jews that Abraham Lincoln undoubtedly heard about were found in the Bible. He took pride in his own biblical name, Abraham, recalling the biblical progenitor of the Jewish people as well as his paternal grandfather, Abraham, who had been brutally murdered by Indian raiders.[3] His uncle, Mordecai, likewise bore an illustrious name from the Bible. Lincoln, as a youth, also became familiar with the biblical figures of Moses and Job, whose life stories in some ways paralleled his own. Indeed, "Father Abraham," as his countrymen would come to call him, may well have been America's most biblically literate president. Throughout his life, he regularly quoted from the Bible in letters, talks to juries, political speeches, and even in day-to-day conversation. He lauded the Bible as "the best gift God has given to man."[4] Like his Puritan ancestors (and unlike Catholics of his time), he considered the Hebrew Bible an equal partner with the New Testament. He quoted, and referenced, the Old Testament about a third more times than he did the New; and in referencing the Deity some 420-plus times, used the phrase "Savior" but six. Likewise, according to the *The Collected Works of Abraham Lincoln*, he mentioned Christ directly only once— "when Christ suffered on the cross—when Moses led Israel through the Red-Sea—nay, even, when Adam first came from the hand of his Maker—then as now, Niagara was roaring here . . ." He never referred directly to Jesus.[5]

Lincoln's parents, Thomas and Nancy, like many Old School Calvinists, considered the Bible inerrant and infallible, the source of Divine Truth. "We believe the Old & New Testaments are the words of God," the constitution of his parents' Pigeon Creek Baptist Church declared. The Bible, their church taught, contained everything "necessary for man's salvation" and supplied all that was required for "faith and practice."[6] In Lincoln's home, as in so many others of his day, life was lived by the "Bible alone."[7]

The Bible was also part of Lincoln's more extended patrimony. His earliest American ancestor, Samuel Lincoln, born in 1622 in the village of Hingham, seventeen miles from Norwich, in East England, sided with the Puritan vicars of his village against the Church of England, and like so many others of his time, crossed the ocean in search of greater independence, congregational autonomy, and economic opportunity. Hingham, Massachusetts, where he built his new home (its name serving as a bridge between his old home and his new one), was a Puritan community deeply influenced by the teachings of John Calvin. Its citizens, like those of Boston, felt especially elected by God. They viewed themselves as part of God's new Israel, characterized by devotion to Scripture ("about as close to literal Biblicism," the Puritan scholar Perry Miller once wrote, "as one can come"[8]), rugged individualism, and a religious commitment to hard work and manual labor. They were fascinated by Jews, and many in the town bore names from the Hebrew Bible. This was especially true of the Lincolns in Hingham, whose names included Abner Lincoln, Abraham Lincoln, Amos Lincoln, Benjamin Lincoln, Enoch Lincoln, Isaac Lincoln, Jeremiah Lincoln, Josiah Lincoln, Levi Lincoln, Mordecai Lincoln, Perez Lincoln, Samuel Lincoln, and Solomon Lincoln.[9]

Growing up in Kentucky and Indiana, Abraham Lincoln knew next to nothing about his Hingham ancestors, but his world, like theirs, was suffused with the Bible. In fact, he learned the English of the King James Bible long before he could read its words for himself. He recalled listening to his mother as she recited Psalms while she worked. He heard the words of Scripture preached in church and was drilled, as all good children were, in the Ten Commandments.[10]

Actual copies of the Bible were expensive and scarce

OPPOSITE

FIRST LECTURE ON DISCOVERIES AND INVENTIONS

The three most important advances in human development, Lincoln said in a nine-page lecture first delivered early in 1858—and repeated, with small revisions, four times over the next year—were writing, printing, and the discovery of America. What most impresses is that while delivered at the invitation of Christian groups, the lecture evidences that the basis of Lincoln's thinking on the world's most important discoveries and inventions was overwhelmingly rooted in the Old Testament; the New Testament is mentioned a scant twice. With commanding ease, Lincoln refers to Old Testament characters and events—including Abraham, Isaac, Jacob, Joseph, Jerusalem—nearly fifty times and spans four out of what he called "the five books of Moses." On describing God's hidden gifts in "the promised land," Lincoln invokes a passage from Deuteronomy: "a land whose stones are iron and out of whose hills thou mayest dig brass."
Meisei University, Tokyo

The Bible makes no other allusion to clothing, before the flood— Soon after the deluge Noah's two sons covered him with a garment; but of what material the garment was made is not mentioned— Gen. 9–23.

Abraham mentions "thread" in su[ch a way as to] indicate that spinning and weaving [were known in] his day— Gen. 14.23— and soon after, [mention of linen] is frequently made— "Linen breeches [...]" 28.42— and it is said "all the wom[en] did spin with their hands "(35.25) [...] hearts stirred them up in wisdom, spun [...] The work of the "weaver" is mention[ed in] the book of Job, a very old book, [...] knows, the "weavers shuttle" is mention[ed]

The above mention of "thread" [is the] oldest recorded allusion to spin[ning] and it was made about two th[ousand years after] the creation of man, and now [...] and years ago— Profane author[s say it ori-] ginated in Egypt; and this is not [...] improbable, by any thing in the Bi[ble; for] of Abraham, mentioned, was not [...] had sojourner in Egypt—

The discovery of the properties [and] making of iron tools, must have [been the] earliest of important discoveries an[d...] scarcely conceive the possibility of [making] anything else, without the use of [...] an iron hammer must have [been] needed to make the first [...]

A stone probably served as [...] How could the "gopher wood" for [...]

gotten out without an axe! It seems to me an axe, or a miracle, was indispensable— Corresponding with the prime necessity, for now we find at least one very early notice of it— Tubal cain was "an instructer of every artificer in brass and iron— Gen: 4–22— Tubal cain was the seventh in descent from Adam; and his birth was about one thousand years before the flood— After the flood, frequent mention is made of iron, and instruments made of iron— Thus "instrument of iron" at Num– 35–16–; "bed stead of iron" at Deut. 3.11— "the iron furnace" at 4–20— and "iron tool" at 27–5— At 19–5– very distinct mention of "the ax to cut down the tree" is made; and also at 8–9, the promised land is described as "a land whose stones are iron, and out of whose hills thou mayest dig brass"— From the somewhat frequent mention of brass in connection with iron, it is not improbable that brass— perhaps what we now call copper— was used by the ancients, for some of the same purposes as now—

Transportation— the removal of persons and goods from place to place— would be an early object, if not a necessity, with man— By his natural powers of locomotion, and without much assistance from Discovery and invention, he could move himself about with considerable facility; and even could carry small burthens, with him— But very soon he would wish to lessen the labor, which he might, at the same time, extend, and expedite the business— For this object, wheel carriages, and water craft— wagons and boats— are the most important inventions— The use of the wheel & axle, has been so long known, that it is difficult, without reflection, to estimate it at its true value.

"a land whose stones are iron, and out of whose hills thou mayest dig brass"— From the somewhat frequent mention of brass in connection with iron, it is not improbable that brass— perhaps what we

in the frontier regions of Kentucky and Indiana when Lincoln was a boy. Whether his parents owned one at that time is uncertain. In any case, his father and many of the Lincolns' neighbors were functionally illiterate. So an oral culture prevailed. Churches encouraged the repetition of Scripture word for word following the preacher. Storytelling, in which Thomas and later Abraham Lincoln excelled, consumed a good deal of leisure time. Schools—known as "blab schools"—required students to repeat their lessons aloud, relying heavily upon memory and rote learning. The goal of preachers and teachers was to train the memory, to instill it with lessons for life; Abraham Lincoln's own life was shaped by those lessons.

Lincoln was also deeply influenced by the schoolbooks that he read and studied as a youngster. Precisely because they were few in number and he read them aloud to himself, those books became deeply imprinted upon his memory. One of them, which he is said to have described as "the best schoolbook ever put into the hands of an American youth,"[11] was Lindley Murray's *The English Reader* (1799). Written by a Pennsylvania Quaker who settled in England, it included well-chosen selections of prose and poetry, many by Scottish Enlightenment writers, and was designed to train students in reading as well as in "some of the most important principles of piety and virtue." A selection that summarized the biblical Book of Esther, for example, described Haman ("a very wicked minister") as "an Amalekite, who inherited all the ancient enmity of his race to the Jewish nation." It contrasted him with "Mordecai the Jew" who, "with virtuous indignation," refused to pay Haman homage. Haman's passions, the text explained, were "so violent and black . . . that he resolved to exterminate the whole nation to which Mordecai belonged." Fortunately, the "conspicuous justice of God" resulted in Haman's "fall and punishment."[12]

The positive estimation of the Jews found in this selection, especially as contrasted with the fate meted out to Haman, reflected the tone of the volume as a whole. Even as it trumpeted Christianity and the New Testament, *The English Reader* also promoted the virtues of religion in general, as well as values like gratitude, integrity, and gentleness to which all could aspire. It praised the beauties of the Psalms ("delivered out as services for Israelites under the Law, yet no less adapted to the circumstances of Christians under the Gospel") and raised up as an example the "clemency and amiable character" of Joseph in the Book of Genesis. It expressed "indignant sentiments" against slavery ("human nature's broadest, foulest blot") and preached "the duty of forgiveness." The absence of overt anti-Jewish sentiments here—in contrast, for example, to those found in William McGuffey's *Eclectic Third Reader* (1837)—may have influenced Lincoln's later attitude toward the Jews. The values he gleaned from Lindley Murray's *English Reader* became ones that, as president, he would internalize and espouse.[13]

As for living, breathing Jews, what most distinguished Abraham Lincoln's upbringing from that of most other Americans of his day was that his parents and members of their church evinced no interest whatsoever in converting Jews to Christianity (or, for that matter, in bringing the gospel to the unchurched anywhere). Instead, they fatalistically believed in predestination, in "election by grace given us . . . before the world began."[14] While America as a whole blazed with religious awakenings and witnessed the creation of countless benevolent organizations that encouraged missions and conversions to promote "truth and

"FOR MRS. LUCY G. SPEED, FROM WHOSE PIOUS HAND I ACCEPTED THE PRESENT OF AN OXFORD BIBLE TWENTY YEARS AGO."

In 1841, a young and depressive Lincoln had been counseled by Lucy Speed, mother of his best friend Joshua, about the healing effects of the Bible—and faith. Remembering her advice to him twenty years later and now one month into his first term as president, Lincoln, for the only known time in his life, personally inscribes a photograph, here with a twenty-word note of gratitude to Lucy.

Shapell Manuscript Collection

For Mrs Lucy G. Speed, from whose pious hand I accepted the present of an Oxford Bible twenty years ago.
Washington, D.C., October 3, 1861   A. Lincoln

[handwritten text] against them — The war is now to them, the gallows of Haman, on which they built for us, and on which they are doomed to be hanged themselves —

righteousness," the Calvinist Baptist church to which Lincoln's parents belonged disdained such movements and considered them utterly futile. One "not elected from the foundation of the world," these so-called Primitive Baptists believed, "was as changeless and as hopeless as if he were already in the bottomless pit."[15]

The American Society for Evangelizing the Jews, established in 1816 in the very month that the Lincolns settled in Indiana, optimistically believed that Jews could be changed. It called upon Americans to "make every possible and proper exertion . . . to bring the Jews to the acknowledgement of Jesus Christ of Nazareth as the true Messiah." Reorganized as the American Society for Meliorating the Condition of the Jews, in 1820, the missionary organization attracted support from the likes of Elias Boudinot, former president of the Continental Congress; John Quincy Adams, a future president of the United States; the heads of Yale, Princeton, and Rutgers universities; and countless other Americans, most of whom had never actually met Jews but worked tirelessly to promote their conversion.[16]

The parents and neighbors of Abraham Lincoln, in contrast, were known as anti-missionary Protestants and complained that missionary societies improperly arrogated to themselves powers that properly lay with God alone. One anti-missionary journal specifically charged that the work of the American Society for Meliorating the Condition of the Jews was "at variance with the providence of God" and that "nearly all the conversions yet affected through the instrumentality of men have proved only worthless." The fate of everyone, including Jews, had long since been decided by God and was not subject to change, missionary opponents like Lincoln's parents believed.[17]

"THE [MEXICAN] WAR IS NOW TO THEM, THE GALLOWS OF HAMAN," JUNE 12, 1848

A line showing Lincoln's familiarity with a portion of Judaic literature less known to most Christians; here Lincoln uses the metaphor of Haman hanging on the gallows, the first of two times that Lincoln would do so in his writings.

The Abraham Lincoln Association

Abraham Lincoln never joined his parents' church or, for that matter, any church in his lifetime, but the Baptist Calvinist atmosphere that pervaded his adolescence left an indelible mark upon him. The conviction that all was predetermined, that "what is to be, will be, and no prayers of ours can reverse the decree," shaped his worldview.[18] That may be why he never associated himself with those who sought to Christianize the Jews or the Constitution. Skeptical of those who "knew" what God wanted, he preferred to make decisions based upon careful reasoning and then to let destiny play out on its own.[19]

Whether missionized or left alone, Jews knew that negative images of themselves and their faith circulated widely in the United States. Jews, even if few in number, commonly experienced prejudice on the part of their neighbors. The Constitution, of course, guaranteed Jews the free exercise of their faith and legal equality on the federal level. President George Washington, in a celebrated letter in 1790, promised Jews that in America they would not just be tolerated but would enjoy religious liberty as an "inherent natural right." "The Government of the United States," he forcefully declared, "gives to bigotry no sanction, to persecution no assistance."[20] But the people of the United States, many of them raised in places where Jews were hated and distrusted, did not always follow the government's lead.

LINCOLN TO ROBERT H. MILROY, JUNE 29, 1863

Lincoln, having for months been frustrated by General Milroy's disobedience and battlefield failures, reprimands him here by employing the Old Testament (Numbers 20:11). Referencing when Moses had faulted in his judgment upon hitting the rock in the desert, Lincoln tells Milroy, "This, my dear general, is I fear, the rock on which you have split." Like Moses, Milroy's mistake had thus irreversibly sealed his own fate.

Courtesy of the Library of Congress

How much popular anti-Jewish prejudice reached the ears of Abraham Lincoln growing up in Kentucky and Indiana cannot be known, but a rare admission of the general situation facing Jews appeared in a German-American newspaper, *The Correspondent*, in 1820, when he was eleven years old. "The Jews are not generally regarded with a favorable eye; and 'Jew' is an epithet which is frequently uttered in a tone bordering on contempt," the newspaper reported. "Say what you will, prejudices against the Jews exist here, and subject them to inconveniences from which other citizens of the United States are exempt."[21] In some cases, such prejudices stood in tension with more positive personal experiences with Jews—a dichotomy, as it were, between the "mythical Jew" and the "Jew next door."[22] Still, as non-Christians, Jews regularly were cast as outsiders in America; they stood apart from the mainstream and were deeply suspected.[23] Lincoln, we shall see, would work to change that. By the time of his death, he had done more than any previous president to promote Jews' advance in American society.

The painful position of Jews was illustrated, in 1809,

just a few months after Lincoln was born, in North Carolina, when a legislator named Jacob Henry, married to a Christian, was threatened with expulsion from his seat in the House of Commons because, as a Jew, he did not accept the divine authority of the New Testament, as required by the state constitution. In a long, celebrated response, Henry declared that "if a man fulfills the duties of that religion, which his education or his conscience has pointed to him as the true one, no person, I hold, in this our land of liberty, has a right to arraign him at the bar of any inquisition." His colleagues, who liked him, agreed to let him keep his seat after that speech, but they refused to change the test oath that should legally have barred him. That remained on the books until after the Civil War.[24]

In Virginia, Thomas Jefferson, in the early nineteenth century, concluded from his wide readings that Jewish ideas of God and His attributes "were degrading and injurious" and that Jewish ethics "were not only imperfect, but often irreconcilable with the sound dictates of reason and morality." Writing to John Adams in 1813, he decried Jews' "wretched depravity of sentiment and manners"—a widely held view in America of that time. To be sure, he did not generalize from this ugly stereotype to the few Jews whom he knew personally. He saluted his friend Joseph Marx, for example, "with sentiments of perfect esteem and respect." He expressed what Marx described as "liberal and enlightened views" on Jewish affairs. In a remarkable letter to the Jewish leader Mordecai Noah, he even admitted that "the prejudice still scowling on your section of our religion . . . cannot be unfelt by ourselves." But so far as he was concerned, Jews were still outsiders. Though they remained so into the mid and late nineteenth century, Lincoln would never treat Jews as such, nor would he ever deride them in any of his writings as Jefferson had done in his letter to Adams.[25]

Perhaps the most broadly discussed controversy concerning American Jews while Abraham Lincoln was growing up took place in Maryland, where a community of over one hundred Jews was denied by state law the right to hold any "office of trust or profit" (including serving as lawyers and jurors) because they would not execute a "declaration of belief in the Christian religion." For twenty-eight years, beginning in 1797, efforts were made to change that provision—so at odds with the spirit of the U.S. Constitution[26]—but rural legislators stood fast, fearing the growing power of Baltimore (where most of Maryland's Jews lived). Opponents of the so-called Jew Bill laced their arguments with anti-Jewish rhetoric and derided Jews and their supporters as "enemies of Christianity." Finally, after newspapers and politicians across the country weighed in, a bill permitting Jews to substitute a declaration of belief "in a future state of rewards and punishments" passed, in 1825, by one vote. It became law on January 5, 1826.[27]

Whether, as a teenager, Abraham Lincoln followed the Maryland Jew Bill controversy or any other episode involving Jews is doubtful but impossible to know for certain. Most likely, his youthful image of the Jew was primarily shaped by what he learned at home, from his parents' church, and from his own reading. Based heavily upon Scripture and hearsay, his understanding of Jews and Judaism lacked the benefit of any real-world experience with the Jewish people. That he would only begin to acquire when he moved to Illinois and met Jews for the first time.

OPPOSITE

"A. LINCOLN AND SON." FEBRUARY 9, 1864

One of only two known signed images of this famous photograph—"A. Lincoln and Son."—has also become a testament to Lincoln's personal convictions. Journalist Noah Brooks noted, "Lincoln explained to me that he was afraid that this picture was a species of false pretense. Most people, he thought, would suppose the book a large clasped Bible, whereas it was a big photograph album . . . Lincoln's anxiety lest somebody should think he was 'making believe to read the Bible to Tad,' was illustrative of his scrupulous honesty."
Shapell Legacy Partnership

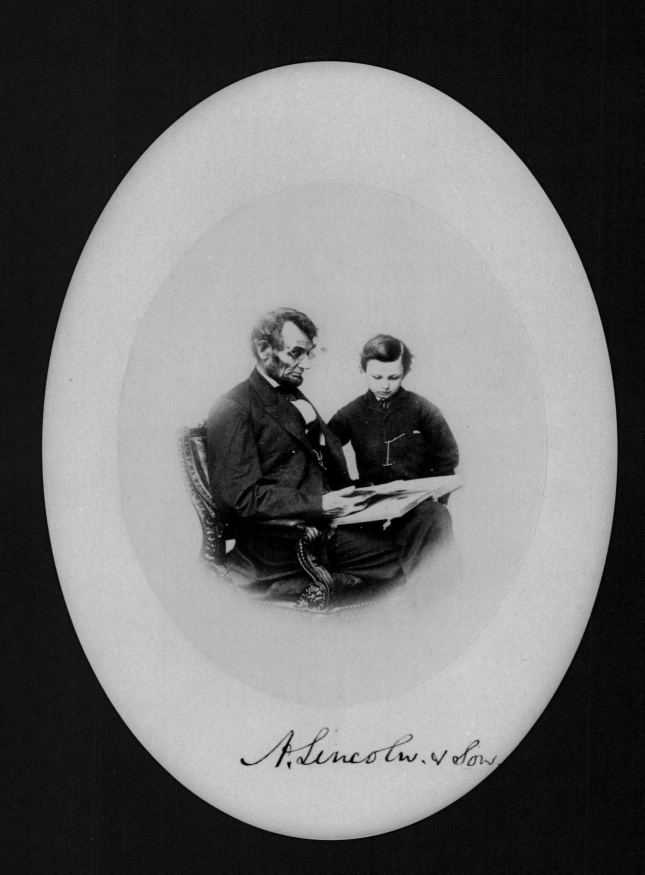

A. Lincoln & Son.

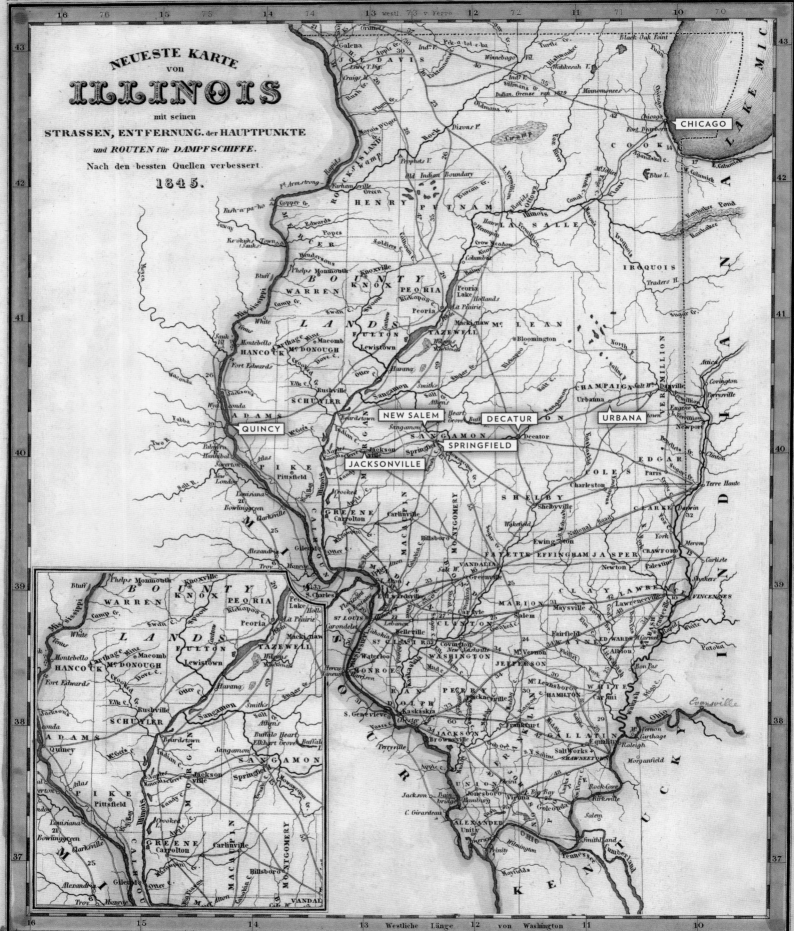

NEUESTE KARTE
VON
ILLINOIS
mit seinen
STRASSEN, ENTFERNUNG. der HAUPTPUNKTE
und ROUTEN für DAMPFSCHIFFE.
Nach den bessten Quellen verbessert.
1845.

CHICAGO

QUINCY

NEW SALEM

DECATUR

URBANA

SPRINGFIELD

JACKSONVILLE

Aus der Geographischen Graviranstalt des Bibliographischen Instituts zu Hildburghausen Amsterdam. Paris u. Philadelphia.

CHAPTER TWO

AND THIS TOO
SHALL PASS AWAY—
NEVER FEAR

1830–1858

Jews preceded Abraham Lincoln's parents in seeking their fortune in Illinois. Back in 1773 and 1775, Jewish merchants—among them several members of the Franks family, Bernard and Michael Gratz, Joseph Simon, and Levi Andrew Levi—formed part of a land company that purchased title from "certain chiefs of the Illinois Indians" to substantial portions of southern Illinois and Indiana. They paid what in today's money would be less than one million dollars. After many years of legal wrangling, the U.S. Supreme Court, in a unanimous 1823 decision written by Chief Justice John Marshall, voided the purchasers' title. Private purchases of Indian land were illegal, the Court ruled, for only the government held the right to sell Indian land. The Jewish merchants lost their entire investment.[1]

OPPOSITE

MAP OF ILLINOIS, 1845

The cities of Springfield, New Salem, Jacksonville, Quincy, Decatur, and Urbana were not only stops on Lincoln's legal circuit, but were also the main locations of Lincoln's early interactions with Jews.

David Rumsey Map Collection, with Shapell Manuscript Collection

Thomas Lincoln proved somewhat more fortunate when he arrived in Illinois in 1830. The land that he settled, on the north bank of the Sangamon River, near Decatur, was undeveloped and available. Aided by his son Abraham, now twenty-one years old and free of legal obligations to his parents, he built a log cabin, a smokehouse, and a barn, broke up acres of land for farming, and put up a fence. Henceforward, Illinois would be the Lincolns' home.

Abraham Lincoln soon relocated to the recently established village of New Salem, Illinois, farther west on the bank of the Sangamon River, partly to get away from his difficult father, and partly to strike out on his own as an adult. There he lived and worked. From there he set forth to defend his land against Indian "invaders" by enlisting to fight in the Black Hawk War.

Once he returned, in 1832, he made his first run for public office from New Salem—and lost. Subsequently, he served as postmaster of New Salem, participated in a public debating society, surveyed land, and frequented public meetings. "Every one knew him; and he knew every one," a local politician recalled.[2] As a result, in

MUSTER ROLL OF CAPTAIN ABRAHAM LINCOLN'S BLACK HAWK WAR COMPANY, APRIL 28, 1832

Lincoln later called his 1832 election as captain by his fellow soldiers "a success which gave me more pleasure than any I have had since." But this win laid the groundwork for a loss, as he was still an active candidate for the Illinois State Legislature. When finally mustered out, his horse was stolen, and he had to canoe and walk home—losing valuable campaign time and thus the election.

Shapell Manuscript Collection

1834, when Lincoln ran for public office again, he was elected to the Illinois state legislature. There, in February 1837, he helped to determine that the capital city of Illinois would be relocated from Vandalia to Springfield. Two months later, on April 15, having passed the bar, he left New Salem and moved to Springfield himself. His life would be exactly half over.

Chartered as a city in 1840, Springfield grew rapidly over the next twenty years; its population, which was less than 2,500 when Lincoln came to town, practically quadrupled. Many of the city's newcomers had emigrated from the German states, including a few Jews.

By 1858, at least one prominent Jewish business considered Springfield its home: Hammerslough and Brothers Clothing, on the north side of the Public Square.[3]

Julius Hammerslough (1832–1908), who headed the family firm, had immigrated to the United States from Hannover in Lower Saxony, clerked in Baltimore, and, in his twenties, established himself in Springfield. There he became one of Abraham Lincoln's numerous acquaintances; likely, Lincoln purchased clothes in his store. Years later, the *New York Times*, in an obituary, described Hammerslough as a "warm friend of Abraham Lincoln." The industry paper *Men's Wear*, after his death, elevated him into one of Lincoln's "closest friends." Isaac Markens, in his seminal 1909 publication, *Abraham Lincoln and the Jews*, recorded that Hammerslough visited Lincoln "frequently at the White House" and once accompanied Mrs. Lincoln's sister, Elizabeth Edwards, to Washington, and also attended Lincoln's first inauguration.[4]

Hammerslough, who was twenty-three years Lincoln's junior, probably admired Lincoln more than he actually befriended him. Hammerslough and Brothers

Clothing prospered during the Civil War, helping to outfit thirty-nine regiments of infantry and nine regiments of cavalry mustered into the Union army and trained at nearby Camp Butler. Subsequently, according to the firm's reports, its military trade "assumed a fabulous dimension," and by 1864 the Hammerslough name was supposedly known "to all the western armies, by each corps, division and by most every soldier." Having prospered, Julius Hammerslough, in 1868, sold his store to his brother-in-law, Samuel Rosenwald (father of the merchant prince Julius Rosenwald of Sears Roebuck fame), and removed to New York. There he became "one of the most prominent clothing manufacturers in the United States, widely known throughout the entire industry." He also founded and headed the Clothiers Association of New York.[5]

Hammerslough, throughout his life, was a proud and engaged Jew. In his twenties, in Baltimore, he served as secretary of Baltimore's Hebrew Assistance Society. In 1865, when Springfield's Jewish community grew large enough to support a synagogue, he became its first president. When funds were sought for a memorial to Lincoln in Springfield, he assumed the role of "special agent" to the "Hebrews" and, as we shall see, requested "their favorable action."[6] According to Markens, who interviewed him, Hammerslough was among those who met the body of the slain president on its return to Springfield.

In interacting with Hammerslough, Abraham Lincoln undoubtedly knew that he was a Jew; everybody in Springfield did. That is why it is so extraordinary that others considered Hammerslough (and he considered himself) to be a friend of Lincoln's. Comparatively few Christians in mid-nineteenth-century America boasted Jewish friends. Fewer than one American in 200, after all, was Jewish. Lincoln, we have seen, had no Jewish friends growing up and mostly knew Jews through the Bible. But once he did meet Jews, he displayed no prejudice whatsoever against them—no religious hatred, no antipathy to them as immigrants, no desire to convert

POSTMASTERS

POSTMASTERS IN LINCOLN'S AMERICA were responsible not only for the transmission of private correspondence but also for the circulation of newspapers, magazines, and government documents. They were in a uniquely advantageous position to exchange information and control the flow of news. The postmaster could also peruse all the printed material that others received, a benefit of which Lincoln took advantage in helping to educate himself. With the mail delivered to the post office a few times a week and people generally coming to call for it in person, the postmaster also had occasion to meet his fellow citizens regularly—that is why politicians coveted the job. Since it not only carried a government salary but also permitted the postmaster to send and receive personal letters for free and to get one daily newspaper delivered for free, it became a plum patronage position.

them. To the contrary, the Jews he befriended during his years in Springfield shaped a positive assessment of Jews on his part. He came to know them as neighbors, clients, and political allies. By the time of his death, he had acquired far more Jewish friends and acquaintances than any American president before him.

From the perspective of those friends and acquaintances, the fact that they had interacted with a future president of the United States, however briefly, was absolutely breathtaking. In central Europe, where they had grown up, the idea that a mere Jew could interact on friendly terms with a future national leader would have been considered laughable. So-called Court Jews, who served as intermediaries between Jews and the government, almost never fully befriended the leaders with whom they interacted; they feared them. Jews who managed estates for aristocratic lords likewise knew "their place" (if not, the lord had his dogs remind them of it).[7] To speak of Lincoln as a friend, the way Hammerslough and many others did, bespoke the democratic ethos that distinguished America from aristocratic Europe. It underscored what Jews could accomplish under freedom.

Before he met Hammerslough, Lincoln had already known Louis Salzenstein, a Jewish storekeeper and livestock trader in Athens (pronounced ay-thens), Illinois, some seven miles from New Salem. Born in the village of Halsdorf in Hessen, Germany, about fifteen miles from Marburg, "Old Salty," as he was later dubbed, moved to Athens around 1843 and became a successful merchant. He was, many believe, the first Jew that Abraham Lincoln ever encountered. As a young man, Lincoln is said to have "often stopped at his store and his residence."[8] Salzenstein's store served as the regional post office. Later, Lincoln represented Salzenstein in a minor lawsuit and represented his litigious kinsman, Elias Salzenstein, in several lawsuits.[9] Salzenstein's clerk, Morris Myers, also a Jew—the families had known each other back in Halsdorf—had two sons, Albert and Louis, who would later purchase Hammerslough's store from Samuel Rosenwald and develop it into Myers Brothers, the largest department store in Springfield. In death, Louis, Elias, and other members of the Salzenstein and Myers families lie buried not far from Abraham Lincoln in Springfield's Oak Ridge Cemetery.[10]

During his Springfield years, Abraham Lincoln maintained far closer connections to another member of the Jewish faith: Abraham Jonas.[11] In all likelihood, Jonas was the first Jew whom Lincoln came to know well; he was the only recorded person in fact whom Lincoln *ever* directly called "one of my most valued friends."[12] The two men shared much in common. Both were named Abraham and known as "Abe." Both had familial roots in England. Both became renowned for their fair-mindedness and wit. Both were postmasters. Both served as Illinois legislators and as country lawyers. Both revered Henry Clay. Both developed into masterful orators. And both began their political lives

as Whigs and moved on to become staunch Republicans. Exactly when they first met is uncertain, but for more than two decades they were friends and political allies.

Born about 1801 into an Orthodox Jewish family in Portsmouth, England, Abraham Jonas followed in the footsteps of his older brother, Joseph, and immigrated as a teenager to the United States, settling in Cincinnati in 1819. Joseph Jonas, the first long-term Jewish settler in Cincinnati, had preceded him there two years earlier. "The fiat had gone forth," Joseph later reported, "that a new resting place for the scattered sons of Israel should be commenced, and that a sanctuary should be erected in the Great West, dedicated to the Lord of Hosts, to resound with praises to the ever-living God."[13]

As if to underscore the religious character of their mission, Joseph and Abraham traveled to New York and married Rachel and Lucia Orah, the daughters of Shearith Israel's venerable religious leader, Gershom Seixas, the foremost Jewish "minister" of his time in North America. Soon afterward, in an effort "to conform as near as possible to the worship and ceremonies of our holy religion," the brothers, in 1824, helped to form Cincinnati's first Jewish congregation, Bene Israel. It is remembered as "the oldest synagogue west of the Alleghenies."[14]

A year later, tragedy struck—the kind of frontier tragedy that Lincoln in his early life knew all too well. First, Abraham and Lucia Orah lost their firstborn son. Then Lucia herself passed away, on June 17, 1825, at the age of twenty. Baby and mother were laid to rest in the city's first Jewish cemetery on the corner of Chestnut Street and Central Avenue in Cincinnati. Abraham must have been devastated by the loss. Years later, after he married Louisa Block, the orphaned daughter of a prominent Jewish pioneer of Richmond, Virginia, and Cape Girardeau, Missouri, he named his firstborn daughter, Lucia.[15]

Subsequently, Abraham Jonas left Cincinnati for the small community of Williamstown, Kentucky, on

*". . . three others
were elected, of whom
I was not one . . ."*

**LINCOLN TO JOHN COULTER,
SEPTEMBER 4, 1860**

*In an autobiographical sketch written while running
for president in 1860, Lincoln noted that his 1832 loss
for the State Legislature was the only time he was ever
beaten by a direct vote of the people. Lincoln blamed no
one and made no excuses; here, with the presidential
election now just two months away, he was forthright
about his loss twenty-eight years before, stating that
four out of the fifteen candidates were elected, "of whom
I was not one." At the same time, he noted his successes
in the campaigns of 1834, 1836, 1838, and 1840.*

Shapell Manuscript Collection

Springfield, Feb. 4 1860

Hon: A. Jonas
My dear Sir:

Yours of the 3rd inquiring how you can get a copy of the debates now being published in Ohio, is received — As you are one of my most valued friends, and have complimented me by the expression of a wish for the books, I propose doing myself the honor of present—

ABOVE

"ONE OF MY MOST VALUED FRIENDS"

A striking example of the close Lincoln-Jonas bond. Lincoln, always a careful and self-conscious wordsmith, uses, for the only known time, a phrase directly acknowledging Abraham Jonas as "one of my most valued friends." Jonas was among the first to suggest in 1858 that Lincoln be the Republican nominee for president in 1860.
Abraham Lincoln Presidential Library & Museum

RIGHT
Abraham Jonas
Wells Family

the road to Lexington about 150 miles northeast of where Lincoln was born. There he opened a store. Striking out on his own, he also embarked upon two pursuits that would claim much of his energy over the next decades: He founded a Masonic lodge and he plunged into politics. Freemasonry offered Jonas a forum where he could interact on an equal footing with non-Jews, emphasizing morality, charity, and belief in a Supreme Being, but nothing overtly Christian. Jews had been Masonic leaders in cities like Newport and Boston in the late eighteenth century, and leading Jews of Jonas's own day, like the New Yorker Mordecai Noah, were Masons as well. In America, unlike in Germany, Jews faced no discrimination in Masonic circles. So it was that in 1827, Jonas, who had once been a Master Mason in Cincinnati, founded Grand Lodge No. 85

and became its first Worshipful Master. Six years later, he was elected Grand Master of the Kentucky Grand Lodge, the highest Masonic position in that state.[16]

His election came at a bad time. A wave of anti-Masonic sentiment swept the country in the late 1820s and early 1830s, following the disappearance of William Morgan, who had allegedly threatened to expose Freemasonry's "secrets" by publishing its rituals. Jonas might have feared that as a Jew and a Mason, his reputation would have taken a pounding, but he actually emerged unscathed. In fact, his personal popularity led to his election to the Kentucky House of Representatives.[17]

As a state legislator, Jonas encountered the greatest Kentucky politician of the day, Henry Clay, thrice speaker of the U.S. House of Representatives and thrice defeated for the presidency of the United States. Jonas idolized him, as did Lincoln, who met Clay at about the same time, and eulogized him in 1852. To Lincoln, indeed, Clay represented "my beau ideal of a statesman."[18] Lincoln and Jonas followed Clay into the Whig Party, studied his oratory, agreed with him concerning the evils of slavery and the need for the government to compensate slave owners in return for freeing their slaves (compensated emancipation), and both sought to emulate his political style. "All legislation, all government, all society, is formed upon the principle of mutual concession, politeness, comity, courtesy; upon these, every thing is based," Clay taught his mentees.[19] Lincoln and Jonas internalized that great lesson. The full extent of Jonas's interactions with Clay remains unknown. Upon hearing the news of Jonas's upcoming move to Illinois, he wrote, "I am truly sorry that you are going to leave us, although I cannot but hope & believe that an exchange of the Dry Ridge for the fertile plains of Illinois must redound to your advantage."[20] In 1842, four years after Jonas had settled in Quincy, Illinois, a growing commercial city at the point where Illinois met the Mississippi River, Clay still corresponded with him and noted, "we . . . miss you very much."[21]

The two would not meet again for several years.

"COMPENSATED EMANCIPATION"

COMPENSATED EMANCIPATION aimed to eliminate slavery by having the government pay slaveholders for the loss of their slave property. First touted by Henry Clay, the plan was aggressively supported by President Lincoln starting in 1862. He argued that this plan would not only end the war if adopted by the southern states, but would be far cheaper for the government than the cost of a prolonged war. Strategically, hoping to bring the war to an early conclusion, Lincoln first approached the border slave states still in the Union, arguing that their adoption of his plan would dash the Confederacy's hopes that these crucial four states (Maryland, Missouri, Kentucky, and Delaware) would secede and join them. The border states rejected compensated emancipation but remained in the Union. Meanwhile, some in the North insisted that slaveholders were undeserving of compensation and that the whole plan was unconstitutional. In the end, Washington, D.C. was the only territory in the United States that actually ended slavery through compensated emancipation. The District of Columbia Compensated Emancipation Act, signed by Lincoln on April 16, 1862, provided Union slaveholders with up to $300 per freed slave, which resulted in freedom for 3,185 slaves.

Meanwhile, Jonas devoted his early years in Quincy to his business and to Freemasonry. He opened a general store, established another business some fifteen miles away in Columbus, Illinois, and engaged in a fruitless effort to boost Columbus by opening a Masonic lodge there and by campaigning to upgrade the village (today home to approximately one hundred people) into a full-fledged county seat. He also helped to establish the Grand Masonic Lodge of Illinois and in 1840 was elected Most Worshipful Grand Master of that lodge. He was becoming known.[22]

Lincoln, with his fine memory and sharp political

HENRY CLAY TO ABRAHAM JONAS, MAY 3, 1838

For Abraham Jonas, like Lincoln, Henry Clay was his "beau ideal of a statesman." That Clay held Jonas in high regard, as well, is evidenced in this letter. Four years later, he would remark that Jonas is still very much missed.
Wells Family

instincts, doubtless took notice. It would also not likely have escaped his notice that Jonas, presumably influenced by his personal experience as a religious outsider and by his family ties with Mormon prophet Joseph Smith's Hebrew teacher, Joshua Seixas, displayed extraordinary sympathy toward local Mormons. Forced from their homes in Missouri, the Mormons had settled in the Illinois city of Commerce, which, in 1840, they renamed Nauvoo. As Grand Master of the Masons, Jonas permitted the establishment of a Masonic lodge in Nauvoo. He presided personally at the lodge installation (with the Mormon Prophet, Joseph Smith, serving as chaplain) and then initiated Smith into the Masonic order and instantly ("on sight") raised him to the rank of Master Mason, a rare honor.[23] "I hope and trust that the people of Illinois have no disposition to disturb unoffending people who have no disposition but to live peacefully under the laws of the country and to worship God, under their own vine and fig tree," Jonas declared, employing the same biblical metaphor that George Washington had used in his famous letter to the Jews of Newport.[24] Lincoln, characteristically, was much more reserved and said nothing about Mormonism until 1857.[25]

Following the murder of Joseph Smith in 1843, Jonas, at the behest of the governor, courageously traveled both to Nauvoo and to surrounding non-Mormon

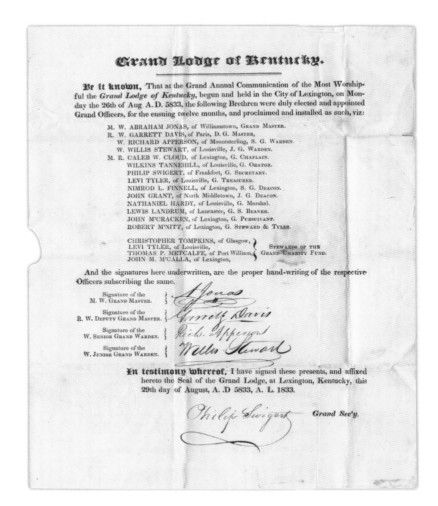

A MASONIC DOCUMENT SIGNED BY ABRAHAM JONAS IN HIS CAPACITY AS GRAND MASTER OF THE GRAND KENTUCKY LODGE, AUGUST 29, 1833

Unlike some fraternal organizations, Freemasonry did not bar Jewish participation. Jonas founded this Kentucky chapter in 1832 and later would go on to found the Masonic Lodge in Quincy, Illinois, in 1846. Lincoln, who was not a Mason, was said to have nonetheless professed respect for the fraternity.

Shapell Manuscript Collection

communities, in a failed attempt to promote peace and restore order.[26] He was by then a familiar figure in the region and (with help from Mormon voters) had won a seat in the Illinois General Assembly.

No later than February 22, 1843, on Washington's Birthday, Abraham Jonas and Abraham Lincoln are known to have been in the same place at the same time. Whether or not the two men had met previously, this is the first recorded instance of them being together in the same location.[27] The annual commemoration of Washington's Birthday was celebrated that year in Springfield's Hall of Representatives. The Springfield Cadets attended, the Masons attended, many legislators attended, and Abraham Lincoln—no longer a legislator but still full of political ambitions—attended as

well, with Jonas, a celebrated orator, delivering one of the principal addresses that day.

Jonas at that time was busy transitioning from commerce to the law. He read law with Orville Hickman Browning, one of Quincy's first and greatest lawyers, a handsome, well-bred Kentucky native who had moved to Quincy in 1831. Browning, in 1843, served as Jonas's colleague in the Illinois General Assembly; both men were Whigs.[28] Jonas also befriended Henry Asbury, another Kentuckian, who had likewise trained under Browning and then became his legal associate. In time, Asbury would leave Browning's firm and on June 1, 1855, become Jonas's law partner.[29] Both Browning and Asbury were friends with Abraham Lincoln—Browning and Lincoln had been friends since at least 1838.[30]

ABRAHAM LINCOLN IN SPRINGFIELD, 1847

The earliest known image of Lincoln, then congressman-elect from Illinois. It is the first of 126 photographic images—40 beardless, 86 bearded—and the only one in which his hair is combed.

Courtesy of the Library of Congress

Once admitted to the bar, on December 20, 1843, Jonas joined this circle and Lincoln befriended him as well.

As lawyers, Browning, Asbury, Jonas, and Lincoln all spent substantial amounts of time out of town, defending clients in Springfield, or in one of the scattered circuit courts. There, lawyers met and interacted, opposing one another in court and merrily fraternizing after court adjourned. Spending long hours in each other's company, they sized one another up, entertained one another (always a Lincoln forte), and talked politics.[31]

That Jonas became part of this select fraternity is no small matter. Dark eyed, slender, with black hair and an aquiline nose, he was always marked as a Jew. Gustav Koerner, a Lincoln acquaintance and an attorney in Belleville, Illinois, who served with Jonas in the General Assembly and later described him as "perhaps the best debater and the best politician on the Whig side,"

did not fail to mention his "Jewish extraction."[32] Nor, by the late 1850s, could anyone else have missed this fact, for the law offices of Jonas and Asbury in Quincy occupied a floor in the Jonas Building at the southeast corner of Fifth and Hampshire, one floor above S. & E. Jonas Hardware, operated by his brothers, and one floor below the Congregation B'nai Abraham synagogue, which the Jonas brothers had helped to establish.[33] Abraham Jonas, unlike some of his brothers, was not an observant Jew. He delivered speeches on the Jewish Sabbath, ate nonkosher foods, and on at least one occasion in 1854 dined openly with Abraham Lincoln and others at an "oyster saloon."[34] But his Judaism was still common knowledge. He was a Jew at heart and in action. Neither his fellow Quincy lawyers nor Abraham Lincoln seem to have held it against him.

Evidence of this may be found in the fact that three Quincy lawyers—Browning, his partner Nehemiah Bushnell, and a third lawyer named Archibald Williams—all supported Jonas when, in 1849, his name was put forward for the position of postmaster—a patronage post. A local blacksmith named Harrison Dills likewise put his own name forward for that position and wrote Lincoln for support. But even Dills conceded that Jonas was "a first rate man." Indeed, in a follow up letter to Lincoln, he offered to drop his candidacy in Jonas's favor: "if thare [sic] is any chance for Mr J," he wrote, "let me pass." That, in fact, is what happened. Thanks to his Whig friends, Jonas served as postmaster of Quincy, under appointments from Presidents Zachary Taylor and Millard Fillmore, from 1849 to 1852.[35]

The patronage job rewarded Jonas for his contribution to the Whig Party. Thanks to his keen mind and formidable oratorical skills he had become a respected party operative and a much-in-demand speaker at political gatherings. Once the Democrats returned to power in 1852, with the election of Franklin Pierce, Jonas naturally lost his position, but his loyalty to the Whigs continued unabated. In 1853, he chaired the party meeting that nominated candidates for local elections to West Point — Please to present my kindest regards to her —

yr friend
Frank Pierce

Hon Wm. C. Clark
Manchester
N.H.

Private

Washington
Apl 9. 1854

My dear Sir

I have just read your letter of the 6th inst.

As to the character of the principles involved in the Nebraska bill and the practical effects, which will undoubtedly flow from their adoption I agree with you entirely, believe that the bill wi

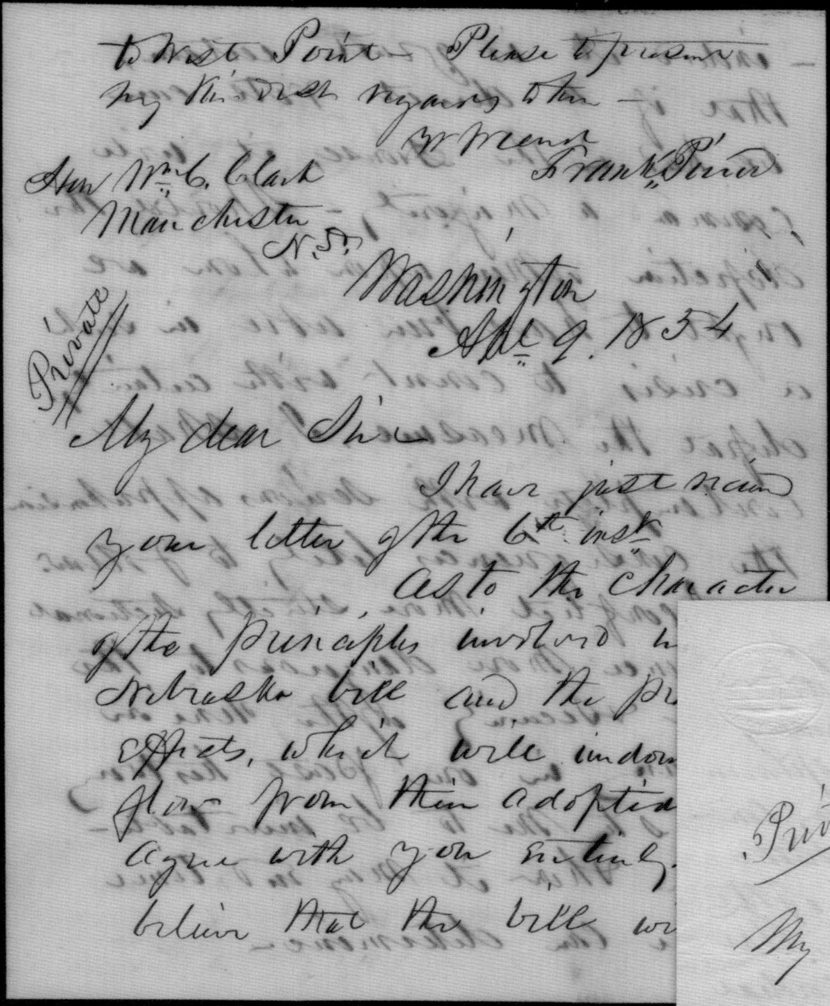

"The bill had not only my cordial assent but... my earnest approbation. I have never seen cause to regret either. Far from it."

Private

Concord
Oct 13, 1860

My dear Sir

Your letter was received two or three days ago and read not without some degree of regret, — as much perhaps on your account, as on my own. It is not easy to conceive, how the expression of an opinion or of a preference — not always matters of volition, could have excited the "anger" of one of my "warmest and most constant friends" as you still subscribe yourself.

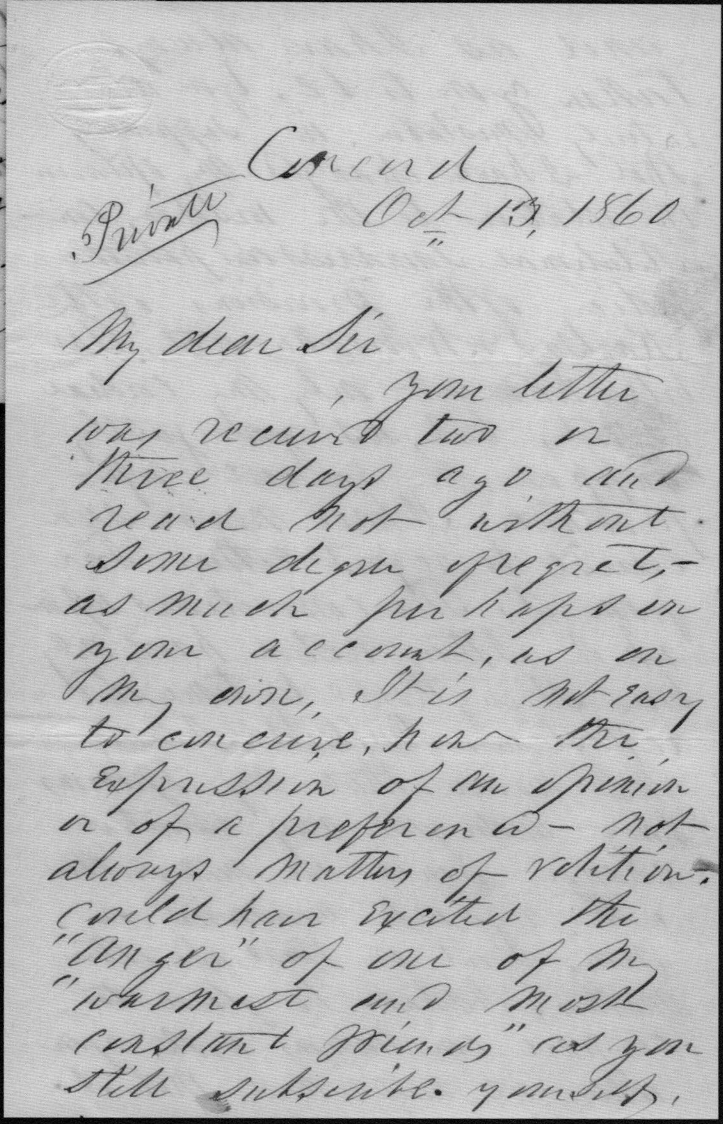

ABOVE

PRESIDENT PIERCE ON THE KANSAS-NEBRASKA ACT, APRIL 9, 1854

RIGHT

PIERCE DEFENDS THE ACT, OCTOBER 13, 1860

President Franklin Pierce, who signed the Kansas-Nebraska Act into law on May 30, 1854, here defends his support for the act. Six years later, on the very eve of rebellion, Pierce still stubbornly swore by "the wisdom, constitutional soundness and patriotic policy of the provisions" of the Kansas-Nebraska Act. "The bill had not only my cordial assent," he wrote, "but . . . my earnest approbation. I have never seen cause to regret either." Lincoln, Jonas, and the emerging Republican Party, however, thought differently. Lincoln would be elected president on the basis of his opposition to the expansion of slavery.

Shapell Manuscript Collection

HENRY ASBURY, IN UNIFORM AS PROVOST-MARSHALL OF THE QUINCY DISTRICT

A rare signed photo of Henry Asbury, Abraham Jonas's law partner for over twenty years. It was at a December 1858 meeting with publisher and power broker Horace Greeley in their law office that Asbury first suggested Lincoln's name as a possible presidential candidate, with Jonas immediately seconding the recommendation. Those two endorsements—the only of the evening—would, soon enough, prove instrumental in Lincoln's rise to the presidency.

Shapell Manuscript Collection

ADVERTISEMENT OF JONAS-ASBURY LAW OFFICES, JUNE 21, 1855

An advertisement in the Quincy Daily Whig *for the law practice of Abraham Jonas and Henry Asbury. Located in the Jonas family-owned building in Quincy, the site was a hive of activity in the 1850s. There was the S. & E. Jonas hardware store on the ground floor; the law offices of Jonas & Asbury on the second—where, on occasion, Abraham Lincoln had probably met with Jonas—and a nascent synagogue on the third.*

Courtesy of Quincy Public Library

A. JONAS.   H. ASBURY.

JONAS & ASBURY
ATTORNEYS AND COUNSELLORS AT LAW,
QUINCY ILLS.

OFFICE over S. & E. Jonas' Iron store N. E. cor. of Public Square.
A. Jonas is Commissioner of deeds for Ohio, Kentucky, Indiana and Missouri.   je4d

in Quincy. A year later, with national elections looming, he turned to the central question of the day—the extension of slavery into Kansas and Nebraska. Amidst what he described as probably "the warmest contest for Congress that we have ever had in this district," he personally "held forth for half an hour" on a cold, rainy night at a political meeting. He also sought to attract a more formidable speaker to boost Whig fortunes. So he wrote to Abraham Lincoln.[36]

Abraham Lincoln had declared himself "thunderstruck and stunned" by Congress's 1854 passage of the Kansas-Nebraska Act and President Pierce's signing of it into law.[37] The act repealed the Missouri Compromise of 1820, which Lincoln and many others considered vital to the limitation of slavery, and left it up to the territory's voters ("popular sovereignty") to decide the question of slavery in Kansas and Nebraska when they applied for statehood. Previously, under the compromise engineered in part by Henry Clay in 1850, slavery in the lands acquired under the Louisiana Purchase had been banned above the Mason-Dixon Line, thirty-six and one-half degrees north of the equator. Now, with both pro- and antislavery advocates clamoring for access to the vast western territories captured in the Mexican War, as well as to the rich farmlands of the prairie; and with industrialists eager to complete the transcontinental railroad in 1854, Congress felt the need to find a different compromise so that these new territories could be opened up and settled—even with slave labor. Stephen A. Douglas, the wily Democratic senator from Illinois and formerly Quincy's representative in Congress, engineered what he thought would be a viable compromise, winning support from a majority of Democrats and Southern Whigs. But opponents of slavery's extension—including Abraham Jonas and Abraham Lincoln—were furious, for Douglas's "compromise" made possible slavery's extension all the way across the Kansas-Nebraska plains to the western shore. There it would have room to spread instead of dying out on its own, as they had previously expected.

Lincoln, as a result, felt "aroused . . . as he had never been before."[38]

By the time Jonas wrote to him, on September 16, 1854, Lincoln had channeled this anger into action. He had immersed himself in the intricacies of the Kansas-Nebraska Act and took up the fight to reverse it. He lent support to the reelection bid of Congressman Richard Yates, who opposed the act. He debated Douglas's friend, John Calhoun, newly appointed surveyor general for the Kansas and Nebraska Territories. And he published an unsigned editorial in the *Illinois Journal* ridiculing the claim that the act did not "require slaves" to be sent into the territories. But he had not yet debated Douglas himself.[39] Moreover, his major statements in opposition to the Kansas-Nebraska Act still lay ahead. So it was extraordinarily prescient of Jonas to think to invite Lincoln to Quincy to counter Douglas and lend support to the Whig candidate, Archibald Williams, who was attempting to unseat Douglas's Democratic friend and successor in Congress, William A. Richardson. "[A]ll the Whigs here, would be much gratified if you could make it convenient and pay us a visit, while the little giant is here," Jonas wrote, using the nickname of the five-foot-four-inch Douglas. "It is believed by all who know you that a reply from you would be more effective, than from any other."[40]

Lincoln promised to come. But weeks before he arrived in Quincy, he took on the arguments of the "Little Giant" elsewhere, notably at the state fair in Springfield and in Peoria. Addressing large crowds, he focused on the immorality of slavery and on how it ran counter to basic tenets of the Declaration of Independence. The nation's founders, he insisted, sought to limit rather than to extend slavery. He called for the Missouri Compromise to be upheld. Audiences quickly warmed to this message. Privately, Douglas characterized Lincoln as "the most difficult and dangerous opponent that I have ever met."[41]

Lincoln arrived in Quincy on the night of October 31, just a week prior to Election Day. It was his first time

THE MISSOURI COMPROMISE AND POPULAR SOVEREIGNTY

THE MISSOURI COMPROMISE, passed in 1820, was an effort to preserve the delicate balance of power in Congress between states where slavery was permitted and ones where it was prohibited. Under its terms, Missouri entered the Union as a slave state and Maine as a free state. Except in Missouri, slavery was prohibited in the Louisiana Territory north of the 36° 30´ latitude line. In 1854, the Missouri Compromise was repealed by the Kansas-Nebraska Act, enacting what Senator Stephen A. Douglas (Illinois) called "popular sovereignty." It opened up the possibility that slavery would spread, since it left the issue of slavery to the vote of local residents.

ever in the city. Abraham Jonas, his host, accompanied him throughout his stay. Orville Hickman Browning took him to dinner and tea. Lincoln addressed a crowd on the Kansas-Nebraska Act, and after his speech, Jonas and others passed another hour with him and walked him to the Quincy House, where he spent the night.[42] The men doubtless talked politics. They knew that Williams's chances of winning were poor, though Lincoln hoped that his speech might give the Whig candidate "a little life."[43] One suspects that they likewise discussed the coming Illinois senatorial contest.

Lincoln's candidates, Williams and Yates, both lost their election bids, but nationally, opponents of the Kansas-Nebraska Act, whom Lincoln had supported, did well—so well, that Lincoln in late 1854 felt emboldened to put his own name forth for the Senate. To win, he needed to secure a majority of votes from members of the state General Assembly who, in those days, were responsible for electing Illinois' senators. He turned to his political friends for help. Abraham Jonas responded at once and also provided critical intelligence concerning other possible candidates, including

Quincy Ills. Sep 16. 1854

A Lincoln Esq—
    Springfield Ills

        My Dr Sir — We are in the midst of
what will probably be the warmest contest for
Congress that we have ever had in this district — if
the election was near at hand — Williams, I think
would be elected beyond a doubt — This district
is to be the great battle field, the defeat of Richardson
at this time, would be the downfall of Douglas,
standing and occupying the same position on the
Nebraska humbug — every foul and unfair means
will be brought to operate against Williams — Douglas is to be here and will in this and other counties of the district — Williams has just left for
Omaha — it being court in Henderson on monday
next — and has requested me to say to you, that
he, as well as all the Whigs here, would be much
gratified if you could make it convenient
and pay us a visit, while the little giant is here
It is believed by all who know you, that a reply
from you, would be more effective, than from
any other — I trust you may be able to pay
us the visit and thereby create a debt of gratitude
on the part of the Whigs here, which they may
at some time, have it in their power, to repay

497

...th — we do not
...will be here —
...we will let
...you to answer
...and be assured
...reatest pleasure
...the Whigs gen-
...visit us — and
...u see old nick
...esent indication
...do better, or I
...t has done for
...a decided ma
...well as on for —
...to is doing all
...e favorable, from
...think will

your assistance, we can check mate them

    Trusting to hear from you soon

        I remain Yrs truly
            A Jonas

OPPOSITE

ABRAHAM JONAS TO LINCOLN, SEPTEMBER 16, 1854

In the earliest known letter between the two men, Abraham Jonas invites Lincoln to speak against the Kansas-Nebraska Act in Quincy. By the terms of the explosive act, slavery would be allowed to spread into the Kansas-Nebraska territories—and the vast new lands captured in the Mexican War—by a vote of the majority of its inhabitants. Emotionally and politically transformed by the act, lawyer Lincoln rushed headlong out of the political wilderness into political activism, catapulting him from the plains to the presidency within six years.

Courtesy of the Library of Congress

RIGHT

LINCOLN TO JEFFERSON L. DUGGER, OCTOBER 29, 1854

Lincoln arranges to speak against the Kansas-Nebraska Act in support of Whig candidate, Archibald Williams. On that road trip through Illinois, Lincoln spent two days with Abraham Jonas: October 31 and November 1.

Shapell Manuscript Collection

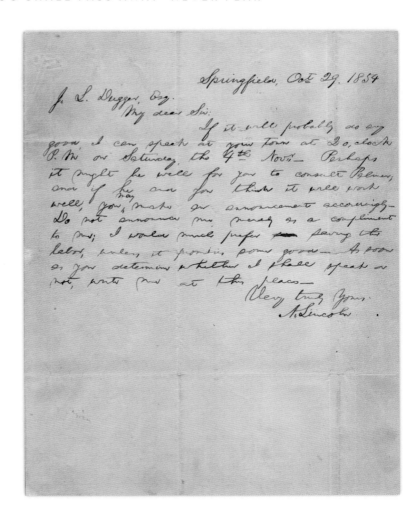

himself. "I have no pretension for that or any other office at this time," he reassured Lincoln, nor, he added, did his fellow Whig lawyers from Quincy, Orville Hickman Browning and Archibald Williams. "I should prefer you to any other," he promised, "and should be pleased to render you any service in my power."[44] As it turned out, Jonas's support did not suffice to win him the position; Lincoln stood a few votes short. So, on the tenth ballot, Lincoln cannily directed his supporters to vote for the Democrat Lyman Trumbull, whom he knew to be as angry at the Kansas-Nebraska Act as he was. He decided, one of his biographers observes, that "the long-term cause of stopping slavery trumped his short-term ambition." Trumbull, thanks to this move, was elected. Lincoln, meanwhile, swallowed his disappointment at being defeated, and within three years

both he and Trumbull stood together in the ranks of the new Republican Party.[45]

Abraham Jonas and many other former Whigs joined them in that party, determined to halt the spread of slavery and promote the spread of freedom. Illinois Republicans eschewed radicalism and nativism, and attempted to build a broad-based coalition, focused around the issue of slavery's containment. They supported the Missouri Compromise, opposed the Kansas-Nebraska Act, and pledged to prevent the admission of any new slave states into the Union. This was likewise the position of explorer John C. Frémont, who became the Republican standard bearer in 1856. Lincoln and Jonas barnstormed on Frémont's behalf, with Lincoln reputedly delivering over fifty campaign speeches, though he did not know the candidate personally.

Jonas hoped that one of those speeches would be in Quincy during the crucial two-week period before the election, but at the last minute Lincoln begged off. "I am here at court, and find myself so 'hobbled' with a particular case, that I can not leave, & consequently, can not be with you on the 23rd," Lincoln wrote sorrowfully. "I regret this exceedingly, but there is no help for it." He asked Jonas to apologize in his name and signed the letter, "Your friend as ever."[46]

The word *hobbled*—set off with quotation marks—most likely clued Jonas as to the true reason why his "friend as ever" could not make it to Quincy. Family business had detained him in Urbana. Lincoln was working there to free his "hobbled" (he was literally crippled) ne'er-do-well stepnephew, Thomas Johnston (the son of his stepbrother, John D. Johnston), who had been jailed in Champaign for stealing a solid-gold watch from a local store owned by the family of William Green. Attorney Henry Clay Whitney of Urbana, one of the many young lawyers whom Lincoln befriended and assisted, recalled that after speaking at a mass meeting in the city, Lincoln had approached him, and the two of them went "on the sly" to the local jail to meet with the unfortunate Johnston, who also faced an earlier charge of theft. "I shall do what I can for him in these two cases," he quoted Lincoln as saying, "but that's the last. After that, if he wants to be a thief, I shan't help him any more."[47] Lincoln persuaded the judge and prosecutor to waive the larceny charges, if William Green and his family agreed not to press the case further, and then visited with the Greens, who, after hearing from Lincoln, seem to have taken pity on the crippled boy and forgave him for his crime. Accordingly, the case was dropped and Johnston released. The other charge of larceny against Johnston was settled in the same fashion. All of this took time, of course, and explains why Lincoln was "hobbled"—a double entendre—and precluded him from speaking in Quincy. The clever wordplay likewise bespeaks Lincoln's intimacy with Jonas. The quotation marks imply that the two

men understood the unhappy family story behind the word *hobbled*. Lincoln had let Jonas in on what was otherwise an embarrassing family secret.[48]

Lincoln and Jonas put their ideological friendship on display in a more public way when both appeared on ballots as Republican electors in 1856. But because of the third-party candidacy of former president Millard Fillmore, representing the anti-immigrant American (Know-Nothing) Party, the Democrat, James Buchanan, eked out a plurality in the state, garnering 44.1 percent of its votes.[49] Buchanan also won the national election—with 45.3 percent of the vote. The election nevertheless proved beneficial to Lincoln, for Republicans won both the state governorship in Illinois and a majority in the General Assembly. As one of the Republican Party's most articulate spokesmen and strategists and runner-up for its vice presidential nomination, he was properly credited with this success, and thanks to press coverage of his speeches, his reputation outside of the state expanded as well. His admirers, like Abraham Jonas, looked to advance Lincoln's career.

Jonas soon had a new reason to admire Lincoln—one that was little known at the time and has been little remembered by biographers but that actually spoke volumes concerning the Republican hopeful's values, particularly his concern for racial justice. In the fall of 1856, a young man named John Shelby, one member of the small community of black residents in Springfield, Illinois (where there were but 171 black residents in 1850), traveled to St. Louis and hired himself out on a steamboat bound for New Orleans. Arriving in port, he clambered ashore without equipping himself with papers attesting to his status as a free person. He was promptly arrested and cast into prison. In New Orleans, it was a crime for blacks to be found on the street after dark without a written pass. While poor Shelby languished in jail, the steamboat that had hired him departed, leaving him at risk of being sold into slavery to pay off his prison expenses.[50]

Fortunately, Lincoln and Benjamin F. Jonas, the

son of Abraham Jonas and a New Orleans attorney,[51] intervened to save him. Young Jonas, in an 1857 letter, indicated that he reached out to Lincoln after Shelby mentioned him as someone "who would take an interest in his behalf." He recognized the name Lincoln as belonging to "an old friend of my father," and contacted him. Benjamin Jonas's sister, Annie, by contrast, wrote some years later that it was Lincoln who actually took the first step, instructing her brother to free Shelby and to "charge the expense incurred to him." Lincoln's law partner, William Herndon, elaborated on that account (though without mentioning Jonas's name), recalling that Shelby's mother "came to us with the story of the wrong done her son and induced us to interfere in her behalf." According to him, the governors of Illinois and Louisiana both refused to act on the matter, so Lincoln and Herndon drew up a subscription list, "collecting funds enough to purchase the young man's liberty." What, in the end, is indisputable is that Lincoln dispatched to Jonas a draft for $69.30 (almost $1,700 in today's money) in order to redeem Shelby. This was enough to purchase his freedom from prison, return him safely to Springfield, and pay off a local official. Both Jonas and Lincoln waived their fees. For Lincoln, who kept the whole matter private, the episode reflected his deepest principles, his belief that "all men are created equal."[52]

LINCOLN AND JONAS ON THE FRÉMONT BALLOT, 1856

Ballots in mid-nineteenth-century America generally listed the name of the presidential candidate at the top, and below it, those of the electors who had been elected to support him. In 1856, Lincoln and Jonas both appeared on the Illinois ballot as presidential electors under the Frémont ticket. Here Lincoln and Jonas represented the new Republican Party, which called itself, among other things, the "Anti-Nebraska Ticket." On Election Day, voters brought to the polling station the ballot of the candidate of their choice, gave their name to the registrar, who checked that they were eligible to vote, and then dropped these preprinted ballots into the ballot box.

Rail Splitter Archives, New York City

FREMONT & BISSELL TICKET.

For Governor.
WILLIAM H. BISSELL.
For Lieutenant Governor.
JOHN WOOD.
For Secretary of State.
OZIAS M. HATCH.
For Auditor of State.
JESSE K. DUBOIS.
For State Treasurer,
JAMES MILLER.
For Superintendent of Public Instruction,
WILLIAM H. POWELL.
For Congress,
ELIHU B. WASHBURNE.

For Presidential Electors.
A. LINCOLN,
FREDERICK HECKER,
ELISHA P. FERRY,
JEROME J. BEARDSLEY,
WILLIAM FITHIAN,
T. JUDSON HALE,
ABRAHAM JONAS,
WILLIAM H. HERNDON,
H. P. H. BROMWELL,
F. S. RUTHERFORD,
DAVID L. PHILLIPS,

COUNTY TICKET.

For Clerk of Circuit Court,
GEORGE T. KASSON,
For District Attorney,
EDWARD S. JOSLYN.
For Sheriff,
JOHN EDDY.
For the Legislature,
LAWRENCE S. CHURCH.
LUTHER W. LAWRENCE.
For Coroner,
NAJAH BEARDSLY.

For Convention.

Urbana, Oct,, 21. 1856

A,, Jonas, Esq
    My dear Sir:
        I am here at court, and find myself so "hobbled" with a particular case, that I can not leave, & consequently, can not be with you on the 23 $\underline{rd}$, I regret this exceedingly, but there is no help for it. Please make the best apology, for me, in your power—
        Your friend as ever
        A,, Lincoln—

"I am here at court and find myself so 'hobbled' with a particular case, that I can not leave."

A VALUABLE LESSON FOR A WAYWARD NEPHEW: "WANTING TO WORK IS SO RARE A MERIT..."

HIS LIFE'S HISTORY, Lincoln said in an 1860 handwritten autobiographical sketch, could be summed up in a single sentence: "The short and simple annals of the poor." Had he chosen to elaborate, he might have added how it was, then, that a child of the impoverished frontier became president: "Work, work, work, is the main thing," he wrote in answer to an 1860 inquiry of how to obtain a thorough knowledge of the law. As much if not more than any other quality, Lincoln valued hard work—in contrast to the thievery of the nephew he was obligated to defend in court. Honest work was, he believed, the essential element in achieving individual success and social advancement.

Interestingly, Lincoln had, eight years before, been down a similar road with the boy's father—Lincoln's stepbrother—when Lincoln tried to lend a helping hand in the face of bad conduct: "You are not lazy, and still you are an idler. I doubt whether since I saw you, you have done a whole day's work in any one day." Lincoln biographer Carl Sandburg referred to the elder Johnston as "the most fascinating braggart and scalawag known to Lincoln's boyhood and youth."

Growing up on the Indiana frontier, Lincoln spent long days working with his father and as a hired hand to neighboring farmers. He taught himself the intricacies of land surveying; and when he decided to become a lawyer, he read and studied diligently; and when a lawyer, rode the circuit six months a year (when prairie lawyers traveled through large sections of Illinois to meet and advise clients who needed representation).

As president, he put in long hours attending to the countless details of running the country. But in running the vast federal bureaucracy, Lincoln discovered that not everyone in government shared his enthusiasm for tireless labor. So, when asked by a needy mother in October 1861 to supply army jobs for her eager boys, the new president was pleased to oblige with this letter of referral. "The lady—bearer of this—says she has two sons who want to work. Set them at it, if possible. Wanting to work is so rare a merit, that it should be encouraged." This brief but defining letter is one of the most personally revealing letters about Lincoln—the man.

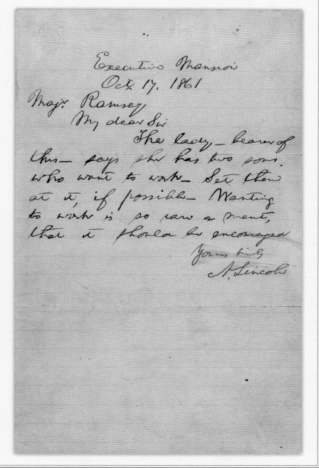

OPPOSITE

LINCOLN TO ABRAHAM JONAS: "HOBBLED," OCTOBER 21, 1856

Busy campaigning for the Republican ticket two weeks before the national election, Lincoln, having shared with Jonas an intimate family matter about a troublesome nephew of his, who was arrested for thievery, shares a humorous pun with Jonas about the situation. Getting the youth—who was, literally, crippled—out of jail, a sarcastic and frustrated Lincoln jokes, has "hobbled" his schedule, so that he cannot meet with Jonas as planned. He signed the letter: "Your friend as ever."

Shapell Legacy Partnership

RIGHT

LINCOLN TO GEORGE D. RAMSEY: "WANTING TO WORK . . . ," OCTOBER 17, 1861

Shapell Legacy Partnership

The Dred Scott case, decided by the U.S. Supreme Court on March 6, 1857, ruled otherwise. Speaking for the Court, Chief Justice Roger B. Taney pronounced blacks "so far inferior, that they had no rights which the white man was bound to respect." Constitutional freedoms, the Court decided, did not apply to blacks. As for the Declaration of Independence's assertion that "all men are created equal," the decision declared "that the enslaved African race were not intended to be included, and formed no part of the people who framed and adopted this declaration." Implicitly, it reduced blacks to a status below that of "all men" and doomed them to perpetual inequality.[53]

Lincoln, when this infamous decision came down, was out of politics. Having spent much of 1856 stumping for Frémont, he needed to focus on his law practice and rebuild his personal assets. But when Stephen A. Douglas, in a celebrated address, vindicated the Court's judgment, declaring that "the signers of the Declaration of Independence . . . referred to the white race alone, and not to the African, when they declared all men to have been created equal," Lincoln felt compelled to reply. Douglas, he knew, would stand for reelection to the Senate in 1858, and he aimed to oppose him. Douglas's views, moreover, were anathema to Lincoln. He predicted, rightly, that the Dred Scott decision would one day be overruled and insisted that the Founders meant what they said when they celebrated the equality of all men. "They did not intend to declare all men equal in all respects," he conceded, but insisted that they did consider them "equal in 'certain inalienable rights, among which are life, liberty, and the pursuit of happiness.'" Thinking beyond the question of blacks, he looked forward to an America that viewed the goal of equality in terms of "progressive improvement." To him, the phrase "all men are created equal" was a "standard maxim for free society," something "constantly looked to, constantly labored for, and even though never perfectly attained, constantly approximated, and thereby constantly spreading and deepening its influence, and

augmenting a happiness and value of life to all people of all colors everywhere."[54]

As Lincoln's law practice and professional reputation expanded and he was drawn back into politics, his circle of Jewish acquaintances expanded as well. Illinois' Jewish population was approaching 3,000 by the late 1850s, many of them involved in business and commerce. Several soon crossed Lincoln's path. A good example is Henry Rice, subsequently a leading figure in the manufacture and distribution of dry goods and in Jewish philanthropy. Born in 1834 in Bamberg, Bavaria, Rice arrived in the United States in 1850. Three years later, he settled in the small community of Jacksonville, Illinois, thirty-five miles from Springfield, and established a clothing store. Rice met Lincoln no later than 1857, when he served as a witness in a court case between Dewitt Gale and the local Morgan County Bank. Gale had sued the bank for nonpayment on a draft; the bank, which Lincoln defended, claimed that it had paid him in cash. Rice's testimony in the case does not survive, but Lincoln's client won the case.[55]

Years later, Rice recalled recommending Lincoln to several Cincinnati firms (probably ones belonging to Jewish relatives of his in that city) that required the services of an Illinois attorney. He also recalled meeting Lincoln again in Springfield following his election. As he recounted the story, the president-elect was on his way to the railroad station to pick up his wife and mentioned, in his typically folksy way, that Mary had been off on a shopping trip "to get some duds." Rice claimed to have called upon Lincoln once at the White House, where, he said, he was invited to stay for supper. In 1861, as we shall see, Lincoln wrote a letter endorsing Rice for the position of sutler, a military storekeeper for the United States Army.[56]

As Lincoln traversed Illinois in 1858, as part of his campaign for the Senate, he continued to meet other Jews. In Chicago, he became acquainted with Henry Greenebaum, one of four prominent Jewish brothers who immigrated to the city from Eppelsheim, Germany, in

AT AN ELECTION

Held at *the house of J Wrights* in *Wrights* precinct, county of *Morgan* state of Illinois, on the *4th* day of November, 1856, the following named persons received the number of votes annexed to their respective names, for the following described offices, to wit:

Names of persons voted for.	Whole number of votes cast for such person.	Name or title of office.
A M Herington	Ninety Six	} Elector at Large.
Chas H Constable	Do	
M L Joslyn	Do	
Hugh Maher	Do	
Milton T Peters	Do	
Robt Holloway	Do	
Jno P Richmon	Do	District Electors
J W Houlton	Do	
O B Ficklin	Do	
W A T Sparks	Do	
John A Logan	Do	
Abraham Lincoln	Fifty Nine	
Frederick Hecker	Do	
Elisha S Ferry	Do	
Jerome J Beardsley	Do	

Abraham Lincoln
Frederick Hecker
Elisha S Ferry
Jerome J Beardsley
William Fithian
J Judson Hale
Abraham Jonas

ILLINOIS POLL BOOK, 1856

In 1856, Lincoln and Jonas were among the organizers of the new Republican Party in Illinois, and their names appear repeatedly in these poll books from various Illinois precincts, evidence of their passionate involvement—always on the same side—in politics. On Election Day, election officials carefully recorded all of the information concerning the election—the candidates, the people who voted, and the sum of the votes— in these individual poll books containing the names of all registered voters.

Shapell Manuscript Collection

the late 1840s. Greenebaum, in his twenties, served as a Democratic alderman in Chicago and had first met Lincoln in 1855. He remembered being "greatly impressed" by Lincoln's "congeniality," his "wealth of humor," and his "remarkable mental endowment." Lincoln, who served as judge in over 300 cases, presided in at least two cases concerning Henry Greenebaum's brother-in-law, German Jew Gerhard Foreman, in 1856 and 1857. In both cases, the court ruled in favor of Foreman's company. In 1858, Greenebaum later recalled, he "accompanied Lincoln on a walk during which he asked me for my support." Since Greenebaum, unlike many other politically engaged Chicago German Jews, was a Democrat and "strong political friend" of Stephen A. Douglas, he turned Lincoln down. Reflecting back years later, he described Lincoln as "the greatest man I ever met."[57]

Lincoln formally kicked off his campaign to unseat Douglas at a special Republican nominating convention held in Springfield on June 16, 1858. There he delivered one of the finest speeches of his life. "A house divided against itself cannot stand," he proclaimed, quoting a well-known teaching from the Gospels.[58] "I believe," he explained, "this government cannot endure permanently half slave and half free." Linking Douglas to what he portrayed as a conspiracy to secure slavery throughout the country, he sought to distance Illinois Republicans from Douglas. Ever distrustful of the leonine "Little Giant," Lincoln insisted that Douglas was a determined opponent of human equality and a staunch advocate of slavery. ("For years he has labored to prove it a sacred right of white men to take negro slaves into the new territories.") Quoting Ecclesiastes (9:4), he declared that "a living dog"—a modest reference to himself—"is better than a dead lion." His own emotions, he knew, had been deeply stirred by slavery's advances; Douglas, by contrast, was indifferent—"He don't care anything about it."[59]

Abraham Jonas and his partner, Henry Asbury, strongly supported Lincoln. In July, Asbury sent the candidate probing questions concerning Douglas's stance on slavery. He particularly urged him to press Douglas. "Don't let him dodge here; he must come out here," he coaxed, encouraging Lincoln to challenge Douglas to explain how slavery might be limited anywhere in the United States.[60] By the time the letter arrived, Lincoln and Douglas had agreed to a series of seven debates across the state of Illinois. The sixth debate was scheduled for Quincy.

Before then, Lincoln agreed to spend a day between his first and second debates on August 21 and August 27, respectively, in the village of Augusta, some forty-one miles from Quincy, where a Republican convention to select a congressional and state senatorial candidate was taking place and Jonas thought that one of Lincoln's "sledge hammer speeches" would "effect wonders." "My mind is at once made up to be with you at Augusta on the 25th," Lincoln promised.[61]

Good to his word, he made the journey, and Abraham Jonas, along with his son Edward, spent time with him. Edward, subsequently the only one of Jonas's sons to fight for the Union, never forgot his encounter with Lincoln, who was drawn to children. "While my father was speaking," Edward recalled, "I suddenly felt a tickling behind my ear. Thinking it a bug or fly I slapped vigorously, but upon its being repeated several times, I became suspicious and turned suddenly and caught the fly. It was Mr. Lincoln with a straw in his hand. He made it all right at once by catching me up with his long arm, drawing me to his side and talking to me very entertainingly until his turn came to address the assemblage." Lincoln went on to address more than 1,200 people on the subject of slavery and then likely took counsel with the elder Jonas and Asbury concerning his forthcoming debate in Freeport, on August 27.[62]

While Lincoln and Douglas were busy debating, Jonas did not sit idle. He was busy campaigning on Lincoln's behalf. In late September, for example, he helped bring 5,000 people to Warsaw, about thirty-four miles from Quincy, to hear Senator Lyman Trumbull speak out for the Republican Party. When Trumbull

to charge a fee of $25, I am at a loss to imagine
as he had nothing to do with the matter— and
so far as I knew, rendered no service whatever.
Again sir permit me to thank
you— and to assure you that any service I
can render you in this part of the world will give
me pleasure—
With much respect
Truly yours
B. F. Jonas

New Orleans La
June 4 1857

Hon. A Lincoln
Springfield Illinois
Dear Sir
Your letter of the 27
ult. enclosing draft for $ 69 30 on the Metropolitan
Bank of NewYork, in full for advances, and fee, in
the matter of the colored boy John Shelly, has just
been received. and permit me Sir, to return my
most sincere acknowledgments for your kind
services in this matter.
I should never have ventured
to trouble you, had not the boy mentioned your
name, as that of one, who would take an interest
in his behalf, and had I not recognized in you
an old friend of my father—
I owe an apology to the
lady, for misinterpreting the cause of her silence
but I was of course disappointed, at receiving
an answer to neither of my letters, and besides
thought my correspondent was a gentleman, as
the boy spoke of Mr Grimsley.
I am glad that he has
returned safe— Should he come south again, be
sure and let him have his papers with him—
and he must also be careful not to go away
from the boat at night— without a pass. which
it is the duty of the Captain to procure for him.
What right Col A P Field had

716

BENJAMIN JONAS TO LINCOLN, JUNE 4, 1857

Who wrote who first is unclear, but together Lincoln and Abraham Jonas's son, Benjamin, worked to get an unjustly held "free man of color" out of a New Orleans jail. Later the younger Jonas would, along with as many as four brothers, join the Confederacy. Nonetheless, he later recalled how "Mr. Lincoln always asked after us when he saw anyone from New Orleans during the war."

Courtesy of Library of Congress

Springfield, Aug: 2. 1858–

A. Jonas, Esq
      My dear Sir
            Yours of the 30th July is
just received– My mind is at once made
up to be with you at Augusta on the 25th
of August, unless I shall conclude it will
prevent my being at Freeport on the 27th
when and where, by appointment, I am to meet
Judge Douglas– I suppose there will be no
difficulty in getting from Augusta to Freeport
in due time–
                              Yours very truly
                              A. Lincoln–

"My mind is at once made up to be

with you at Augusta on the 25th..."

was delayed, Jonas himself rose to speak, addressing the crowd for two hours, "in which," a sympathetic local paper reported, "he held his audience spell bound."[63]

When Lincoln arrived in Quincy to debate Douglas, on October 13, Jonas, as chair of the local Committee on Arrangements, was one of his hosts. The law office of Jonas and Asbury, according to a retrospective account, served as "a kind of Lincoln headquarters."[64] Contemporary newspaper advertisements, signed by Jonas, encouraged voters to travel to Quincy for the debate, to "hear the true principles of the Republican Party expounded and the unsound doctrines of the Douglas Democracy exposed."[65] Jonas, who appreciated the importance of pageantry, also made sure that when Lincoln arrived on the morning train from Macomb, an elaborate procession accompanied him to the courthouse. Following the debate, doubtless also at Jonas's initiative, a "splendid torchlight procession" brought him to the patrician home of Orville Hickman Browning, where he spent the night (though Browning himself was away at court in Carthage).[66] The debate itself did not break new ground but did offer Lincoln an opportunity to spell out in pithy fashion the difference, as he saw it, between his Republican Party and Douglas's Democrats: "the difference of opinion, reduced to its lowest terms, is no other than the difference between the men who think slavery a wrong and

OPPOSITE

LINCOLN TO JONAS, AUGUST 2, 1858

Summoned by Abraham Jonas in July 1858 to give another of his "sledge hammer speeches" on behalf of the Republican congressional candidates in Augusta, Illinois, Lincoln— although himself immersed in his own grueling race against Stephen A. Douglas for the Senate—heeded Jonas's political call to show up and speak. "My mind is at once made up to be with you at Augusta on the 25th," he replied here. It is noteworthy that Lincoln, who would first debate Douglas on the 21st and again, the second time, on August 27th, took Jonas's advice.

Abraham Lincoln Presidential Library & Museum

Daily Whig & Republican.

QUINCY ILLINOIS.
TUESDAY, AUGUST 24.
REPUBLICAN TICKET.

For State Treasurer,
JAMES MILLER,
OF MCLEAN COUNTY.

For Superintendent of Public Instruction,
NEWTON BATEMAN,
OF MORGAN COUNTY.

AUGUSTA, AHOY!

We understand that a very large delegation, accompanied by Steig's Brass Band, will leave on the morning train on Wendesday, the 25th, for Augusta, to attend the Congressional Convention and the Mass Meeting, to meet and hear LINCOLN. We hope every good Republican, that can do so, will be on hand. TRUMBULL is also expected to be there. Those who intend forming part of the crowd on the occasion, from this city, are requested to obtain their tickets at the office, under the Quincy House, to-day or to-morrow, so as to enable the Rail Road agents to be prepared with sufficient accommodation for the crowd. We learn that some 50 are expected to join the train at Camp Point. A glorious time is anticipated.

Huzza for Abe Lincoln!!!

DELEGATES TO THE REPUBLICAN CONGRESSIONAL CONVENTION TO BE HELD AT AUGUSTA, WEDNESDAY, 25th.

A. Jonas, Henry Asbury, B. M. Prentiss, S. P. Delano, J. K. Van Doorn, A. Buddee, J. S. Loomis, J. Tilson, J. Rice, T. Crocker, E. A. Dudly, Capt. J. V. Hanks, Jas. M. Crawford, T. Killam, J. Benton, Col. J. B. Chittenden, J. Byler, T. B. Warren, J. J. Kirkpatrick, A. M. Smith, G. P. Phinney, J. Pearce, G. W. Williams, A. H. Pettit, J. Q. Adams, S. S. Meacham and R. G. Kay.

THE *QUINCY DAILY WHIG*, AUGUST 24, 1858

"Augusta Ahoy!" The local Quincy newspaper announces Lincoln's upcoming visit to Augusta: "Huzza for Abe Lincoln!!!"

Courtesy of the Quincy Public Library

**EDWARD JONAS,
"I SUDDENLY FELT A
TICKLING BEHIND
MY EAR . . ."**

*As Lincoln and Abraham Jonas's son
Edward sat listening to the elder
Jonas speak at an Augusta political
event in the week between the first
and second debates, the younger Jonas
was playfully teased, he later recalled,
by Lincoln himself.*

Collection of John E. Boos

those who do not think it wrong. The Republican party think it wrong—we think it is a moral, a social and a political wrong."[67]

By the time he uttered those words in Quincy, Lincoln may have sensed that he was fighting a losing battle. Douglas's campaign chest was far richer than his, and years of gerrymandered voting districts and malapportioned seats in Illinois gave the Democrats a clear electoral advantage; the rule of "one man one vote" was not yet in force. In addition, Lincoln proved too radical

for some voters. They feared, despite his denials, that a vote for him was a vote for abolition. Perhaps in an effort to steel himself (even as he reassured others that "we shall carry the day") Lincoln told one of those who met with him at Quincy, the humorist David R. Locke, that he would win the popular vote "but that Douglas would, nevertheless, be elected to the Senate, owing to the skillful manner in which the State had been districted in his interest." That is precisely what happened on Election Day. Lincoln won the popular

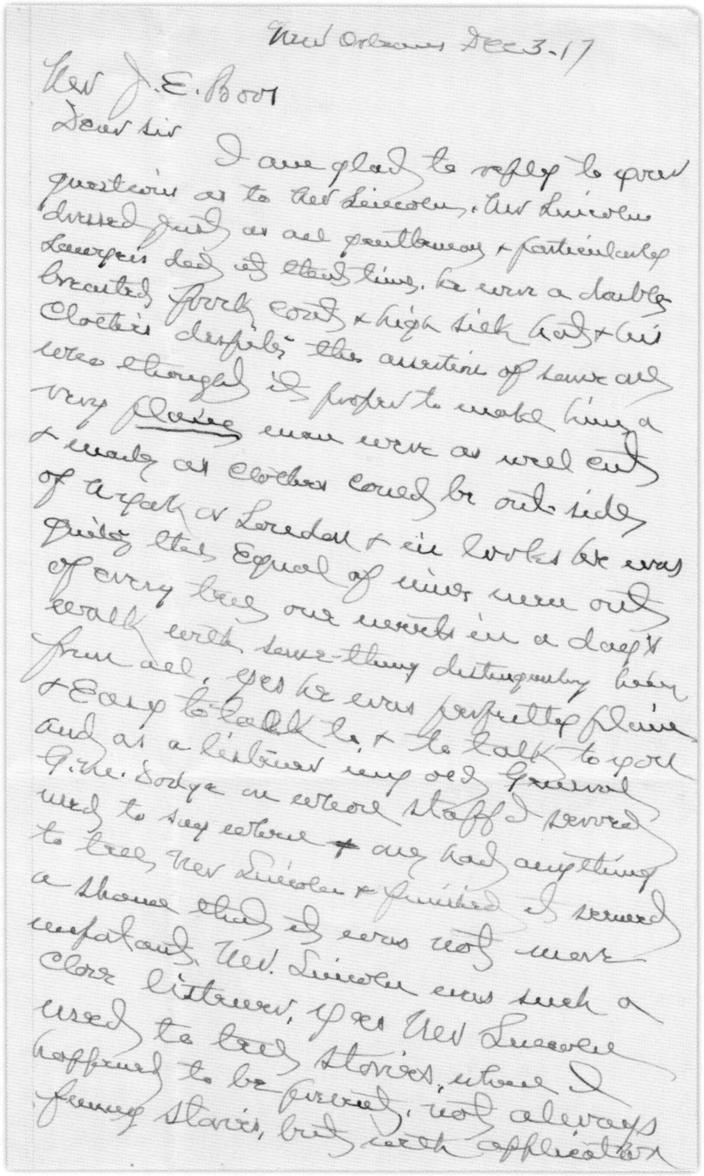

[Handwritten letter, largely illegible cursive, dated "New Orleans Dec 3-17," addressed to "Rev J. E. Boot / Dear Sir"]

EDWARD JONAS RECALLS HIS FATHER'S FRIEND

The youngest Jonas son, Edward, the only son of Abraham to fight for the Union, fondly recalls in 1917 how Lincoln dressed, talked, listened, and debated in Quincy, fifty-nine years before: "Yes he was perfectly plain & easy to talk to . . . Mr. Lincoln was such a close listener. Yes Mr. Lincoln used to tell stories, when I happened to be present . . ."

Shapell Manuscript Collection

vote but Douglas became senator. Yet even as he lost his Senate bid, Lincoln knew that he had advanced the cause of human equality, attracted nationwide attention to himself and his platform, and inflicted great political damage upon Douglas. "You can't overturn a pyramid," he reputedly observed, "but you can undermine it; that's what I have been trying to do."[68] In the aftermath, Henry Asbury wrote to thank Lincoln "for your noble canvass in behalf of Freedom." Speaking, one suspects, for his law partner Abraham Jonas as well,

he encouraged Lincoln not to "be persuaded by soreheads to abandon the positions you and we assumed in the late canvass until we have fought out the battle," a hint that another, even more decisive electoral contest lay ahead. "I simply write to say," Asbury concluded, "you have been and are right." Lincoln sent him back a reassuring reply. "The fight must go on," he agreed. "The cause of civil liberty must not be surrendered at the end of one, or even, one hundred defeats."[69] He expressed similar sentiments to the chair of the Republican state

THE FRIENDS OF

HON. ABRAHAM LINCOLN

In the city and country are invited to rally in their strength, at QUINCY, on Wednesday, Oct. 13th. ABRAHAM LINCOLN and JUDGE DOUGLAS will address the masses then assembled. MR. LINCOLN is expected to arrive at Quincy on a special train, from the north, on the morning of the 13th, at half-past 9 o'clock, at which time the Republicans from the city and country, under the charge of the Marshal of the day, will proceed in procession, to receive our champion at the depot, and conduct him to the Court House. It is hoped our country friends will be in the city in time to co-operate with the Republicans of the city. The programme and order of procession will be published by the Marshal in a day or two.

All who desire to hear the true principles of the Repuplican party expounded, and the unsound doctrines of the Douglas Democracy exposed, are invited to attend.

By order of the Republican Committee of Arrangements,

A. JONAS, Ch'n.

central committee, his friend and de facto campaign manager, Norman B. Judd. "Let the past as nothing be," he wrote him in the election's aftermath. "For the future my view is that the fight must go on." A day later, he consoled Judd with wisdom from the East, sometimes attributed to King Solomon and deeply important to his own psychological well-being. "And this too shall pass away," he wrote, "Never fear."[70]

Confessing to Judd that in the wake of his defeat he was "absolutely without money now for even household purposes," Lincoln took a long view of his situation—much as he would repeatedly do later, following defeats in the Civil War. Looking ahead, he even promised to contribute $250 toward discharging his party's debt from the election, but only after a real estate investment he had earlier made with Judd was settled.[71]

"I write merely to let you know that I am neither dead nor dying," Lincoln wrote reassuringly to a friend on December 12, 1858. His defeat still stung and he experienced moments of dark depression, but in one interview, he compared himself to a boy who, having had his finger squeezed pretty badly, "felt too big to cry and too badly hurt to laugh." He understood, in short, that he had not been wounded nearly as seriously as first he thought. "We shall," he vowed, "beat them in the long run."[72]

The passage of time, the renewal of his law practice, and a rising stream of much-needed income all likely contributed to Lincoln's improved demeanor. He also

ABOVE

THE *QUINCY DAILY WHIG*, OCTOBER 7, 1858

Jonas, as the Republican chairman of the committee for the Lincoln-Douglas debate in Quincy, published this invitation in the local papers: "The Friends of Hon. Abraham Lincoln . . . are invited to rally in their strength . . . to hear the true principles of the Republican Party expounded, and the unsound doctrines of the Douglas Democracy exposed." Jonas not only signed the printed invitation but introduced Lincoln to the crowd.

Courtesy of the Quincy Public Library

OPPPOSITE

**LINCOLN TO NORMAN B. JUDD, "NEVER FEAR,"
NOVEMBER 16, 1858**

Following his defeat in the epic 1858 Senate contest, Lincoln writes to campaign manager Judd. "You are feeling badly— And this too shall pass away'—Never fear." The phrase came from an Eastern folktale attributed to King Solomon. Judd's disappointment would indeed soon pass away: within six weeks Lincoln would be proposed as a possible presidential candidate in the 1860 election.

Shapell Manuscript Collection

Springfield, Nov. 16. 1858

Hon: N. B. Judd
My dear Sir
Yours of the 15th is just received. I wrote you the same day. As to the pecuniary matter, I am willing to pay according to my ability; but I am the poorest hand living to get others to pay. I have been on expences so long without seeing any thing that I am absolutely without money now for even household purposes. Still, if you can put in two hundred and fifty dollars for me towards discharging the debt of the committee, I will allow it when you and I settle the private matter between us. This, with what I have already paid, and with an outstanding note of mine, will exceed my subscription of five hundred dollars. This too is exclusive of my ordinary expences during the campaign, all which being added to my loss of time and business, bears pretty heavily upon one no better off in world's goods than I; but as I had the post of honor, it is not for me to be over-nice.
You are feeling badly. "And this too shall pass away." Never fear.
Yours as ever
A. Lincoln

"You are feeling badly—'And this too shall pass away'—Never fear."

discovered, perhaps to his surprise, that he had become something of a national celebrity. Some even discerned in him presidential timber.

Abraham Jonas, whose political instincts were widely admired, promoted Lincoln's candidacy for the nation's highest office. When Horace Greeley, editor of the *New York Tribune* and one of the most influential political figures in the country, showed up in Quincy on December 26, 1858, Jonas called together his Republican friends to meet with him in the law offices of Asbury and Jonas. The talk dealt with "political matters," and Jonas, as well as the others in the room, openly criticized Greeley for his "benevolent attitude" toward Douglas in the senatorial campaign. When the talk turned to the upcoming presidential contest, various names were bandied about including William Seward of New York, Edward Bates of Missouri, and the elderly Supreme Court justice John McClean, whose dissent in the Dred Scott case made him a Republican hero. "Gentlemen, there is one name you have not mentioned," Henry Asbury recalled interjecting when he wrote of the meeting years later. "I mean Abraham Lincoln." The suggestion initially fell flat, Asbury remembered, but then his Jewish partner, Abraham Jonas, reinforced it. "There may be more in Asbury's suggestion than any of us now think," Jonas declared, as if in echo of Lincoln's "And this too shall pass away. Never fear." Events would soon prove both men correct.[74]

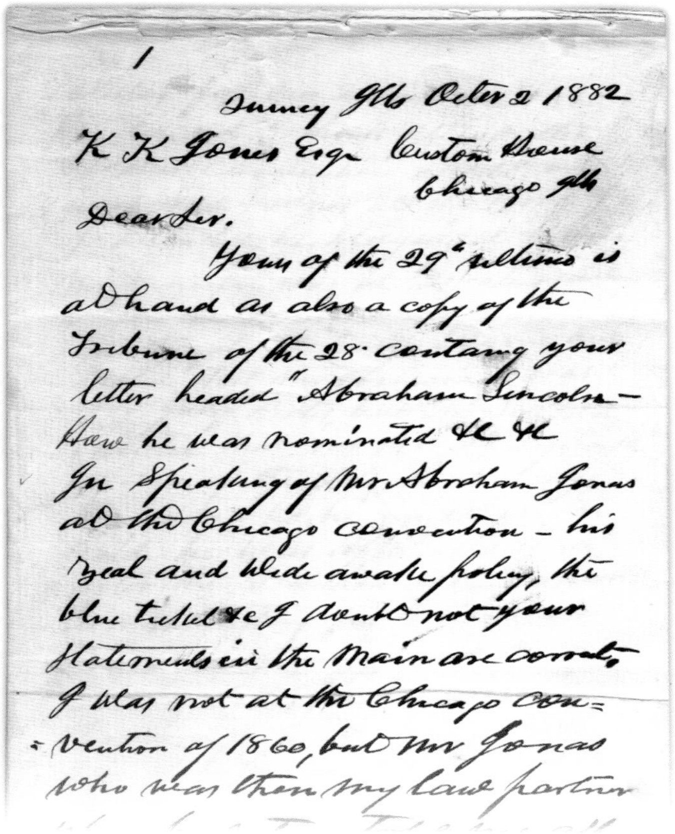

Quincy Ills Octor 2 1882

K K Jones Esq. Custom House
                              Chicago Ills
Dear Sir.

Yours of the 29" ultimo is
at hand as also a copy of the
Tribune of the 28 containing your
letter headed "Abraham Lincoln—
How he was nominated &c &c
In Speaking of Mr Abraham Jonas
at the Chicago Convention—his
zeal and wide awake policy, the
blue ticket &c I doubt not your
Statements in the Main are correct,
I was not at the Chicago Con=
=vention of 1860, but Mr Jonas
who was then my law partner

*"Gentlemen, there is
one name you have not
mentioned, one that I think
we shall all hear of before
long . . . I said Gentlemen
I mean Abraham Lincoln
of Illinois."*

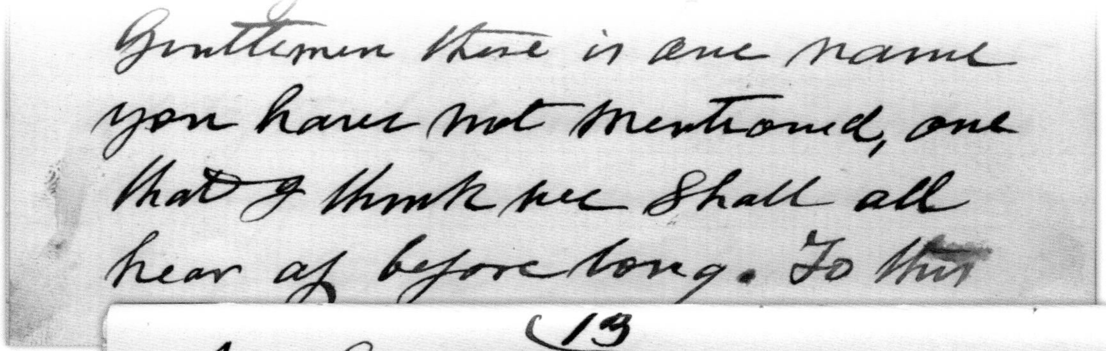

Gentlemen there is one name
you have not mentioned, one
that I think we shall all
hear of before long. To this

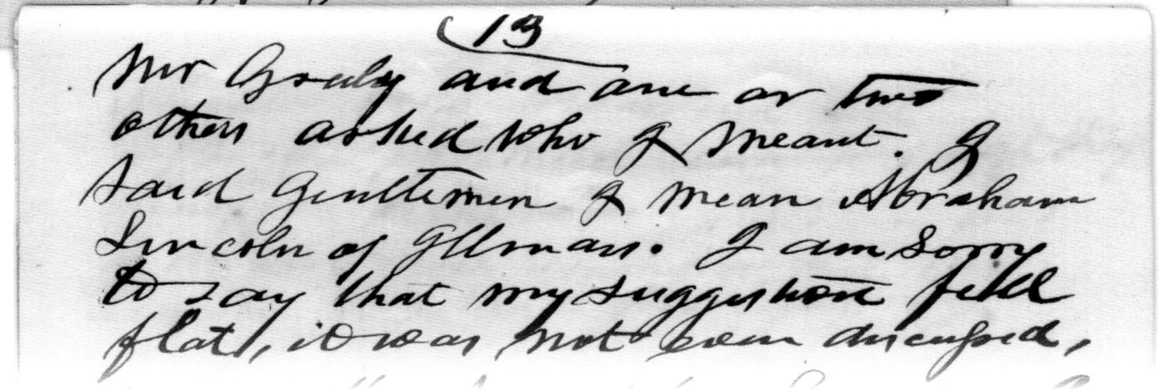

13

Mr Greely and one or two
others asked who I meant. I
said Gentlemen I mean Abraham
Lincoln of Illinois. I am sorry
to say that my suggestion fell
flat, it was not even discussed,

Yours truly
A. Lincoln.

CHAPTER THREE

ONE OF MY MOST VALUED FRIENDS

1858–1860

"We have no chance in the world for the Catholics," Abraham Jonas argued, as he laid out a strategy for winning new recruits into the Republican Party's ranks. Writing to Senator Lyman Trumbull on the same December day as he talked politics with Horace Greeley in Quincy, Jonas urged the party to focus on political outsiders. Specifically, he proposed an effort, "preparatory to the fight of 1860," to win over "the liberal and freethinking Germans," the anti-Catholic "Know-nothings," and most interesting of all, "the Israelites."[1]

OPPOSITE

ABRAHAM LINCOLN, 1858

The self-proclaimed "homeliest man in the State of Illinois" is generally thought to have sat for this beardless portrait in 1858, in Peoria. A slight variant of this pose, taken at the same sitting, was used in the 1860 presidential campaign poster about which young Grace Bedell, whose father had brought home the poster, famously wrote to Lincoln with advice on how to obtain more votes: "if you will let your whiskers grow . . . you would look a great deal better for your face is so thin . . . then you would be President."

Shapell Manuscript Collection

The context for Jonas's plan was "the Jewish abduction case at Rome," known as the Mortara Affair. Six-year-old Edgardo Mortara had been secretly baptized as an infant by his nursemaid in Bologna and, as a consequence, was torn away from his parents' Jewish home in 1858 and handed over to the Church to be raised as a Catholic. The case provided grist for the anti-Catholic mill in America and attracted enormous public attention. Yet when American Jewish leaders sought help from Secretary of State Lewis Cass and President James Buchanan in freeing the youngster, they were rebuffed. The administration solemnly explained that the United States had "neither the right nor the duty . . . to express a moral censorship over the conduct of other independent governments." In reality, the concern was that foreign governments might link the Mortara Affair to American slavery, which similarly turned a blind eye to the forcible separation of (slave) children from their parents. Fearful of being criticized for America's own immoral behavior, its leaders resolved not to criticize others.[2]

This decision to take no action on Edgardo Mortara's behalf, according to Jonas, "offended all my

ABRAHAM JONAS STRATEGIZES WITH SENATOR LYMAN TRUMBULL, DECEMBER 26, 1858

The votes of 50,000 American Jews, Jonas contended, were up for grabs in 1860. The Buchanan administration, which had mishandled the outrageous Mortara Affair—in which a Jewish child was secretly baptized and then kidnapped and raised as a Catholic in Rome— had offended, Jonas declared, "all my church."

Courtesy of the Library of Congress

church" and presented the Republicans with a golden opportunity. "Could you not," he asked Trumbull, "introduce some Resolution into the Senate on the subject and get the Republican vote for it?" A vigorous resolution that was "anti-Cass in sentiment," he promised, would "make in this county [Adams County, Illinois] a change of 100 votes, and unite the Jewish [sic] all over the Union." Since he calculated that "in the free states there are 50,000 Jewish votes, two thirds of whom vote the democratic ticket," his goal, with the help of a Senate resolution, was to get those votes "all on our side" by Election Day.[3]

While Jonas was working behind the scenes to boost the Republican Party's ranks, Abraham Lincoln was busy with his law practice. His run for the Senate had, as he had earlier explained to Norman Judd, greatly reduced his income in 1858, and he was working hard to recoup. That meant fewer political engagements. "I regret the necessity of declining," he wrote in response to Judd's request to speak in Morris, Illinois. "This year I must devote to my private business." In a more colorful letter, he apologetically informed a prominent Republican who sought his presence in Keokuk, Iowa, that "I shall go to the wall for bread and meat, if I neglect my business this year as well as last."[4]

Attending to business, however, did not preclude Lincoln from keeping abreast of politics. "When you can find leisure, write me your present impressions of Douglas's movements," he wrote Lyman Trumbull early in 1859.[5] A few months later, he warned Republicans in Chicago not to be taken in by Stephen A. Douglas's ideas: "Judge Douglas," he charged, "would lead us inevitably to the nationalization of slavery."[6] Promoting the Republican Party and opposing the spread

Springfield, Ills. July 6. 1859.

Hon: Schuyler Colfax:

My dear Sir:

I much regret not seeing you while you were here among us— Before learning that you were to be at Jacksonville on the 4th. I had given my word to be at another place. Besides a strong desire to make your personal acquaintance, I was anxious to speak with you on politics, a little more fully than I can well do in a letter— My main object in such conversation would be to hedge against divisions in the Republican ranks generally, and particularly for the contest of 1860. The point of danger is the temptation in different localities to "platform" for something which will be popular just there, but which, nevertheless, will be a firebrand elsewhere, and especially in a national convention— As instances, the movement against foreigners in Massach... ... paper, to make obedience to ... law, punishable as a ...

... or at least say nothing on points where it is probable we shall disagree—

I write this for your eye only; hoping however that if you see danger as I think I do, you will do what you can to avert it— Could not suggestions be made to the leading men in the State and Congressional Conventions; and so avoided, to some extent at least, these apples of discord?

Yours very truly

A. Lincoln

... to repeal the Fugitive Slave law; and squatter sovereignty in Kansas— In these things there is explosive matter enough to blow up half a dozen national conventions, if it gets into them; and what gets very rife outside of conventions is very likely to find its way into them— What is desirable, if possible, is that in every local convocation of Republicans, a point should be made to avoid everything which will distract republicans elsewhere— Massachusetts republicans should have looked beyond their noses; and then they could not have failed to see that tilting against foreigners would ruin us in the whole North-West— New-Hampshire and Ohio should forbear tilting against the Fugitive Slave law in such way as to utterly overwhelm us in Illinois with the charge of enmity to the constitution itself— Kansas, in her confidence that she can be saved to freedom on "squatter sovereignty," ought not to forget that to prevent the spread and nationalization of slavery is a national concern, and must be attended to by the nation— In a word, in every locality we should look beyond our noses;

"We should look
beyond our noses"

LINCOLN TO SCHUYLER COLFAX,
JULY 6, 1859

Lincoln's strategy in 1860 was to avoid regional issues, which were likely to distract and divide Republicans and ruin their chances for a victory—what he called "apples of discord"—and instead "look beyond our noses" by focusing on the great issue that united them, namely to prevent the spread and nationalization of slavery.

Shapell Manuscript Collection

of slavery were Lincoln's primary political goals at this time. In response to those who sought to promote him as a candidate in the 1860 election, he modestly replied, "I do not think myself fit for the Presidency."[7]

Evidence of nativism in the Republican ranks raised grave suspicions about the party, particularly among Germans and Jews, that threatened to upset Lincoln and Jonas's political calculations. Lincoln was particularly worried about "the movement against foreigners in Massachusetts," where, with Republican support, a popular initiative looked to impose upon foreigners a further two-year wait, following their naturalization, before they could vote or hold office. Lincoln urged Republicans to resist "the temptation in different localities to 'platform' for something which will be popular just there, but which, nevertheless, will be a firebrand elsewhere."[8] Nativists, however, ignored him.

Once the Massachusetts initiative passed, German-American papers expressed outrage at the new law, particularly since no similar wait time was imposed upon ex-slaves or free blacks who moved to the state. Carl Schurz, a leader of the German-American community (and a friend of many Jews and later of Lincoln) who had battled for social rights in his home country before escaping to the United States, delivered a celebrated address at Faneuil Hall in Boston entitled "True Americanism," where he spoke out boldly in favor of "toleration" and "equality of rights" and against the state initiative.[9] Other leaders of the German immigrant community demanded that Republicans everywhere speak out in opposition to what Massachusetts had done. The German-American vote, they hinted, hung in the balance. In a letter to Theodore Canisius, editor of Springfield's German newspaper, the Illinois *Staats-Anzeiger*, Lincoln lost no time ("I have written this hastily") in complying. His statement aimed not only to distance himself from nativism but to stress the consistency of his thinking, and his desire to elevate people of all kinds, blacks and foreigners included:

As I understand the Massachusetts provision, I am against its adoption in Illinois, or in any other place, where I have a right to oppose it. Understanding the spirit of our institutions to aim at the elevation of men, I am opposed to whatever tends to degrade them. I have some little notoriety for commiserating the oppressed condition of the negro; and I should be strangely inconsistent if I could favor any project for curtailing the existing rights of white men, even though born in different lands, and speaking different languages from myself.[10]

Lincoln's law partner, William H. Herndon, delivered a major address on this same subject, published in the *Daily State Journal* on May 17, 1859, which explicitly included Jews among those deserving of equality. In distancing the Republican Party from nativism, he set forth a capacious vision of "freedom and justice to all" that ran parallel to Lincoln's own and was, for its time, extraordinary:

I know of no distinction among men, except those of the heart and head. I now repeat that, though I am native born, my country is the World, and my love for man is as broad as the race, and as deep as its humanity. As a matter of course I include native and foreign people, Protestant and Catholic, "Jew and Gentile." I go the full length of justice to all men—equality among all American citizens and freedom to the race of man.[11]

Two weeks later, on May 30, Lincoln, using his own funds, purchased a printing press and type for the German-language Illinois *Staats-Anzeiger*, with the proviso that it promote Republican Party policies. His goal was to win over German Americans and to ensure that German-speaking voters, Gentiles and Jews alike, would be welcomed into the Republican camp.[12]

Meanwhile, Stephen A. Douglas was stumping for the Democrats. In Ohio, where both the governor

LINCOLN'S FRIEND—AND ADVOCATE FOR JEWS—CARL SCHURZ

Carl Schurz
Courtesy of the Library of Congress

CARL SCHURZ, like Lincoln, was intimately acquainted with Jews and had come to know and respect them. His appreciation for Jews began back with his father in Liblar, Germany, who had a close Jewish friend whom he revered as honest and wise. Schurz befriended Jews at the University of Bonn and in German revolutionary circles, where he achieved great renown. Later, in America, where he settled in 1852, one of his closest friends was the pioneering Jewish pediatrician Abraham Jacobi. Schurz's wife, Margarethe Meyer, likewise grew up among Jews, and in America was sometimes mistaken for one. During the Civil War, Schurz, a staunch Republican, served as a brigadier general. The 82nd Illinois Infantry Company C, a Jewish company, served under him, and he often boasted of its commander, Edward S. Salomon.

Schurz remained close to the Jewish community throughout his life and spoke out frequently against anti-Semitism. "Jews have done as much as any other class of citizens,—nay . . . the Jews have, in proportion to their numbers, done far more," he declared in a salute to Jews in 1888 upon the dedication of a Jewish charity home. "I repeat this with all the greater willingness, as I have recently had occasion to observe the motive springs, the character and the aims of the so-called 'Anti-semitic movement'—a movement whose dark spirit of fanaticism and persecution insults the humane enlightenment of the nineteenth century. . . ."

and the legislature were on the ballot in 1859, Lincoln agreed to counter Douglas's appeals to "popular sovereignty" by delivering five public speeches over two days in Columbus, Dayton, Hamilton, and Cincinnati. The last of these, at Fifth Street Market in Cincinnati on September 17, 1859, attracted a crowd of thousands; it was "one of the best-attended events in Lincoln's career before he became president."[13] Cincinnati was by far the largest Ohio city at that time, with a population of some 160,000. As many as 10,000 of those residents were Jews; no Jewish community west of the Alleghenies was larger.[14] How many of those Jews turned out to hear Lincoln is unknown, but a lithograph produced for the event's fiftieth anniversary preserves the name "Rosenbaum" on a store sign atop the building from whose portico he spoke.[15] Jews must have heard something about his speech for it was broadly covered in the press and, according to one historian, "was the most widely read speech of his pre-presidency."[16]

In his more than two-hour-long address, Lincoln sought to calm those who accused him of dividing the country. He made clear that the Republicans had no intention of interfering with slavery where it already existed, such as across the river in Kentucky, but only opposed slavery's extension into new territories. Countering Douglas's ahistorical view that the nation's founders had allowed each state's citizens to decide the issue of slavery on their own, Lincoln reminded Cincinnatians that the reason why they had no slaves, unlike their across-the-river neighbors in Kentucky, was because the Founders had made that decision for them. The Northwest Ordinance of 1787 explicitly banned slavery and involuntary servitude in the territories that became Ohio, Indiana, Illinois, Michigan,

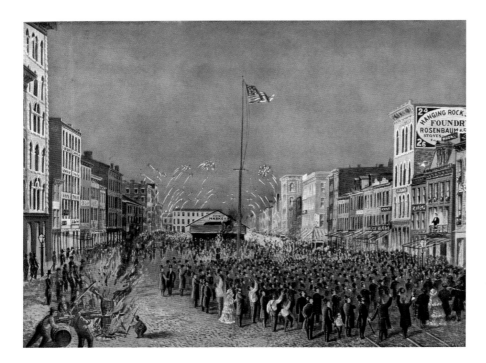

LINCOLN IN CINCINNATI

This lithograph commemorates the famous speech Lincoln gave there on September 17, 1859. "I think slavery is wrong, morally and politically," Lincoln declared. "I desire that it should be no further spread in these United States, and I should not object if it should gradually terminate in the whole Union."

Cincinnati Museum Center

and Wisconsin. Finally, Lincoln turned to the coming presidential election. Insisting that principles, not sectional issues, would determine who the Republican candidate was, he reassured his listeners that "there are plenty of men in the slave states that are altogether good enough . . . to be either President or Vice President." But he also warned against compromising principles or putting forth a man, like Douglas, who sought to be all things to all people. "He who is not for us is against us," he concluded, quoting the Gospels.[17] "He who gathereth not with us scattereth."

"How would you feel if we nominated you for President?" a visitor asked Lincoln on the morning following his Cincinnati speech.[18] Lincoln's response to this enticing question is not known, but the widely publicized address catapulted Lincoln back into the presidential fray, positioning him in the ideological center of the Republican Party. Over the next seven months, he delivered thirty speeches in eight states and the Kansas Territory, greatly enhancing his national visibility and broadening his own familiarity with the country.[19] Consistent with the strategy that Jonas had laid out early in the campaign, Lincoln often met with "liberal and freethinking Germans" as well as "Israelites" on these trips; sometimes they were the same people.

So it was when Lincoln traveled to the Kansas Territory in December 1859. This was the farthest west that he ever traveled, and he did so at the invitation of some fifty-three Republican merchants, bankers, and businessmen, organized by Lincoln's friend and distant relative Mark W. Delahay. Their goal, with the coming presidential election in mind, was to win Kansas, "bleeding" from pitched battles between proslavery and antislavery activists, for the Republican Party. They assured Lincoln, who himself had plenty of experience in frontier communities, that they would try to make his "expenses light," his "visit agreeable," and his "welcome hearty."[20] Significantly, one of the signatories on this invitation was a pioneering Leavenworth Jew named Jonas (James) Wollman (1824–1905). The famed Wollman Skating Rink in New York is named for the Wollmans, whose descendants included the two brothers who founded the tax preparation company

THE WOLLMAN SHOP

On his visit to Leavenworth in 1859, which included a dinner or two with the Jewish leader and scholar Jonas Wollman and his family, Lincoln was quoted in the New York Daily Tribune *as saying he regarded it as "one of the happiest events of his life."*
The Kansas State Historical Society

H&R Block. Born in Kempen-in-Posen, Prussia, where at one time he planned to become a rabbi, Wollman had arrived in the United States in 1851 and moved to Leavenworth soon after his marriage to Betty Kohn of St. Louis, in 1855. There he took advantage of the opportunities created by the Kansas-Nebraska Act and opened up a clothing store to service the many newcomers flooding into the well-located city. He soon expanded into dry goods, jewelry, books, and rubber goods. He also played an active role in the development of Jewish institutions in the city, including its first synagogue and cemetery. Wollman courageously sided with the minority in Leavenworth, many of them German immigrants like himself, who staunchly opposed the spread of slavery into the state. For a time, his store even occupied the same building as Delahay's antislavery newspaper, the *Territorial Register*. When "border ruffians" supportive of slavery's spread destroyed that paper in 1855, Wollman was taken into protective custody. He and his family were threatened with harm repeatedly; for a time, the Wollmans were driven from the city by proslavery forces and on several occasions

his wife and infant daughter were detained. All this goes far to explain why Lincoln, who so vigorously opposed the spread of slavery into Kansas, sat down to dinner with the Wollmans on his visit to Leavenworth. Some sources claim that he dined with them and another local Jewish merchant family, Simon and Amalia Abeles, at the Delahay home. Others insist that it was the Wollmans themselves who hosted the dinner for Lincoln. Family lore holds that Betty Wolman was deeply impressed with Lincoln and predicted, when he departed, that someday the "great man" would "be President of the United States." It likewise recalls that Lincoln cradled the Wollmans' sixteen-month-old son, Henry, in his arms. What seems indisputable is that such interactions as he had with the Wollmans helped to further acquaint Lincoln with Jews. He understood that "Israelites" like them could form part of a new Republican coalition.[21]

Lincoln similarly met with Jews when he visited New York. He had been invited to New York in October 1859 in the wake of his widely publicized success in the Midwest. "We want to hear a speech from

ABRAM J. DITTENHOEFER

When Jewish lawyer Dittenhoefer met Lincoln on the day of the Cooper Union Address, he was impressed, and when they met again at Lincoln's hotel the day after, he was congratulatory—although Lincoln himself felt unsure his speech had been a success. In the 1864 reelection campaign, Dittenhoefer would become a Republican elector for Lincoln.
Museum of the City of New York

for Southern markets. Many of them also had friends and relatives in the South. Unsurprisingly, therefore, they tended to sympathize with the South. Even if they expressed no personal support for slavery, preservation of the Union was still their paramount concern. As a result, the majority of Jews sided with the Democrats. A significant minority, however, especially Jewish liberals, freethinkers, and young people, vigorously disagreed. Horrified by the specter of slavery's spread, they gravitated toward the Republican Party. They were particularly interested in what a man like Abraham Lincoln had to say.[25]

How many Jews sat among the audience of over 900 that listened to Lincoln's address at Cooper Union is impossible to know.[26] But at least one, a young attorney named Abram J. Dittenhoefer (1836–1919), was actually sitting on the platform that night. Years later, he recounted what he had seen:

> Mr. Lincoln never ranted, but gave emphatic emphasis to what he wished especially to "put across" by a slowness and marked clearness of enunciation. His voice was unpleasant, almost rasping and shrill at first. Perhaps that was due to the fact that he found it necessary to force it. A little later, he seemed to control his voice better, and his earnestness invited and easily held the attention of his auditors.[27]

him, such a one as he delivered in Cincinnati," a New York lecture promoter explained to William H. Bailhache, coeditor of the Illinois *State Journal.*[22] Easterners hardly knew Abraham Lincoln, and he was excited by the opportunity to introduce himself but felt that he needed time to prepare.[23] His address, delivered on February 27, 1860, in the Great Hall of Cooper Union in New York City, was one of the most important of his career up to that time, and has been described as "the speech that made Abraham Lincoln president."[24]

New York City was home to the largest Jewish community in the United States in 1860. Some twenty-seven synagogues and over forty-four Jewish charitable and educational societies served the city's 40,000 Jews. One out of every twenty New Yorkers was Jewish, the bulk of them recent immigrants from central Europe. Many of New York's Jews worked in the clothing trade. They depended for their livelihood upon Southern cotton and produced clothes destined

Dittenhoefer was only twenty-three when he witnessed the Cooper Union Address, but he had already made a name for himself in Republican circles. Born in the South, he had converted to antislavery in college, stumped for Frémont four years earlier, and then converted his father, a merchant, to the Republican cause. Explicit Jewish considerations, he confessed, prompted his conversion. Having read how Senator Benjamin Wade characterized Judah Benjamin, the proslavery Jewish senator from Louisiana, as "an Israelite with Egyptian principles," it struck Dittenhoefer

LINCOLN AT COOPER UNION

On the night of February 27, 1860, at least 900 people heard Lincoln give one of the most famous speeches of his life. "No man ever before made such an impression," Horace Greeley proclaimed, "on his first appeal to a New York audience." The speech, punctuated by lyrical phrases, including "right makes might," made Lincoln, overnight, a national candidate.
Cooper Union

"with great force that the Israelite . . . whose ancestors were enslaved in Egypt, ought not to uphold slavery in free America, and could not do so without bringing disgrace upon himself."[28]

Dittenhoefer warmed toward Lincoln after hearing him at Cooper Union, especially when he forthrightly declared slavery wrong and opposed its spread yet promised, in moderate tones, "to let it alone where it is, because that much is due to the necessity arising from its actual presence in the nation." As for Lincoln's famous closing line, which reversed the standard aphorism and declared, "Let us have faith that right makes might and in that faith, let us, to the end, dare to do our duty as we understand it," Dittenhoefer recalled that he and those around him responded less than enthusiastically. Many, he concluded, "left the auditorium that night, as I did, in a seriously thoughtful mood." The next morning, according to Dittenhoefer, Lincoln himself questioned his performance—indeed, he was a harsh critic of his own speeches, even his greatest ones. "I am not sure," Dittenhoefer quoted him as saying, "that I made a success."[29]

Subsequently, after the speech had been widely reprinted and discussed, Dittenhoefer knew better; he described the Cooper Union address as "epoch-making."

Most scholars agree. According to historian Harold Holzer, for example, "Abraham Lincoln did triumph in New York. He delivered a learned, witty, and exquisitely reasoned address that electrified his elite audience and, more important, reverberated in newspapers and pamphlets alike until it reached tens of thousands of Republican voters across the North. He . . . departed politically reborn."[30]

As Lincoln's bid for the Republican nomination gathered steam in 1860, requests poured in for copies of his major speeches, particularly his 1858 debates with Stephen A. Douglas. Voters who had not heard Lincoln with their own ears wanted to have the opportunity to read what he said, and Lincoln's supporters wanted to be able to quote him verbatim in speeches they made on his behalf. Lincoln had received requests for transcripts of his debates with Douglas at least as early as January 1859, but at that time he expressed no interest in their publication beyond the press. By late March, he was enthusiastic about publishing the debates ("I would really be pleased with a publication substantially as you propose"). He insisted, consistent with his character, that the publication be "mutual, and fair," reproducing transcripts from each side "as reported by his own friends."

Lincoln himself worked hard on the volume, which,

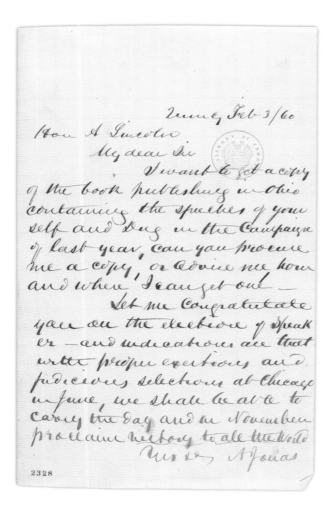

2328

**ABRAHAM JONAS TO LINCOLN,
FEBRUARY 3, 1860**

*Eager to obtain a copy of the Lincoln–Douglas debates book,
Jonas predicts his friend's ascension to the presidency: ". . . at
Chicago in June, we shall be able to carry the day and in
November proclaim victory to all the World."*

Courtesy of the Library of Congress

**LINCOLN TO ABRAHAM JONAS: "...ONE OF MY
MOST VALUED FRIENDS," FEBRUARY 4, 1860**

*Replying to Jonas's request from the previous day for a copy of
the Lincoln–Douglas debates, Lincoln writes, for the only known
time in his life, a phrase directly acknowledging what Jonas's
friendship meant to him: "As you are one of my most valued
friends, and have complimented me by the expression of a wish
for the book, I propose doing myself the honor of presenting you
with one, as soon as I can."*

Abraham Lincoln Presidential Library & Museum

like many a book, took longer than expected to appear.
By February 1860, Abraham Jonas was impatient to
obtain a copy and wrote directly to Lincoln: "I want to
get a copy of the book publishing in Ohio containing
the speeches of your self and Douglas in the Campaign
of last year, can you procure me a copy, or advise me,
how and where I can get one—"? Lincoln responded at
once, reporting that the books "would not be out before
March." In fact, they did not appear until April, just a
month prior to the Republican Convention. In a particularly warm and impressive letter to a member of the
Jewish community, Lincoln then proceeded, revealingly,
to express his friendship for Jonas in singularly intimate terms ("you are one of my most valued friends")
and to promise him one of the hundred gratis copies
that had been allocated to him by the publisher. He
kept his word. The copy he personally inscribed to Jonas
of *Political Debates Between Hon. Abraham Lincoln and
Hon. Stephen A. Douglas, In the Celebrated Campaign of
1858 in Illinois* survives to this day. The debates themselves went through eight editions, with some 50,000
copies distributed prior to the election, and became a
campaign bestseller.[31]

As one of Lincoln's most valued friends, Jonas was
determined to see Lincoln nominated by the Republican Party for the presidency. Senator William H.
Seward of New York, however, was the front-running
candidate for that position. A staunch opponent of
slavery, Seward in 1858 had incautiously warned of a
coming "irrepressible conflict" between the North and
the South. "The United States," he declared, "must and
will, sooner or later, become either entirely a slaveholding nation, or entirely a free-labor nation." Fearing that
such militant talk could doom his electoral chances,
his advisors dispatched him on an eight-month tour
of Europe and the Middle East, including, in September 1859, Jerusalem.[32] During that voluntary exile, Lincoln delivered his well-publicized speech in Cincinnati,
which led to the success at Cooper Union and greatly
improved his own chances for nomination.

Springfield, Feb. 4 1860

Hon: A. Jones
    My dear Sir:
              Yours of the 3rd inquiring how you can get a copy of the debates now being published in Ohio, is received— As you are one of my most valued friends, and have complimented me by the expression of a wish for the book, I propose doing myself the honor of presenting you with one, so soon as I can— By the arrangement our Ohio friends have made with the publishers, I am to have one hundred copies gratis— When I shall receive them I will send you one by Express— I understand they will not be out before March, and I probably shall be absent about that time. So that you must not be disappointed if you do not receive yours, before about the middle of that month.
                              Yours very truly
                                      A. Lincoln

"As you are one of my most valued friends . . ."

The other major Republican candidates for the presidency were Edward Bates of Missouri, Simon Cameron of Pennsylvania, and Salmon P. Chase of Ohio. With long careers in politics behind them, all of these men had significant enemies, personal and political. Lincoln, with much less national experience, aimed to be everybody's second choice. His plan was "to give no offence to others—leave them in a mood to come to us, if they shall be compelled to give up their first love."[33]

As Republicans gathered on May 16 for their convention in Chicago's cavernous 18,000-square-foot Wigwam—so-called because it was built to resemble an Indian loghouse—the goal of Jonas and other Lincoln supporters was precisely to encourage delegates "to give up their first love" and shift to favorite son Lincoln as an electable second choice. To do that, they had to prevent Seward from carrying the convention on the first ballot. Seward's supporters felt supremely confident. They enjoyed superior manpower, ample funding, and long political experience. But they underestimated the opposition, including Abraham Jonas. Though not himself a delegate, Jonas was present in Chicago and actively promoted Lincoln's cause among Midwest delegations. Jonas's law partner Henry Asbury's retrospective account, published by an Illinois party operative named K. K. Jones, reveals that beyond that first auspicious meeting with Horace Greeley, Jonas continued to play an important backstage role in the maneuverings that led to Lincoln's nomination.

"The evening before and the day of the nomination," Jones recalled, "it had become apparent that the Seward forces, abetted by the then Chairman of the National Committee [Edwin D. Morgan of New York], had manipulated the 'blue tickets' so that it was feared there would be a large majority of Seward men in the Wigwam when the nominating speeches were made. They were prepared for a grand display of enthusiasm when William H. Seward should be named, and intended thus to 'boom things.'" A huge pro-Seward demonstration, his supporters believed, would persuade wavering delegates to vote for Seward on the first ballot so as to align themselves with a winner. Abraham Jonas, according to Jones, got wind of the plan and "took it upon himself to counteract this nicely laid scheme." Some 10,000 people from Central Illinois and Indiana were rounded up to stage an even bigger convention demonstration when Lincoln's name was placed in nomination. To ensure that these outsiders could gain admission to the Wigwam, Lincoln's supporters did just what Seward's had done: they "manipulated" the blue admission tickets, printing extras which they distributed to their friends in order to pack the hall. "I have got the thing all fixed," Jones quoted Jonas as telling him. "Our friends are stationed in every part of this Wigwam, and when 'Old Abe' is put in nomination we will show our Eastern brethren what Western vim, Western endurance and Western enthusiasm can do." That, in fact, is what happened.

The nomination of Seward touched off, as expected, a "grand demonstration"—what the convention minutes describe as "prolonged applause and cheers." To the surprise of everyone, however, the nomination of favorite son Abraham Lincoln resulted in another grand "outburst of enthusiasm," described in the convention minutes as "immense applause and cheers." This was taken as a signal of the convention's fervor for Lincoln, especially since demonstrations on behalf of Bates, Chase, Cameron, and other candidates proved far more muted. Seward, as a result, failed to win the nomination on the first ballot. As Lincoln's supporters had hoped, numerous delegates then abandoned their "first love" and embraced Lincoln. He won the nomination on the third ballot.[34]

In addition to Jonas and Dittenhoefer, who attended the Republican convention in nonvoting capacities, at least one Jewish delegate actively participated and voted in the convention: Lewis Naphtali Dembitz (1833–1907) of Louisville, Kentucky. An Orthodox Jew, attorney, and polymath (he read twelve languages), Dembitz immigrated to the United States,

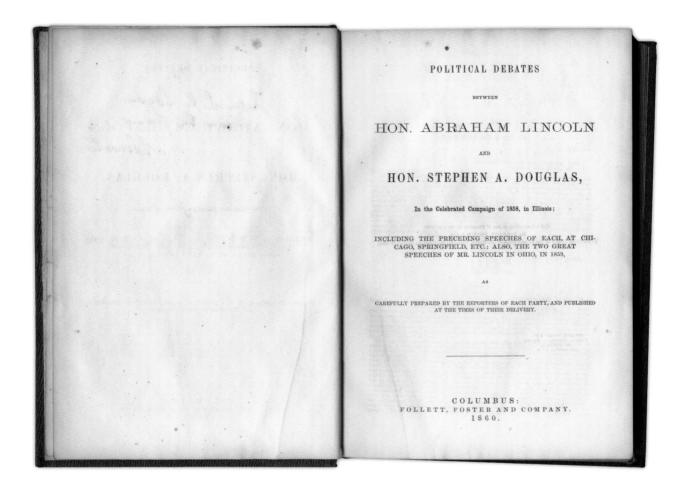

POLITICAL DEBATES

BETWEEN

HON. ABRAHAM LINCOLN

AND

HON. STEPHEN A. DOUGLAS,

In the Celebrated Campaign of 1858, in Illinois;

INCLUDING THE PRECEDING SPEECHES OF EACH, AT CHI-
CAGO, SPRINGFIELD, ETC.; ALSO, THE TWO GREAT
SPEECHES OF MR. LINCOLN IN OHIO, IN 1859,

AS

CAREFULLY PREPARED BY THE REPORTERS OF EACH PARTY, AND PUBLISHED
AT THE TIMES OF THEIR DELIVERY.

COLUMBUS:
FOLLETT, FOSTER AND COMPANY.
1860.

along with relatives named Brandeis and Wehle, in response to the failed 1848 liberal revolutions in central Europe. He fervently opposed slavery and, like Lincoln and Jonas, revered Henry Clay; he even named one of his sons after him (another would later be named after Abraham Lincoln). At twenty-seven, he was already a significant Republican political leader in Kentucky and one of the city's leading lawyers. Consequently, he was appointed to the select committee that prepared the order of business for the convention. Tradition holds that he delivered a nominating address for Lincoln at the convention, but if so that was not recorded in the official proceedings. Dembitz did vote for Lincoln at the convention but never had the opportunity to meet him. Later, in addition to authoring many distinguished publications, he greatly influenced his talented nephew, the future Supreme Court justice Louis

ABOVE AND BELOW (DETAIL)

INSCRIBED LINCOLN TO ABRAHAM JONAS DEBATE BOOK, 1860

Of the hundred copies of the debates given to Lincoln by the publisher to distribute to friends, forty-two presentation copies are now known to exist, most of which are inscribed in pencil. Four copies, however, are in ink. Apparently, Lincoln noticed that the paper tended to absorb the ink, creating a spread-out, "feathery" pattern, and he therefore switched from pen to pencil.

Abraham Lincoln Presidential Library & Museum

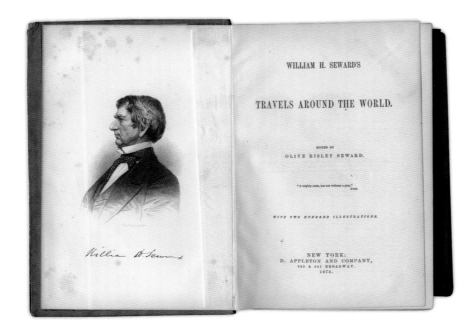

**WILLIAM H. SEWARD
GOES TO JERUSALEM**

*In late 1859, as the front-runner
for the Republican nomination,
Senator Seward of New York
traveled abroad, which included a
trip to Jerusalem. The trip coincided
with Lincoln's rise to prominence,
and his transformative Cooper
Union address. Seward visited the
Holy Land a second time, in 1871.*

William H. Seward's Travels
Around the World, 1873

**THE "WIGWAM"
CONVENTION HALL,
CHICAGO, MAY 18, 1860**

*In the Wigwam, on Lincoln's home
turf of Illinois, Abraham Jonas and
Henry Asbury played an important
backstage role in the orchestrations
that led Lincoln to maneuver the
nomination away from Seward.*

Courtesy of the Library of Congress

D. Brandeis, who changed his middle name to Dembitz in his uncle's honor.[35]

The other Jewish delegate[36] at the convention was Moritz Pinner (1828–1911). Born in the Prussian province of Posen (today Poznan, Poland) and the son of a rabbi, Pinner immigrated to America in 1851 and soon became involved in abolitionism. He was one of those quintessential "liberal and freethinking Germans" and "Israelites" whom Jonas sought for the Republican coalition. In strife-torn Kansas, Pinner edited the uncompromisingly antislavery *Kansas Post* (which, when published in Kansas City, Missouri, was known as the *Missouri Post*.) At the state Republican convention in Missouri, reputedly attended by only 134 people, he played an active role, speaking out on behalf of his fellow Germans and opposing efforts to compel Republican delegates to cast their vote for the state's favorite son, Edward Bates. Though acquainted both with Bates and with Lincoln, Pinner favored William Seward. He resigned from Missouri's delegation when denied the right to vote his conscience and subsequently worked to undermine Bates at the Chicago national convention, greatly to Lincoln's advantage. As a result, he was not officially listed as a conference delegate from Missouri and did not cast any ballots.[37]

Pinner, like many of the other Jews committed to the Republican Party, spent the months following the Republican national convention campaigning for Abraham Lincoln. "I am satisfied with Mr. Lincoln," he wrote to abolitionist Wendell Phillips. "I hold that out of Republ[ican] ranks no better man could have been selected. He is opposed to slavery in the abstract, is free in the expression of his sentiments on all subjects, is honest and therefore reliable."[38] Abram Dittenhoefer recalled that he himself threw all his energy into the campaign, "and though young . . . was frequently making several speeches during a day and evening." Days before the election, at Cooper Union, he claimed to have sung out "We are coming, Father Abraham, five hundred thousand strong," as if in anticipation of James Sloan Gibbons's famous 1862 Civil War poem of an almost identical name, set to music by Luther Orlando Emerson.[39] Abraham Jonas likewise addressed a series of meetings and rallies in Illinois, including ones in Quincy and Marceline. At a rally in Stones Prairie in Adams County, he spoke "eloquently" for an hour on "the principles of the Republican Party and in refutation of the false and slanderous assertations of the Douglasites," reputedly before 10,000 people—some of whom, later in the day, staged an ugly riot.[40]

Jonas's devotion to Lincoln and the Republican cause at that time was further evidenced in his confidential letter to Lincoln dated July 20, 1860, informing him that Illinois' Democratic congressman, Isaac Newton Morris, was "engaged in obtaining aff[i]davits and certificates of certain Irish men that they saw you in Quincy come out of a Know-Nothing Lodge." Central European immigrants opposed to slavery, like

ABRAHAM JONAS TO LINCOLN, JULY 20, 1860

Jonas writes to Lincoln to warn him that the Democrats are trying to paint him as anti-immigrant by gathering "aff[i]-davits" of Irishmen who claim they saw him coming out of a Know-Nothing Lodge in Quincy.

Courtesy of the Library of Congress

Moritz Pinner, Abram Dittenhoefer, and Lewis Dembitz, were a key component of Lincoln's coalition, and they despised the anti-Catholic and anti-immigrant Know-Nothings. Tying Lincoln to an appearance in a Know-Nothing Lodge in 1854, Jonas knew, was a Democratic ploy to "work on the Germans." However much Jonas was prepared to welcome Know-Nothings into the Republican coalition, he worried that tying

LINCOLN TO JOSHUA SPEED: NOT A "KNOW-NOTHING," AUGUST 24, 1855

Nearly five years before his presidential campaign, Lincoln writes to his close friend Joshua Speed of his intense dismay for the "despotism" of the Know-Nothings, who, if in control, would maintain "all men are created equal, except negroes, and foreigners, and catholics"—the "foreigners," a term common at the time that included Jews.
Courtesy of the Massachusetts Historical Society

Lincoln directly to the Know-Nothing cause might cost his close friend many votes.[41]

Lincoln must likewise have been worried, for he replied within twenty-four hours with a confidential letter of his own. "I suppose as good, or even better men than I may have been in American or Know-Nothing lodges," he observed, thereby distancing himself from the kind of guilt-by-association politics that Congressman Morris and so many others engaged in. "But in point of fact, I never was in one, at Quincy or elsewhere." Reminding Jonas that he "was never in Quincy but one day and two nights while Know-Nothing lodges were in existence, and you were with me that day and both those nights," Lincoln traced with astonishing precision his movements during that 1854 visit. He felt sure that affidavits from "respectable men . . . would put the matter at rest."[42]

Lincoln did not mention to Jonas that in a remark-able private letter to his friend Joshua F. Speed, back in 1855, he had unequivocally distanced himself from Know-Nothingism:

I am not a Know-Nothing. That is certain. How could I be? How can any one who abhors the oppression of negroes, be in favor of degrading classes of white people? Our progress in degeneracy appears to me to be pretty rapid. As a nation, we began by declaring that "all men are created equal." We now practically read it "all men are created equal, except negroes." When the "Know-Nothings" get control, it will read "all men are created equal, except negroes, and foreigners, and catholics." When it comes to this I should prefer emigrating to some country where they make no pretence of loving liberty—to Russia, for instance, where despotism can be taken pure, and without the base alloy of hypocrisy.[43]

*"It was in 1854, when I spoke
in some Hall there, and after
the speaking, you, with others,
took me to an oyster saloon,
passed an hour there . . .
and you walked with me . . ."*

**LINCOLN TO ABRAHAM JONAS,
JULY 21, 1860**

*Replying confidentially to Jonas's letter of
the previous day, Lincoln rebuts the charge
that he was ever in a Know-Nothing Lodge.
Lincoln recalls that Jonas was in fact the
witness for his alibi: while indeed in Quincy
at the time in question, he was with Jonas in
an oyster saloon.*

Abraham Lincoln Presidential Library & Museum

Springfield, Ills., May 26, 1860

Hon. C. M. Clay.

My dear Sir:

Yours of the 21st is received, and for which I sincerely thank you— The humblest of all whose names were before the Convention, I shall, in the canvass, and especially afterwards, if the result shall devolve the administration upon me, need the support of all the talent, popularity, and courage, North and South, which is in the party; and it is with sincere gratification that I receive this early indication of your unwavering purpose to stand for the right.— Your Obt. Servt.

A. Lincoln

LINCOLN TO CASSIUS M. CLAY: "THE HUMBLEST OF ALL," MAY 26, 1860

A week after receiving the nomination, Lincoln, here referring to himself as the "humblest of all whose names were before the convention," appeals to Cassius Marcellus Clay, a former rival for the nomination, in order to enlist his support in the upcoming campaign, and salutes his "unwavering purpose to stand for the right."

Shapell Legacy Partnership

Yet, Lincoln cautioned Jonas to be discreet. "Our adversaries think they can gain a point if they could force me to openly deny the charge, by which some degree of offence would be given to the Americans," Lincoln wrote, referring to members of the nativist American Party, many of whose members (some of them also Know-Nothings) supported him. "For this reason it must not publicly appear that I am paying any attention to the charge." Jonas, himself a consummate politician, understood. Lincoln sought to personally disassociate himself from the taint of prejudice but could not afford, as a candidate, to lose the votes of those less enlightened than he was.[44]

Having been nominated as his party's candidate, Lincoln, consistent with the custom of his times, did not personally leave home to campaign. Within four days of his nomination he understood that "it will scarcely be prudent for me to leave home much, if any" until after the election.[45] Instead, as his correspondence with Jonas about the Know-Nothings indicates, he managed his campaign from Springfield. Thousands of supporters, including Moritz Pinner, came to visit him there.[46] He also received stacks of mail and telegrams from around the country and posed agreeably for photographs and portraits.

"Lincoln bears his honors meekly," Orville Hickman Browning, who was friendly with both Lincoln and Jonas, reported in his diary after meeting with the nominee.[47] This was a characteristic trait of Lincoln's and was especially evident during the almost six months

Springfield, July 2 1860
D. L. Phillips, Esq
My dear Sir
Yours of the 27th. was received yesterday— Herewith is a general letter of introduction, such, I hope, as meets your view—
Just now, the skies look bright— What clouds may hereafter rise, we know not—
Yours as ever
A. Lincoln

LINCOLN TO DAVID L. PHILLIPS: "JUST NOW, THE SKIES LOOK BRIGHT," JULY 2, 1860

"Just now, the skies look bright. What clouds may hereafter rise, we know not," Lincoln writes to political operative David L. Phillips. While the sentiment would prove prophetic of the coming storm of war, he also reflects on his improving chances for victory in November.

Shapell Manuscript Collection

between his nomination and election that Lincoln spent in Springfield. Perhaps, at age fifty-one, this humility sprang from his painful early life, lack of formal education, absence of wealth, and want of influential friends. Perhaps, he still saw himself as something of an outsider, like the Germans and Jews whom he befriended. Whatever the case, he described himself in a letter to the somewhat vainglorious antislavery reformer Cassius Marcellus Clay, cousin of Henry Clay, as "the humblest of all whose names were before the convention."[48]

Having lived his entire life, prior to his whirlwind elevation to national notice, as an ordinary person, Lincoln saw himself as unexceptional. He had been a day laborer, a small shopkeeper, a lawyer—and, politically, for most of his life, a failure. Now he was poised to

claim the highest office in the land—and still he did not think himself, as he put it back in 1859, "fit for the presidency."[49] So, when the learned Pennsylvania judge William D. Kelley, an acquaintance and leading Republican, sought permission to inscribe a new legal work to him, Lincoln gratefully accepted the proffered honor, "begging only that the inscription may be in modest terms, not representing me as a man of great learning, or a very extraordinary one in any respect."[50]

During this time, as the Democratic Party split along sectional lines and contentiousness spread through its ranks, Lincoln grew increasingly hopeful concerning his election chances. The Democrats, unable to unite, held two conventions in Baltimore: Northern Democrats, after a clamorous debate, nominated

Stephen A. Douglas on the fifty-seventh ballot, on June 18, while Southern Democrats nominated John C. Breckinridge on June 23. Against this background, on July 2, Lincoln wrote to David L. Phillips, a distant relative of abolitionist Wendell Phillips and, according to one scholar, "the leading Republican of Southern Illinois," that "just now, the skies look bright. What clouds may hereafter rise, we know not."[51] The poetic turn of phrase reflected long years of accumulated experience. Lincoln knew that bright political skies could darken at any time, and he may even have had a premonition of coming sectional strife. Still, he sensed, as he wrote later that same month to his vice presidential running mate, Hannibal Hamlin, that "the prospect of Republican success now appears very flattering."[52] By October, the die seemed cast. As congressional elections on October 9 swept the Republicans to victory in key Northern states, Lincoln wrote exultantly to William H. Seward three days later that "it now really looks as if the Government is about to fall into our hands. Pennsylvania, Ohio and Indiana have surpassed all expectation, even the most extravagant."[53]

The prediction, based on a careful analysis of voting trends, proved accurate. On November 6, 1860, Election Day, Lincoln won the four-way presidential contest with slightly less than 40 percent of the popular vote, capturing 180 out of 303 electoral votes. The Northern free states from Maine to Minnesota, plus California and Oregon, formed the core of his majority. This basically vindicated the electoral strategy that Jonas had crafted in his letter to Senator Trumbull back in December 1858. Lincoln, according to one analysis, "did especially well among younger voters, newly eligible voters, former nonvoters, rural residents, skilled laborers, members of the middle class, German Protestants, evangelical Protestants, native-born Americans, and most especially former Know-Nothings and Whig Americans."[54] How many Jews voted for him is hard to determine. He lost New York City, the largest Jewish community in the United States, and some estimates

claim that German immigrants there, as well as Jews, voted against him by a two-to-one margin.[55] He also had trouble in other large Northern urban areas: only four of the North's eleven most populous cities (where Jews tended to live) gave him a majority. Unsurprisingly, he received very few votes—Jewish or non-Jewish—in the South. On the other hand, a study of the Chicago Jewish community (probably less than a thousand voters) determined that "the majority of the Chicago Jewish community . . . supported Lincoln over Douglas."[56] On balance, even if more Jews voted Democratic than Republican in 1860, the 50,000 or so Jewish voters made no difference whatsoever in the election results. Jews like Jonas and Dittenhoefer, however, did make a difference in helping to shape the six-year-old Republican Party's first national victory.

One of the 180 electors whose votes in the Electoral College made Lincoln's election to the presidency official was known to be Jewish. His name was Sigismund Kaufmann of New York (1826-1889). A prominent German-American who left Germany in the wake of the failed liberal revolutions of 1848, Kaufmann was active in the turnvereins, the German-American gymnastic societies founded by German liberals to promote sound bodies and sound minds. The socialistic Turnerbund that he established and headed in New York was not only dedicated to physical activity, but

OPPOSITE

LINCOLN TO WILLIAM D. KELL[E]Y: ON THE VERGE OF VICTORY, A TIMELESS LESSON, OCTOBER 13, 1860

Lincoln agrees to having a forthcoming legal book dedicated to him, though he tempers the honor by referencing his humble origins and lack of formal education: ". . . that the inscription may be in modest terms, not representing me as a man of great learning, or as a very extraordinary one in any respect." Though Lincoln was unschooled, he was not uneducated, having taught himself law, surveying, and military strategy.
Shapell Legacy Partnership

Private

Springfield, Ills. Oct— 13. 1860

Hon. William D. Kelly

My dear Sir:

Yours of the 6th.,
asking permission to inscribe your
new legal work to me, is received.
Gratefully accepting the proffered
honor, I give the leave, begging only
that the inscription may be in modest
terms, not representing me as a man
of great learning, or a very extraordinary one in any respect—

Yours very truly

A. Lincoln.

"... not representing me as a man of great learning,
or as a very extraordinary one in any respect."

Springfield, Ills. Oct. 12. 1860
Hon. W. H. Seward.
My dear Sir

Your kind note of the 8th is received. I am quite satisfied with what you said, at Chicago, upon the point I mentioned to you; and I am much obliged to you for saying it—I hope it did not give you much trouble weaving it into the general web of your discourse—

I shall look up the speech made at DeBuque and published in the N. Y. Times—

I have had no fears of New York recently; though, of course, I am glad to have the expression of your continued confidence. It now really looks as if the Government is about to fall into our hands. Pennsyl—

"*. . . the government is about to fall into our hands*"

LINCOLN TO WILLIAM H. SEWARD, OCTOBER 12, 1860

As congressional elections sweep the Republicans to victory in key Northern states, Lincoln writes to Seward that "the government is about to fall into our hands"—a phrase that suggests a sureness, a literal grasp, that he would use again at another heightened, hard-won, and long-sought moment: writing at the end of the Civil War, he says, "It is certain now that Richmond is in our hands."

Shapell Legacy Partnership

also "strongly encourage[d] true freedom, prosperity and education for all classes."[57] Kaufmann belonged to a synagogue and was involved in Jewish charitable activities but devoted most of his efforts to furthering the interests of the German immigrant community. As a political radical and staunch opponent of slavery, he strongly advocated the importance of German Americans voting for the Republican Party. This probably explains why he was rewarded with the opportunity to serve as a presidential elector. Lincoln and Kaufmann met, likely for the first time, at a reception

for members of the Electoral College on February 19, 1861 in New York, and the president-elect "pleasantly remarked that he knew enough of German to know that the name [Kaufmann] meant merchant."[58] Subsequently, Kaufmann obtained Lincoln's autograph for a friend and advocated for German Americans in government and in the military. Tradition holds that President Lincoln offered him the post of minister to Italy but that he declined "on the ground that he could be more useful to his party at home."[59]

Before the electoral votes of Kaufmann and his

fellow presidential electors were formally counted at a joint session of Congress on February 13, 1861, the results of the November election had unleashed a frenzy of political activity across the South. Fearing that Lincoln's ascension portended slave revolts and a perilous threat to the whole Southern way of life and the slave system that made it possible, the cry went out for secession. Declining to write for publication, so as not to exacerbate the seething tension, Lincoln stuck to his guns on secession, choosing to make his views known only through confidential letters. "My opinion is that no state can, in any way lawfully, get out of the Union, without the consent of the others."[60]

Just three days later, however, on December 20, 1860, South Carolina, the state with proportionally the largest black population in the country (57 percent), repudiated Lincoln's view. It became the first of seven states in the Deep South to secede from the Union prior to his inauguration. "South Carolina has resumed her entire sovereign powers, and, unshackled, has become one of the nations of the earth," the

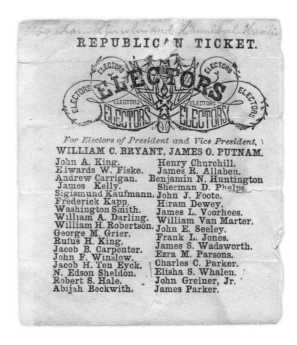

TOP RIGHT

SIGISMUND KAUFMANN, NEW YORK REPUBLICAN ELECTORAL BALLOT, 1860

When Lincoln first met the fiery Jewish refugee from the German Revolution of 1848, he knew enough German (or, some say, Yiddish) to say that he understood that "kaufmann" meant "merchant"—and "schneider" meant "tailor." Sigismund Kaufmann, however, was neither: instead, as a lawyer, he led New York's German Jews in supporting Lincoln and cast an electoral vote for him in 1861.

Rail Splitter Archives, New York City

BOTTOM RIGHT

LINCOLN TO SIGISMUND KAUFMANN, ESQ, THE COMMONALITY OF TWO LAWYERS, DECEMBER 24, 1861

On Christmas Eve, 1861, Lincoln does a favor for the influential representative of the German-Jewish Republican element, Sigismund Kaufmann. "Below is the autograph for your friend," Lincoln writes, "as you request."

Shapell Manuscript Collection

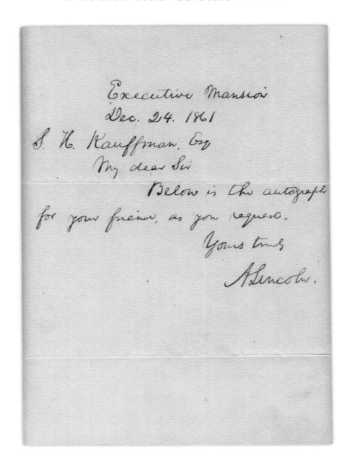

Charleston Mercury reported.[61] Eleven days afterward, Judah P. Benjamin, the senator from Louisiana whom Abram Dittenhoefer had heard called "an Israelite with Egyptian principles," delivered a spellbinding farewell to his Senate colleagues, expounding upon what he termed "The Right of Secession." "What may be the fate of this horrible contest, no man can tell, none pretend to foresee," he emotionally concluded, "but this much I will say: the fortunes of war may be adverse to our arms; you may carry desolation into our peaceful land, and with torch and fire you may set our cities in flames . . . but you never can subjugate us; you never can convert the free sons of the soil into vassals paying tribute to your power; and you never, never can degrade them to the level of an inferior and servile race. Never! Never!"[62]

As the nation teetered toward civil war, rumors of plots against the president and vice president-elect circulated. One of them reached Abraham Jonas in Quincy, and on December 30, 1860, he hastened to inform Lincoln. Expressing "great anxiety in regard to your personal safety and the preservation of our national integrity," Jonas reminded the president-elect that he had a "very large family connection in the south," including six children and other "near relatives" in New Orleans. Divided as those relatives were politically, they still maintained close familial ties. Jonas reported in confidence that he had learned from one of those relatives—he did not say which one, but it is tempting to think that it was his son, Benjamin, who had earlier worked with Lincoln to free John Shelby—"that there is a perfect organization, fearful in numbers and controuled [*sic*] by men of character and influence, whose object is to prevent the inauguration of Lincoln . . . if by no other means, by using violence on the person of Lincoln—men engaged in this measure are known to be of the most violent character, capable of doing any act necessary to carry out their vile measures." Alarmed, Jonas urged "precautionary measures," adding the salutation "with great devotion."[63] A day earlier, Sen.

William H. Seward, soon to become Lincoln's secretary of state, passed along similar intelligence concerning a plot to seize the capital on or before the inauguration on March 4 ("you must not imagine that I am giving you suspicions and rumors—Believe that I know what I write.")[64] So it was that in a December 31 letter to Ohio governor Salmon P. Chase, soon to be nominated secretary of the Treasury, that Lincoln, as if summing up the last two weeks of 1860 and anticipating the even worse year to come, evoked the apocalyptic language of the Book of Daniel (9:25): "these troub'lous times."[65] On that last day of 1860, the image he saw reflected in the lion's den may well have been his own.

President James Buchanan, chastened by the election and aware that he had but a few months left in office, was by no means blind to these same "troub'lous times." In a message to the American people, he designated Friday, January 4, 1861, as a day to be "set apart for Humiliation, Fasting and Prayer throughout the Union."[66] In response, Rabbi Isaac Mayer Wise of Cincinnati, who considered the results of the 1860 election "one of the greatest blunders a nation can commit," was openly scornful. "Pray, Sir? No, it is too late. Either the Republican party must go overboard or the Union be dissolved."[67] For the most part, though, synagogues were "exceedingly well attended" on the fast day, with Jews reputedly just as focused on "the importance of the Union and the duty of its preservation" as their non-Jewish neighbors.[68]

Rabbi Morris Raphall (1798–1868) of New York's B'nai Jeshurun Congregation delivered the most memorable sermon of the fast day—so memorable that he was invited to repeat it eleven days later before the New-York Historical Society. An ordained Orthodox rabbi with impressive university credentials, Raphall possessed dazzling oratorical skills, and was once described as the first celebrity rabbi in American Jewish history. He had supported Douglas against Lincoln, opposed abolitionism, and distrusted those who justified anti-slavery on the basis of the Bible. "How dare you, in the

Private & confidential.

Springfield, Ills. Dec. 17- 1860

Hon. Thurlow Weed

My dear Sir

Yours of the 11th was re-
ceived two days ago— Should the convocation of Governors, of which you speak,
seem desirous to know my views on the
present aspect of things, tell them
you judge from my speeches that I
will be inflexible on the territorial
question; that I probably think
either the Missouri line extended,
or Douglas' and Eli Thayer's Pop. Sov.
would lose us every thing we gained
by the election; that filibustering
for all South of us, and making
slave states of it, would follow in
spite of us, under either plan.

Also, that I probably think all
opposition, real and apparent, to the
fugitive slave clause of the Constitution
ought to be withdrawn.

I believe you can pretend to find
but little, if any thing, in my speeches,
about secession; but my opinion is
that no state can, in any way lawfully,
get out of the Union, without the
consent of the others; and that
it is the duty of the President, and
other government functionaries to run
the machine as it is—

Yours very truly
A. Lincoln—

"No state can, in any
way lawfully, get out of
the Union, without the
consent of the others."

LINCOLN TO THURLOW WEED,
DECEMBER 17, 1860

Just three days ahead of South
Carolina's secession on December 20,
Lincoln maintains his consistent
posture: "No state can, in any way
lawfully, get out of the Union,
without the consent of the others,"
he declares. Lincoln also refers to
Douglas's dreaded favorite slogan:
Popular Sovereignty.

Shapell Legacy Partnership

THE UNION IS DISSOLVED

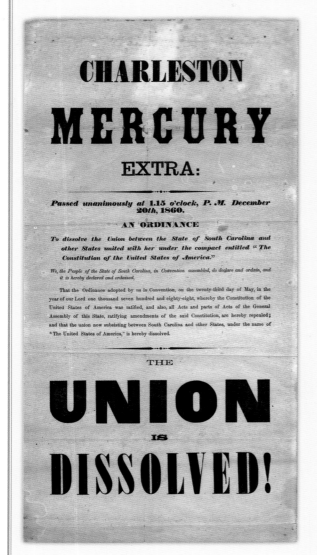

CHARLESTON MERCURY

EXTRA:

Passed unanimously at 1.15 o'clock, P. M. December 20th, 1860.

AN ORDINANCE

To dissolve the Union between the State of South Carolina and other States united with her under the compact entitled " The Constitution of the United States of America."

We, the People of the State of South Carolina, in Convention assembled, do declare and ordain, and it is hereby declared and ordained,

That the Ordinance adopted by us in Convention, on the twenty-third day of May, in the year of our Lord one thousand seven hundred and eighty-eight, whereby the Constitution of the United States of America was ratified, and also, all Acts and parts of Acts of the General Assembly of this State, ratifying amendments of the said Constitution, are hereby repealed; and that the union now subsisting between South Carolina and other States, under the name of " The United States of America," is hereby dissolved.

THE UNION IS DISSOLVED!

DECEMBER 20, 1860

Some seven weeks after Lincoln's election, South Carolina became the first Southern state to secede from the United States. This broadside, published by the Charleston Mercury, *announces the unanimous adoption by South Carolina of an ordinance of secession, at 1:15 P.M., December 20, 1860.*

Shapell Manuscript Collection

IN 1860, THE AMERICAN EXPERIMENT in democracy was less than ninety years old: no other government in the world was headed by an elected figure. Lincoln, profoundly conscious of his roles as both leader of the states and the preserver of their unity, insisted in December 1860 that no state could lawfully leave the Union without the consent of the others and had stressed in his Cooper Union address that this was indeed the intent of the Founders. To Lincoln, that the Union might be dissolved from within was no less than anathema. This is, perhaps, why the headline in the *Charleston Mercury*, "Union Is Dissolved," had not so much to do with slavery, which he so abhorred, but with democracy, which he so loved. Secession, to Lincoln, was an attack on the foundations of self-governance; and, looming ominously, raised the possibility of a catastrophic defeat for the cause of human liberty. "My paramount object in this struggle is to save the Union," he made clear to Horace Greeley in his famous August 22, 1862, letter, "and is not either to save or to destroy slavery. If I could save the Union without freeing any slave I would do it, and if I could save it by freeing all the slaves I would do it."

Lincoln, however, had other things to consider—pragmatic ones. His view of his official duty as president contrasted, he made clear, with his personal position on slavery. "I intend no modification of my oft-expressed personal wish that all men every where could be free," he told Greeley. Yet he clarified, in an April 4, 1864, letter to a Kentucky newspaper editor, that "if slavery is not wrong, nothing is wrong. I cannot remember when I did not so think and feel." But his lifelong goal of abolishing slavery would have to wait, for had he made the war only about slavery and not about secession, he would have lost the slaveholding border states, still in the Union, to the Confederacy—and perhaps the war itself. "I hope to have God on my side," Lincoln is reported to have said, "but I must have Kentucky."

Lincoln walked, then, a fine line indeed, for even if the war was fought over states' rights and secession, those rights included owning slaves and allowing the expansion of slavery into the western territories. Without slavery, there would have been no war between North and South. And what congressional legislation could not fix in the 1850s on the slavery question, war—and Lincoln's pen—ultimately would.

**ABRAHAM JONAS
TO LINCOLN,
DECEMBER 30, 1860**

*Jonas warns Lincoln of a
plot to assassinate him before
Inauguration Day. His warnings
did not go unheeded: Lincoln
was smuggled into Washington,
arriving in the dead of night ten
days before the Inauguration.*
Courtesy of the Library of Congress

face of the sanction and protection afforded to slave property in the Ten Commandments—how dare you denounce slaveholding as a sin?" he challenged the abolitionist preacher Henry Ward Beecher in his sermon. His own analysis of the Bible led him to believe that (1) slavery had existed since antiquity; (2) that it was "no sin," as slave property was expressly placed under the protection of the Ten Commandments; and (3) that the slave should be considered a person with rights "not conflicting with the lawful exercise of the rights of his owner." This, he believed offered a sound basis for sectional reconciliation: "If our Northern fellow-citizens, content with following the word of God, would not insist on being 'righteous overmuch,' or denouncing 'sin' which the Bible knows not, but which is plainly taught by the precepts of men—they would entertain more equity and less ill feeling towards their Southern brethren," he thundered. "And if our Southern fellow-citizens would adopt the Bible view of slavery, and discard the heathen slave code, which permits a few bad men to indulge in an abuse of power that throws a stigma and disgrace on the whole body of slaveholders—if both North and South would do what is right, then God . . . would mercifully avert the impending evil, for with Him alone is the power to do so."[69]

Raphall's address echoed familiar Protestant

Springfield, Ill., Dec. 31. 1860

Hon. S. P. Chase

My dear Sir

In these troub'lous
times I would much like a
conference with you— Please
visit me here at once—

Yours very truly

A. Lincoln—

"In these troub'lous times"

THE ANTI-SEMITIC ABOLITIONISTS

BY DEFINITION, *abolitionism* was understood to mean, in its simplest form, the movement to achieve immediate and total abolition of slavery, and to many it also carried with it connotations of altruism, liberal-mindedness, tolerance, and respect for blacks. But there was another side—a darker side—to abolitionism, and that was the abolitionists themselves. Yes, blacks could be free, but they should be free blacks somewhere else. Colonization of blacks in foreign lands, outside the borders of the U.S., formed a big part of their beliefs. And for good measure, they were, to varying degrees, also anti-Semitic, especially the most famous of them, William Lloyd Garrison, who once called his opponent Mordecai Noah "a lineal descendant of the monsters who nailed Jesus to the cross . . ." Well-known clergyman Theodore Parker also often had vicious words for the Jews: their "intellect was sadly pinched in those narrow foreheads," he wrote—and, another time, said of Jews that "they did sometimes kill a Christian baby at the Passover or the anniversary of Haman's famous day."

arguments and was properly described as "very forcible if not novel."[70] Yet coming as it did from a learned rabbi, it received wide circulation, sparking fierce debate in both Jewish and non-Jewish circles. "Child of a thrice delivered race," one Christian poet scolded, "hast thou/ no tears for those who still in bondage bow?"[71] The key debate concerned how the Bible should be interpreted and read. Within the Jewish community, supporters of Lincoln who opposed slavery condemned Raphall's literal reading of the biblical text and insisted on a more contextualized reading or one that focused on the spirit rather than on the letter of divine law. The radical reform rabbi David Einhorn, for example, who fiercely opposed slavery, argued vehemently that "the spirit of the law of God" enshrined in the creation story, where "God created man in his image" [Gen. 1:27], "can never approve of slavery."[72] The lay Jewish

OPPOSITE

**LINCOLN IN THE LION'S DEN,
DECEMBER 31, 1860**

Secession, assassination, and war: as the country tore itself apart, Lincoln, in Springfield, strove to put together his cabinet. Now immersed "in these troub'lous times," Lincoln, echoing the biblical Daniel, acknowledges in a letter to Salmon P. Chase, the impending danger from all sides.

Shapell Manuscript Collection

biblical scholar Michael Heilprin, whose brother was Lincoln's optician in 1864, mischievously wondered whether Raphall would support polygamy and concubinage, since both were also accepted by the Bible and practiced by the patriarchs.[73] On the other hand, one enthusiastic Protestant minister was so persuaded by Raphall's close textual reading, based on the Hebrew original, that he declared the rabbi's lecture to be "as true almost as the word of God itself."[74]

Raphall was far from being the only Jewish apologist for slavery. Rabbi Bernard Illowy in Baltimore used his Fast Day sermon to attack Lincoln and the Republicans. "Who can blame our brethren of the South," he declared, "for seceding from a society whose government can not, or will not, protect the property rights and privileges of a great portion of the Union against the encroachments of a majority misguided by some influential, ambitious aspirants and selfish politicians who, under the color of religion and the disguise of philanthropy, have thrown the country into a general state of confusion?" He, like Raphall, defended slavery on the basis of the Bible.[75]

Even Abraham Jonas's older brother, Joseph Jonas, in an address before the Ohio House of Representatives, defended slavery. He argued, likewise from the Bible, that the Negro slave descended from the serpent in the Garden of Eden and was cast into "slavery, without the power of rising in the scale of nations." Abolitionists, he charged, were sinfully "flying in the face of Providence, who has, for some grand purpose . . . condemned this race to slavery."[76]

The controversy over Morris Raphall's sermon brought unprecedented publicity to the supposed "Jewish view" on the slavery issue but only underscored, in the end, the complexity of the issue and the many different ways that biblical texts could be parsed. On the issue of slavery, the question of how properly to understand the Bible, and most other controversial issues through the Civil War years, the Jewish community did not speak, as Abraham Jonas had hoped they would, with a single voice. Instead, some Jews supported Lincoln and opposed slavery; some supported the Union and sought to compromise on slavery; and some justified slavery and hated Lincoln with a passion.

Chicago Jewish leader Abraham Kohn (1819–71) became one of those who supported Lincoln. Born and educated in Bavaria, Kohn immigrated to the United States in 1842. For a time, he peddled in New England, but in 1843 or 1844 he moved to Chicago and became the proprietor of a clothing store. On the Day of Atonement in 1845, Kohn participated in the first known Jewish religious service held in Chicago and subsequently helped to found its first synagogue, of which he was later president. In 1860, he also became the city's first Jewish clerk. By then, he had become active in politics as a staunch Republican, dubbed by his enemies "one of the blackest Republicans and Abolitionists."

Abraham Lincoln was introduced to Kohn as a Jewish leader by his friend, newly elected congressman Isaac N. Arnold, probably on his trip to Chicago following the election (November 21–25, 1860), and the two men spoke of their common devotion to the Bible.[77] Ten weeks later, when Kohn wrote Lincoln to recommend the appointment of a local attorney, Republican leader John W. Waughop, a Methodist, as resident minister to the Hague, he reminded Lincoln of his Jewish connections. "Being well acquainted with the Hebrew population of the City of Chicago," he assured the president-elect, "I know that the appointment of Mr. Waughop to that position would give entire satisfaction, indeed they would rejoice in it." "Mr. Waughop," he explained, "has taken great pains to encourage the Hebrews in the support of the Republican cause." While there is no evidence that Lincoln acted on the recommendation, one of his aides docketed the letter as coming "from a leading Jew" and appended a revealing note to the bottom of the letter, further evidence of the special interest Lincoln took in Jews: "I regard Mr. Kohn," it read, "as the best authority for his countrymen in Chicago."[78]

Later that same month, Kohn (described by one newspaper as "a Hebrew of the Hebrews") sent Lincoln a present, one of many he received as he prepared to leave his home in Springfield to take up residence in the White House. It was, according to one reporter, "an exquisitely executed picture of the American flag, with a Hebrew inscription filling the entire extent of the white stripes." The reporter described the gift as "gracefully designed, delicately executed, felicitously presented, and gratefully accepted." The Hebrew inscription, according to multiple contemporary sources, consisted of "the passage in the first chapter of Joshua; the 4th to the 9th verses inclusive." Lincoln and Kohn, who knew their Bible so well, understood how apt that passage was for a new leader about to cross the country to take up his duties in Washington under the threat of a looming war. Even reporters found the inscription "to be very appropriate." One supplied readers with an English translation from the King James Bible. "Be strong and of a good courage," the text concluded. "Be not afraid, neither be thou dismayed: for the Lord thy God is with thee whithersoever thou goest."[79]

LEFT

ABRAHAM KOHN, CIRCA 1865

A German-born Chicago clothier and city official, Kohn met Lincoln during the presidential campaign of 1860—and, as both an ardent Republican and devout Jew, saw in him, his daughter recalled, a leader like Moses, destined to free the slaves and save his nation.

KAM Isaiah Israel Congregation, Chicago, Illinois

BELOW

KOHN FLAG

To his new friend Lincoln, departing to Washington as president-elect, Kohn sent this painted flag. In the white bars of the flag Kohn inscribed, in Hebrew, verses 4 through 9 of Joshua I, including: "Be strong and of a good courage...Be not afraid, neither be thou dismayed: for the Lord thy God is with thee whithersoever thou goest."

Courtesy of the Chicago History Museum

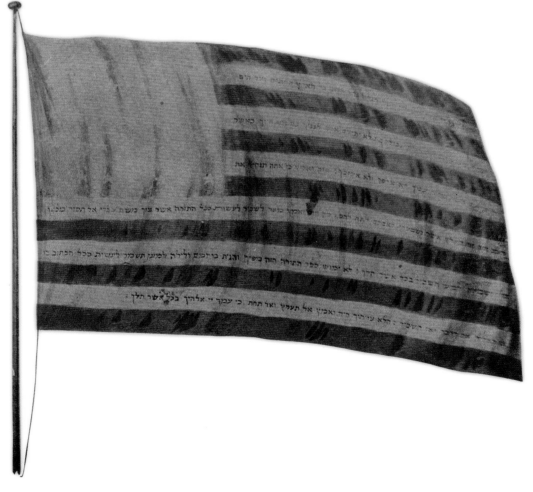

CAPTURING LINCOLN

Lincoln understood the political importance of his image. He sat for his photo some fifty times, including for the Jewish photographer Samuel G. Alschuler, with whom he met on at least two occasions. The images here reflect not only how Lincoln looked but how, approaching the presidency, that look changed: in 1860, he grew a beard.

Why Lincoln grew a beard is anyone's guess, but he himself gave the nod to an eleven-year-old girl named Grace Bedell. She wrote him that his face was too thin and that he would look better if he let his whiskers grow. Women like beards, Grace reasoned, so they would tease their husbands to vote for him. She promised, meanwhile, to try and get her older brothers to vote for him as well. Charmed by her letter, Lincoln, with his characteristic love of children, replied to "My dear Little Miss." "As to the whiskers," he wrote, "having never worn any, do you not think people would call it a piece of silly affection [sic] if I were to begin it now?" Though Lincoln was concerned about vanity and affectation, he nevertheless took her advice, though he had already realized a week earlier, that with "the government about to fall into our hands," he did not grow his beard to gain votes. He did, however, change the fashion of the times: for the next fifty years, all elected U.S. presidents, save for William McKinley, would have facial hair.

While famous for its connection to Lincoln's beard, Lincoln's letter to little Grace also shows Lincoln in a moment of quiet personal reflection: in response to her question about children, as the father of four sons he replies, "I regret the necessity of saying I have no daughters."

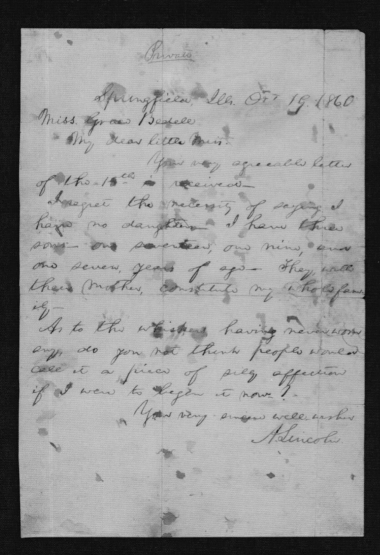

ABOVE

1858

Samuel Alschuler lent Lincoln his own velvet-trimmed coat for this photo taken by Alschuler in Urbana, Illinois, on April 25, 1858.

Courtesy of the Library of Congress

LEFT

LINCOLN'S FAMOUS LETTER TO GRACE BEDELL, OCTOBER 19, 1860

Shapell Legacy Partnership

*"in behalf of
Mr. Alschuler . . .
I gave him a sitting."*

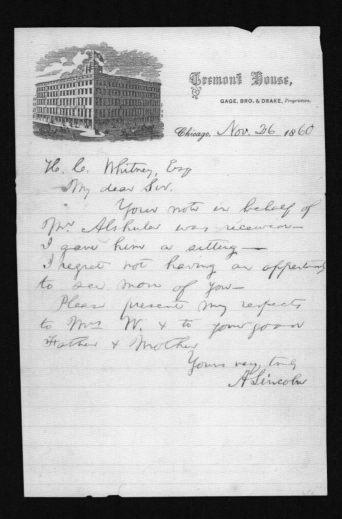

 ABOVE
1860
Lincoln, now president-elect and with an early
beard, again sits for Alschuler, in Chicago, on
November 25, 1860.
Courtesy of the Library of Congress

TOP RIGHT
President-elect Lincoln recalls sitting for
Alschuler on the previous day; written
on Fremont House Chicago stationery,
November 26, 1860.
Abraham Lincoln Presidential Library & Museum

BOTTOM RIGHT
1861
Lincoln, in a signed photograph taken by
Christopher German in Springfield, Ilinois,
dated January 26, 1861, now with a full beard.
Shapell Manuscript Collection

CHAPTER FOUR

WE HAVE NOT YET APPOINTED A HEBREW

1861–1862

Needing every ounce of the strength and the courage that Abraham Kohn, invoking the biblical Joshua, had wished upon him, Abraham Lincoln set forth on February 11, 1861, the eve of his fifty-second birthday, for Washington, D.C. Some one thousand people gathered early in the morning at Springfield's Great Western Railroad depot to see him off. Henry Greenebaum, the Jewish Democrat whom Lincoln had earlier wooed in Chicago, happened to be in Springfield for a legislative hearing that day and joined them. "I now leave," he heard Lincoln say, "not knowing when, or whether ever, I may return." In what Greenebaum recalled as "a very solemn

OPPOSITE

INAUGURATION DAY, MARCH 4, 1861

Amid unprecedented military security and accompanied by President James Buchanan, Lincoln spoke movingly of peace and reconciliation with the rebellious South. "We are not enemies, but friends," he pleaded in his inauguration speech. Nonetheless, six weeks later, the Confederates fired on Fort Sumter, and the war began.

The Granger Collection

and impressive speech," the president-elect described the task awaiting him as even "greater than that which rested upon Washington." South Carolina, Mississippi, Florida, Alabama, Georgia, Louisiana, and Texas had all by then seceded from the United States, and, on February 8, the Confederate States of America, "invoking the favor of Almighty God," had formed a provisional constitution. Lincoln, affirming his own trust in God, "who can go with me, and remain with you and be every where for good," confidently hoped "that all will yet be well." He bid "an affectionate farewell" to everyone, and, according to Greenebaum, "moved us to tears."[1]

Lincoln's train stopped repeatedly along the route, a conscious effort to promote calm and acquaint Americans with their new president—"that I may see you," he said, "and that you may see me." Everywhere he was greeted by large crowds. In Cincinnati, where he left his train for the night, Rabbi Isaac Mayer Wise watched the eager throngs and was appalled. "The Philistines from all corners of the land congregate around their Dagon and worship him . . . ," he complained,

HENRY GREENEBAUM

The German-born Greenebaum was an intimate friend of Stephen A. Douglas in Illinois, but he knew and liked Lincoln, becoming a Republican with the advent of the Civil War. Lincoln, he recalled, had "very broad views, had no prejudices whatever against any nationalities or classes and many of the most prominent Jews of Illinois supported him for the Presidency."

Chicago History Museum

ISAAC MAYER WISE

Though not denying Lincoln's honesty and intelligence, Rabbi Isaac Mayer Wise, a leading figure in the American Jewish community, was repulsed by Lincoln's primitive manner. A Northern Democrat, Wise was fearful of radicalism on both sides; and while not antislavery, his primary aim was to hold the Union together.

Jacob Rader Marcus Center of the American Jewish Archives, Cincinnati, Ohio

employing a biblical metaphor that, ironically, Lincoln himself might well have appreciated. "We can not tell why these extraordinary demonstrations, processions, banquets, &c., should be made." To Wise, an immigrant and a Democrat, the president-elect appeared inadequate; he described him, evoking a central European metaphor, as looking like "Der Landjunker das erste Mal in der Stadt, which [means], in good English, 'like a country squire for the first time in the city.'" "We have no doubt he is an honest man and, as much as we can learn, also quite an intelligent man," he concluded, "but he will look queer in the white house, with his primitive manner."[2]

Abram Dittenhoefer, the Jewish lawyer who had worked so hard to elect Lincoln, naturally disagreed. He was present on February 20 when the Democratic mayor of New York, Fernando Wood, hosted Lincoln, and described the president-elect as "more grave and serious" than before, an indication either of "fatigue or anxiety regarding the future." Lincoln, he sensed, was "a man carrying a burden that grew heavier day by day," understandably so in the wake of Jefferson Davis's inauguration two days earlier as provisional president of the Confederate States. Lincoln's remarks in response to Wood, in which he analogized the Union to a ship with passengers and cargo, and hinted that in order to save the ship it might be necessary to throw "cargo overboard," suggested to Dittenhoefer that the president-elect "had become bolder in the expression of his feeling against the continuance of slavery in the South." Looking back, he described what Lincoln said that day as an anticipation of the future, "the first gleam of emancipation."[3]

Many other Jews also gazed upon Abraham Lincoln as trains carried him across the country, a journey that covered 1,904 miles and the tracks of eighteen different railroad lines. In Philadelphia, in sight of the hall where the Declaration of Independence and the Constitution were originally framed, Lincoln repeated an ancient Jewish oath, inspired by Psalm 137. "May my

Philadelphia Pa
Feb. 21st 1861.

Hon, Erastus Corning
Dear Sir!
Col. Sumner
having engagements this
evening, and having just
received your favor of
Yesterday, in relation to
the subject of Mr Lincoln
& family — & Suite. Stopp
-ing at Willards — he requ
-ested me to answer your
letter — We have decided
after consulting with
Mr. & Mrs Lincoln — to
go to Willards —
Mr. Washburn & friends
had secured a private
house for him but
after Consultation

Mrs Lincoln is decidedly
of opinion that there
will not be suffi
cient room for the
family in the house
they have secured
Can Judge Davis &
myself get rooms
adjoining the rooms
intended for Mr.
Lincoln & family?
very
Respy Yours

Ward H Lamon

ABOVE

LINCOLN IS SAFELY DELIVERED TO WASHINGTON, FEBRUARY 21, 1861

Eight weeks after Abraham Jonas expressed concern over Lincoln's safety prior to the inauguration, Lincoln's friend and bodyguard Ward Lamon confirms that the president-elect will stay at a public hotel, Willard's, in Washington, for the ten days prior to his move into the Executive Mansion. Sadly, Lamon would be out of town four years later when the inadequately protected Lincoln was shot at Ford's Theatre.

Shapell Manuscript Collection

RIGHT

FIRST WASHINGTON SITTING, FEBRUARY 24, 1861

One day after sneaking into Washington from Baltimore under cover of darkness, Lincoln, exhausted and pensive, sits as president-elect for this photo—his first taken in Washington— by Alexander Gardner at Mathew Brady's studio.

Shapell Manuscript Collection

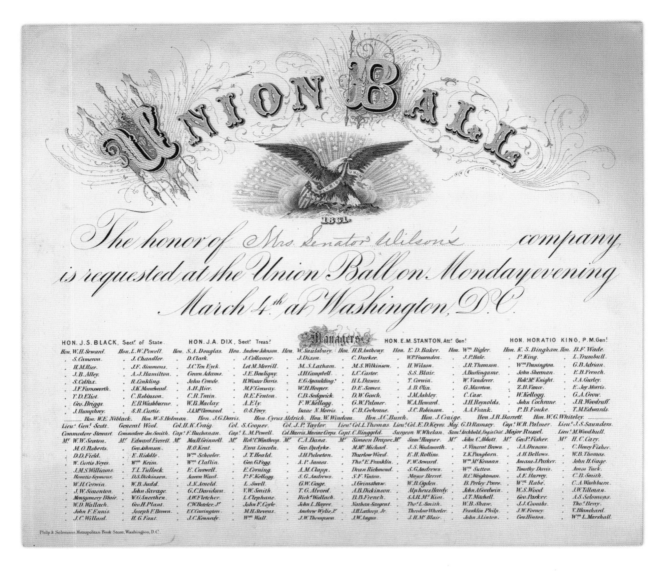

ABOVE AND RIGHT (DETAIL)

INAUGURAL BALL INVITATION, MARCH 4, 1861

Listed as a "Manager" of Lincoln's celebratory Union Ball, to be held the night of the swearing-in, is Jewish activist, philanthropist, and businessman Adolphus Simeon (A. S.) Solomons.

Shapell Manuscript Collection

right hand forget its cunning and my tongue cleave to the roof of my mouth," he declared, thinking of what the Founders had created, "if ever I prove false to those teachings." Implicitly, he here linked the most sacred documents of the United States to the sacred city of Jerusalem; Lincoln was very likely aware of how the portion of Psalm 137 continues: "If I do not remember you, if I do not consider Jerusalem, my highest joy."[4]

Inspired as some were by Lincoln's biblically inflected rhetoric, Jews remained divided in their views concerning the incoming president. As such, they were a microcosm of the nation as a whole. This was particularly evident in Baltimore, where, in order to avoid a suspected assassination plot, Lincoln arrived under cover of darkness at about 3:30 A.M. on Saturday morning, February 23, and made himself inconspicuous as he switched trains for the last leg of his journey to Washington. Baltimore at that time was home to as many as 7,000 Jews, and they spanned the spectrum. Some of the city's oldest and most Orthodox Jews, like the majority of the Cohen and Friedenwald families and Rabbi Bernard Illowy, loathed the Republican Party and openly sympathized with the slaveholding South. Radical Jews like Rabbi David Einhorn and his followers, many of whom had supported the failed 1848 revolutions in Europe, detested slavery and cheered on its Republican opponents (as a result, Einhorn would be forced to flee the city in April). The majority of Jews, in the middle, having voted for the Democrats, promoted peace and reconciliation. They sought at all costs to stem the secessionist tide that Lincoln's nomination had precipitated.[5]

Ten days following his arrival in Washington, Abraham Lincoln was inaugurated as the sixteenth president of the United States. His celebrated inaugural address likewise sought to stem the secessionist tide. He promised his "dissatisfied fellow countrymen" that he would uphold the laws, and reiterated his promise not "to interfere with the institution of slavery in the States where it exists." His remarkable peroration, a literary masterpiece, pleaded for national reconciliation:

PHILP & SOLOMONS STATIONERY EMBOSSMENT

Imprint from the firm of Philp & Solomons, founded by Jewish printer Adolphus S. Solomons. Official Executive Mansion stationery had never before been employed in the White House, and Lincoln wrote many of his first personal and official letters as president on plain Philp & Solomons imprinted stationery. A year after taking office, Lincoln received the first printing of official Executive Mansion-embossed stationery. Lincoln continued to use Philp & Solomon's stationery—including for one of five handwritten copies of the Gettysburg Address.

We are not enemies, but friends. We must not be enemies. Though passion may have strained, it must not break our bonds of affection. The mystic chords of memory, stre[t]ching from every battle-field, and patriot grave, to every living heart and hearthstone, all over this broad land, will yet swell the chorus of the Union, when again touched, as surely they will be, by the better angels of our nature.[6]

Unremarked, except by Jews, was Lincoln's specific reference to Christianity as a basis for resolving the sectional crisis. "Intelligence, patriotism, Christianity, and a firm reliance on Him, who has never yet forsaken this favored land," he declared, "are still competent to adjust, in the best way, all our present difficulty."[7] A dozen letters poured into the office of the *Israelite* protesting the president's remarks. "Why not take

"MR. LINCOLN," HIS WIFE WROTE, "is almost a monomaniac on the subject of honesty." "On no terms would either male or female receive his signature to enable them to profit by our Government." In fact, even before he became president, tales concerning his integrity and magnanimity circulated, whether as a shopkeeper in New Salem or as a hardworking lawyer in Springfield collecting judgments for his clients. As president, he demanded the same standards of honesty from others whom he appointed to government office.

On April 5, 1861, he sent a memo that illustrates those exacting standards. "On to-day," he wrote, "and on the ~~first~~ fifth of each month, please to send me a Warrant for the amount of my salary as President of the United States." He had been inaugurated on March 4, and lest he be paid for four days (March 1–4) when he had not yet assumed office, he corrected the memo in his own hand and stipulated that his salary should thereafter be paid on the fifth of every month.

Two weeks later, on April 19, he displayed his standards of probity once again. "I am annoyed to know that my Bill at your house has not yet been paid," he wrote to the proprietor of Willard's Hotel, where he had stayed prior to his inauguration. "Receipt it & hand it to Mr. Nicolay & he will give a check for the amount." By the nineteenth, a week after hostilities began, Fort Sumter had fallen, and Lincoln, on that very day, was proclaiming a blockade of the South. Nevertheless, he took time out from his busy schedule to make certain that an overdue bill was paid.

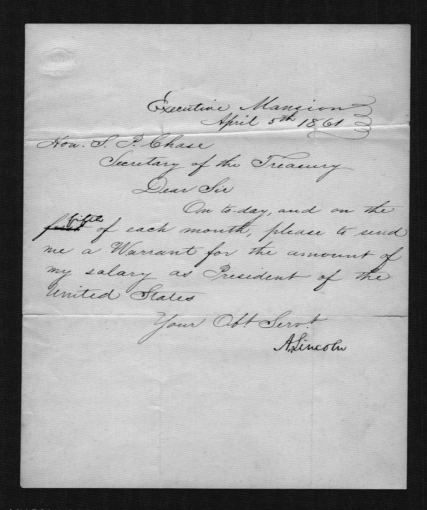

LINCOLN'S TELLING ONE-WORD REVISION OF HIS SALARY VOUCHER

Shapell Legacy Partnership

**THE CHECK, SHOWING THE CORRECT DATE—APRIL 5, 1861,
WITH LINCOLN'S ENDORSEMENT**

U.S. National Archives & Records Administration

Executive Mansion
April 19, 1861

Messrs. Willards
Gents.
I am annoyed to
know that my Bill at your
house has not yet been paid.
Receipt it hand it to Mr.
Nicolay & he will give a
check for the amount
Yours &c
A. Lincoln

LINCOLN PAYS HIS BILL TO WILLARD'S HOTEL

Shapell Manuscript Collection

the advice of the writings and doings of Thomas Jefferson," one of them asked. It called upon Lincoln to speak out "in the name of humanity and not Christianity." Giving voice to perennial Jewish fears concerning the use of state power to advance the Christian faith to the disadvantage of others, the letter writer worried that Lincoln, in the future, might prove sympathetic to nationwide efforts to strengthen Christian Sunday closing ("blue") laws, as well as to the campaign to have "Christ be acknowledged by the Constitution."[8]

Though no partisan of the president, Rabbi Isaac Mayer Wise, the editor of the *Israelite*, urged calm. "In Springfield religion is called Christianity," he wrote reassuringly, "because people there do not think of any other form of worship, hence Mr. Lincoln uses the same word to express the same sentiment." Observing that Lincoln's supporters at the polls included many infidels and atheists, he suggested that his "words must not be criticized too closely." "By and by," he patronizingly predicted, "he will learn the precise use and import of terms."[9]

The precise meaning of "Christianity" at that time was actually somewhat complex. Some in Lincoln's day used the word narrowly as a synonym for Protestantism, others as a synecdoche for religion as a whole. The status of religious outsiders, such as Catholics, Jews, Mormons, and Native Americans, lay much in dispute.[10] Moreover, for all of his appeal to Christianity, Lincoln may not even have considered himself a Christian. He grew up, we have seen, among Calvinist Baptists who believed in predestination. True Christians, according to them, had been selected as such when the world came into being. "I am not a Christian—God knows I would be one," he allegedly told Illinois' state superintendent of public instruction, Newton Bateman, in 1860.[11]

As for Jews, while they were known to be a distinctive "class" of Americans, much like Germans and Catholics, the fact that they were not Christian became an issue only when Jews felt excluded.[12] Otherwise, they mostly played down their religious differences and sought to fit in. Many of them, indeed, were better

known as Germans than as Jews. Lincoln, from his previous interactions with Jews, had no reason to know that his reference to "Christianity" would offend them. Over time, as we shall see, he learned better.

Meanwhile, a call had gone out in the *Jewish Messenger* for "our people" to be "well represented" at the grand Union Ball held on inauguration night. However much Jews viewed themselves as a people apart ("our people"), they looked to participate as equals in public events of this sort. Over eighty Jewish families reputedly lived in Washington at that time. The noted Washington printer and bookstore owner Adolphus S. Solomons, who was Sabbath-observing and Orthodox, was even listed as a "manager" on the ball's official invitation. "The tickets are to be $10 each," the *Messenger* drolly reported, "admitting a gentleman and as many ladies as he may have the moral courage to bring with him."[13]

Some of those who paid to dance at the inaugural ball were office seekers. Prior to the 1883 Pendleton Civil Service Reform Act, patronage dominated most levels of government in the United States, on the theory that "to the victor belongs the spoils." Presidents rewarded their acquaintances and supporters with government jobs to cement their hold on power and promote party loyalty. As a result, within days of the inauguration, thousands of job seekers, of every faith and no faith, thronged the White House. Abraham Lincoln spent long hours seeking to identify whom he could depend upon to work hard and resist corruption.[14]

Ethnic and religious group leaders naturally paid close attention to presidential appointments, hoping that members of their own flock received their due. Jews were no exception. "The present government . . . has not given one single office to an Israelite," Rabbi Isaac Mayer Wise complained four weeks after Lincoln took office.[15] By then, Lincoln was actually preparing to make his first official appointment of a Jew to public office. On May 24, Wise himself happily announced the news: "Abraham Jonas has received the appointment of Post Master of Quincy by the direct

diate power, if it would, to change either. If it were admitted that you who are dissatisfied, hold the right side in the dispute, there still is no single good reason for precipitate action. Intelligence, patriotism, Christianity, and a firm reliance on Him, who has never yet forsaken this favored land, are still competent to adjust, in the best way, all our present difficulty.

7744 In *your* hands, my dissatisfied fellow countrymen, and not in *mine*, is the momentous issue of civil war. The government will not assail *you.* You can have no conflict, without being yourselves the aggressors. *You* have no oath registered in Heaven to destroy the government, while *I* shall have the most solemn one to "preserve, protect and defend" it.

I am loth to close. We are not enemies, but friends— We must not be enemies. Though passion may have strained, it must not break our bonds of affection. The mystic chords of memory, stretching from every battlefield, and patriot grave, to every living heart and hearthstone, all over this broad land, will yet swell the chorus of the Union, when again touched, as surely they will be, by the better angels of our nature.

nomination of President Lincoln."[16] Jonas, we have seen, had served in that position before, under Presidents Taylor and Fillmore. Having worked so hard to elect Lincoln, he sought the remunerative position once again. Soon after the November election, the *Quincy Daily Herald* reported that a petition was circulating in the community, "asking Abe Lincoln to appoint Abe Jonas postmaster." Democrats signed the petition as well. Orville Hickman Browning, in a letter to Lincoln in December, added his weight to the effort: "I would be glad to have our mutual friend Abram Jonas remembered in connection with the Post office at Quincy. He wishes the place, and, I think, ought to have it." Lincoln, preoccupied by the fall of Fort Sumter and the outbreak of war, seems to have delayed the appointment. Once he acted favorably, though, Jonas lost no time in extending patronage to friends of his own: "The new Post Master, Mr. Jonas has made the following appointments," the *Quincy Whig Republican* reported on May 25. "Edward Jonas, Principal Assistant; Simon

P. Cohen, Book-Keeper; John Kinkle, Clerk." Two of those three early appointments went to Jews, one of whom was Jonas's own son.[17]

Abraham Lincoln found himself engaged with matters concerning Jews thrice more around the time that Jonas became Quincy's postmaster, a sign of the growing numbers and significance of Jews in the United States, of Lincoln's own predilections, and of the president's changing priorities and responsibilities with the onset of the Civil War. On May 26, he dashed off a note to Secretary of War Simon Cameron concerning a Jew named Max Einstein. "I am very much

307

To the Senate of the United States.

I nominate Abraham Jonas
to be Deputy Postmaster at Quincy, in the
county of Adams, and State of Illinois,
in place of Wm H. Carlin removed; the said Abraham
Jonas having been appointed during the last recess of the
Senate.

Abraham Lincoln

Washington,
July 10. 1861.

inclined to accept Col. Einsteins Regiment," he wrote "and wish you would have it mustered into service as soon as possible."[18]

Einstein (1822–1906), who immigrated to America from Württemberg in 1844, owned a successful ribbon and silk store in Philadelphia, but his passion was the military. During the 1850s, he served in various Pennsylvania militias and helped to found and lead the Philadelphia Flying Artillery Company, a unit that specialized in fighting on horseback, using recently introduced lightweight artillery. He also developed extensive political connections. As war loomed, in 1861, Einstein helped to organize the 27th Pennsylvania Volunteer Infantry Regiment: at least half of its volunteers were German immigrants, and about 10 percent Jews. Embarrassed when rioters attacked the unprepared volunteers in Baltimore as they sought to make their way to Washington, the regiment was reorganized as a light artillery company, with Einstein, who was experienced in that area, serving as colonel. He personally traveled to Washington amid the patriotic fervor that swept the North following the fall of Fort Sumter, so as to offer his troops to Secretary of War Cameron, whom he had previously known as Pennsylvania's senator.

Although it was officially up to "state authorities" to supply militiamen in response to the call for 75,000 volunteers to suppress the Confederacy, Lincoln encouraged Cameron to accept the regiment anyway. At the first battle of Bull Run (Manassas), which the Union lost, the 27th Regiment covered the military's retreat, and according to some reports at the time, "Colonel

OPPOSITE

LINCOLN NOMINATES ABRAHAM JONAS, JULY 10, 1861

At the recommendation of Orville Hickman Browning, Lincoln nominates his long-time friend and political supporter, Abraham Jonas, to the position of Deputy Postmaster of Quincy, Illinois.

U.S. National Archives & Records Administration

Einstein's Regiment behaved gallantly." But Major General George B. McClellan, with whom Einstein had apparently clashed, wanted the regiment placed under new leadership. When, allegedly without authorization, Einstein traveled to Philadelphia to procure clothing and shoes for his troops, McClellan had him arrested. Subsequently, McClellan told Cameron that "the interests of the service demand Colonel Einstein's dismissal" since he was "in no respects fit to be a colonel." Accordingly, Einstein was honorably discharged on October 2, 1861. Yet Lincoln was apparently far from convinced of his unfitness, for less than twelve weeks later he nominated him to be U.S. consul to Germany at Nuremberg. The existing consul, Philip Geisse, whom Einstein was slated to replace, was appalled. Among other things, he complained that Einstein's "being an Israelite is much to his prejudice here." Ultimately, the Senate rejected Einstein's nomination.[19]

Anti-Semitism likewise bedeviled another one of Lincoln's consular appointees from that time, Charles L. Bernays. Editor of an antislavery German newspaper in Missouri, Bernays had been a delegate to the 1860 Republican convention and was one of several sympathetic editors whom Lincoln rewarded with consulships. In early June, Lincoln appointed him consul to Zurich, and the recess appointment subsequently sailed through Congress. Jews of the day seem not to have paid much attention to the appointment. Bernays, scion of a distinguished Jewish family, was nominally a Lutheran, baptized and confirmed as a child in Germany prior to his immigration, and was known in Missouri as a freethinker. According to Isaac Mayer Wise, "nobody" would consider him an "Israelite." Nevertheless, several Swiss citizens protested Bernays's nomination, both because they considered him a Jew and because he had criticized Switzerland for discriminating against Jews. Within six months, Lincoln prudently shifted him to Helsingør (Elsinore), Denmark, where his Jewish parentage seems not to have been an issue.[20]

The third matter concerning Jews that engaged

Abraham Lincoln around the time that Abraham Jonas took office involved a European Jewish banking family, the Rothschilds. On May 28, Lincoln received a letter from the prominent New York attorney and former Democratic congressman Francis Brockholst Cutting, advising him "that impressions beneficial to our country will be produced by continuing to communicate with Europe, thro' the medium of the Messrs Rothschild."[21] One of Lincoln's greatest fears at that time was that Great Britain, which was dependent upon Southern cotton, angered by America's recently raised protectionist tariff (the Morrill tariff), and happy to see the United States weakened, might grant official recognition to the Confederacy in a bid to weaken America still more. Salomon James de Rothschild, the somewhat irresponsible twenty-six-year-old son of Baron James Mayer de Rothschild of France, who was on a prolonged visit to America, advocated precisely that policy in a letter home: "The sooner the great European powers recognize the Confederacy . . . ," he wrote, "the sooner they will have fulfilled a mission of peace and humanity. Even more, it is in their own interest to do so, for the independence of the South will bring about free trade and will create an immense outlet for all our products and for those of England. . . . I am therefore begging you to use all your influence to have the Confederacy recognized as quickly as possible."[22]

What Cutting had discovered and revealed to Lincoln, however, was that the elder Rothschild's own Jewish agent in the United States, August (Aaron) Belmont (1813–1890), strongly disagreed with Salomon. The German-born Belmont, who mixed in high society, and was married (in a church) to the daughter of Commodore Matthew Perry, was a leading figure in the Democratic Party.[23] Opposed to Lincoln's election, he was nevertheless outraged by the attack on Fort Sumter and strongly advocated for the Union. "Your Statesmen & your press have at all times taken the most violent & uncompromising stand against Slavery," he reminded Baron Lionel de Rothschild, England's first Jewish

member of Parliament, "and it is more than strange to see the British Government now give its moral countenance to a power, which . . . is based upon Slavery as its principal fundamental strength." Rebutting arguments by Lord John Russell and others that favored British recognition of the Confederacy, Belmont insisted that the South had rebelled from "a fear that their peculiar institution of slavery may hereafter be interfered with by the party which put Mr Lincoln into power." He warned that British interference would "only prolong the fratricidal war and entail ruin not only upon both sections of our country but upon the material interests & commerce of the world." Never a shrinking violet, he made sure that his letter would be read both by the British prime minister, Lord Palmerston, and by Salomon's father, Baron de Rothschild of Paris.[24]

Belmont visited Washington in June, offering advice on how to fund the war (he thought it would require "from 50 to 60 millions of dollars"—Belmont was off in his estimate by a factor of one hundred).[25] He also met privately with Abraham Lincoln. He even seems to have undertaken a secret mission into Confederate territory, though details of his trip remain shrouded in mystery. Later, from Paris, he conveyed to Lincoln confidential "impressions & convictions of highplaced & wellfavored parties" in England and France concerning foreign intervention, and offered suggestions on how to export enough cotton across the Atlantic to prevent the Europeans from entering the conflict.[26] Belmont's call for "an earnest effort towards reconciliation and peace," as if the Southern states have not seceded at all, later distanced him from Lincoln: "Broken eggs," Lincoln replied, employing a metaphor that he memorably used following the Emancipation Proclamation, to underscore that there could be no return to the earlier status quo, "can not be mended." As head of the Democratic Party, in 1864, Belmont actively opposed Lincoln's reelection.[27] Even when they clashed, however, Lincoln—unlike so many others of his time—never disparaged Belmont as a Jew. By contrast, former president James Buchanan (whom

Washington D.C. May 26th 1861.

Hon. Simon Cameron
                    Ser. of War.

Dear Sir,

        I am very much inclined to accept Col. Einsteins Regiment and wish you would have it mustered into service as soon as possible if in any way consistent with our arrangements.

                    Yours Truly
                    A. Lincoln

LINCOLN'S APPOINTMENTS TO JERUSALEM

LINCOLN, WHO, according to his wife, Mary, told her on April 14, 1865, that he wanted to see Jerusalem before he died, shared a similar fate with his October 1861 choice for consul at Jerusalem: neither one of them ever got there. "If the Consul at Jerusalem has resigned, (as I believe he has)," Lincoln wrote, then he obliges the appointment of Josiah S. Weyer. But Weyer, of Iowa, had been trumped months earlier by a more politically viable candidate, Franklin Olcott of New York. Lincoln had simply forgotten that Olcott had been chosen. Albert Rhodes, who was appointed on February 23, 1864, was the last of four different consuls who served under Lincoln in the Holy Land.

RIGHT

LINCOLN'S ENDORSEMENT OF JOSIAH S. WEYER ON A LETTER FROM WILLIAM MCKEE DUNN, OCTOBER 29, 1861

Shapell Manuscript Collection

BELOW

APPOINTMENT OF ALBERT RHODES AS CONSUL AT JERUSALEM, FEBRUARY 23, 1864

Brown University Library

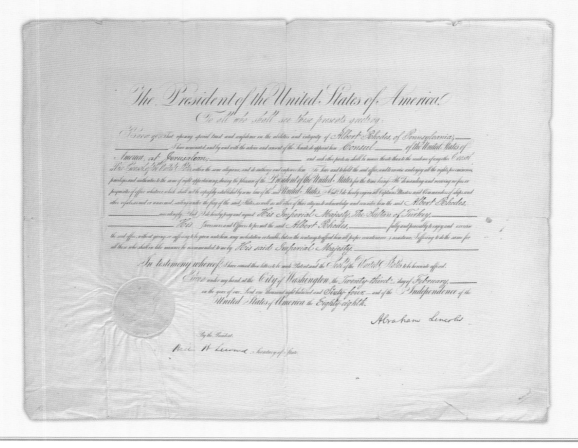

Belmont had helped to elect back in 1856) once privately described him as a "speculating German Jew." The *New York Times* portrayed him as "the agent of foreign Jew bankers." A colonel named Max Langenschwarz dismissed him as "Jew-President Belmont."[28] Lincoln sometimes respected Belmont and sometimes not, but never commented on his ancestry or religion.

Nor did ancestry and religion initially play much role in Lincoln's military appointments, which became increasingly numerous and significant in the months following the fall of Fort Sumter. As we previously noted, he appointed people, as far as possible, on the basis of merit. Such was certainly the case with regard to Alfred Mordecai, Jr., whom Lincoln, on August 10, 1861, appointed a second lieutenant.[29] Mordecai, twenty-one, was the scion of a distinguished and close-knit American Jewish family that dated back from before the American Revolution; he had relatives in both the North and the South. His father, Alfred Mordecai, Sr., received a classical and Jewish education, graduated first in his class at West Point in 1823, was a leader in the field of weapons and ammunitions development, and was probably the highest-ranking Jew of his day in the army. Varina Davis, the wife of Jefferson Davis, met him in the 1850s when her husband was U.S. secretary of war and was so impressed by the "Hebrew" that she felt she could understand, after seeing him, "how that race had furnished the highest type of mankind." In her memoirs, she went on to describe Mordecai's "habits of thought," "moral nature," and "private life" as being most admirable and praiseworthy; he was, she gushed, echoing the New Testament (John 1:47), "an Israelite without guile."[30]

Heavily recruited by the Confederacy once the Civil War began, even as he was overseeing the manufacture of cannon carriages meant to pound the Confederacy into submission, the elder Mordecai resolved his painful sectional dilemma by resigning from the military and sitting out the war in Philadelphia, forgoing honor and a comfortable salary. In so doing, he

AUGUST BELMONT

The wealthy German-born August Belmont was a New York Democrat who, as an international banker, was primarily concerned with preserving a peaceful economy. After Fort Sumter, however, he supported the Union cause and helped raise and equip the first German-American regiment.
Courtesy of the Library of Congress

sought to "spare the feelings" of his wife and children, who favored the North; forbear taking up arms against his mother, siblings, and extended family, who all lived in and sided with the South; and preserve his ties to the army and the Union to which he had sworn loyalty.[31] None applauded his decision. Mordecai's son and namesake, whom Lincoln appointed, faced no similar dilemma. Likewise a West Point graduate ("near the top of his class"), and a lifelong Northerner, he identified with his Jewishness far less than his father (after the war, he was married, in a church, to a Christian).[32] His skills commended him to Lincoln.

The same was true of the Jewish quartermasters whom Lincoln appointed. Quartermasters during the Civil War were responsible for the housing ("quarters"), transportation, clothing, and supplies of the troops. Their labors were described as "incessant." "The

LINCOLN AND THE JEWS

success of all military operations," one Civil War era study concluded, depended "in a great measure" upon the "promptness and efficiency" of the quartermaster.[33] Since a successful quartermaster required business and management skills in abundance, it comes as no surprise that a disproportionate number of Jews, many of whom had mercantile backgrounds, were called upon to fill these positions. One of the first whom Lincoln is known to have appointed was Moritz Pinner, the Jewish delegate from Missouri who had been present at the Republican national convention that nominated Lincoln for president in 1860. Pinner possessed both military and business experience, and General Philip Kearny of the First New Jersey Brigade asked that he be "appointed Quarter Master of his staff." In reply, Lincoln scrawled on the back of the letter, "Let Gen. Kearney be obliged, if it can be done consistently," and

HEBREW, ISRAELITE, JEW

AT DIFFERENT TIMES in his correspondence, Abraham Lincoln spoke of "Jews," of "Hebrews," and of "Israelites." All three terms were commonplace in his day, and they frequently were used interchangeably. Given the negative associations many Christians had with the word *Jew*, some considered *Hebrew* and *Israelite* more respectful terms. A name change, they thought, would improve Jews' overall status. Others, however, remained loyal to the word *Jew*, which had deep historical resonance. Revealingly, nineteenth-century American Jewish newspapers carried names like the *Jewish Messenger*, as well as the *Hebrew Leader* and the *American Israelite*.

The word *Jew*, in the end, did not disappear from the American lexicon. Instead, context generally determined whether it was being used respectfully, descriptively, or disparagingly. In Lincoln's case, whether he wrote about Jews, Hebrews, or Israelites, he never did so, as far as is known, in a disrespectful way.

forwarded it on to Simon Cameron. Pinner received his commission a week later.[34]

Some fifty other Jews served as quartermasters for the Union during the Civil War, but with a single exception no mention of their being Jewish accompanied their appointment; they were appointed on the basis of their merit or connections.[35] In the Confederacy, there were also many Jewish quartermasters, including the quartermaster general of the entire army (derided by his enemies as "Jew Quarter-Master General"), Col. Abraham Charles Myers, for whom Fort Myers, Florida, is named.[36]

On one remarkable occasion—the "single exception" noted above—Lincoln appointed an assistant quartermaster precisely because he was a Jew. The individual involved, Cheme (Cherie) Moise Levy, was the son-in-law of Rabbi Morris J. Raphall of New York's Congregation B'nai Jeshurun. Before the war, as we have seen, Raphall defended slavery as biblically sanctioned, but once the war began he evinced ardent patriotism. His son, Alfred, was commissioned an officer and served with distinction in the Union army, later losing an arm in the fighting near Devil's Den at the Battle of Gettysburg.[37] The elder Raphall's son-in-law, probably with his father-in-law's backing, applied to be a quartermaster. "I believe we have not yet appointed a Hebrew," Lincoln responded in a note to Secretary of War Edwin M. Stanton on November 4, 1862. In fact, he was quite wrong in that belief, for, as we have seen, he had already appointed numbers of Jews, including quartermasters. Levy, however, was different: being Orthodox and well respected in New York, he was a public and visible Jew. That, indeed, is why Lincoln appointed him, because he was a "Hebrew" and because he was "well vouched as a capable and faithful man" (the word *faithful*, with typical Lincoln wordplay, carried a double meaning.) "Let him be appointed an Assistant Quarter-Master, with the rank of Captain," Lincoln ordered.[38]

Levy was soon hard at work in the capital and, on the side, distributed food and clothing to Jewish

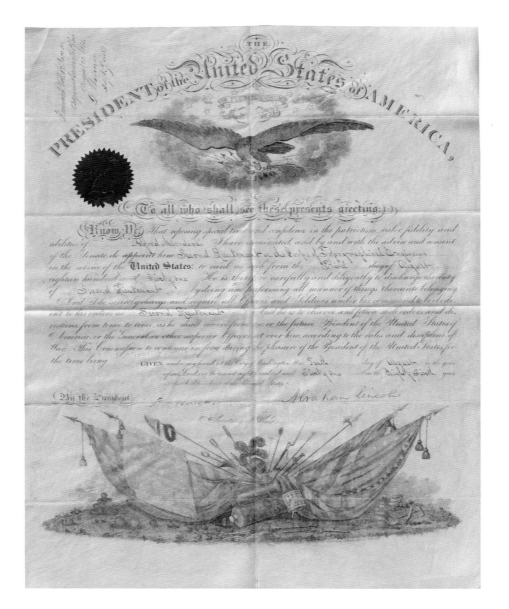

ABOVE

LINCOLN APPOINTS ALFRED MORDECAI, JR. A SECOND LIEUTENANT, AUGUST 10, 1861

Mordecai, a Jewish West Pointer, would go on to become one of the best-known ordnance officers in the United States Army; he retired as a general.

Shapell Manuscript Collection

LEFT

Alfred Mordecai, Jr.

Collection of Robert Marcus

93

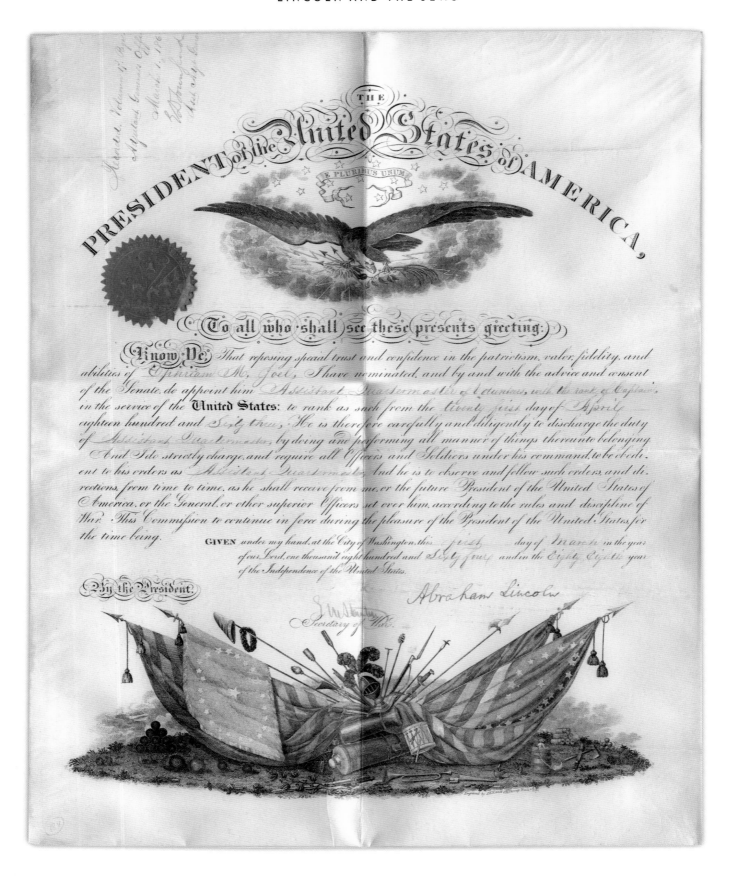

OPPOSITE

LINCOLN PROMOTES JOEL QUARTERMASTER WITH THE RANK OF CAPTAIN, MARCH 1, 1864

Lt. Ephraim M. Joel, having been commended for his conduct at the end of the Vicksburg campaign, when he appropriated Confederate cannons for use by Union troops in the battle, is with this document raised by Lincoln to the rank of captain.

Shapell Manuscript Collection

LEFT

JOEL CONTINUES TO RISE IN THE RANKS, AUGUST 18, 1864

Lincoln appoints Ephraim M. Joel "now A.Q.M. to be Corps Q.M. with rank of Lt. Col. at the request of General Francis Preston Blair."

Shapell Manuscript Collection

PHILIP KEARNY TO LINCOLN, SEPTEMBER 3, 1861, WITH LINCOLN'S ENDORSEMENT OF MORITZ PINNER

At the request of General Philip Kearny, Lincoln endorses the appointment of Moritz Pinner, who had been active in electing Lincoln the year before, as quartermaster for Kearny's staff.

William Clements Library,
University of Michigan

patients in Washington area hospitals.[39] Within less than a year, however, he was charged with "conduct prejudicial to good order and military discipline," for signing a false certificate relating to the pay of men under his command. He secretly withheld half of one clerk's pay—upon the order of a commanding officer, he claimed—allegedly to prevent the man "from squandering one hundred dollars per month [on alcohol] to his own destruction." The sum involved was small, and Senator Samuel C. Pomeroy of Kansas apparently sought to intervene on Levy's behalf. Lincoln, however, was persuaded of Levy's guilt: "it makes too bad a record to admit of my interference—in fact, it could not be worse," he wrote. "To interfere, under the circumstances, would blacken my own character." Levy was therefore deprived of his rank and office in the army and "forever disqualified to hold any office of trust or profit in the United States."[40] Later, however, after hearing favorable reports on Levy from, among others, Richard Busteed (whom he had just appointed a U.S. district judge) and, it seems, after meeting personally with Rabbi Raphall, Lincoln reconsidered.[41] Justice was more important to him than being proven wrong.

On January 16, 1864, Lincoln renominated Levy as assistant quartermaster with the rank of captain. "Permit me to offer my sincere and heartfelt thanks for the generosity and justice with which you have treated my son-in-law Captain C. M. Levy," Raphall wrote him in gratitude. "My whole family unites with me in feeling that you are indeed his true benefactor."[42] Congress investigated and confirmed Levy's appointment, but Stanton blocked it; to him, "forever disqualified" meant just that. Senator Pomeroy protested to Lincoln that the original court martial was "an unjust imputation" and pleaded for Levy's reinstatement, but to no avail. It took another five years until, on February 18, 1869, outgoing president Andrew Johnson removed Levy's disability.[43]

If quartermasters like Levy needed business experience (and connections) to be appointed, so did sutlers,

MORRIS RAPHALL

A powerful New York rabbi, he was both a defender of slavery and a Unionist. In 1861 Raphall became the first rabbi invited to deliver an opening prayer before Congress—which he did, to the dismay of some, in a prayer shawl and skullcap, and partly in Hebrew. He was also one of four rabbis to have had face-to-face meetings with Lincoln in the White House.
Collection of Robert Marcus

and a disproportionate number of them turn out to have been Jewish as well. Sutlers were not military personnel but civilians licensed by military commanders to market provisions to soldiers in the field. Theirs was a dangerous but lucrative line of work with a long history. In William Shakespeare's play *Henry V*, set in the Hundred Years' War, a soldier named Pistol declares, "I shall sutler be Unto the camp, and profits will accrue."[44] The word *sutler* comes from a root meaning "to follow a mean or low occupation" (the word *soot* comes from the same cognate), the implication being that the sutler profited from the harsh conditions of war. Perhaps for that reason, Jews had long been permitted to serve as sutlers, even in Europe. Yet, however scorned and distrusted they were, sutlers—much like frontier peddlers of the day—were also indispensable. They offered for sale necessary and desirable items—food, clothing, personal supplies, reading material, religious articles,

Executive Mansion,

Washington, Nov. 4 , 1862.

Hon. Sec. of War.

Sir

I believe we have not yet appointed a Hebrew — A. Cherie, Mr. Levy, is well vouched, as a capable and faithful man, let him be appointed an Assistant Quarter. Master, with the rank of Captain.

Yours truly,

A. Lincoln

"I believe we have not yet appointed a Hebrew."

88

32

To the Senate of the United States

I nominate C. M. Levy of New York to be Assistant Quarter-master with the rank of Captain in the Volunteer forces of the United States.

Abraham Lincoln

January 16, 1864.

OPPOSITE

LINCOLN TO EDWIN M. STANTON: APPOINTING A "HEBREW," NOVEMBER 4, 1862

Lincoln makes a historic military appointment: because he has "not yet appointed a Hebrew," he names C. M. Levy—the son-in-law of New York's leading Ashkenazi rabbi, Morris Raphall—an assistant quartermaster with the rank of captain.

Shapell Manuscript Collection

RIGHT

LINCOLN AGAIN NOMINATES C.M. LEVY, JANUARY 16, 1864

In October 1863, Captain C. M. Levy was dismissed from the army on grounds of "conduct prejudicial to Good order and military discipline." Lincoln here renominates Levy for the same position he had nominated him for fourteen months earlier.

U.S. National Archives & Records Administration

and even, in one famous case, Passover provisions—not otherwise available where soldiers camped.[45]

During the first year of the Civil War, generals sought Lincoln's approval for the appointment of sutlers. "I have never had my attention particularly drawn to the appointment of Sutlers," Lincoln confessed in September 1861.[46] In the case of Henry Rice, the Jewish clothier from Jacksonville, Illinois, mentioned in Chapter 2, whom he and General John A. McClernand knew personally, the president wrote three months later that he did "not distinctly understand how Sutlers are

appointed" and would "be obliged" if the War Department "would make or cause to be made" his appointment as a sutler.[47] Sutler tokens in denominations of 5, 10, 25, and 50 cents from the brigade of Illinois volunteers organized by General McClernand bear Rice's name, as well as McClernand's. Later, when the War Department wisely decided that commissioned officers should choose sutlers on their own, Jews continued to be disproportionately selected. At least two dozen Civil War sutlers are known definitively to have been Jews, and others had distinctively Jewish names, like Isaacks

Brigade Head Quarters.
Camp Cairo. Oct 29th 1861.
Henry Rice, late of Jacksonville, Illinois,
is hereby appointed Sutler of my brigade
of Illinois Volunteers— designated and rank-
ing by virtue of General Order No. issued
by Brigadier General Frank Commanding
the South East District of Missouri as the
first brigade in said district—with all
the rights and privileges and subject to
all the restrictions, obligations and duties
usually and properly appertaining to said
office.
John A. McClernand
Brig. Genl. Comg.

JOHN A. McCLERNAND APPOINTS HENRY RICE, OCTOBER 29, 1861

Union General John A. McClernand appoints Henry Rice a sutler of his brigade of Illinois Volunteers.

Abraham Lincoln Presidential Library & Museum

and Kohn.[48] What was essential, from Lincoln's perspective, was not religion or ethnicity but that a sutler, above all, be "a worthy and competent business man."[49]

Where religion did matter most was in the military chaplaincy. Chaplains had accompanied American soldiers into battle since colonial days. They served in the Revolutionary War and in each subsequent American military engagement, including the Black Hawk War, in which Lincoln had fought. Regiments generally elected their own chaplains—people whom they looked up to for spiritual sustenance, psychological support, and moral uplift—and most of those selected, unsurprisingly, were Protestant. While some opposed the chaplaincy as unconstitutional, a violation of church-state separation, Congress rejected that view, believing chaplains necessary to meet soldiers' religious needs. On the eve of the Civil War, some thirty post chaplains were authorized to serve in the armed forces of the United States.[50]

The outbreak of the Civil War led to a rapid buildup of the armed forces. To this end, in the summer of 1861, Congress provided for the appointment of new chaplains, one per regiment, to be elected by "vote of the field officers and company commanders." In a bid to ensure that only bona fide clergy were selected, Congress proposed an eligibility requirement: "The chaplain . . . must be a regular[ly] ordained minister of a Christian denomination."[51] A suggestion to make special provisions for the appointment of Roman Catholic chaplains, since so many Union recruits were Catholic, was voted down. Congressman Clement Vallandigham, an Ohio Democrat who opposed abolition and supported the South's right to secede, then moved to "strike out the words 'Christian denomination' . . . and in lieu thereof, to insert 'religious society.' " He explained that "there is a large body of men in this country . . . of the Hebrew faith" who were "excluded by this section." He also deemed the eligibility requirement a violation of the no-establishment clause of the First Amendment. His own proposal, he explained, would open the chaplaincy "to those at least who are of the Hebrew faith, and who, by the terms of the bill, are unjustly and without constitutional warrant, excluded from it."

General Mc'Clernand wishes Henry Rice to be Sutler at Cairo. I do not distinctly understand how Sutlers are appointed; and hence will be obliged if the War Department will make, or cause to be made, this one above mentioned.

A. Lincoln

Dec. 6, 1861.

**LINCOLN APPROVES HENRY RICE
AS SUTLER, DECEMBER 6, 1861**

Rice, a German-born Jewish merchant from Jacksonville, Illinois, knew Lincoln personally. Rice had on occasion recommended Lincoln as a lawyer and later, during the war, dined with him at the White House. Lincoln approved the appointment of Rice as sutler in a handwritten note. He became, after the war, a leading philanthropist in New York City.

Shapell Manuscript Collection.

Vallandigham, however, was something of a congressional gadfly; many of his colleagues despised him, and later in 1863 he would be banished to the Confederate lines for the duration of the war. Moreover, having just voted down a special provision to aid Catholics, Congress was in no mood to think about Jews. The Vallandigham amendment was thus summarily rejected.[52]

President Lincoln, on July 22, happily signed the congressional measure that expanded the armed forces. He apparently paid no attention to the eligibility requirement for chaplains. General Orders promulgated by the War Department back in May contained virtually the same requirements ("The chaplain . . . must be a regularly ordained minister of some Christian denomination"), and nobody had complained.[53] Most Americans imagined that the bulk of their countrymen were Christians of one sort or another. Vallandigham himself was conscious of this. His convoluted effort to explain why the bill's use of the term *Christian* was problematic is telling:

> While we are in one sense a Christian people
> and yet in another sense not the most Christian
> people in the world, this is yet not a "Christian
> Government," nor a Government which has
> any connection with any one form of religion in

ABOUT SUTLERS

SUTLERS, ALTHOUGH CIVILIANS, were critical to the success of the army in the field. They sold what soldiers wanted, and they usually sold it on credit, which, to men who went an inordinate amount of time between paydays, was a blessing. At the sutler's store they could buy necessities like paper, ink, soap, polish, needles, and thread, as well as luxuries like sweets, tobacco, magazines, and sometimes even liquor. Sutlers, in fact, were the Civil War's equivalent of post exchanges—with one exception: they issued their own currency.

On the battlefield, soldiers without cash bought from the sutler. They would request a certain amount; the sutler would pay it out in tokens; and the soldiers would sign an order to the paymaster to repay the sutler (with interest) when funds arrived. Even when soldiers had money, they usually received their salaries in gold and silver coins in large denominations; there was a terrific shortage of small change. Sutlers solved that problem, too. They exchanged the large coins and bills for sutler tokens in the small amounts necessary to purchase the 5-, 10-, 25-, and 50-cent items that soldiers preferred.

LEFT

A CIVIL WAR SUTLER AT HIS PLACE OF BUSINESS IN THE FIELD

Courtesy of the Library of Congress

BELOW

HENRY RICE SUTLER TOKENS

A form of regimental currency used on the battlefield by soldiers—as credit and small change both—with which to buy what the army did not provide: notions, niceties, and often, in poorly equipped units, necessities. Here, we see all denominations from sutler Henry Rice.

Shapell Manuscript Collection

preference to any other form—I speak, of course, in a political sense alone.[54]

Isaac Mayer Wise, who was something of a one-man Anti-Defamation League in his day, had no similar difficulty in articulating his objections to the bill's language. "We were," he complained, "positively and unjustly deprived of a constitutional right."[55]

Proof of this deprivation was not long in coming. On July 18, four days before Lincoln signed the congressional measure, the 65th Regiment of the 5th Pennsylvania Cavalry (known as the Cameron Dragoons), which was commanded by a Bavarian-born Jew named Max Friedman and included over thirty Jewish mounted cavalrymen, elected Michael M. Allen, a liquor dealer, as its regimental chaplain. Though not ordained, Allen had studied Hebrew and the Code of Jewish Law in Philadelphia and was a capable lay reader of the liturgy as well as an active figure in Jewish communal life. Impressing his colleagues with his piety, concern for others, and abilities as a preacher, he apparently won their confidence. As chaplain, Allen led nondenominational services for the troops on Sunday and lectured on topics like "Peace and Harmony." He also translated letters and taught English to those "not very well conversant with the English language." Being a regimental and not a Jewish chaplain, he never led Jewish services but instead traveled when he could to nearby synagogues on Saturdays and Jewish holidays. Still, since he was neither a Christian nor a regularly ordained minister, his service as a chaplain contravened regulations. When the breach was brought to the public's attention by a visiting worker from the Young Men's Christian Association (YMCA), Allen had no legal basis for remaining in office. On September 23, the fifth day of the Jewish holiday of Sukkot, he wrote in his daily journal, "sent in my Resignation as Chaplain."[56]

The field officers and company commanders of the Cameron Dragoons, several of whom were themselves Jewish, soon elected another member of the Jewish

MICHAEL ALLEN

The first Jew to serve as a regimental chaplain, Allen was elected to the post by the soldiers of the 5th Pennsylvania Cavalry, known as the Cameron Dragoons.

Jacob Rader Marcus Center of the American Jewish Archives, Cincinnati, Ohio

faith as their chaplain. One suspects that they did so purposely, as a test case, for the man they selected, Arnold Fischel, served as "teacher and lecturer" at New York's congregation Shearith Israel and was regularly described by the press as a "Reverend Doctor." His credentials exceeded those of many a Christian chaplain at that time, a few of whom were illiterate and impious. Secretary of War Simon Cameron, the namesake of the Dragoons, had no choice, nevertheless, but to reject Fischel's appointment. "You are respectfully informed . . . that the Chaplain appointed by 'the vote of the field officers and company commanders, must be a regular ordained minister of some Christian denomination,'" he informed Fischel on October 23. Had it not been for this legal impediment, he assured him, "the Department would have taken your application into its favorable consideration."[57]

A CIVIL WAR SEDER IN WEST VIRGINIA

THE CRITICAL ROLE played by sutlers in meeting the needs of troops in the field is well illustrated by the following story, recounted by Joseph A. Joel in the March 30, 1866, issue of the *Jewish Messenger*, of how a "thoughtful sutler," most likely G. W. Forbes, who was a "co-religionist," made it possible for twenty Jews in the 23rd Ohio regiment to observe the Passover seder in West Virginia in 1862. The commanding officer who permitted those troops to "keep the holydays" was General Rutherford B. Hayes, who went on to become the nineteenth president of the United States. Joel remained friendly with him and named one of his sons in his honor.

"Being apprised of the approaching Feast of Passover, twenty of my comrades and co-religionists belonging to the Regiment, united in a request to our commanding officer for relief from duty, in order that we might keep the holydays, which he readily acceded to. The first point was gained, and, as the Paymaster had lately visited the Regiment, he had left us plenty of greenbacks. Our next business was to find some suitable person to proceed to Cincinnati, Ohio, to buy us Matzos. Our sutler being a co-religionist and going home to that city, readily undertook to send them. . . . About the middle of the morning of erev Pessach [the Eve of Passover] a supply train arrived in camp, and to our delight seven barrels of Matzos. On opening them, we were surprised and pleased to find that our thoughtful sutler had enclosed two Hagodahs and prayer-books. We were now able to keep the seder nights, if we could only obtain the other requisites for that occasion. We held a consultation and decided to send parties to forage in the country. . . . About the middle of the afternoon the foragers arrived, having been quite successful. We obtained two kegs of cider, a lamb, several chickens and some eggs. Horseradish or parsley we could not obtain, but in lieu we found a weed, whose bitterness, I apprehend, exceeded anything our forefathers 'enjoyed' . . .

There, in the wild woods of West Virginia, away from home and friends, we consecrated and offered up to the ever-loving God of Israel our prayers and sacrifice. . . . enacting this commemoration of the scene that transpired in Egypt."

A RARE ASSOCIATION WITH AN 1862 BATTLEFIELD PASSOVER SEDER: A G.W. FORBES CIVIL WAR SUTLER'S TOKEN

Shapell Manuscript Collection

Cameron's letter, for all of its surface courtesy, mortified American Jews, for it confirmed that by official regulation and simply on account of their religion they were barred from the military chaplaincy. This placed the thousands of Jewish troops at a great disadvantage vis–à–vis their Christian counterparts, whose spiritual and pastoral needs were met by qualified chaplains. It also undermined constitutional guarantees of religious equality in which Jews had placed great faith. Since chaplains were "the most numerous, visible, and direct representatives of organized religion in the camps of the Civil War armies," the requirement that they be "of some Christian denomination" in effect rendered the whole Jewish faith illegitimate.[58]

Rabbi Isaac Mayer Wise looked to Congress to remedy this unhappy situation. He called upon Jews to "petition that body from all parts of the U. S.," to solicit signatures from their non-Jewish neighbors, and to send completed petitions "to your representative or senator." Six times in one issue of his newspaper, the *Israelite*, he

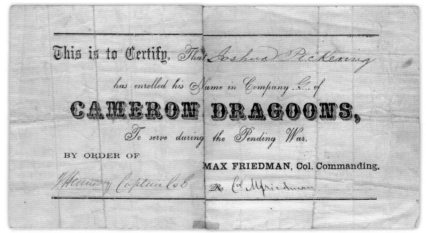

TOP RIGHT

**PATRIOTIC COVER DEPICTING
COLONEL MAX FRIEDMAN**

*Colonel Max Friedman was the
founder of the 65th Regiment, 5th
Cavalry—also known as the Cameron
Dragoons—in which Jews were largely
represented.*

Shapell Manuscript Collection

BOTTOM RIGHT

CAMERON DRAGOONS

*Into this largely Jewish regiment is
enlisted one Joshua Pickering, on or
about August 10, 1861; he served
with Company G until his death at
Darbytown Road, Virginia, on October
7, 1864. His commanding officer, Max
Friedman, certifies his enlistment.*

Shapell Manuscript Collection

printed the line "Forget not to attend to the petition to the Congress of the United States."[59] In response, a mass of petitions descended upon Congress, some from large communities like Baltimore (where Jews joined 700 Christians in urging a change in the law), and others from tiny communities like Columbus, Iowa, and Edinburgh, Indiana, where few if any Jews lived at all.[60]

The grandly named Board of Delegates of American Israelites, established in 1859 as the representative body of America's Jews but actually representing no more than a fifth of America's synagogues, believed that only President Lincoln's personal intervention would fix the problem. Though the Board too sent a "memorial" to Congress, it also took the unprecedented step of sending Rev. Dr. Fischel himself to Washington as its representative. His assignment was to lobby legislators, meet with the president, and, in addition, "take charge of the

spiritual welfare of our coreligionists in the Camps & hospitals attached to the Department of the Potomac." Wisely, Fischel obtained letters of introduction from two non-Jewish friends of Lincoln's: the young U.S. district attorney of New York, Edward Delafield Smith, and former congressman and Republican stalwart Moses Hicks Grinnell. He also employed some back channels to get the president's attention. As a result, even though Lincoln's private secretary, John Nicolay, warned that prior to the adjournment of Congress Lincoln would have no time to read Fischel's letter, let alone see him, and even though hundreds of other petitioners were anxiously awaiting a moment of the president's precious time, Fischel refused to be discouraged. On Wednesday, December 11, 1861, he boldly called at the White House at 10:00 A.M. in hopes of gaining an audience with the president. Doubtless to the surprise of many, he was, according to the breathless letter he sent to the Board of Delegates that very day, "at once invited to his room and was received with marked courtesy." Lincoln read Fischel's materials, questioned him, and told him, according to Fischel, that "he fully admitted the justice of my remarks, that he believed the exclusion of Jewish chaplains to have been altogether unintentional on the part of Congress," and that he agreed "that something ought to be done to meet this case." With Congress in session, he refused to act unilaterally—as he had done in October, when without congressional authorization he made "a sort of quasi appointment" of three Protestant and two Catholic clergy to serve as hospital chaplains.[61] Instead, he told Fischel "that it was the first time this subject had been brought under his notice, that it was altogether new to him, [and] that he would take the subject into serious consideration." He then invited Fischel to call again "tomorrow morning" to hear his views.[62]

Instead of meeting with Fischel the next day, the president set aside time to consider a plan sent to him by George H. Stuart, chair of a newly formed Christian Commission, "to promote the spiritual and temporal welfare of the brave men in arms." The commission sought permission to distribute Bibles, hymnals, tracts, and other Christian religious publications to the troops and to sponsor prayer meetings and sermons of a revivalist nature. Lincoln, eager as usual to promote religious faith and charity, gave the plan his full support. "Your Christian and benevolent undertaking for the benefit of the soldiers, is too obviously proper, and praise-worthy, to admit any difference of opinion," he wrote. "I sincerely hope your plan may be as successful in execution, as it is just and generous in conception."[63]

In endorsing the work of the Christian Commission, however, Lincoln—who construed the word *Christian* very broadly—did not imagine that he was in any way shortchanging the needs of Jewish soldiers. To the contrary, two days later he reassured Fischel with the following letter: "My dear Sir: I find that there are several particulars in which the present law in regard to

Chaplains is supposed to be deficient, all of which I now design presenting to the appropriate Committee of Congress. I shall try to have a new law broad enough to cover what is desired by you in behalf of the Israelites."[64]

The representatives of the YMCA were appalled.[65] Subsequently, one evangelical paper, which construed the word *Christian* narrowly, complained that if the law were changed, "one might despise and reject the Savior of men . . . and yet be a fit minister of religion." It warned that "Mormon debauchees, Chinese priests, and Indian conjurors" would stand next in line for government recognition—a tacit admission that the central issue under debate concerned the religious rights of non-Christians.[66]

Lincoln, working behind the scenes, effected a compromise. Instead of actually repealing the language requiring that a chaplain be of "some Christian denomination," congressional leaders acquiesced to let it stand. Then, they reinterpreted that language by construing it to read exactly as Jews and Lincoln wanted: "That no person shall be appointed a chaplain in the United States Army that is not a regularly ordained minister of some religious denomination." They won additional rank-and-file support by coupling this change to an amendment, strongly supported by the YMCA, that sought to improve the quality of the military chaplaincy as a whole by requiring candidates to present "testimonials of . . . present good standing" as well as a recommendation "from some authorized ecclesiastical body" or "five accredited ministers belonging to said religious denomination." These revised qualifications, quietly buried in a bill that became law on July 17, 1862, entitled "An Act to define the Pay and Emoluments of certain Officers of the Army and for other Purposes," finally opened the military chaplaincy to non-Christians. It represented a major political victory for the Jewish community, serves as a case study in Lincoln's consummate political skills, and remains a landmark in the legal recognition of America's non-Christian faiths.[67]

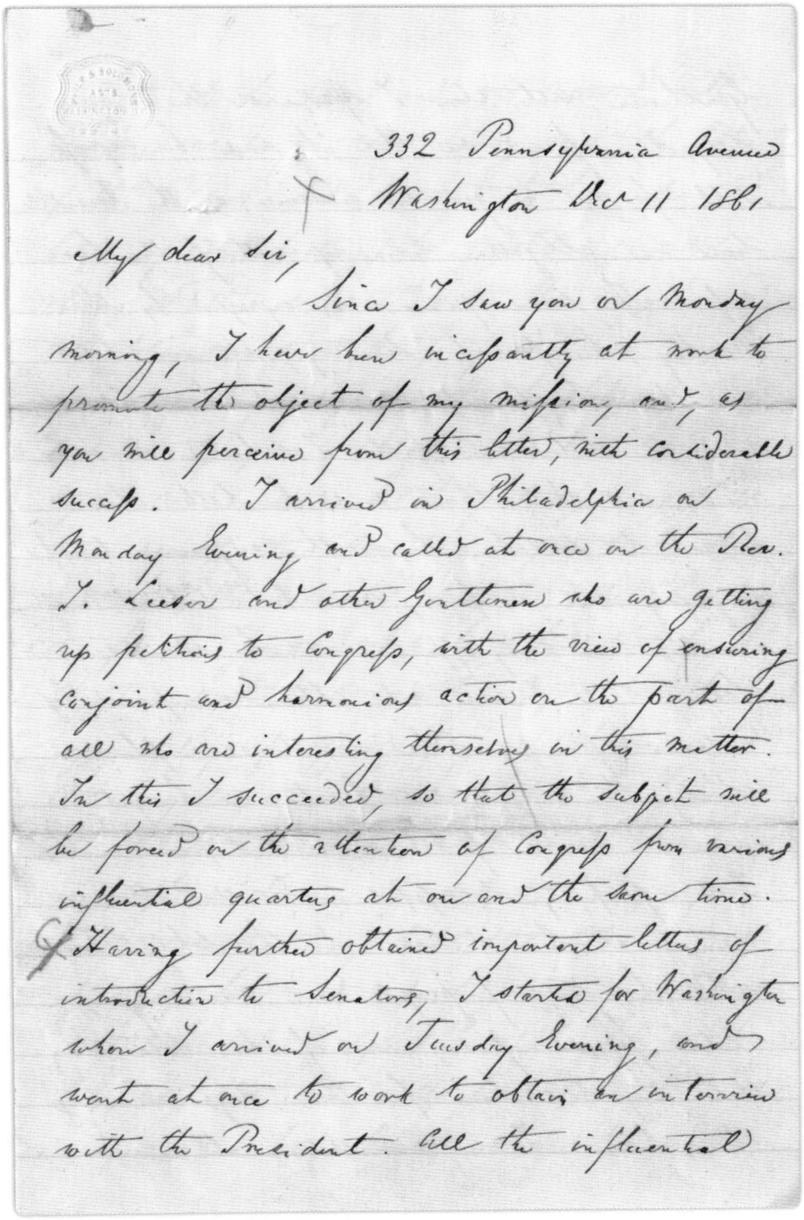

332 Pennsylvania Avenue
Washington Dec 11 1861

My dear Sir,

Since I saw you on Monday morning, I have been incessantly at work to promote the object of my mission, and, as you will perceive from this letter, with considerable success. I arrived in Philadelphia on Monday Evening and called at once on the Rev. I. Leeser and other Gentlemen who are getting up petitions to Congress, with the view of ensuring conjoint and harmonious action on the part of all who are interesting themselves in this matter. In this I succeeded, so that the subject will be forced on the attention of Congress from various influential quarters at one and the same time. Having further obtained important letters of introduction to Senators, I started for Washington where I arrived on Tuesday Evening, and went at once to work to obtain an interview with the President. All the influential

ABOVE

ARNOLD FISCHEL

Although the War Department had denied his request to become the Cameron Dragoon's military chaplain, as the regiment wished, a groundswell of Jewish insistence that Jews serving their country be allowed their own chaplains—and Fischel's own direct lobbying of Lincoln—led to a change in the law restricting military chaplaincies to Christians only.

American Jewish Historical Society

LEFT

LINCOLN RECEIVES FISCHEL, DECEMBER 11, 1861

Fischel writes to Henry Hart, president of the Board of Delegates, that despite a long line of people, some of whom had been waiting for three days, Fischel is, almost unbelievably, immediately received by Lincoln, who promises to take the matter into consideration, and requests to see Fischel again the following day.

American Jewish Historical Society

Abraham Lincoln demonstrated his support for the new legislation by appointing Jewish chaplains as soon as he was requested to do so. When, on August 21, Isaac Leeser and the Board of Ministers of the Hebrew Congregations of Philadelphia petitioned for a Jewish chaplain to meet the needs of the growing number of wounded Jewish servicemen in their area, Lincoln's secretary, John Hay, made clear to the surgeon general that the President would like this to be done. When, in short order, the surgeon general obligingly declared that it was "both legal and proper," the Board of Ministers recommended Rev. Jacob Frankel of Rodef Shalom congregation for the position. Lincoln accepted the recommendation, and in so doing fulfilled his promise to Fischel of nine months before. On September 18, 1862, Frankel became the first Jewish military chaplain in American history.[68]

The administration failed to be so obliging three

"I shall try to have a new law broad enough to cover what is desired by you in behalf of the Israelites."

DECEMBER 15, 1861

Fischel's handwritten copy of Lincoln's famous chaplaincy letter written the previous day. "I shall try to have a new law broad enough to cover what is desired by you in behalf of the Israelites," Lincoln momentously wrote. Lincoln's original letter has apparently disappeared.

American Jewish Historical Society

weeks later when leaders of the Board of Delegates of American Israelites belatedly requested the appointment of a Jewish hospital chaplain in Washington, D.C. The man recommended, Arnold Fischel, was by all accounts highly deserving, having led the battle to amend the chaplaincy law, but a survey of the city's hospitals by the medical inspector general of the army located "but 7 Jews" and concluded that wounded Jewish soldiers were so few in number and so scattered "that it would be impracticable for a clergyman to find and attend to them." Lincoln, as a result, could make no appointment, and Fischel, whom the board had not paid and who was without funds, soon returned to Holland.[69]

Lincoln did appoint two other Jewish chaplains during the course of the war. On April 10, 1863, he appointed the first regimental Jewish chaplain, Rabbi Ferdinand Leopold Sarner, following the rabbi's election to that post by the heavily German-speaking 54th New York Volunteer Regiment. Sarner's impressive academic credentials (a Ph.D. from the University of Hesse) coupled with his ability to preach in florid German seem to have had more to do with his appointment than his Judaism. In fact, some mistakenly considered him a German Lutheran! That he was actually a rabbi seems not to have impeded him from ministering to the needs of his mostly Christian regiment. Like Michael Allen and a host of subsequent Jewish chaplains, he apparently learned the art of nondenominational preaching.[70] A month later, on May 6, 1863, Lincoln appointed Rev. Bernard Gotthelf, the (unordained) leader of Louisville's Adas Israel congregation, to be a hospital chaplain in that city. Congressman Robert Mallory, a Lincoln ally, recommended the appointment, according to contemporary reports, because " a very respectable number of Jewish soldiers have been or are still receiving medical treatment at our hospitals." Local newspapers cheered the appointment, and Gotthelf ultimately served eighteen army hospitals, ministering to Jews and Christians alike.[71]

Lincoln's approach to the question of appointing

ISAAC LEESER

German-born American, author, editor, and publisher of The Occident *and* American Jewish Advocate, *Leeser was one of the most important Jews in nineteenth-century America, well known as the first translator of the Jewish Bible into English. The idea that Jews, North and South, would kill one another, was anathema to him. Throughout the conflict, then, he confined himself to strictly Jewish issues—and when he finally did write to Lincoln, it was merely to request the appointment of a Jewish hospital chaplain in Philadelphia.*
Courtesy of the Library of Congress

Jews as chaplains bespoke his attitude not only toward Jews but toward religion generally. On the one hand, he was not initially troubled by the Christian provision in the chaplaincy law, for, as we have seen, the word *Christian* to him excluded no religious denomination. Nor did he display any compunction about endorsing the work of the "Christian Commission." Yet, evidence that Jews faced discrimination in the chaplaincy at once elicited his sympathy. To his mind all people of faith deserved to be treated equally. Thus, in addition to appointing Jews to the chaplaincy, Lincoln put forth the name of a Universalist minister named James Shrigley to be a hospital chaplain—upon the recommendation, among others, of Jewish congressman Leonard Myers.

LINCOLN APPOINTS A JEWISH CHAPLAIN

Jacob Frankel of Philadelphia, commissioned a hospital chaplain by Lincoln, became the country's first Jewish military chaplain on September 18, 1862.

Congregation Rodeph Shalom

YMCA members opposed his appointment, Shrigley later recalled, because they considered him "not sound in his theological opinions." Among other heresies, they charged, he believed "that even the rebels themselves will finally be saved." Lincoln, however, was unmoved. "Well, gentlemen," Shrigley quoted him as replying, "if that be so, and there is any way under heaven whereby the rebels can be saved, then, for God's sake and their sakes, let the man be appointed"—and he was.[72]

In November 1864, Lincoln expressed willingness to make an even more controversial appointment. The 1st Wisconsin Heavy Artillery unanimously elected a Spiritualist medium named Ella E. Gibson (Hobart) as their chaplain; she was ordained a minister by the Religio-Philosophical Society of St. Charles, Illinois. "She is a woman," Lincoln pointed out to Secretary of War Edwin M. Stanton, when the nomination came to his attention. "The President has not legally anything to do with such a question, but has no objection to her appointment." Stanton, though, declined to appoint her "on account of her sex."[73] Still, the fact that Lincoln himself had no objection to the appointment bespeaks the breadth of his religious vision. Perhaps because he himself grew up as something of a religious outsider, he considered other religious outsiders—Jews, Universalists, and Spiritualist women among them—to be worthy of inclusion not only within the panoply of American religion but within the military chaplaincy as well.

From a Jewish perspective, Lincoln's frequent appeal to Americans as a "Christian people" nevertheless remained problematic. This was brought home in late 1862 when he issued an executive order concerning Sabbath observance within the armed forces. "The importance for man and beast of the prescribed weekly rest, the sacred rights of Christian soldiers and sailors, a becoming deference to the best sentiment of a Christian people, and a due regard for the Divine will," Lincoln declared, "demand that Sunday labor in the Army and Navy be reduced to the measure of strict necessity." Christian religious leaders from New York had lobbied for such an order, and in issuing it Lincoln echoed George Washington, who in 1776 had urged his troops "to live and act as becomes a Christian soldier defending the dearest rights and liberties of his country."[74]

There were, however, a hundred times more Jews in the country and in the armed forces than there had been in Washington's day, and to them, Lincoln's declaration was an affront. "Are we equals in this land?" Isaac Leeser demanded in his newspaper soon after the order appeared. He wondered in an editorial why those who observed the Sabbath on Sunday were protected, "while everything is done to make the observance of the Seventh day burdensome to the Jew." "Is this equality," he asked, "or are the rights of the minority of no importance in the eyes of the law-makers and the law-dispensers?"[75]

To reinforce his point, Leeser reprinted a moving letter to Lincoln (dated December 4, 1862) by a German-Jewish immigrant named Bernhard Behrend, the father of Adajah Behrend, an enlisted hospital steward. "I gave my consent to my son, who was yet a minor, that he should enlist in the United States army," Behrend wrote. "I thought it was his duty, and I gave him my advice to fulfill his duty as a good citizen, and he has done so. At the same time I taught him also to observe the Sabbath on Saturday, when it would not hinder him from fulfilling his duty in the army. Now I do not want that he shall be dragged either to the stake or the

DOCKET BY JOHN HAY ON A LETTER FROM ISAAC LEESER TO LINCOLN, AUGUST 23, 1862

Tasked with writing Lincoln during the ongoing chaplaincy legislature reform, Leeser declared that as "Many Israelites are serving in the army of the United States . . . it is to be expected that not a few persons of our persuasion will . . . require spiritual no less than bodily care." A Jewish chaplain appointed by the president was needed now, he told the president. Lincoln's secretary, John Hay, directing Leeser's letter to the surgeon general, noted that the president wanted this to be done. And, within a matter of days, so it was.

Courtesy of the Library of Congress

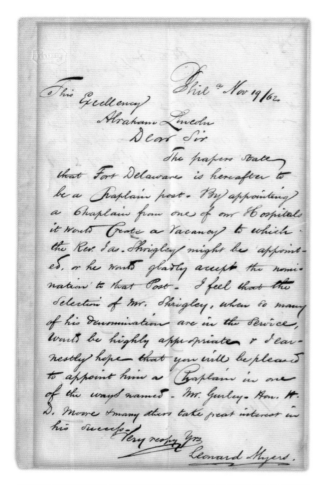

LEONARD MYERS TO LINCOLN, NOVEMBER 19, 1862

To the Jewish Civil War-era Republican congressman Leonard Myers goes this distinction: he was elected from a district with notably few co-religionists. This helps to explain, then, his request as a newly elected congressman on behalf of James Shrigley, a Gentile clergyman seeking appointment. On December 2, 1862, Lincoln forwards Myers's request and begins a correspondence with Myers that would last through the rest of Lincoln's life.

Shapell Manuscript Collection

church to observe the Sunday as a Sabbath." Pleading for "justice," Behrend asked Lincoln "to proclaim in another order, that also all those in the army who celebrate another day as the Sunday may be allowed to celebrate that day which they think is the right day according to their own conscience."[76] No reply from Lincoln is extant. Nor is Behrend's letter included in standard collections of Lincoln's correspondence. One suspects, however, that the Jewish community's complaints reached Lincoln's ears. Significantly, he never again, in his official correspondence, referred to Americans as a "Christian people," nor did he pay further heed to those who sought to publicly identify the government with Christianity. Instead, within a few weeks, Isaac Mayer Wise heard Lincoln reassure Jewish leaders that he would by no means allow any citizen to be "wronged on account of his place of birth or religious confession."[77]

Lincoln's reassurance to Jewish leaders came in response to the most notorious official act of anti-Semitism in American history. On December 17, 1862, General Ulysses S. Grant issued a sweeping order, known as General Orders No. 11, expelling "Jews as a class" from his war zone (the Department of the Tennessee), stretching from Northern Mississippi to Cairo, Illinois, and from the Mississippi River to the Tennessee River.[78]

For months, Grant had been worried about cotton speculators and smugglers in the area under his command. Since some of the men his troops caught were Jews, he became persuaded that all smugglers, speculators, and traders were Jews, whether they were actually Jewish or not. Just as Southerners dubbed all Northerners "Yankees," whether or not they hailed from New England, so Grant and others in the military often characterized all smugglers and traders as "Jews." Grant wanted as few of them in the area under his command as possible.

In July 1862, Grant ordered the commander of the District of the Mississippi to "examine all baggage of all speculators coming South," and to turn back those who were carrying gold ("specie"). "Jews," he admonished, "should receive special attention." In August, a soldiers' newspaper quoted Grant as calling Jews "a nuisance." It intimated that he had plans to "abate" that nuisance. Nothing happened for several months, but on November 9, as he prepared to move south in preparation for the decisive battle at Vicksburg, Grant tightened his regulations against Jews: "Refuse all permits to come south of Jackson for the present," he ordered. "The Isrealites [*sic*] especially should be kept out." The very next day he strengthened that order: "no Jews are to be permitted to travel on the Rail Road southward from any point . . . they are such an intolerable nuisance that the Department must be purged for [*sic*] them." Writing in early December to General Sherman, whose quartermaster had created problems by selling cotton "to a Jew by the name of Haas," Grant explained that "in consequence of the total disregard and evasion of orders by the Jews my policy is to exclude them so far as practicable from the Dept."[79]

But until December 17, Grant had not gone so far as to expel Jews from his department. Indeed, when Colonel John Van Deusen Du Bois, on December 8, 1862, angrily ordered "All Cotton-Speculators, Jews and other Vagrants having no honest means of support, except trading upon the miseries of their Country" to leave Holly Springs, and gave them "twenty-four hours or they will be sent to duty in the trenches," Grant insisted that the draconian order be rescinded. "Instructions from Washington," he reminded Du Bois, "are to encourage getting Cotton out of the country."[80] Notwithstanding his private opinions and actions, Grant understood that he still had to publicly uphold President Lincoln's policy, which permitted those loyal to the Union to trade in cotton.

All that changed on December 17. Grant, according to multiple sources, received a visit that day from his sixty-eight-year-old father, Jesse R. Grant, accompanied by members of the prominent Mack family of Cincinnati, significant Jewish clothing manufacturers.

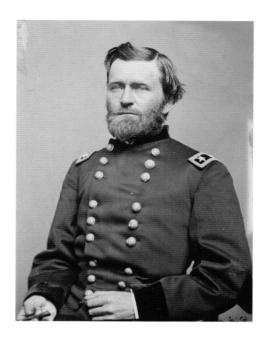

ULYSSES S. GRANT

Having failed in the antebellum military—failed, even worse, in civilian life—his rise from colonel to general in chief of the Armies of the United States was, perhaps, the unlikeliest, but most deserved, in military history. Yet his issuance of what he would later call his "Jew Order," expelling the Jews from parts or all of the states of Tennessee, Kentucky, Illinois, and Mississippi, tarnished his reputation.
Courtesy of the Library of Congress

Harman, Henry, and Simon Mack, as part of an ingenious scheme, had formed a secret partnership with the elder Grant. In return for 25 percent of their profits, he agreed to accompany them to his son's Mississippi headquarters, act as their agent to "procure a permit for them to purchase cotton," and help them secure the means to transport that cotton to New York.[81]

According to journalist Sylvanus Cadwallader, an eyewitness, General Grant waxed indignant at his father's crass attempt to profit from his son's military status and raged at the Jewish traders who "entrapped his old father into such an unworthy undertaking." He refused to provide the permit, sent the Macks homeward "on the first train for the north," and in high dudgeon, immediately issued the order expelling "Jews as a

WILLIAM T. SHERMAN TO PHILEMON B. EWING, NOVEMBER 2, 1862

Written just two days before Lincoln's official handwritten request for the appointment of C.M. Levy, a "Hebrew," and during a time of intense anti-Semitism, Sherman reports in passing, "A great deal of smuggling is going on in the Holly Spring Army, but this is mostly managed by Union men and Jews instigated by a sense of gain." This pervasive prejudice would help give rise, a month later, to Grant's notorious General Orders No. 11, whereby all Jews were to be driven from his area of control. The order would be countermanded by Lincoln immediately after it first was brought to his attention.

Shapell Manuscript Collection

class" from his territory.[82] Jesse R. Grant's involvement in this scheme provides "a psychological explanation" for General Orders No. 11, according to John Y. Simon, the scholarly editor of *The Papers of Ulysses S. Grant.* In a classic act of displacement, the general "expelled the Jews rather than his father."[83]

Fortunately for the thousands of Jews who lived in the territory under his command, Grant was soon distracted. Less than seventy-two hours after what Grant would later call his "Jew order"[84] was issued, his forces at Holly Springs were raided by 3,500 Confederate

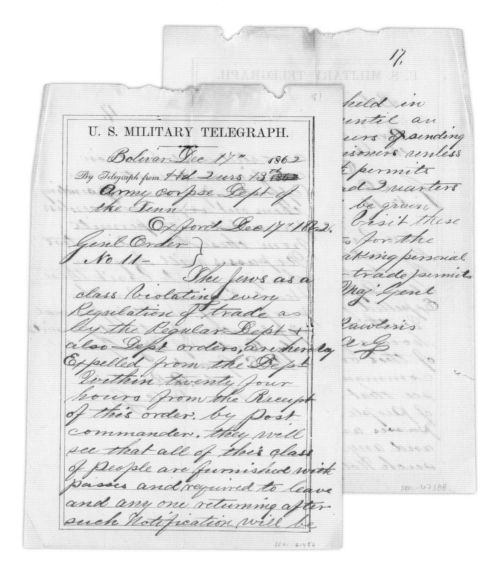

GENERAL ORDERS NO. 11

When Grant expelled the Jews "as a class" from the area under his command, he perpetrated the most blatant state-sanctioned act of anti-Semitism in American history. Later, when Lincoln rescinded the order, and later still, when running for president, Grant claimed the "order was made and sent out without any reflection." In fact, he said, it had been drafted by a subordinate and that he, Grant, in the press of warfare, had approved the decree without even looking at it.

Chicago History Museum

troops led by Major General Earl Van Dorn. Simultaneous raids to the north by troops of the dreaded Confederate cavalryman General Nathan Bedford Forrest, inflicted significant damage to Grant's army and tore up fifty miles of railroad and telegraph lines. Communications to and from Grant's headquarters were disrupted for weeks by these surprise attacks. As a result, news of Grant's order expelling the Jews spread slowly and did not reach army headquarters in a timely fashion—sparing many Jews who might otherwise have been banished.[85]

To be sure, some Jewish traders in the vicinity of Grant's army in northern Mississippi were treated roughly. A "Mr. Silberman" from Chicago, temporarily in Holly Springs, was reportedly imprisoned for twelve hours just for the "crime" of seeking to telegraph General Grant to find out if the expulsion order he received was genuine. An unnamed young Jewish trader and his fiancée, traveling through Grant's department on their way east, described in the *Jewish Record* how they were detained, forbidden to change out of wet clothes, robbed of their horse and buggy, verbally abused, and also had

HENRY MACK

In December 1862, Grant's frustration and anger with the cotton speculators and rapacious businessmen trading illegally in the conquered areas of the South was only exacerbated by the knowledge that his father, Jesse Root Grant, was one of them. Henry Mack, Jesse's partner, was a prominent Jewish clothing manufacturer from Cincinnati.

Jacob Rader Marcus Center of the American Jewish Archives, Cincinnati, Ohio

one of their trunks burned and their pockets picked in the wake of the order. Their expulsion, if not their mistreatment, was explained by Brigadier General James Tuttle, commander of the Union garrison in Cairo, Illinois, with the utmost simplicity: "you are Jews, and . . . neither a benefit to the Union or Confederacy."[86]

But it was only when Grant's order reached Paducah, Kentucky, eleven days after it was issued, that a whole community of Jews found itself expelled. On Sunday, December 28, 1862, Paducah's provost marshal, L. J. Waddell, sent Cesar Kaskel and every other Jew in the city an official notice ordering them "to leave the city of Paducah, Kentucky within twenty-four hours after receiving this order." Women and children were expelled too, and in the confusion—so it was recalled years later—one baby was almost forgotten, and two dying women had to be left behind in the care of neighbors.[87]

As they prepared to leave their homes, Cesar Kaskel and several other Jews sent a telegram to President

Lincoln, describing their plight and pronouncing themselves "greatly insulted and outraged by this inhuman order, the carrying out of which would be the grossest violation of the Constitution, and our rights as good citizens under it."[88]

The president, in all likelihood, never saw that telegram because of the attacks on the telegraph lines. He was also at this time busy preparing to issue the Emancipation Proclamation (January 1, 1863). The irony of his freeing the slaves while Grant was expelling the Jews was not lost on some contemporaries. The *Memphis Daily Bulletin* published the two documents one above the other. The juxtaposition of these events also shaped the responses of several Jewish leaders to Grant's order. They feared that Jews would replace blacks as the nation's stigmatized minority. [89]

Fearing the worst, Kaskel wasted no time. "On my way to Washington, in order to get this most outrageous and inhuman order of Major General Grant countermanded," he announced in the press. He begged the journalists to whom he told his story "to lend the powerful aid of the press to the suffering cause of outraged humanity [and] to blot out as quick as possible this stain on our national honor."[90]

Arriving in the nation's capital just as the Jewish Sabbath was concluding on January 3, Kaskel called at once upon Cincinnati's outgoing Republican congressman, John Addison Gurley, who enjoyed ready access to the White House. Together, they immediately went over to see President Lincoln.

Lincoln turned out to have no knowledge whatsoever of the order, for it had not reached Washington. According to an oft-quoted report, he resorted to biblical imagery in his interview with Kaskel, a reminder of how immersed he was in the Bible and how, like many nineteenth-century Americans, he linked Jews to ancient Israel, and America to the Promised Land:

LINCOLN: And so the children of Israel were driven from the happy land of Canaan?

GENERAL ORDERS NO. 11: "THE WISEST ORDER YET MADE BY A MILITARY COMMAND"

ANTI-SEMITISM was not only evident among Lincoln's cabinet and generals; it also was apparent in members of Congress. Elihu Washburne, an associate of Lincoln's since their days as attorneys in Illinois and a long-standing congressman from that state, as well as a frequent correspondent with the president, wrote immediately to Lincoln on the day that Lincoln revoked Grant's order expelling the Jews, hoping the report of its revocation was incorrect. "I consider it the wisest order yet made by a military command." Believing it "necessary," he pressed Lincoln to reconsider before it was made official. Washburne, a committed abolitionist, ironically, supported emancipation for blacks yet expressed contempt for Jews.

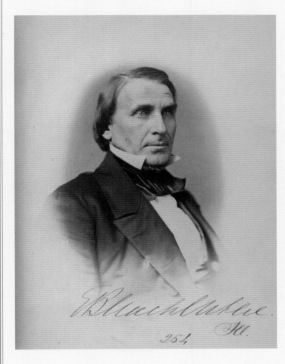

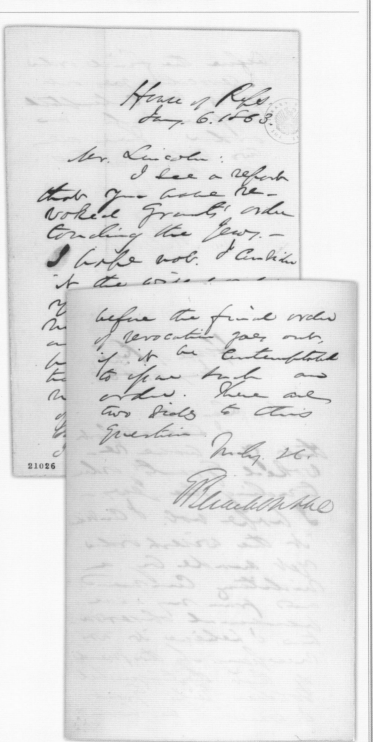

ABOVE
Elihu Washburne
Courtesy of Library of Congress

RIGHT
Elihu Washburne to Lincoln, January 6, 1863
Courtesy of Library of Congress

KASKEL: Yes, and that is why we have come unto Father Abraham's bosom, asking protection.

LINCOLN: And this protection they shall have at once.[91]

Whether or not such a conversation actually took place, when Lincoln did hear about the order, he instantly instructed the general in chief of the army, Henry Halleck, to countermand General Orders No. 11. On January 6, 1863, several urgent telegrams went out from Grant's headquarters in obedience to that demand. "By direction of the General in Chief of the Army at Washington," they read, "the General Order from these Head Quarters expelling Jews from this Department is hereby revoked."[92]

Some days after Lincoln acted, an eloquent plea from B'nai B'rith's Missouri lodges, addressed to the president, reached Washington. It described Jews as a "class of loyal citizens" who had been "driven from their homes, deprived of their liberty, and injured in their property without having violated any law or regulation" and who were "sacrificing their lives and fortunes for the union and the suppression of this rebellion." It called upon the president "to annul the Order and to protect the liberties even of your humblest constituents." Disappointingly, Attorney General Edward Bates, who forwarded this poignant document to Lincoln, expressed "no particular interest in the subject."[93]

Lincoln proved far more solicitous. When on January 7 a delegation of Jewish leaders arrived in Washington to thank him for revoking General Orders No. 11, he carved out time to meet with them. According to Isaac Mayer Wise, who participated in the meeting and wrote a widely circulated account of what transpired, the president reaffirmed that he knew "of no distinction between Jew and Gentile" and promised that he would allow no citizen to be "wronged on account of his place of birth or religious confession." "To condemn a class," he emphatically continued, "is, to say the least, to wrong the good with the bad. I do not like to hear a class or nationality condemned on account of a few sinners."[94]

By revoking General Orders No. 11, ensuring that the chaplaincy was opened up to Jews, and appointing numerous Jews to public and military positions of trust, Lincoln dramatically improved the status of Jews in the United States. He impressed even those like Rabbis Raphall and Wise who had earlier opposed his election. Many who regularly interacted with Lincoln—including military men, Evangelical leaders, even his own attorney general—displayed no similar sympathies. They exhibited unabashed prejudice against Jews and Judaism. By contrast, during his first two years in office, Lincoln displayed extraordinary sensitivity toward Jews and Jewish interests. More than any previous president, he befriended Jews, defended Jews, and promoted Jewish equality.

> " . . . tho a Jew, is
> a man of personal
> respectability
> in St. Louis."

**ISIDOR BUSH TO EDWARD
BATES, JANUARY 6, 1863**

*The B'nai B'rith petition had been
sent to Lincoln by acquaintance Isidor
Bush, in care of Attorney General
Edward Bates, who, in forwarding
the petition to the president, noted that
Bush "tho a Jew, is a man of personal
respectability in St. Louis."*
Courtesy of the Library of Congress

THE ANTI-SEMITIC GENERALS

Generals Butler, Sherman, McClellan, and Grant were, Lincoln knew, prejudiced at best and persecutory at worst. The letters illustrated here bear unhappy but vivid witness to the anti-Semitism of Lincoln's military leaders.

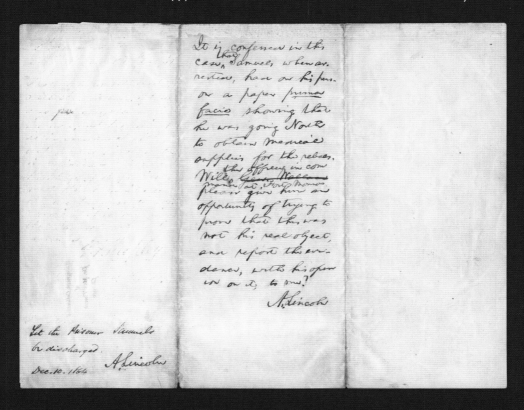

BENJAMIN F. BUTLER TO LINCOLN, SEPTEMBER 15, 1864

Butler—whose anti-Semitism had been called to Lincoln's attention in the past, in particular in an instance involving Jews who fell into Butler's hands at Fortress Monroe—arrested Abraham Samuels, a Jewish Virginian accused in 1864 of trying to pass through the Union lines to obtain medical supplies for the Confederate army. While trusting Butler as a general, Lincoln nonetheless ordered Butler on September 15, 1864 to give Samuels the "opportunity of trying to prove" that his objective was not criminal, and then, having reviewed the evidence, Lincoln ordered him freed on December 10, 1864. It would take two orders—and three months—until Butler finally acceded to Lincoln's request to free Samuels.

Shapell Manuscript Collection

ROBERT EMMETT RODES

Anti-Semitism was also rampant in the South during the war. Confederate general Robert Emmett Rodes requests on March 21, 1862 that an AWOL "Jew" be arrested and sent to him at once; he proceeds to describe Major Salomon S. Bamberger in the most unflattering terms—and suggests he may be found in a brothel.

Shapell Manuscript Collection

CHAPTER FIVE

I MYSELF HAVE A
REGARD FOR THE JEWS

1863

Another year commenced, and with it per-haps a new era in the history of the country, certainly a new era for liberty," a nineteen-year-old Jewish telegraph operator named Edward Rose-water wrote in his diary on January 1, 1863.[1] Rosewater, born in Bohemia, had immigrated to the United States with his parents when he was thirteen years old and in the summer of 1862 began work as an army telegrapher in the War Department telegraph office, located in the old library opposite the office of Secretary of War Edwin Stanton. He was one of eight operators working there and the only Jew. Abraham Lincoln spent a great deal of time in the telegraph office. "Every morning about 8 o'clock [he] comes in to read Dispatches which are

OPPOSITE

FIRST READING OF THE EMANCIPATION PROCLAMATION OF PRESIDENT LINCOLN

Lincoln, as portrayed in Francis Bicknell Carpenter's famous rendering of the event, reads to his cabinet his preliminary Emancipation Proclamation on September 22, 1862.

U.S. Senate Collection

copied into books," Rosewater wrote to his future wife, Leah. "His house being next to this, he is here often." Rosewater and the other young telegraphers enjoyed many an interaction with the president. "Sometimes," he wrote Leah, "he tells an anecdote, or reads a Story aloud and laughs (You could hear him ½ mile)."[2]

On January 1, Rosewater joined a large crowd of local residents at the president's traditional New Year's Day reception at the Executive Mansion. "The President looked rather cheerful," he recorded. "His whiskers cut within an inch of his face, [he] stood in [the] center of [the] room and shook hands with everyone."[3] Fol-lowing the reception, at 4:00 P.M., Rosewater reported to his post at the telegraph office. Lincoln, meanwhile, ascended to his study. His hands still quivering from the hours spent shaking hands at the reception, he prepared to affix his signature to the Emancipation Proclamation. "I never in my life," he declared, "felt more certain that I was doing right than I do in signing this paper." Though his arm remained "stiff and numb," he was determined that no trembling be reflected in his signature, lest some conclude that "he had some compunctions." The document is signed in a bold, clear hand.[4] At eight that evening, Rosewater, who was still on duty, transmitted the official text of the Emancipation Proclamation from the telegraph office. As Lincoln watched, he tapped out the epoch-making words that freed over 3 million slaves: "And upon this act, sincerely believed to be an act of justice, warranted by the Constitution, upon military necessity, I invoke the considerate judgment of mankind, and the gracious favor of Almighty God."[5]

Rosewater, a staunch opponent of slavery, had every reason to be proud of his role in telegraphing to the world news of the "new era for liberty." He became a Republican politician after the war, then served for years as editor of the *Omaha Bee*. Other Jews, however, doubted the president's actions. *The Jewish Record* of New York, for example, deplored the Emancipation Proclamation. "To proclaim the African equal to the surrounding races, would be a farce," it declared.[6] Isaac Mayer Wise, noting support for the Proclamation from groups that aimed to write Christianity into the Constitution, likewise warned against those who sought "to free the black and enslave the white man."[7] Isaac Leeser, recalling Grant's order expelling the Jews, wondered whether the ultimate aim of the proclamation was "to give freedom to the negro, only to bring expulsion from the Union territory to the descendants of the Hebrew race."[8] On the other hand, the young Washington Jewish lawyer Simon Wolf personally congratulated Lincoln on the historic proclamation. In his memoirs, he quoted Lincoln's perceptive reply: "It was not only the negro that I freed, but the white man no less."[9] Rabbi Henry Vidaver of Warsaw, who arrived in America on the eve of the Civil War, marshaled biblical language to describe the Emancipation Proclamation to readers of the Hebrew newspaper *Hamagid* in Europe: "All slaves purchased in perpetuity by residents of the South are from this day forth free men," he exulted. He understood, as Lincoln himself did, that the Emancipation Proclamation was transformative and final.[10]

Lincoln explained just how final the Emancipation Proclamation was in a letter to Major General John A. McClernand, a friend and fellow lawyer from Illinois, who deemed the action a mistake. "I have issued the emancipation proclamation, and I can not retract it," Lincoln explained, recalling a biblical injunction from the Book of Esther ("… for the writing which is written in the king's name, and sealed with the king's ring, may no man reverse.")[11] To drive the point home, he also employed what he called a "coarse but an expressive" figure of speech that, we have seen, he employed only once before, in a letter to the Jewish political powerbroker August Belmont: "Broken eggs can not be mended."[12]

On the very same day—January 1, 1863—that Edward Rosewater transmitted Lincoln's Emancipation Proclamation over the telegraph lines, Lincoln's podiatrist (the nineteenth-century term was chiropodist), Issachar Zacharie, his closest Jewish friend after Abraham Jonas and a "favored family visitor at the White House,"[13] began his brief career as a spy, appointed by the president himself. Zacharie was something of a mystery man; historians consider him one of Lincoln's "most enigmatic intimates."[14] He spelled his name in multiple ways (Issachar, Issacher, Issachor, Isachar, Zacharie, Zacharia, Zachariah). He concealed the year of his birth; it was more likely 1825 than oft-cited later dates.[15] He hid the place of his birth; although sometimes listed as Charleston, it was actually Chatham in North Kent, England. He also provided conflicting stories concerning his immigration. Only thanks to a surviving ship's manifest, do we now know that he arrived from England

OPPOSITE

THE LELAND-BOKER EMANCIPATION PROCLAMATION

Lincoln authorized this signed souvenir edition of his keystone Emancipation Proclamation to be sold at Philadelphia's Great Central Fair in June 1864, in order to raise money for the war effort. At $10 apiece, however, not all of them sold—and those that remained were given away to libraries. Today, of the forty-eight copies signed by Lincoln, only twenty-six are known to exist.
Shapell Manuscript Collection

BY THE PRESIDENT OF THE UNITED STATES OF AMERICA.

A Proclamation.

Whereas, on the twenty-second day of September, in the year of our Lord one thousand eight hundred and sixty-two, a proclamation was issued by the President of the United States, containing, among other things, the following, to wit:

"That on the first day of January, in the year of our Lord one thousand eight hundred and sixty-three, all persons held as slaves within any State or designated part of a State, the people whereof shall then be in rebellion against the United States, shall be then, thenceforward, and forever, free; and the Executive government of the United States, including the military and naval authority thereof, will recognize and maintain the freedom of such persons, and will do no act or acts to repress such persons, or any of them, in any efforts they may make for their actual freedom.

"That the Executive will, on the first day of January aforesaid, by proclamation, designate the States and parts of States, if any, in which the people thereof, respectively, shall then be in rebellion against the United States; and the fact that any State, or the people thereof, shall on that day be in good faith represented in the Congress of the United States, by members chosen thereto at elections wherein a majority of the qualified voters of such State shall have participated, shall, in the absence of strong countervailing testimony, be deemed conclusive evidence that such State, and the people thereof, are not then in rebellion against the United States."

Now, therefore, I, ABRAHAM LINCOLN, PRESIDENT OF THE UNITED STATES, by virtue of the power in me vested as commander-in-chief of the army and navy of the United States, in time of actual armed rebellion against the authority and government of the United States, and as a fit and necessary war measure for suppressing said rebellion, do, on this first day of January, in the year of our Lord one thousand eight hundred and sixty-three, and in accordance with my purpose so to do, publicly proclaimed for the full period of one hundred days from the day first above mentioned, order and designate as the States and parts of States wherein the people thereof, respectively, are this day in rebellion against the United States, the following, to wit: ARKANSAS, TEXAS, LOUISIANA, (except the Parishes of St. Bernard, Plaquemines, Jefferson, St. John, St. Charles, St. James, Ascension, Assumption, Terre Bonne, Lafourche, St. Mary, St. Martin, and Orleans, including the City of New Orleans,) MISSISSIPPI, ALABAMA, FLORIDA, GEORGIA, SOUTH CAROLINA, NORTH CAROLINA, AND VIRGINIA, (except the forty-eight counties designated as West Virginia, and also the counties of Berkeley, Accomac, Northampton, Elizabeth City, York, Princess Ann, and Norfolk, including the cities of Norfolk and Portsmouth,) and which excepted parts are for the present left precisely as if this proclamation were not issued.

And by virtue of the power and for the purpose aforesaid, I do order and declare that all persons held as slaves within said designated States and parts of States are and henceforward shall be free; and that the Executive government of the United States, including the military and naval authorities thereof, will recognize and maintain the freedom of said persons.

And I hereby enjoin upon the people so declared to be free to abstain from all violence, unless in necessary self-defence; and I recommend to them that, in all cases when allowed, they labor faithfully for reasonable wages.

And I further declare and make known that such persons, of suitable condition, will be received into the armed service of the United States, to garrison forts, positions, stations, and other places, and to man vessels of all sorts in said service.

And upon this act, sincerely believed to be an act of justice warranted by the Constitution upon military necessity, I invoke the considerate judgment of mankind and the gracious favor of Almighty God.

In witness whereof I have hereunto set my hand and caused the seal of the United States to be affixed.

[L. S.]   Done at the CITY OF WASHINGTON this first day of January, in the year of our Lord one thousand eight hundred and sixty-three, and of the Independence of the United States of America the eighty-seventh.

By the President: *Abraham Lincoln*

William H Seward   Secretary of State.

A true copy, with the autograph signatures of the President and the Secretary of State.

Jno G. Nicolay
Priv. Sec. to the President.

on August 24, 1832, in care of his parents, Jonathan and Amelia Zacharia.[16] He especially tried to mask his lack of education, pretending to have studied with great doctors and to have written learned books, when in fact he had trouble writing standard English (most of his letters were written for him by others) and admitted to friends that "I lack education."[17] In 1844, in another act of concealment, he married Mary Anne Lawson in Philadelphia in a ceremony performed by a Baptist minister.[18] For some time, he lived with his wife's non-Jewish family, but like many intermarried Jews of the time, he also maintained ties with members of the Jewish community, later insisting that "I have always been proud to acknowledge that I was an Israelite." Abraham Lincoln certainly knew him as a Jew.[19]

A central mystery concerning Zacharie concerns how he became such a skilled and successful chiropodist, celebrated by such luminaries as Henry Clay, John C. Calhoun, and, of course, Lincoln himself. Chiropody was a brand-new field in Zacharie's day—the word had only come into existence in 1785—and it was far from a respectable one. Medical science paid scant attention to foot discomforts, and surgeons considered problems like corns and bunions beneath their dignity; they relegated them to lowly "corn cutters" some of whom dabbled in folk medicine and dentistry on the side. The skills needed to alleviate foot discomforts were thus learned from those experienced in the field and were often passed down from parents to children.[20]

The first serious English-language medical text on foot care, *A Treatise on Corns, Bunions, the Diseases of Nails, and the General Management of the Feet* (1845), was written by a proud and communally active Jew named Lewis Durlacher, of London, who served as "surgeon-chiropodist" to three successive British monarchs and was also the son, father, and grandfather of chiropodists. An American edition of his well-regarded work was published in Philadelphia soon after the London edition appeared.[21]

Another early British chiropodist, a German immigrant of uncertain background named John Eisenberg, likewise published a book on chiropody in 1845. Entitled *Surgical and Practical Observations on the Diseases of the Human Foot with Instructions for their Treatment to which is added Advice on the Management of the Hand*, the volume was expensively produced and elegantly written, but its contents (including veiled attacks on Durlacher) were greeted with scorn. "Fine semblance, no substance," the reviewer for the *British and Foreign Medical Review* concluded. "We warn our readers all and sundry against meddling with the charming cheat."[22] A medical journal for surgeons dismissed the work as "scarcely deserving of even the brief attention we have given to it."[23] Little more is known about Eisenberg, but in 1860, Issachar Zacharie would pirate his book and publish most of it under his own name in America. He also borrowed six illustrations from Durlacher's book for his own, again without any acknowledgment.[24]

Much as he undoubtedly learned from these books, Zacharie must also have had a teacher to train him in the science and art of chiropody. Who that was remains another of Zacharie's many mysteries. On one occasion, he published a "certificate," purportedly from the great English surgeon Sir Astley Paston Cooper (1768–1841), dated 27 June 1837, attesting that "I. Zacharie studied the profession of Chiropodist under me."[25] Since Zacharie was no more than twelve years old in 1837 and living in poverty in the United States, while Cooper died in England in 1841, that claim is easy to reject. Zacharie dedicated both editions of his book *Surgical and Practical Observations on the Diseases of the Human Foot* (1860, 1876) to the great American surgeon Valentine Mott, who had studied under Cooper. "I am indeed rejoiced that this tribute of my respect and admiration has been accepted by you, and that you consider the labors of an humble individual, upon a neglected branch of knowledge, not unworthy [of] your kind protection and consideration," he wrote. Strangely, that dedication is dated 1844, sixteen years before the first edition of his volume had even appeared in the United States,

"... broken eggs can
not be mended.
I have issued the
emancipation
proclamation and
I can not retract it."

**LINCOLN TO JOHN
A. McCLERNAND,
JANUARY 8, 186[3]**

*Lincoln would later tell the artist
Francis Bicknell Carpenter that
"as affairs have turned out," the
Emancipation Proclamation was
"the central act of my administration,
and the great event of the nineteenth
century." But the "turning out"
was not without contention, and
Lincoln emphatically defended his
proclamation: "broken eggs can not be
mended," he declared. "I have issued the
emancipation proclamation, and I can
not retract it."*

Shapell Legacy Partnership

Executive Mansion,

Washington, January 8. , 1862.

Major General McClernand

My dear Sir

Your interesting communication by the
hand of Major Scates is received. I never did ask more,
nor ever was willing to accept less, than for all the
States, and the people thereof, to take and hold their
places, and their rights, in the Union, under the Constitution of the United States. For this alone have
I felt authorized to struggle; and I seek neither more
nor less now. Still, to use a coarse, but an expressive
figure, broken eggs can not be mended. I have issued
the emancipation proclamation, and I can not retract it.

After the commencement of hostilities I struggled nearly
a year and a half to get along without touching the
"institution"; and when finally I conditionally determined
to touch it, I gave a hundred days fair notice of my
purpose, to all the States and people, within which time they
could have turned it wholly aside, by simply again becoming good citizens of the United States. They chose to dis-

As to any dread of my having a "purpose to enslave, or exter-

safety, so far as I am concerned.
I think you would better not make this letter public;
but you may rely confidently on my standing by whatever
I have said in it. Please write me if anything more
comes to light.

Yours very truly
A. Lincoln.

and it stops short of saying that Zacharie himself had studied with Mott, which he almost certainly did not.[26] It seems more likely that Zacharie studied chiropody in Philadelphia where the first chiropody office ever known in the United States was opened in 1841 by an English-born Jew named Julius Davidson.[27] Had he, as an obituary claims, also studied under Dr. Thomas Dent Mutter, the eminent professor of surgery at Philadelphia's Thomas Jefferson Medical College, he would not likely have considered himself lacking in education.[28] Much still remains mysterious about Zacharie's life and training, but this much is known with certainty: he was living in Philadelphia with his wife's family and his own two small children when the census taker found him in 1850, and beginning several years before then, in his twenties, he started taking testimonials from public figures whose feet he successfully treated.[29]

Shrewdly, Zacharie began by soliciting commendations from doctors in Philadelphia and nearby Baltimore. They attested, in testimonials dating as early as August 27, 1846, that his "method"—avoiding use of the knife, spilling no blood, minimizing pain, maximizing comfort, and operating quickly—was "rational" and "scientific." They also addressed him as "Doctor," a professional degree that he ambitiously aspired to but never actually attained.[30] On a trip to the nation's capital, the freshly titled "doctor" courageously employed his method on the corns of Lincoln's "beau ideal," Senator Henry Clay. "I take pleasure in saying," Clay wrote in a January 29, 1848, testimonial, "that Dr. Zacharie operated on me for Corns, with perfect comfort, and to my entire satisfaction, and I derived great and immediate benefit from the exercise of his skill and judgment."[31] That commendation naturally opened many doors to the young chiropodist, and within the year he had won additional testimonials from such luminaries as Senators Lewis Cass, Thomas Hart Benton, and John C. Calhoun.[32]

For several years during the gold rush, Zacharie and his family lived in California. He was the only chiropodist listed in the San Francisco city directory of 1856 and is remembered as the "pioneer practitioner in that city."[33] Much like Abraham Jonas when he moved to Kentucky, he also became a leader in Freemasonry, a meeting ground where upwardly mobile Jews and Protestants could safely interact. In keeping with the air of mystery that he so frequently projected, he became especially devoted to Masonry's Order of the Secret Monitor, influenced by Dutch Masonry, which focused upon mutual assistance ("to search out and call upon any Brother who may be in danger or distress, or who may have fallen into ill health or may be in need of fraternal monition, sympathy, consolation or assistance"). Years later he would bring that secretive order back to England, becoming its first Supreme Ruler.[34]

In 1858, Zacharie returned from California and took up residence in New York. By then, he boasted of having collected some "1500 certificates" attesting to his skills from "some of the most eminent men in the United States." Though still only in his thirties, he was well on his way to becoming chiropody's foremost American booster. The *New York Atlas* characterized him that year as "the most successful operator of his class ever known in New York" and gushed that "professors of chiropody" of his type were nothing less than "benefactors of the human race."[35]

One of the "eminent men" whose feet Zacharie treated in New York was the esteemed poet and longtime editor of the *New-York Evening Post*, William Cullen Bryant. Known to be "an indefatigable walker," Bryant regularly tramped three miles to and from work and was once said to have walked forty miles in a single day.[36] So it is, perhaps, not surprising that he became particularly interested in chiropody. "Diseases of the feet," he knew, were the cause "of great suffering and inconvenience, and few persons are wholly exempt from them." After watching Zacharie in action in 1859, Bryant praised his "knowledge of the structure of the human foot and the consummate dexterity of his operations." He also became one of his patients.[37]

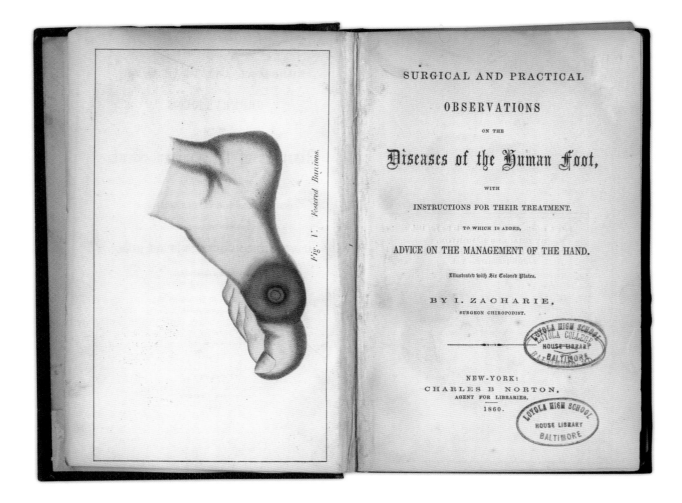

Fig. V. Festered Bunions.

SURGICAL AND PRACTICAL

OBSERVATIONS

ON THE

Diseases of the Human Foot,

WITH

INSTRUCTIONS FOR THEIR TREATMENT.

TO WHICH IS ADDED,

ADVICE ON THE MANAGEMENT OF THE HAND.

Illustrated with Six Colored Plates.

BY I. ZACHARIE,

SURGEON CHIROPODIST.

NEW-YORK:
CHARLES B NORTON,
AGENT FOR LIBRARIES.
1860.

INSCRIBED COPY OF ZACHARIE'S BOOK

Zacharie published Surgical and Practical Observations on the Diseases of the Human Foot *in 1860—which shared, at the very least, the exact same title of a book published abroad, by another chiropodist, years earlier. While his authorship is suspect, he was nonetheless an expert healer, not only of foot complaints but of hand and back maladies as well.*
Shapell Manuscript Collection

In the summer of 1862, with the Civil War raging, Northern morale ebbing, and William A. Hammond, an energetic young surgeon general newly installed in Washington committed to the establishment of a permanent hospital and ambulance corps for the military,[38] a plan was hatched, perhaps by Zacharie himself, to improve the lives of soldiers by establishing a chiropody corps "to inspect the feet of the men and keep them in order for marching." Bryant, who loved the idea, agreed to recommend Zacharie to be its chief. "His skill in this branch is truly astonishing," he informed Secretary of War Edwin Stanton and then expounded at length on the "importance of maintaining the feet of our soldiers."[39] On the same day, August 21, 1862, Bryant provided Zacharie with a personal letter of introduction to Abraham Lincoln. He had been one of Lincoln's earliest New York supporters, served as emcee when Lincoln spoke at Cooper Union, and often corresponded with him. He expected that his recommendation would carry weight with the president, and probably for that reason, his carefully chosen words focused more on Zacharie's medical skill than on his executive abilities:

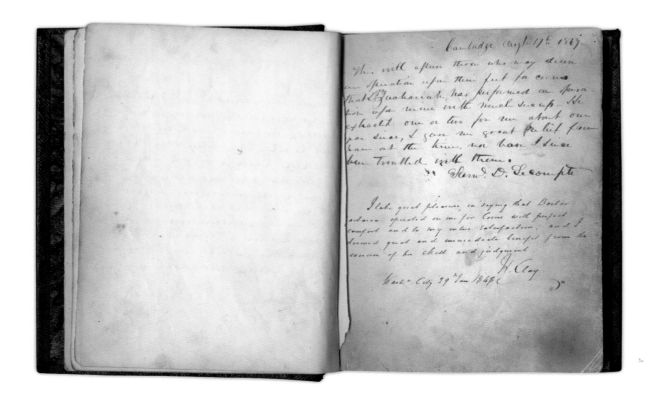

THE INTRODUCTION, AUGUST 21, 1862

With this letter of introduction to Lincoln, Issachar Zacharie began his unique connection with the president—the end of which, just as at the beginning, would see him as a man of mystery. Here William Cullen Bryant, the powerful editor of the New-York Evening Post, *tells the president of the chiropodist's "marvelous skill."*

Shapell Manuscript Collection

TESTIFYING TO ZACHARIE

Some of the 1500 testimonials of Issachar Zacharie's skill that he had personally assembled, which included Henry Clay, John C. Calhoun, Lewis Cass, Thomas Hart Benton, William H. Herndon, as well as top Union generals.

Shapell Manuscript Collection

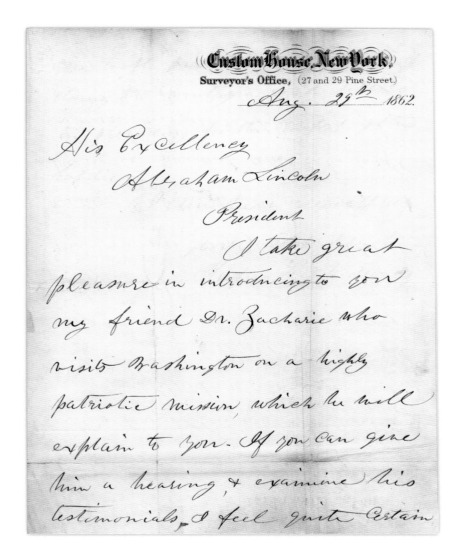

THE CATALYST FOR THE FIRST MEETING, AUGUST 29, 1862

Adding to the recommendation from William Cullen Bryant just a week before, New York Custom House official Rufus F. Andrews also recommends Dr. Issachar Zacharie to Lincoln— this time, as a friend "who visits Washington on a highly patriotic mission." This missive was most likely the catalyst for the first meeting between Lincoln and Zacharie three weeks later.

Shapell Manuscript Collection

The bearer of this note, Dr. I. Zacharie, a chiropodist of marvelous skill, as I have had occasion to experience, has desired that I would say to you what I know of him. He is a regularly educated surgeon, whose operations on the feet are performed with a nicety, delicacy and dexterity which is truly surprising. If you or any of your family are incommoded with any disease whatever of the feet, he will be happy to give proof of his skill.[40]

These letters became part of a small-scale lobbying effort on behalf of Zacharie and the proposed chiropody corps. George Opdyke, the Republican mayor of New York City, penned a letter of his own to Lincoln in praise of Zacharie ("I beg to commend him to your favorable consideration as the Chief of a Corps of Chiropodists which, I learn, and I hope truly, is to be organized for the benefit of the country, by keeping in good marching condition, the feet of those who go forth to fight our battles").[41] Rufus F. Andrews, surveyor of the Port of New York, gave Zacharie a letter of introduction to Lincoln as well, most likely the catalyst for the first meeting between Lincoln and Zacharie three weeks later.[42] The *New-York Evening Post* and the *New York Herald* likewise published articles favoring the chiropody corps.[43] The *Herald* colorfully depicted

Zacharie as being "distinguished by a splendid Roman nose, fashionable whiskers, an eloquent tongue, a dazzling diamond breastpin, great skill in his profession, an ingratiating address, a perfect knowledge of his business and a plentiful supply of social moral courage."[44] Zacharie himself, meanwhile, kept Stanton and Hammond informed of these tributes, and pleaded for "favorable consideration."[45]

In September, Zacharie traveled to Washington to argue his case in person. According to published reports, he treated the feet of three generals, George McClellan, Ambrose Burnside, and most important of all in terms of his later career, Nathaniel P. Banks. He also treated Secretary of State William Seward, and other members of the cabinet.[46] Then, on September 20, he met with Abraham Lincoln, probably for the first time, and in the course of just five days would treat Lincoln for back, wrist, and foot problems. "Dr. Zacharie, has, with great dexterity, taken some troublesome corns from my toes," the president wrote in a testimonial striking for its lack of pretentiousness. "He is now healing me, and I believe with success, for what plain people call back-ache. We shall see how it will end."[47]

Apparently it ended well, for two days later, on September 22, the very day that he delivered the preliminary Emancipation Proclamation to his cabinet, announcing his decision to emancipate slaves on January 1, 1863, Lincoln made time during a momentous week to pen a more formal testimonial attesting that he had met with Dr. Zacharie in the Executive Mansion. Presumably, Zacharie presented to him his plan for the chiropody corps; he also again treated Lincoln's famously painful feet. "Dr. Zacharie has operated on my feet with great success, and considerable addition to my comfort," Lincoln wrote.[48]

Three days after that, on September 25, which happened to be the first day of Rosh Hashanah, the Jewish New Year, the president invited Zacharie back into his office seeking treatment for a sprained wrist.[49] In the meanwhile, on September 23, Lincoln had co-signed,

along with William Seward, yet another testimonial for Zacharie, this one likely written with Surgeon General Hammond in mind. Noting "numerous testimonies of the highest character," as well as their own "personal experience," Lincoln and Seward endorsed Zacharie's "very great success . . . in operating upon corns, bunions & other troubles of the feet," and expressed their "desire that the Soldiers of our brave army may have the benefit of the Doctor's surprising skill."[50] Stanton followed that up the next day with a thirty-day pass to Zacharie, "for the purpose of operating upon the feet of the soldiers for corns, bunions" in and around Washington.[51]

New Yorkers seem to have assumed, following all of these testimonials and accolades, that Zacharie's mission had been crowned with success. *Vanity Fair*, a humorous

OPPOSITE TOP

THE FIRST LINCOLN TESTIMONIAL, SEPTEMBER 20, 1862

Of all the hundreds of testimonials affirming the wondrous talents of Issachar Zacharie, this is the most interesting: "Dr. Zacharie, has, with great dexterity, taken some troublesome corns from my toes—He is now treating me, and I believe with success, for what plain people call back-ache. We shall see how it will end." It is the first of three such testimonials Lincoln would write for Zacharie, written within three days of one another, and suggests that from the very beginning, Lincoln found something compelling in the able and affable doctor. It also serves as yet another example of Lincoln's striking humility: for having been for the first twenty-one years of his life a manual worker, he had yet to forget what "plain people call back-ache."

Shapell Manuscript Collection

OPPOSITE BOTTOM

THE SECOND TESTIMONIAL: A SURPRISING GESTURE ON A LANDMARK DAY, SEPTEMBER 22, 1862

Within five days of Antietam, the single bloodiest battle in American history, and on the very day that Lincoln issued his preliminary Emancipation Proclamation to his cabinet, he found time to gratify Zacharie's request for a second endorsement.

Shapell Manuscript Collection

Dr. Zacharie, has, with great dexterity, taken some troublesome corns from my toes— He is now treating me, and I believe with success, for what plain people call back-ache. We shall see how it will prove.

Sep. 20. 1862.   A. Lincoln

"*Dr. Zacharie . . . is now treating me, and I believe with success, for what plain people call back-ache.*"

Dr. Zacharie has operated on my feet with great success, and considerable addition to my comfort.

A. Lincoln

Sep. 22. 1862.

Executive Mansion
Washington. D.C.

From Numerous testimonials
of the highest Character and
from personal experience — we
approve the very great success
of Dr J. Zacharie in Operating
upon Corns bunions & other
troubles of the feet, by which
instant relief is afforded, &
we desire that the Soldiers
of our brave Army may
have the benefit of the
Doctors surprising skill

A. Lincoln.

William H. Seward,

Sep. 23. 1862.

"... we desire that the soldiers of our
brave army may have the benefit of
the Doctor's surprising skill."

New York weekly, went so far as to publish an anonymous "Ode to Dr. Zacharie"—might it have been the work of William Cullen Bryant?—praising the chiropodist's skill and celebrating his appointment to the military.[52]

Surgeon General Hammond, who like so many surgeons seems to have held chiropody in low esteem, paid no heed to any of this. He received any number of well-intentioned suggestions from politicians and citizens extolling treatments and remedies of every kind (Bryant, for example, was a great devotee of homeopathic medicine[53]), and with his elevated sense of professionalism, Hammond proceeded to reject most all of them—even when they came addressed to him from the president of the United States.[54] Just a few days after he met with Zacharie, to take one instance, Lincoln specifically requested Hammond to allow a Dr. S. W. Forsha of Ohio to treat soldiers with a special "balm" that, Forsha had promised, would "insure ninety percent of all the flesh wounds to be well and the Soldiers to be in a healthy condition and fit for duty within thirty days." Hammond ignored the request; when it was repeated, he bluntly informed the president that Forsha was nothing but "an ignorant quack."[55] What Hammond thought of Zacharie at the time has not been preserved, but in 1864, when he was dismissed, the surgeon general admitted that he had refused to sanction the "corn doctor['s] . . . entrance into the army, although he was supported by the President and other prominent politicians."[56] As a result, notwithstanding all of the many endorsements

Zacharie collected, including those of Lincoln and Seward, no chiropody corps came into being.

Nevertheless, Lincoln, Seward, and Banks—new friends whom the affable chiropodist made in Washington after treating their feet successfully—all tried to assist him. Banks, on October 6, recommended Zacharie's skills ("I have experienced the benefit of his professional skill and commend him to your favor") to the commander of Fort Monroe, John A. Dix. Zacharie later claimed to have relieved the feet of some 5,000 soldiers at the Virginia fort. He published an advertisement claiming that "all soldiers having corns, bunions or bad nails upon their feet, can have them cured without pain" and declared in capital letters that he was serving "UNDER THE AUTHORITY OF THE SECRETARY OF WAR."[57] But there is no evidence that he received any such authority or military commission, and he never was paid. In 1874, when he sought retroactive compensation for his work, Congress's Committee on War Claims scornfully turned him down, insisting that he had been merely "plying his vocation; and voluntarily sought to pursue the same in the lines of the Union Army."[58]

Zacharie, who made up in ambition, imagination, and determination whatever he lacked in education, returned to Washington after seven weeks at Fort Monroe with a new and highly secretive plan. After meeting with Lincoln, who appreciated his skills and took a personal liking to him, Zacharie exultantly wrote Seward that, pending a kind word from him, he would "obtain what I desire": the opportunity to accompany General Banks to New Orleans.[59] The very next day, on November 25, Lincoln wrote a revealing letter to Banks providing his consent:

> Dr. Zacharie, whom you know as well as I do, wishes to go with you on your expedition. I think he might be of service, to you, first in his peculiar profession, and secondly, as a means of access to his countrymen, who are quite numerous in some of the localities you will probably visit. This, however, is

[October 18, 1862.

ODE TO DR. ZACHARIE.

KING of Chiropodists, salaam !
Thy skill provides a sovereign balm
    For every toe cornuted.
BOOTES shone bright when thou wast born
To bless a shoe-pinched world forlorn,
And tenderly of toughest horn
    Relieve the tender-footed.

Our soldiers for the South *en route*
Are cursed with corns that sharply shoot
    As SHARP'S sharp-shooting rifle;
And, as their way they slowly pick,
Too often, goaded to the quick,
Find words suggested by old NICK
    Quite difficult to stifle.

But thou eftsoons canst pare away
Each hard excrescence, so they say,
    As pears are pared, or onions.
Then, well rid of this growing ill,
Each soldier Pilgrim's Progress will
Be brisker far, o'er dale and hill,
    Than CHRISTIAN'S was in BUNYAN'S.

When first thou didst arrive in town,
The gracious ABE his foot put down,
    A foot of full ten inches,
And in his Roman manner said :
" ZACHARIE, old fellow, go ahead !
Let soldiers corns be re-mo-*ved*
    Wherever the shoe pinches."

And now, O man of dexterous fist !
Thou'rt U. S. A. Chiropodist,
    And drawest pay and ration :
Millions of toe-joints are thy care,
Oh ! keep them all in good repair,
That they our gallant boys may bear
    To Treason's castigation.

"ODE TO DR. ZACHARIE": OCTOBER 18, 1862

From the first, and short-lived, incarnation of Vanity Fair *magazine—then a Manhattan-based humorous weekly published between 1859 and 1863—came this "Ode to Dr. Zacharie," celebrating his well-known friendship with President Lincoln. Though published anonymously, it may have been authored by William Cullen Bryant.*

Vanity Fair

not an order, nor a request even, for you to take him; but a permission merely, excepting his case from a general prohibition which I understand to exist.[60]

Banks, at the time, was collecting men and matériel for a secretive expedition, by boat, to New Orleans. Lincoln had appointed him to replace the unpopular General Benjamin F. Butler as commander of what was then known as the Department of the Gulf. A key goal of Banks's mission was to pacify the population and win its goodwill so as to entice Louisiana back into the Union.[61] As Lincoln clearly knew, Jews (many of them intermarried and assimilated) played an outsized role in the politics of the region. On the eve of the Civil War, Judah P. Benjamin had been Louisiana's U.S. senator; Henry M. Hyams, its lieutenant governor; and Edwin Warren Moise, the speaker of its legislature— all of them Jews.[62] Overall, as many as 2,000 Jews lived in New Orleans. Butler, a notorious anti-Semite, had alienated Jews during his tenure, jailing several of them and insulting all of them ("my experience with men of the Jewish faith or nation," the general explained, "has been an unfortunate one."[63] Butler, in a letter to the attorney general in October 1862, wrote: "They are Jews who betrayed their Savior & also have betrayed us."[64])

Lincoln, who understood what a great mistake that policy had been, hoped that Zacharie, being Jewish himself and with his Jewish connections in New Orleans,[65] could win back the affections of his Jewish "countrymen" by surreptitiously promoting pro-Union sentiments among them. He assumed that Zacharie's chiropody skills would come in handy for Banks as well. As to the "general prohibition" to which Lincoln referred in his letter to Banks, that seems to have been a reference to General Ulysses S. Grant's orders of November 9 and 10 barring Jews from traveling south. "Refuse all permits to come south of Jackson for the present," the general had ordered. "The Isrealites [*sic*] especially should be kept out."[66]

Zacharie received his official instructions from

General Banks on January 1, 1863, when his intelligence mission commenced. "In pursuance to your instructions from the President," the general wrote, "I desire you during your continuance in the city to mingle freely with its people of all classes, especially with your own countrymen; to ascertain and report as far as possible the nature of its public opinion, as well as the opinion of individuals." In addition, like any spy, he was instructed to be on the lookout for "the plans of the public Enemy, the character of his troops . . . the extent of their supplies and ammunition, and the different organizations of which their army may be composed." "Spare no expense in obtaining that which is of importance," Banks added.[67]

Zacharie soon set to work. He collected information on firms sending supplies to the Confederacy. He passed along reports (some accurate, some not) on Confederate troop movements. He gathered information on the misdeeds of General Butler. He promoted the work of his patron, General Banks, whom he fawningly compared, in one of his letters to Lincoln, to the man he knew Lincoln idealized, Henry Clay.[68] And, just as he had been instructed to do, he spent a great deal of time aiding Jews. He befriended Jews whom General Butler had offended and hired selected Jews to gather intelligence for him. He met with the most revered Jewish religious leader in New Orleans, Rev. James K. Gutheim, a prominent Confederate supporter who faced banishment to the Confederacy for refusing to take the oath of allegiance to the man he called "the Dictator of Washington," and offered him kind words of reassurance. To his superiors, he soothingly explained that "in his heart" Gutheim "wishes the Union restored. . . . It is his wife who influences him."[69] He also met with scores of other Jews who, as "registered enemies," needed to leave town. "The Doctor," the *New York Herald* reported, "appears to have taken them under his wing; for he has been beset with them morning, noon and night, and his elegant apartments at the St. Charles Hotel have sometimes been crowded with Israelites, waiting his

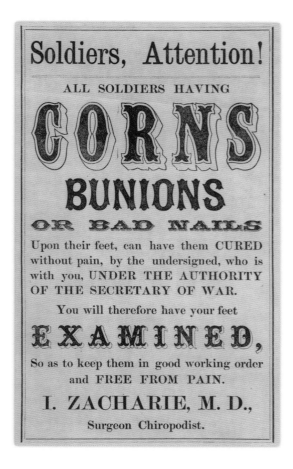

ZACHARIE BROADSIDE

Under the imprimatur of "the Authority of the Secretary of War," Zacharie advertises his painless podiatry in this broadside, circa 1862.

Maine Historical Society

leisure, in order to obtain his advice as to what they should do."[70] Amid these exertions, he reassured the president that he was meeting with success, "not only among my own people but among the most wealthy & influential of citizens." Radiating optimism, he wrote that "the people every day are becoming more favorably disposed to the Government."[71] He sent similar reports to Banks and Seward.[72]

Empowered to hire assistants to help him gather intelligence, Zacharie hired local Jews of long acquaintance and had the inspired idea of disguising them as peddlers to give them some "good excuse" for their travels through the state. He thought that providing them with "merchandise for sale" would provide "a cloak to their real object."[73] Other intelligence gatherers in New Orleans, like George S. Denison, the acting collector of customs and undercover spy for Treasury secretary Salmon P. Chase, knew nothing of this and deeply suspected Zacharie. The chiropodist's own Jewish background only compounded such suspicions; one scholar writes of Denison's "lack of tolerance for foreigners in general and Jews in particular."[74] In correspondence with Chase, Denison wrote derisively that one of Zacharie's "Israelite friends" sought to "take a large stock of goods to Donaldsonville. The reason given is the same as before—that the Dr. wants his friends' cooperation, which would be imperfect unless said friend pretends to be selling goods." Denison, of course, did not "believe a word of it." He described Zacharie as a "vulgar little scoundrel . . . who takes bribes, and whose only object is to make money."[75] Louisiana's military governor, George F. Shepley, viewed Zacharie's activities, including his allegiance to Banks, as proof that "the Christ killers . . . have it all their own way."[76] Even former congressman Michael Hahn, who was born of Jewish parents but did not identify as Jewish, expressed doubts about Zacharie. "The general report prevails here," he wrote Lincoln, "that he obtains important commercial and other privileges from the government officers here for persons who pay him heavy sums of money &c. This should be stopped."[77]

Whether Zacharie actually succumbed to the corruption and theft that characterized the Department of the Gulf while he was there, or whether instead his financial dealings served as camouflage for the larger goal with which Lincoln had entrusted him is disputed.[78] When he departed, even General Banks, who knew of the accusations against him, seemed uncertain. "Doctor Zacharie," he wrote Seward, "has been the subject of remark on the part of some parties here who suspect him of speculation. There is much crimination and recriminations among officers of the government on this subject in which I have no part and of which I have no knowledge. I can only say that Doctor Zacharie has had no favors whatever from the Government and has asked for none at my hands."[79]

In March, Zacharie was called east to confer with the president. "Will have the honor of seeing you in day or two," he telegraphed him from New York soon after he arrived there.[80] Their meetings were secret, but it is known that the former Democratic Jewish congressman, Emanuel B. Hart (who was friendly with Seward), was present. Zacharie had agreed to help set up an exchange of Southern cotton for Northern goods and that was likely on the agenda. Zacharie may also have been involved in an abortive plan to buy cotton directly from Southern planters to help overcome the drastic shortage of cotton affecting mills both in the North and in Europe. There may even have been some more ambitious plan afoot to find an end to the war— for when the meetings concluded, Seward authorized an enormous $5 million line of credit for Banks for an unspecified purpose (the funds were never used).[81] Whatever the case, Zacharie departed "quite agitated on account of the great responsibility" resting upon him, and expressed the hope to Lincoln, who placed so much trust in him, that "everything will be consummated to realize your best wishes."[82]

Coincident with the meetings with Zacharie in March 1863, Lincoln was visited by a long-bearded Canadian self-proclaimed prophet with fiery eyes and hair below his shoulders. His name was Henry Wentworth Monk (1827–96), and his object was nothing less than to end the Civil War, restore the Jews to Palestine, save mankind from doom, and promote world peace. After close study of the Book of Revelations, Monk, in 1852, had renounced property and wealth, ceased to cut his hair or adorn his body, and became a man with a mission. He set off for the Land of Israel, arriving on New Year's Day, 1854, and joined the Christian agricultural settlement established by the Anglican convert John Meshullam in Artas, near Bethlehem. It was there that Monk met the young Pre-Raphaelite painter William Holman Hunt, who painted his portrait and used him as his model for Christ. Monk returned to Canada after eighteen months and published his *A Simple Interpretation of the Revelation* (1857). He thought to settle permanently in Jerusalem until Hunt's patron, the great English art critic John Ruskin, challenged him to prove his prophetic powers by bringing the American Civil War to an end. That challenge explained Monk's sudden appearance at Lincoln's door.[83]

Standing among the crowd that regularly gathered in hopes of winning an audience with the president, Monk's Christ-like appearance naturally caught Lincoln's attention; he was ushered in. According to the description of what followed, quoted from a contemporary letter by Monk's biographer, Monk presented his peace plan, which entailed each side giving up its central war objective, and Lincoln jocularly dismissed it. He then inquired how Canadians viewed his Emancipation Proclamation. That led to a remarkable exchange:

MONK: Why not follow the emancipation of the Negro by a still more urgent step—the emancipation of the Jew?

LINCOLN: The Jew—why the Jew? Are they not free already?

MONK: Certainly, Mr. President, the American Jew is free, and so is the English Jew—but not the European. In America we live so far off that we are blind to what goes on in Russia and Prussia and Turkey. There can be no permanent peace in the world until the civilized nations, led, I hope by Great Britain and the United States, atone for what they have done to the Jews—for their two thousand years of persecution—by restoring them to their national home in Palestine, and making Jerusalem the capital city of a reunited Christendom.

LINCOLN: That is a noble dream, Mr. Monk, and one shared by many Americans. I myself have a regard for the Jews. My chiropodist is a Jew, and he has so many times "put me on my feet" that I would have no objection to giving his countrymen "a leg up." But the United States is, alas, at this moment a house divided against itself. We must first bring this dreadful war to a victorious conclusion, which no compromise can do— and then, Mr. Monk, we may begin again to see visions, and dream dreams. Then you will see what leadership America will show to the world![84]

Lincoln's parting comment to Monk, an apt and clever wordplay that subtly poked fun at the dreams of the self-proclaimed prophet, drew upon the ancient words of the Hebrew prophet, Joel: "Your old men shall dream dreams, your young men shall see visions."[85] Joel's promise of restoration in the aftermath of the punishing blows inflicted by "my great army which I sent among you" may also have provided solace to the beleaguered president. He was already looking forward to leading America in a post–Civil War world.

Even more significant was Lincoln's unequivocal assertion that "I myself have a regard for the Jews," the most direct statement of respect for Jews attributed to him during his lifetime, and one that comports with his friendships and actions since he first became personally acquainted with Jews back in New Salem.

Many, including Generals Butler, Sherman, McClellan and Grant, held different views. A visiting English lawyer, strategist, and scholar named Edward Yates similarly warned Lincoln in a letter that the Jews were the "most venomously opposed" to his administration, the "perpetual enemies of liberty [and] progress, . . . animated by the worst feelings toward the communities on which they prey & fatten & for which they never labor or fight," and were "the spies & most malignant aiders of the Rebels & of every corrupt thing." He urged that not "a single Jew shd on any pretense be allowed to pass or be within or near the lines."[86] Lincoln's "regard for the Jews" though led him systematically to ignore all such suggestions. Earlier, as we have seen, he had appointed a "Hebrew" as an assistant quartermaster just two days after General Sherman had warned against smuggling on the part of "Jews instigated by a sense of gain."[87] He had also appointed Jewish chaplains and abrogated an order expelling Jews "as a class," over the objection of cabinet members and generals. As for Zacharie, not only did the president describe him to Monk as "my chiropodist," he also indicated that his feet benefited from Zacharie's gentle ministrations "many times"— far more often than standard chronologies of his day-to-day activities preserve.[88] The clever wordplay ("he has so many times 'put me on my feet' that I would have no objection to giving his countrymen 'a leg up'") is vintage Lincoln and reprises the very word—countrymen—that Lincoln had previously used in characterizing Zacharie's fellow Jews. The account indicates that Zacharie was on Lincoln's mind at that time and hints at his belief that through Zacharie he could reach out to other Jews— Zacharie's "countrymen"—as well.

It was likely this belief that brought Zacharie, in September 1863, face-to-face with the most prominent

I MYSELF HAVE A REGARD FOR THE JEWS

The self-proclaimed "Prophet" Henry Wentworth Monk, here depicted in 1858 by William Holman Hunt, shared a conversation with Lincoln about restoring Jews to their homeland, in which Lincoln proclaimed, "I myself have a regard for the Jews."

National Gallery of Canada

Jew and the highest-ranking member of the Confederate cabinet: its secretary of state, Judah P. Benjamin. Zacharie's patron, General Banks, had long advocated a negotiated settlement to end the Civil War "with honor to the North and without humiliation to the South." He thought that a deal based upon gradual emancipation, with compensation for the loss of slave property, might end the bloodshed and also cast him in the role of peacemaker and statesman, perhaps even propelling him to the presidency.[89] In July 1863, Banks sent his first emissaries into the Confederacy to talk peace. Zacharie was supposed to have been among them and spent two hours with Abraham Lincoln setting forth his plans, but officials in Washington eventually denied him a pass—partly because they distrusted him and partly because the more radical members of the cabinet opposed negotiations with the Confederacy.[90] Zacharie's friends Martin Gordon Jr. of New Orleans (a relative of Jefferson Davis)[91] and David Pretts did make it to Richmond, and Gordon reported back that many Southerners wanted peace and were sympathetic to just the kind of plan that Banks had proposed.[92] Meanwhile, Lincoln secretly recalled Zacharie

to Washington, sat closeted with him for two days, and promised him "every facility to carry out my plans." He also provided him with an introduction to Major General John Gray Foster at Fort Monroe, mentioning the "high degree" of confidence in which Banks held Zacharie. In coded language ("any kindness you may show him will be appreciated by me"), he ordered Foster to help Zacharie pass through the lines to the Confederate capital of Richmond. Zacharie, in evident excitement, shared the news with Banks, whose presidential dreams he artfully fed. "If I am successful," he assured him, "you as well as I are made for life."[93]

On September 27, 1863, Zacharie met with Judah P. Benjamin—once in the company of several other Confederate leaders, and then, unexpectedly, again at night alone. The recent Confederate surrender of Vicksburg, coupled with the bloody defeat at Gettysburg, where 20,000 Confederate soldiers fell in battle, had darkened the mood in Richmond. Benjamin's hopes for European intervention on the Confederacy's behalf were dimming fast. Still, Benjamin insisted to visitors that "self-government" had to be the basis for any peace—"All we are struggling for is to be let alone."[94] Whether, in private conversation, he intimated to Zacharie that further concessions were possible is unknown, but whatever transpired when they met face-to-face, the chiropodist came away from the encounter overcome with excitement. The fawning letter that he sent to Benjamin the very next day shows him eager to ingratiate himself with the Jewish secretary of state. He expressed joy "that the confederate flag was waving over my head," treacherously declared that "I would gladly join the armies of the confederacy if I did not know that I could be of more service to you from where I am," and closed suggestively with the hope that Benjamin would "never regret the interview we had last night."[95] A day later—having been denied the opportunity to visit his father in Savannah—Zacharie was safely back in the Union. "Just returned," he telegraphed Lincoln. "Will be with you tomorrow afternoon."[96]

Zacharie spent two hours debriefing the president. During that time, he later reported to Banks, Lincoln "lock[ed] his doors . . . preventing any person from having access to him" and "seemed to be delighted with my revelations." According to the *New York Herald*, those revelations included a far-fetched plan, a variant of one suggested by the respected political leader Francis Preston Blair Sr., to restore the Confederate states to the Union while assisting the Confederate government and armies to capture Mexico for the Confederacy, with Jefferson Davis to be its president. Lincoln's cabinet, which had not received prior notice of Zacharie's mission, was unenthusiastic—especially in the wake of the battlefield successes that made Union victory so much more likely. "Send for Genl. Banks. He is your friend and you can trust him with your confidence in carrying out any negotiation, and let me go down and tell Benjamin," Zacharie implored.[97] Lincoln found the conversation exhausting. "I have been so worn down today," he wrote, begging the forgiveness of chemist and patent officer Benjamin Sherwood Hedrick, for not meeting with him. Though Lincoln promised to reflect on Zacharie's "happy thought," he clearly had no intention

of handing the role of peacemaker over to a potential rival. Instead, he and Seward ordered Zacharie to "lay quiet until the time arrives for them to act."[98] Zacharie, meanwhile, became more and more impatient. Lincoln, he complained, "reminds me of the man that won the Elephant at a Raffle. He does not know what to do with it."[99] A week later, he concluded that the president "lacks stability. He has it in his powers to stop all fighting in 24 hours if he would follow out my program."[100] By the end of December 1863, having still heard nothing from Lincoln and Seward, Zacharie expressed "no confidence in them—they are affraid [*sic*] if they make Peace—that their party will not like it."[101] By then, Zacharie understood that his hopes of seeing Benjamin again and negotiating, along with General Banks, an end to the Civil War were effectively dead. Before long, ads promising that "corns, bunions, inverted nails, enlarged joints, and diseases of the foot cured without pain or inconvenience to the patient by Dr. Zacharie" returned to New York's newspapers.[102]

What briefly drew Zacharie back to Washington early in 1864 was the age-old Jewish commandment to redeem the captive. A request came to him to help free Goodman L. Mordecai, a young Jewish Confederate from Charleston who had been imprisoned in Washington, D.C. The twenty-four-year-old Mordecai was the son of one of South Carolina's wealthiest Jewish merchants, Benjamin Mordecai, remembered for his "magnificent" donation of $10,000 (the equivalent in today's money of about $250,000) to advance the interests of his "noble commonwealth" when it seceded

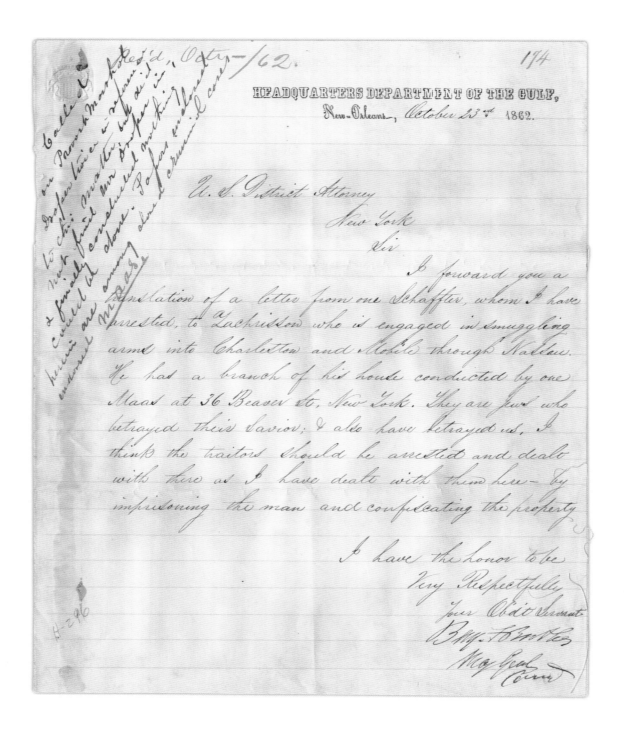

"They are Jews who betrayed their

Savior; & also have betrayed us."

JUDAH P. BENJAMIN, FEATURED ON THE CONFEDERATE $2 BILL

Judah Philip Benjamin's appearance as the first Jew on American currency was not his only remarkable achievement. The second Jewish United States senator, he was the first to serve as a professing Jew and the first Jew to be considered for nomination to the United States Supreme Court (he declined two offers). When his home state of Louisiana seceded, he became the first Jewish cabinet member, serving the Confederacy as attorney general, secretary of war, and, until its collapse, secretary of state. After the war Benjamin fled to England, where he became a successful barrister.

Courtesy of the Library of Congress

from the Union. The younger Mordecai had also loyally served the Confederate army and then worked as a commercial agent for South Carolina blockade runners. While attempting to cross the Potomac Bridge into Washington, he was captured and incarcerated in the Old Capitol prison. Friends of Mordecai's, including the prominent New York Jewish businessman and communal leader Samuel A. Lewis (whose niece, Ada, was Mordecai's fiancée), interceded with Lincoln, and Zacharie personally visited with the president to procure the young man's release. On February 4, when Mordecai and Zacharie came to Lincoln's office to say thank you, the garrulous chiropodist let drop that Mordecai "had fought against the government and that [his] father at that time was prominent in the Confederacy."

According to the account Mordecai published many years later, Lincoln grasped his hand and responded, "I am happy to know I am able to serve an enemy!"[103]

Six weeks later, after another plea from Zacharie, Lincoln also freed the chiropodist's Savannah nephew Jacob [James] G. Cohen, who was imprisoned in Philadelphia—either justly, for running the blockade, or, as he insisted, unjustly, while trying to escape from the Confederacy. Cohen, in a letter, had pleaded with his "dear uncle" to "properly represent my case to the President at Washington & get my release," and on March 16, writing on that same letter, Lincoln responded with typical magnanimity: "Let this man take the [loyalty] oath of Dec. 8 and be discharged."[104]

Lincoln's magnanimity on these two occasions restored Zacharie's devotion to the president and probably explains the two gifts that he sent to the Executive Mansion in 1864: a barrel of hominy in February ("eat it with much enjoyment"), and a box of fine pineapples in May.[105] His success in freeing Jewish captives likewise explains the highly unusual testimonial reception accorded him on May 7, 1864, at his private residence in New York. There he was thanked for exerting "his influence" and employing his "power through the clemency of the President, to aid many . . . and enable them to return to the North and to freedom," as well as "for his efforts" during the war "to soften the hardships

TOP LEFT
SEPTEMBER 29, 1863

A telegram from Zacharie to Lincoln stating, "Just returned. Will be with you tomorrow afternoon."
Courtesy of the Library of Congress

BOTTOM LEFT
"WORN DOWN," SEPTEMBER 30, 1863

Lincoln spent two hours with Zacharie on September 30, 1863, behind closed doors, discussing the latter's secret peace mission, and afterward, Lincoln was too "worn down," he writes here, to even meet with another caller—and so begs to be excused. That the card is written in pencil, rather than the more labor-intensive process of pen and ink, suggests his exhaustion.
Shapell Manuscript Collection

and alleviate the distresses of our [Southern] co-religionists." The lavish present tendered him on that occasion by those "in whose behalf [his] noble and fraternal efforts were so successfully used," makes clear how many felt indebted to him for using his position and influence with the president to render important "services towards the Israelites of America."[106]

While Issachar Zacharie was tending feet, collecting intelligence, assisting Jews caught up in the fighting, and working to end the war, thousands of other Jews, at least 20 percent of eligible Jewish males, were serving as battlefield soldiers. Lincoln was well aware of their contributions. When he revoked Ulysses S. Grant's order expelling the Jews, he explicitly explained, through General Halleck, that he did so because it "proscribed an entire religious class some of whom are fighting in our ranks."[107] He also knew about the heavily immigrant 82nd Regiment in his home state of Illinois, commanded by one of his German-American political friends, Friedrich Hecker. It included what became known as the "Jewish Company" in the Civil War, Company C. Chicago's Jews raised $11,000 (equivalent to about $250,000 today) in recruiting bonuses for those who signed up to fight in the company's ranks, and a high proportion of its soldiers, as well as its company commander, Colonel Edward S. Salomon, were Jews.[108]

The 82nd Illinois Regiment made its reputation at the Battle of Gettysburg, Pennsylvania (July 1–3, 1863), when, according to a standard account, "Colonel Salomon with the 82nd, made a charge upon the pits in

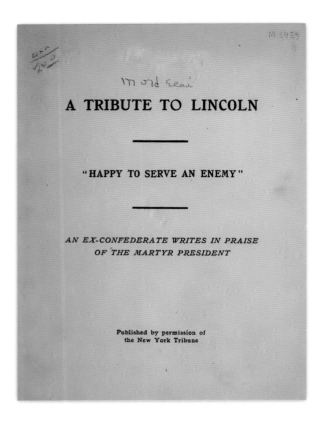

"HAPPY TO SERVE AN ENEMY"

Confederate Prisoner of War Goodman Mordecai's grateful account of how Zacharie, "an influential friend of the President," procured his release from jail. Lincoln, he recorded, was "happy to serve an enemy."
New York Daily Tribune

his front, driving the Confederates back. . . . During the three days' fighting, Colonel Salomon had two horses shot from under him while leading his regiment." Some 131 of the soldiers under his command were killed, wounded, or captured during the battle.[109]

One hundred forty miles away, in Philadelphia, Sabato Morais, the religious leader of Mikveh Israel Congregation, mounted the podium to speak on Saturday, July 4, not knowing how the battle in Gettysburg had turned out. "The murky clouds which have long hovered all over the American horizon [are] gathered at length menacingly nearer to our houses," he cried. "Behold, my hearers! The deplorable consequences and weep. The dust raised by the feet of invasion has

tarnished our escutcheon. Havoc and devastation rage in our borders." Unusually that year, the anniversary of America's independence coincided with the seventeenth day of the Hebrew month of Tammuz, the anniversary of the day when the walls of Jerusalem were breached prior to the destruction of the Second Temple. That mournful commemoration and the fear that the same Confederate forces that had penetrated into Northern territory in Gettysburg might soon threaten Philadelphia, Baltimore and Washington, D.C., led Morais to a fervent prayer: "Encircle Pennsylvania with Thy Mighty shield, protect the lives of her inhabitants." Still, in spite of all the gloom, he remained mindful of July 4 and what that meant. His sermon memorably recalled independence as "the event which four score and seven years ago brought to this new world light and joy."[110]

Whether Abraham Lincoln borrowed the phrase "four score and seven years ago" from Morais for the commemorative address that he delivered at Gettysburg on November 19 cannot be known.[111] While both may independently have reworked the famous King James translation of Psalm 90:10 ("The days of our years are threescore years and ten; and if by reason of strength they be fourscore years"), it is also possible that Lincoln read Morais's sermon, which was published in the *Jewish Messenger*. Other Morais sermons certainly made their way to the president. The prominent Philadelphia publisher Abraham Hart, who was the president of Mikveh Israel, sent him one in April 1862 because he thought that Lincoln would appreciate how it "breathes Loyalty to the Union without exultation, or being Triumphant over the loss of our misguided Brothers in the South."[112] He also sent him a later Morais sermon advocating sympathy and charity for Civil War victims and their families. It was acknowledged on January 9, 1864, by John Hay.[113]

Far more important for Jews than the adaptation of the biblical quote was the fact that Lincoln, in his Gettysburg Address, managed to strike an appropriately religious tone without being in any way parochially

Christian. While Edward Everett, in his two-hour oration at Gettysburg, invoked Christianity no fewer than five times,[114] Lincoln, having been enlivened to Jewish sensitivities, may purposely have employed the novel and more inclusive phrase "this nation, under God." In so doing, he paid silent homage to the Jews who had fallen side-by-side with Christians at Gettysburg and reimagined America in language that embraced Jews as equals.

Eight weeks after the Battle of Gettysburg, on Saturday, August 29, 1863, Jews and Christians once again fell side-by-side. This time, though, they were executed as deserters by order of the United States government. The executions took place before 25,000 troops assembled at Beverly Ford on the Rappahannock River in Virginia. The five men shot included two Protestants, two Catholics, and one Jew.[115]

Desertion plagued the Union army during the Civil War: some 200,000 soldiers reputedly deserted just between 1863 and 1865. Ideology motivated some of these deserters. Others deserted to take care of family. Still others deserted because they were mistreated, or not paid, or frightened, or because they suffered from what would today be called combat fatigue. A few, though, sought to enrich themselves by enlisting, pocketing recruitment bounties, and then deserting in order to "enlist" again, usually under a different name. Desertion, whatever its cause, sapped military morale and endangered the war effort. Seeking to combat it,

A FAVOR FOR ZACHARIE, MARCH 16, 1864

Zacharie's nephew J. G. Cohen, a rebel accused of blockade-running, would owe much to his uncle's friendship with Lincoln, beginning with this note, written on the back of Cohen's impassioned plea for help from his uncle, forgiving his allegiance to the Confederate army. "Let this man take the oath of Dec 8 and be discharged," a common and required oath of loyalty to the Union.

U.S. National Archives & Records Administration

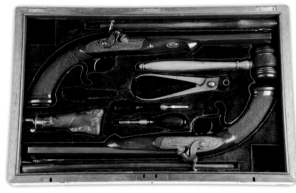

TOP LEFT

EDWARD SELIG SALOMON

Colonel Edward Selig Salomon was a German-Jewish immigrant who enlisted in the 24th Illinois as a first lieutenant. A hero of Gettysburg and Atlanta, he won quick promotions for battlefield bravery and rose to command the 82nd Illinois, Hecker's German and Jewish regiment organized in Chicago. Later brevetted a brigadier general, he remained active in veterans' affairs for the rest of his life.

Collection of Robert Marcus

LEFT AND BELOW

SALOMON'S PISTOLS

Popular with those above and those below, Edward Salomon gravitated after the war to politics, first becoming the clerk of Cook County, Illinois, a role in which he was celebrated and honored by the local citizens with the presentation of these dueling pistols.

Shapell Manuscript Collection

military leaders urged that deserters be tried and publicly executed, as a warning to others.[116]

Abraham Lincoln preferred to be merciful when it came to deserters. "When I think," he once explained to Congressman Henry L. Dawes, "of these mere lads, who had never before left their homes, enlisting in the enthusiasm of the moment for a war of which they had no conception and then in the camp or on the battle field a thousand miles from home, longing for its rest and safety, I have so much sympathy for him that I cannot condemn him to die for forgetting the obligations of the soldier in the longing for home life. There is death and woe enough in this war without such a sacrifice."[117] Lincoln therefore spared the lives of many condemned soldiers, especially if they were willing to reenlist and fight.

The Jewish lawyer Simon Wolf recounted the story of one such reprieve in his memoirs. Wolf, accompanied by Republican Thomas Corwin, a former Ohio senator who was a lawyer in Washington at the time, came to the White House at 2:00 A.M. to plead for the life of a condemned Jewish soldier. The soldier had deserted his unit allegedly in order to be with his mother, "who was

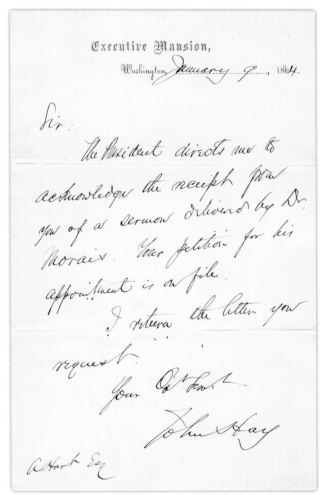

TOP RIGHT
SABATO MORAIS

The Italian-American rabbi Sabato Morais, passionately antislavery and pro-Lincoln, preached on Lincoln's, and the nation's, suffering.

Courtesy of the Library at the Herbert D. Katz Center
for Advanced Judaic Studies, University of Pennsylvania

BOTTOM RIGHT
**JOHN HAY TO ABRAHAM HART,
JANUARY 9, 1864**

Lincoln's secretary, John Hay, thanks Abraham Hart, the president of Mikveh Israel synagogue, for sending Lincoln a Thanksgiving sermon by Dr. Sabato Morais. The letter was written six weeks after the Gettysburg Address, in which Lincoln's indelible line of "four score and seven years ago" might have been directly borrowed from Morais's July 4 sermon, given earlier that year.

Shapell Manuscript Collection

JEWISH SOLDIERS SERVING LINCOLN:
A SAMPLING

THE WAR PROVIDED one of the most central and crucial meeting points for Lincoln to interact with Jews and they with him: over 7,000 Jewish men served Lincoln in the Union army. The broader documentation of Lincoln's involvement with Jewish soldiers is the evidence of this meeting point of the thousands of Jews who faithfully served Lincoln and the Union cause. Jewish patriotism was a product of a number of instrumental factors, namely: high rates of Jewish immigration to the U.S. in the late 1850s, the strong desire of Jews to integrate into American society, of Jews identifying with the values Lincoln was embodying in fighting the war, and a sense that Lincoln was welcoming them into his army.

The *Shapell Roster of Jews in the Service of the Union and Confederate Armies and Navies During the American Civil War period of 1861–1865* is based on a parallel section in Simon Wolf's, *The American Jew as Soldier, Patriot and Citizen,* and provides remarkable evidence of Jewish patriotism—on both the Union and Confederate sides. With military records now consolidated and placed under the control of the U.S. National Archives and Records Administration, the Shapell Manuscript Foundation was able to expand and correct the Wolf study by about 1,500 Jewish names, while also eliminating numerous duplicate entries.

**BREVET LIEUTENANT ISAAC MOSES
OF NEW YORK**

Collection of Robert Marcus

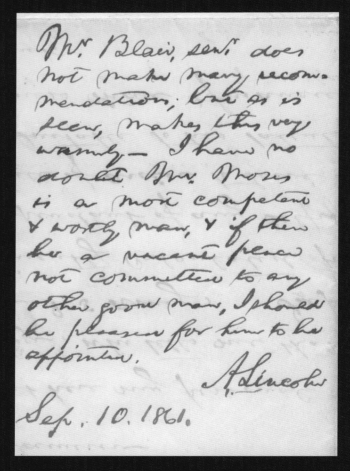

**LINCOLN RECOMMENDS ISAAC MOSES: "I HAVE
NO DOUBT MR. MOSES IS A MOST COMPETENT
& WORTHY MAN," SEPTEMBER 10, 1861**

Courtesy of the Library of Congress

**BADGE OF BREVET CAPTAIN
AARON LAZARUS OF PENNSYLVANIA**

Shapell Manuscript Collection

**COLONEL MARCUS M. SPIEGEL OF OHIO
WAS MORTALLY WOUNDED DURING
THE RED RIVER CAMPAIGN**

Collection of Jean Powers Soman

**SERGEANT LEOPOLD KARPELES OF PENNSYLVANIA,
WINNER OF THE MEDAL OF HONOR**

Collection of Robert Marcus

**BREVET BRIGADIER GENERAL FREDERICK KNEFLER
OF INDIANA, CONSIDERED THE HIGHEST
RANKING JEW IN LINCOLN'S ARMY**

Courtesy of the Jacob Rader Marcus Center
of the American Jewish Archives, Cincinnati, Ohio

**LEOPOLD NEWMAN OF NEW YORK,
WAS WOUNDED AT THE BATTLE OF
CHANCELLORSVILLE, AND REPORTEDLY
RECEIVED THE COMMISSION OF
BRIGADIER GENERAL WHILE ON HIS
DEATHBED—FROM LINCOLN HIMSELF**

Collection of Robert Marcus

Office U. S. Military Telegraph,
WAR DEPARTMENT.

The following Telegram received at Washington, 4 H 3 P M. Aug 26th 1863.

From Camp 11th Regt P.V. near Beverly Ford. M.

Dated, Aug 26th 1863.

His Excellency the President of the United States.

We the undersigned sentenced to suffer death for desertion on Saturday next, humbly beg that you exercise your authority to commute, our sentence, to imprisonment, & hard labor, for any term of years, you may see fit, as we each have wives & children, depending upon us.

Charles Walter,
John Rainese,
John Faline,
Emile Lae. & George Kuhne.

25862

WALTER, RAINESE, FALINE, LAE, AND KUHNE TO LINCOLN: "HUMBLY BEG," AUGUST 26, 1863

The five condemned men appeal to Lincoln for clemency in a telegram dated August 26, 1863.
Courtesy of the Library of Congress

on her death bed." She had begged to see him so as to "give him a parting blessing." Lincoln, Wolf recalled, listened sympathetically but explained that he was under pressure from Secretary of War Stanton to crack down on military deserters and that it was "impossible to do anything." Wolf nevertheless made a final plea: "Mr. President," he entreated, "what would you have done under similar circumstances? If your dying mother had summoned you to her bedside to receive her last message before her soul would be summoned to its Maker, would you have been a deserter to her who gave you birth rather than a deserter in law but not in fact to the flag to which you had sworn allegiance?" Lincoln, perhaps recalling being summoned to the bedside of his own dying mother when he was just nine years old, was clearly moved. He "ordered a telegram to be sent

to stop the execution." The reprieved soldier, according to Wolf, returned to his regiment and died heroically at the Battle of Cold Harbor.[118]

Stories like that of Wolf circulated widely during Lincoln's presidency. In addition to all of his other duties, Lincoln became the "pardoner-in-chief," extending clemency to hundreds of prisoners convicted by civil courts and hundreds more convicted by military ones. Where judges and generals called for justice, he often responded with mercy.[119]

But the case of the five men sentenced to die at Beverly Ford proved different. They were charged with being "bounty jumpers," for they had enlisted and been paid to serve as substitutes for conscripted men, in exchange for payments of hundreds of dollars, and then deserted. Unlike most deserters, in this

LINCOLN TO GEORGE MEADE: "THEIR APPEAL IS DENIED," AUGUST 27, 1863

At 9:00 A.M., Lincoln responds to the appeal of the soldiers condemned to death by allowing General George Meade, in the face of these "flagrant cases," to proceed as he deems fit.

Abraham Lincoln Presidential
Library & Museum

GEORGE MEADE TO LINCOLN, AUGUST 27, 1863

General Meade confirmed Lincoln's telegram of a half hour earlier, and added that he had postponed the execution in order to procure the services of a Roman Catholic priest; curiously, Meade made no mention to Lincoln of the need for a rabbi.

Courtesy of the Library of Congress

BENJAMIN SZOLD

The Hungarian-born rabbi Benjamin Szold of Baltimore lobbied Lincoln to commute the death sentence of a Jewish bounty jumper. Still leaving the door open, the final decision, the president insisted, had in this case to be made by General Meade—and he wished him success on his mission. It is likely that only with Rabbi Szold's visit did Lincoln come to know that one of the deserters was Jewish.
Jewish Museum of Maryland

case, prosecutors claimed, it was greed—not fear—that drove them to run away. The five had signed up with the 118th Pennsylvania and were caught and arrested on August 13, 1863. Seven days later, they were court-martialed and sentenced to die by firing squad. On August 25, the men pleaded with General Meade to defer their sentence, since there were neither priests nor rabbis available to help them "in preparing to meet our God." They sought mercy on behalf of their wives and children and asked that their sentences be commuted "to hard labor instead of death, as we think we have been wrongfully sentenced; as we, being foreigners, were led astray by other soldiers, who promised us there would be no harm done."[120] Meade was unmoved. He was determined, he wrote Lincoln, to execute the men to "deter others from imitating their bad conduct."[121]

The following day, August 26, the condemned men sent a telegram to Lincoln, likewise requesting commutation of their sentences to "imprisonment & hard

labor, for any term of years."[122] Unaccountably, they failed to repeat to the president the reason why they felt, as foreigners, that they had been wrongfully sentenced, likely sealing their fate. Since they appealed for mercy "without giving any ground for it whatever," Lincoln turned them down at 9:00 a.m. the next day: "I understand these are very flagrant cases," he informed Meade in a telegram, "and that you deem their punishment as being indispensable to the service. If I am not mistaken in this, please let them know at once that their appeal is denied."[123]

Meade responded at once: The "execution was postponed by my order till Saturday the 29th that time might be given to procure the services of a Roman Catholic Priest to assist them in preparing for death. They are substitute conscripts who enlisted for the purpose of deserting after receiving the bounty, and being the first of this class whose cases came before me, I believed that humanity the safety of this Army, and the most vital interests of the Country, required their prompt execution as an example. . . . In view of these circumstances I shall therefore inform them their appeal to you is denied."[124]

Father Constantine L. Egan, a Catholic chaplain, came to accompany the doomed Catholic men. Even though Meade's telegram to Lincoln made no mention of a rabbi, Baltimore's Rabbi Benjamin Szold was asked to accompany the condemned Jew, a twenty-two-year-old private named George Kuhne. Hoping to arrange clemency, Szold "hurried to the White House, hoping to have a personal interview with the President." Lincoln was closeted with his cabinet at the time, so the quick-thinking rabbi, perhaps believing that Kuhne deserted out of fear, marked in his Bible the verse in Deuteronomy that reads, "What man is there that is fearful and fainthearted? Let him go and return unto his house lest his brethren's heart faint as well as his heart (20:8)." It was delivered to the president with a short note. Before long, Lincoln emerged laughing heartily. "If I were to follow the instructions laid down

THE ARMY OF THE POTOMAC—EXECUTION OF FIVE ... IN THE FIFTH CORPS.—Sketched by Mr. A. R. Waud.—[See Page 622.]

HARPER'S WEEKLY

General Meade, who had sent out a press release ahead of the executions, was looking for wide coverage of the case, and he achieved it: all of the major Northern newspapers were on the scene. The image shows one of the men, likely Kuhne, having been the first to march out, still sitting up following the shots. Despite the executions, the rate of desertion only continued to rise, and the effort in deterrence was a failure.

Shapell Manuscript Collection

here," he smiled, "I would not have a man in the field in a week's time." Lincoln sent Szold to talk to the general himself, who listened patiently but turned down the plea for clemency. Szold, disregarding Sabbath restrictions, then traveled to the condemned man, and the two recited Psalms and prayers. As the time neared, Szold "kissed the accused, who convulsively clung to him."[125]

A solemn procession, accompanied by the military band playing the death march, paraded the condemned prisoners, "their coffins carried in front of them and their hands tied behind them," before the assembled 25,000 troops ordered to watch the grisly scene.

The Jewish prisoner, along with Rabbi Szold, occupied the right-most position and marched out first, for Judaism was recognized as being "the most ancient of religious creeds." Soldiers at the scene, as well as military and press accounts, highlighted the unusual presence of multiple religious leaders ("a Catholic priest, a Jewish Rabbi and a Methodist preacher") at the execution, evidence of how novel it was, at that time, to witness "the minister, the priest and the rabbi engaged in earnest, fervent prayer."[126] Each prisoner was then seated at the edge of his coffin with eyes bandaged. While the troops watched, fifty muskets simultaneously fired. The two Protestants, the two Catholics, and the Jew were shot to death. "It made me feel worse," one soldier wrote two weeks later, "to see those five men

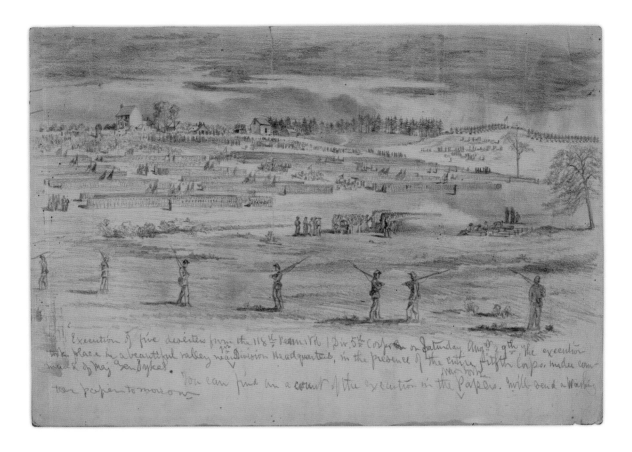

shot that day than to see a thousand men shot down in battle."[127] The eerie scene was concluded with the band playing "The Girl I Left Behind Me," an enlivening military marching tune. The soldiers were then required to march "by the bodies to see that the work of the executioner had been effectually done."[128]

Whether justice was actually "effectively done" when the five unfortunate bounty jumpers were summarily tried and shot is doubtful.[129] Judging from the many subsequently published lists of "substitutes enlisted at headquarters . . . who have deserted," the executions, for all of the publicity that they garnered, had far less of a deterrent effect than General Meade had hoped. What Meade did teach his troops at Beverly Ford was an enduring lesson in religious pluralism. Deserters, he showed, could be Protestant, Catholic, or Jewish, and however harshly they themselves might be punished, their faith and their clergy would still be accorded the greatest of respect.

ABOVE

EDWIN FORBES DEPICTS THE LANDSCAPE OF THE EXECUTION

Forbes's drawing of the execution of five deserters from the 118th PA Volunteers in Beverly Ford, Virginia, shows the grim scene witnessed by 25,000 soldiers.
Courtesy of the Library of Congress

OPPOSITE

JAMES CLOSSEN TO HIS MOTHER: "ACCOMPANIED BY A CATHOLIC PRIEST, A JEWISH RABBI AND A METHODIST PREACHER," SEPTEMBER 3, 1863

Clossen, a soldier who witnessed the execution, described the scene with remarkable detail, which is echoed in the image by Edwin Forbes. He also described the interfaith service: "The men were brought out and marched through the whole corps, their coffins carried in front of them and their hands tied behind them, and a brass band playing the dead march, they were dressed in white shirts blue pants and caps, they were accompanied by a Catholic priest, a Jewish Rabbi and a Methodist preacher."
Shapell Manuscript Collection

Camp near Beverly Ford Va
September 5/62

Dear Mother

Yours of the 30th August I recd yesterday
I am sorry to learn that you are sick and little
James also, the sudden changes from extreme heat
to such cool weather as we have had lately will cause
a great deal of sickness throughout the country.
You say there is a bill for taxes on my income.
You must not pay that, officers in the army pay
taxes on their income every time they are paid off.
it is deducted from their pay on the rolls.
On the afternoon of the 29th August our whole corps
were ordered out to witness the execution of
five deserters from the 118th PV they were substitutes
for drafted men, the day was beautiful and
the appearance and maneuvers of the troops grand,
the troops were massed on the side of a hill about
one mile from Beverly Ford, the graves of the condemned men were dug under a tree on the rise
of ground opposite. a small stream running between
the troops and the place of execution, we got into position directly opposite at 2½ oclock, at 3 oclock

[they were brought] out and marched through the
[line] coffins carried in front of them
[guard] behind them, and a brass band
[on the] march, they were dressed in white
[pants and] caps, they were accompanied
[by] a Jewish Rabbi and a Methodist
[when] they arrived at the place of execution
[set on] their coffins in front of their
[graves conv]ersed with the clergy, and bid their
[friends adieu,] one of them prayed or spoke loud
[b]ut I could not understand him
[so]me of the others fainted while
[al]l seemed deeply affected.
[at] 4 oclock their eyes were bandaged
[the guard] advanced to within 6 paces of the
[men the] command Ready, aim fire was
[given at] 4 oclock, their deaths were instan-
taneous. I hope their fate may be a warning
to all others, a man that would desert his country
at a time like this and particularly a substitute
deserves to be shot,
I wrote Josiah a long letter some time ago let me
know in your next whether he recd it.
I must now close, your affectionate son
James H Closson

"The troops were massed on the side of a hill about one mile from Beverly Ford, the graves of the condemned men were dug under a tree on the rise of ground opposite a small stream running between the troops and the place of execution . . ."

CHAPTER SIX

ABOUT JEWS

1863–1865

Abraham Lincoln provided the model for the public display of religious pluralism that General George Meade staged at Beverly Ford. Having stated his own "regard for the Jews," and having promised that no citizen would "be wronged on account of his place of birth or religious confession,"[1] he continued to interact with a wide variety of Jews during the final eighteen months of his presidential term—evidence of their widening role in national life. At a time when it was commonplace in America to identify Jews as such when describing them, and Jews in many parts of the country experienced prejudice,[2] Lincoln turned a blind eye to stereotypes. So it was in November 1863,

OPPOSITE

LINCOLN AT GETTYSBURG, NOVEMBER 19, 1863

Photographer David Bachrach, a member of Baltimore's tightly knit German-Jewish community, was the only photographer to successfully set up the frame with the purpose of capturing Lincoln sitting on the dais just prior to or immediately after giving his famous remarks at the Gettysburg battlefield, November 19, 1863.

Courtesy of the Library of Congress

when Lincoln submitted to the secretary of war and general-in-chief of the army a recommendation that William Mayer, a Jewish immigrant from Austria, be elevated to the rank of brigadier general. Mayer was reputedly the "most efficient officer" engaged in quelling the notorious July 1863 antidraft riots in New York City. Coming just ten days after the battle of Gettysburg, the riots injured 2,000 people and killed at least 120. Considered one of the worst civil insurrections in American history, the riots began as an expression of discontent against those able to afford to pay others to substitute for them in the military and rapidly escalated into horrific attacks against the city's black residents. Many white Northerners were willing to fight to preserve the Union, but being compelled to fight—and die—in order to end slavery drove some to violence.

Mayer, in a bid to restore order, reportedly went without sleep or rest while he directed troops and was "constantly on duty both night and day." He courageously faced down mobs and was credited with leading children from the Colored Orphan Asylum onto a police boat, thereby saving their lives when the orphanage was

Washington, D. C., *July 7*, 1863.

I, ABRAHAM LINCOLN, President of the United States of America, and Commander=in=chief of the Army and Navy thereof, having taken into consideration the number of volunteers and militia furnished by and from the several States, including the State of *New York*, and the period of service of said volunteers and militia since the commencement of the present rebellion, in order to equalize the numbers among the Districts of the said States, and having considered and allowed for the number already furnished as aforesaid, and the time of their service aforesaid, do hereby assign *Four Thousand Five Hundred and Thirty-eight* as the first proportional part of the quota of troops to be furnished by the *Sixth* DISTRICT OF THE STATE OF *New York* under this, the first call made by me on the State of *New York*, under the act approved March 3, 1863, entitled "An Act for Enrolling and Calling out the National Forces, and for other purposes," and, in pursuance of the act aforesaid, I order that a draft be made in the said *Sixth* DISTRICT OF THE STATE OF *New York* for the number of men herein assigned to said District, and FIFTY PER CENT. IN ADDITION.

IN WITNESS WHEREOF, I have hereunto set my hand and caused the seal of the United States to be affixed.

Done at the City of Washington, this *Seventh* day of *July*, in the year of our Lord one thousand eight hundred and sixty-three, and of the independence of the United States, the eighty-eighth.

Abraham Lincoln

torched. Lincoln, in the months that followed, wrote two separate notes recommending Mayer for promotion and another urging that he be permitted to raise troops and reenter the service after he was mustered out.

He made no mention of Mayer's religion in any of those letters.[3] Lincoln likewise refused to take religion into account when Jews were prosecuted by military authorities. On one notorious occasion, in 1864,

OPPOSITE

JULY 7, 1863

Lincoln's Order that sparked the New York City draft riots: it would, within a week, cause one of the largest civil insurrections in American history. The riots lasted three days, and calm was restored in large part by the intervention of troops bravely led by William Mayer.

Shapell Manuscript Collection

TOP RIGHT

"MAYER'S COMPANY WAS FIRED ON FROM THE HOUSETOPS..."

AUGUST 1, 1863

Colonel William Mayer raised a regiment from New York during the Civil War. For heroic service in putting down the New York City draft riots in 1863, Mayer received praise from Lincoln: on August 28, 1863, Lincoln wrote that "Col. Wm. Mayer, named within, was the most efficient officer in suppressing the late New-York riots," and furthers his request to be made a brigadier general.

Harper's Weekly

MIDDLE AND BOTTOM RIGHT

HORATIO SEYMOUR TO LINCOLN, OCTOBER 5, 1863, WITH LINCOLN'S ENDORSEMENT ON THE LETTER FIVE WEEKS LATER

Four days before traveling to Gettysburg, Lincoln considers the petition of New York Governor Horatio Seymour for the promotion of Austrian-born Jewish colonel William Mayer to brigadier general—even though Mayer, who immigrated in 1857, would become a U.S. citizen only in June 1864. Nevertheless, he received his commission to brigadier general. Lincoln also wrote a longer letter on Executive Mansion stationery to Stanton again that day about Mayer's desire to raise troops—a request that was granted.

Shapell Manuscript Collection

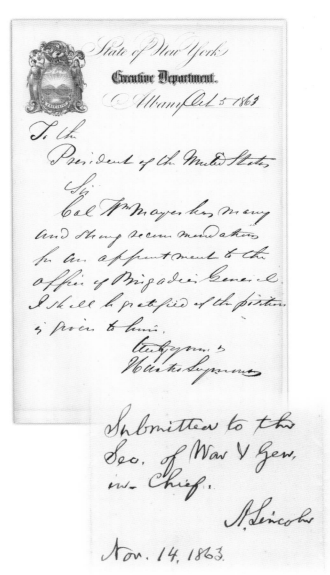

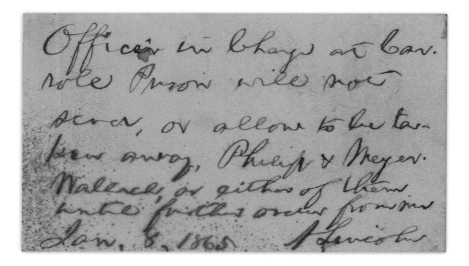

LINCOLN PERSONALLY INTERVENES IN THE CASE OF TWO JEWISH MERCHANTS, JANUARY 8, 1865

Lincoln interjected himself into the case of Philip and Meyer Wallach, two Jewish merchants charged with selling goods to blockaders. First, on January 8, 1865, Lincoln, acting with concern and unusual caution, instructs that they were not to be sent for or be moved "until further order from me"; four days later, he directs that their case be reviewed, and finally, on February 17, he orders that they be given a "jubilee" and released.

Shapell Manuscript Collection

JANUARY 12, 1865

Lincoln endorses the Wallach brothers' court-martial transcript.

U.S. National Archives & Records Administration

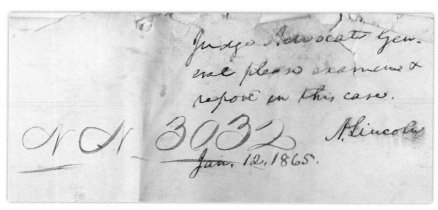

a Jewish clothier in Washington, D.C., named Moses Waldauer was tried for "[s]elling citizens clothing to soldiers to enable them to desert." In trial, it transpired that Waldauer and his daughter had been tricked by the soldiers. Two of them falsely stated that they were awaiting discharge and needed the clothes, and a third fraudulently claimed to be a sergeant and vouched for the men. Waldauer eloquently defended himself before the court. He pointed to the "extraordinary precautions" he took to observe the law, listed a myriad of factual errors in the allegations made against him, and showed that his motive was not to assist desertion but rather to help soldiers who he thought required civilian clothes. Was he, he wondered, supposed to presume "every non-commissioned officer and soldier, however honorable his cause and profession, to be a liar and a scoundrel until he has proved himself otherwise?" Nevertheless, he was found guilty on September 15, 1864, and sentenced to six months in prison plus a fine of fifty dollars. Friends apparently appealed on his behalf, and Lincoln asked the judge advocate general for a report on the case. "This man is a Jew," Joseph Holt's reply began, as if intending to sway Lincoln against the defendant. However, even before Holt's reply was received, Waldauer had been released "by direction of the President."[4]

In another case involving Jewish clothiers, Lincoln likewise proved sympathetic. On January 8, 1865, he ordered the officer in charge of the Old Capitol (Carroll) Prison not to "send or allow to be taken away Philip and Meyer Wallach, or either of them, until further orders from me." The two Jewish merchants had been

"I propose giving them a jubilee."

**LINCOLN TO JOSEPH HOLT,
FEBRUARY 17, 1865**

Lincoln frees the Wallachs.

Huntington Museum

convicted for selling contraband goods to the Confederacy and sentenced to a fine plus three years in jail in Albany. The case was one of several, following a sweep of clothing manufacturers in Baltimore and Washington, instigated by a blockade runner and double agent named Pardon Worsley, who claimed that the defendants, many of them Jews, knowingly sold him goods destined for the enemy. Petitions flooded into the Executive Mansion, attesting to the loyalty and patriotism of the men, including a request for clemency from the brothers' relative and mayor of Washington, D.C., Richard Wallach. Lincoln, after ordering an investigation, expressed doubt as to their guilt. "In regard to the Baltimore and Washington Merchants—clothes dealers—convicted mostly on the testimony of one Worsley (I believe) I have not been quite satisfied," he wrote. "It is very unsatisfactory

to me that so many men of fair character should be convicted principally on the testimony of one single man & he of not quite fair character." Lincoln therefore proposed "giving them a jubilee," using a biblical term for their release, and that was accomplished on February 18, "by order of the President of the United States."[5]

In still a third case, Lincoln admitted that an injustice had been done to a Jewish justice of the peace named Nehemiah H. Miller. Rather than covering up the mistake, he immediately moved to restore Miller's reputation and position. Born in Frankfurt, Germany, in 1832, Miller had arrived in the United States about 1857, studied law, and won appointment, on January 12, 1864, as justice of the peace for Washington, D.C.[6] Ten months later, he was removed from office for malfeasance in "exercising extra-judicial authority" and

Washington 27 May 1862

To the President

I take pleasure in bearing willing testimony to the general good standing of the two Bambergers (Brothers) whose petition for relief I herewith present — The parties are all Jews —

I do not believe that the Bambergers have been, or ever intended to be guilty of any offence —

The facts as I learn them stand thus — They found a Frenco — a man of their own religious faith in prison — charged with treason — anxious to serve him they went upon his bond for his appearance to answer — believing that he would appear and that the offence did not amount to treason —

Any of us would have done as much for a friend — Knowing them as I do to be among the best of their faith, among us and believing them to be loyal men I hope you will grant their petition

Referring you to the papers & praying for them a favorable response I am

as ever

J. F. Speed

*"The parties are all Jews . . . knowing them
as I do to be among the best of their faith . . .
I hope you will grant their petition."*

JOSHUA SPEED TO LINCOLN, MAY 27, 1862

Lincoln's close friend Joshua Speed successfully petitioned him to address an unfair judgment against Simon and Emanuel Bamberger; they had posted a $5,000 bond on a co-religionist from New Orleans, Herman Franks, and, when Franks failed to show up, what should have been a simple "case dismissed" resulted in their bond being forfeited. "The parties are all Jews," Speed wrote to Lincoln. "Knowing them as I do to be among the best of their faith . . . believing them to be loyal men I hope you will grant their petition." Lincoln supported Speed's petition, and the men were eventually pardoned in March 1863.

U.S. National Archives & Records Administration

LINCOLN SIGNS THE PARDON OF EMANUEL AND SIMON BAMBERGER

U.S. National Archives & Records Administration

ANOTHER PARDON, JANUARY 22, 1863

Herman Koppel, a tailor hailing from the heart of the Jewish community in Charleston, supplied "cheap, excellent and serviceable" fatigue uniforms to Confederate units. Lincoln wrote a memorandum concerning Koppel, who had appealed to the president to remit proceeds of property condemned by the court. Lincoln reviewed the facts, which included blockade running as a method of Koppel's escape, and asked, "Admitting this all to be true, is it both lawful and proper . . . ?"

Courtesy of Library of Congress

DAVID K. CARTTER AND ANDREW WYLIE TO LINCOLN, DECEMBER 5, 1864, WITH LINCOLN'S ENDORSEMENT OF DECEMBER 9, 1864

Lincoln, writing to Attorney General (and brother of Joshua) James Speed, endorses the reappointment of German-born Miller, whom Lincoln twice appointed a justice of the peace in Washington, D.C. Miller would, on the night of April 14, 1865, be the first justice of the peace to take sworn statements from witnesses to Lincoln's murder.

U.S. National Archives & Records Administration

falsely stating that two Egyptian nationals had lived in the country for two years, entitling them to a passport, when in fact they had lived in the country for but two months.[7] Subsequent to Miller's removal, a witness provided an affidavit that, according to the same judges who had earlier removed him, went "very far to relieve Miller of any intentional misbehavior in the matter." The judges informed the president that "had that evidence been before us on the trial, and not contradicted, our decision would have been different." In the face of this evidence of injustice, Lincoln reacted unhesitatingly. "Let him be reappointed," he wrote, and he was.[8]

Not all Jews, of course, proved so fortunate. A

Jewish businessman named David Hirsch, for example, complained to Lincoln in late 1863 that General Stephen A. Hurlbut, the military governor of Memphis, had unjustly fined and expelled him from the city. While he had left the army of the Confederacy, Hirsch explained, he had nonetheless taken an oath to not take up arms against it, and he therefore felt compelled to refuse Hurlbut's demand that he enroll in the local Union militia. The punishment he incurred for not violating his oath—a $500 fine (equivalent to over $7,000 in today's money) and expulsion from the city— seemed to him cruel and unjust. In fact, Hirsch was one of a series of Memphis Jews whom Hurlbut abused and persecuted; the general is remembered for being corrupt, arbitrary, and anti-Semitic. Hirsch hoped that Lincoln would restore both his money and his status. He had "not come to ask for favors," he wrote when he asked for an appointment with the president, "but merely for an act of justice, sincerely hoping to find it here." He left disappointed, however, for the secretary of war ultimately ruled against him.[9]

Other Jews who asked for personal favors fared better. A Republican Jewish businessman from Louisville, Kentucky, named Sigmund Griff came to see Lincoln in September 1864 "for the purpose of obtaining some trade facilities." Since he carried strong recommendations from people Lincoln trusted, he was rewarded with three different presidential notes, all written within two days of each other, one asking the secretary of the Treasury to "please see and hear him," one asking the same of the secretary of war, and a third promising to "see and talk with the Secretary of War on the subject." The records have not preserved what "trade facilities" came under discussion, but Griff clearly had the satisfaction of knowing that his proposal was taken seriously.[10]

That same month, Lincoln asked Gideon Welles, secretary of the navy, to accommodate a request made by Jewish congressman Leonard Myers, who represented Philadelphia during the war, to appoint one of his constituents to the "Naval School," then temporarily housed at Fort Adams, in Newport, Rhode Island. "I really wish this done," Lincoln reiterated.[11] Five months later, Lincoln again obliged Congressman Myers, this time in pardoning a bounty jumper, "because Mr. Myers requests it."[12] Myers was part of the first generation of American Jews to serve in Congress, being one of three Jews to serve during Lincoln's presidency, the others being Michael Hahn as a representative from Louisiana, and Myer Strouse, likewise of Pennsylvania. All three men were remembered as Jews but did not identify with the Jewish community. Myers, who possessed a profound sense of civic duty, was dedicated to protecting the rights of immigrants, laborers, inventors, soldiers, sailors, and

"PLEASE SEE & HEAR HIM"

The German-born Jew Sigmund Griff left the Democratic Party because of Stephen A. Douglas's position on the extension of slavery. He became a staunch Lincoln supporter in 1860. As a clothing manufacturer in Louisville, Kentucky, he came so highly recommended to Lincoln that Lincoln wrote three notes, within two days in 1864, to secure him a favor.
Courtesy of David Benjamin Family Collection

former slaves and corresponded with Lincoln over at least three years, with Lincoln consistently supporting his appeals.

In December, Lincoln presented a note to Joseph Stiner, then a captain in the Union army and later a lawyer, politician, judge, member of the Grand Army of the Republic, and a founder of the Hebrew Union Veterans Association, introducing him to Secretary of the Treasury William P. Fessenden. "Please see and hear this gentleman," the president wrote. What Stiner said to Fessenden has been lost, but Stiner did carefully preserve the card, writing on the reverse, "given to me personally by President A. Lincoln, December 2, 1864."

The fact that the president of the United States personally took the time to handwrite a card recommending him to the Secretary of the Treasury clearly left a lasting impression. Stiner took pride in having been treated by Lincoln as an equal.[13]

Indeed, it was these small courtesies extended to Jews that helped to cement Lincoln's reputation among them. In another such case, Mary Lincoln wrote to General Marsena R. Patrick, provost marshal for the Army of the Potomac, seeking a favor for "Herman Grau, from whose family," she wrote, "I have received much politeness."[14] Herman, along with his brother Jacob, his nephew Maurice, and other members of the distinguished Grau family, pioneered musical theater and grand opera in the United States. They acted as agents, managers, promoters, theater directors, and troupe organizers for a wide array of celebrated performers and performances of opera and popular music that were presented throughout the country. In Washington, they often invited the Lincolns as their guests. Lincoln, under their tutelage, was said to have become "a devotee of Italian Opera."[15] Apparently, Herman Grau

TOP LEFT

LEONARD MYERS

Leonard Myers, the young congressman who represented Philadelphia during the Civil War and the early years of Reconstruction, was also a cousin of the American composer and virtuoso pianist Louis Moreau Gottschalk—who was a favorite of Lincoln's and performed for him many times.
Shapell Manuscript Collection

BOTTOM LEFT

LINCOLN TO GIDEON WELLES: "I REALLY WISH THIS DONE," SEPTEMBER 9, 1864

Lincoln, writing on Executive Mansion stationery, seems to have consistently attended to Leonard Myers's requests with a marked interest; here, forwarding a routine appeal for a "Naval School" appointment, the president notes, "let it be done. . . . I really wish this done." Four months later, the warm relationship between the two men was again evident, "I will do it," Lincoln responds to an appeal, "because Mr. Myers requests it."
Shapell Manuscript Collection

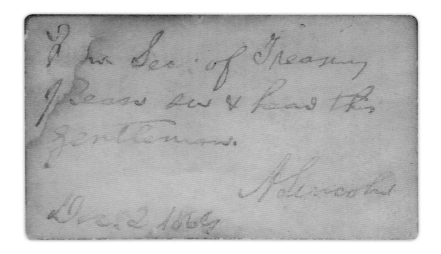

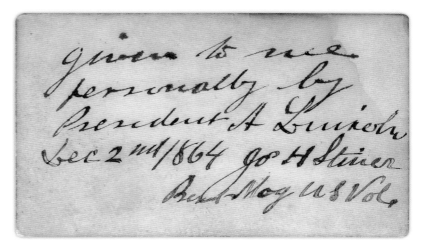

"GIVEN TO ME PERSONALLY BY PRESIDENT A. LINCOLN"

On December 2, 1864, Lincoln writes an introduction for New York Jewish soldier Joseph Stiner.

Shapell Manuscript Collection

sought to open a stage at City Point (now Hopewell) in Central Virginia, where General Ulysses S. Grant had set up field headquarters during the long Petersburg Campaign and some 100,000 troops were encamped. This required General Patrick's permission, and Mary, who felt indebted to Grau and saw "no good reason to refuse this," asked for his "prompt consent."[16]

In another case of presidential courtesy directed at a Jew, on July 15, 1864, Lincoln personally thanked the Philadelphia Jewish leader Lazarus J. Lieberman for sending him an elegant made-to-measure suit. The suit had been prepared to Lincoln's large measurements by one of the city's top clothing contractors, Rockhill & Wilson, which flourished thanks to lucrative government contracts to make military uniforms, and the suit

had then been donated as a benefit for the United States Sanitary Commission to aid sick and wounded soldiers. Funds were contributed at Philadelphia's Great Central Fair to purchase the suit for Lincoln, and the donors asked Lieberman, of Mikveh Israel and himself a significant wholesale and retail clothier, to forward the suit to the president. "I am happy, honored Sir, to be the medium of presentation," Lieberman wrote. Lincoln replied in his own hand, asking both Lieberman and "Messrs. Rockhill & Wilson" to "please accept my thanks."[17]

On May 4, 1864, Lincoln purchased a pair of eyeglasses from the shop of Jewish optician Isaac Heilprin, brother of the outspoken liberal Jewish opponent of slavery, Michael Heilprin. The Washington, D.C., shop, Franklin & Co., was located four blocks from the

"I HAVE RECEIVED MUCH POLITENESS,"
SEPTEMBER 24, 1864

*Mary Lincoln requests that Herman Grau, a
Jewish theater director, be allowed to open a
business at City Point, Virginia.*

Shapell Manuscript Collection

White House. "Lincoln was a regular customer and a warm friendship developed" between optometrist and president.[18]

These and similar interactions between Lincoln and Jews might, on their own, seem trivial. For the most part, they have escaped historians' notice. Aggregated, however, they form a pattern. The president of the United States, they show, insisted on treating Jews on the same basis as everybody else. For Lincoln, we have seen, this was nothing new. It continued the example he had set when he first encountered Jews back in New Salem, Illinois. The fact that his network of friends had, for years, been diverse and pluralistic helped to inoculate him against ethnic and religious hatred; "contact among people of different but salient social groups," modern social psychologists know, "reduces prejudice."[19]

Lincoln's early friendship with Abraham Jonas was a particularly shaping influence. Jonas served for him as an enduring model of what it meant to be a Jew and was someone he knew he could now count upon. This explains why, as president, in December 1862, when testimonies were sent to the Executive Mansion on behalf of an attorney named Thomas Thoroughman of St. Joseph, Missouri, who had been arrested for disloyalty and shipped off to Quincy, Illinois, Lincoln placed the case in the hands of Jonas and his Quincy law partner,

LINCOLN TO LAZARUS J. LIEBERMAN: "PLEASE ACCEPT MY THANKS," JULY 15, 1864

Messrs. Rockhill & Wilson, clothiers, made the president a suit of clothes. To Jewish civic leader L. J. Lieberman went the honor of presenting the gift. Here Lincoln thanks him and all concerned and handwrites not only the letter but the envelope, replete with frank (free postage accomplished with the president's signature).

Shapell Manuscript Collection

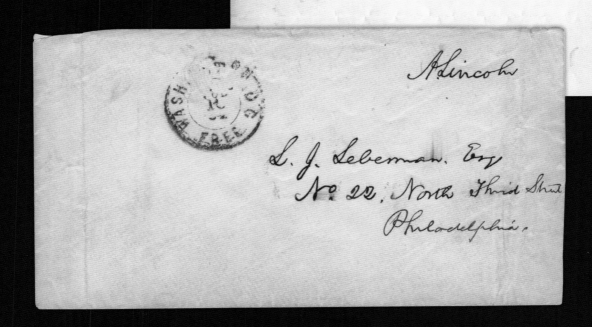

Executive Mansion,

Washington, July 15, 1864.

L. J. Leberman, Esq.

My dear Sir:

The suit of garments sent by you, on behalf of Messrs. Rockhill & Wilson, came duly to hand; and for which you and they will please accept my thanks.

Yours truly
A. Lincoln

A. Lincoln

L. J. Leberman, Esq
No. 22, North Third Street
Philadelphia.

ISAAC HEILPRIN AT FRANKLIN & CO.

This check, from May 4, 1864, is for a pair of eyeglasses that Lincoln purchased from Franklin & Co, the shop of Jewish optician Isaac Heilprin. The glasses cost $2.50 and were for farsightedness.

Christie's Images Limited

Henry Asbury, "both of whom I know to be loyal and sensible men." Upon their recommendation, Thoroughman was paroled and permitted to return home. He rose to become a colonel in the Confederacy.[20]

Jonas had children of his own fighting for the Confederacy. He and his daughter, Annie, nevertheless supported the Union—so strongly that in one speech he declared that there would be no peace until the rebels "give up their leaders to be hung."[21] Such family divisions as plagued the Jonases were common in the Civil War, especially in cases, familiar to many Jews and to Lincoln's own wife, where kinfolk lived on both sides of the sectional divide.[22] The emotional cost nevertheless remained high. When, early in the war, Quincy's Democratic newspaper questioned whether, as the father of rebel soldiers, Jonas should continue as the city's postmaster, his pained response spoke volumes:

> If it be true, as they say, that two of my sons are
> in the rebel army, however grieved I may be at
> the knowledge thereof, all true men who know

me will sympathize with me and admit that I have no control in the matter. My five boys were in the South many years before the rebellion, and when last heard from were all loyal to the Union. That two of them, like hundreds of other loyal men, should have been compelled to join the rebel army I am not prepared to deny, since I have not received a line from any one of them since the commencement of this unhappy war.[23]

Adding to Jonas's pain was the fact that his teenage son, Edward, his "principal assistant" as postmaster, the young man whose ear Lincoln had tickled four years earlier, enlisted on the side of the Union, faced his own brothers on the battlefield, and was taken prisoner at the Battle of Shiloh on April 6, 1862. He was freed in a prisoner exchange and returned home to a celebration six months later.[24]

Nine months after that, on July 9, 1863, Jonas's eldest son, Charles, who lived in New Orleans and fought for the Confederacy, was captured at Fort Hudson, Louisiana. He would remain imprisoned, along with other Confederate officers, at the U.S. Military Prison on Johnson's Island near Sandusky, Ohio, for some twenty months, until exchanged on March 14, 1865.[25]

Meanwhile, perhaps affected by the stresses of war, Abraham Jonas's health suddenly took a turn for the worse. Orville Hickman Browning, on August 10, 1863,

both of whom I know to be loyal and sen-sible friend,

A Lincoln

Dec. 13. 1862.

described his friend's condition as "perilous" ("entirely imbecile—knows nothing—is very feeble and nervous, and seems to be in danger of paralysis or congestion of the brain.")[26] Jonas recovered enough to pen a letter to Lincoln seeking, "in consideration of our old friendship," permission to visit his imprisoned son. "His mother and myself desire to see him," he wrote the president, "not only for the purpose of affording him necessary aid, but also hope to induce him, again to seek protection under the glorious flag of our country." On the same day, Browning wrote to Stanton recommending that the request be granted.[27] Nevertheless, a low-level bureaucrat in the office of the Commissary General of Prisoners rejected the request, and Lincoln may never even have seen it.[28]

By late May 1864, Jonas was unable to travel, for his condition had deteriorated and turned hopeless. His daughter Annie, knowing how much her father still wanted to see his eldest son before he died, wrote to Browning in Washington to see if he might intercede with Lincoln to have Charles released on a temporary furlough. Browning agreed and "went immediately to the President, the Secretary of War, and the Commissary General of Prisoners."[29] Lincoln's handwritten

"BOTH OF WHOM I KNOW TO BE LOYAL AND SENSIBLE MEN."

On December 13, 1862, Lincoln asked that a case of disloyalty be adjudicated by and entrusted entirely to the judgment of Quincy law partners Abraham Jonas and Henry Asbury. Thomas Thoroughman, a lawyer, was wrongly accused of a crime, Jonas and Asbury determined, and so he was exonerated and duly paroled. The condition of the card is noteworthy in that the original, upper portion was unfortunately removed—and presumably lost—many years ago.

Shapell Manuscript Collection

order, a testament to his long friendship with Jonas, followed at once: "Allow Charles H. Jonas, now a prisoner of war at Johnson's Island, a parol[e] of three weeks to visit his dying father."[30] After promising that he would "do no act or thing prejudicial to the Government of the United States," Charles hastened to Quincy. He arrived on June 8, 1864, just in time to be "recognized and welcomed" by his father, who died later that day.[31] Burial followed at the Jewish Sunset Cemetery in Quincy, with an impressive Masonic service. The long friendship between the two Abrahams, which began in the Illinois legislature over twenty years before, and was punctuated by Jonas's pivotal roles in the Quincy

ABOVE

SIDNEY (SAMUEL) ALROY JONAS

Sidney Jonas, the middle son of Abraham and Louisa Jonas, fought for the Confederacy, though it "grieved" Abraham that two of his sons should fight for the rebel army. By the end of the war, five of the Jonas sons had at one time served in the Confederacy. One, Edward, remained entirely loyal to the Union.

Collection of Robert Marcus

OPPOSITE, TOP

ABRAHAM JONAS TO LINCOLN, ". . . IN CONSIDERATION OF OUR OLD FRIENDSHIP," OCTOBER 22, 1863

Three months after Charles Jonas's capture by Union forces, his father, Abraham, appeals to his longtime friend, President Lincoln, to allow him passage to visit his son.

U.S. National Archives & Records Administration

OPPOSITE, BOTTOM

ORDER OF PAROLE OF CHARLES H. JONAS: A FAREWELL GESTURE TO AN OLD FRIEND, JUNE 2, 1864

After hearing of it from Orville Hickman Browning, Lincoln lost no time in accommodating the request from the Jonas family to allow Charles to travel home from a Union prison before his father's death. Had Lincoln not acted in haste to grant the request, Charles would not have made it back in time to see his father alive.

Shapell Manuscript Collection

debates and—after the 1858 lost Senate bid—in Lincoln's successful climb to the presidency, had now come to a close.

On June 10, Browning went at night to the Executive Mansion, to tell Lincoln about the death of their mutual friend and to make a further request, which was granted: "I . . . got his promise to appoint Mrs. Jonas Post Mistress at Quincy in place of her deceased husband." Just two days later, the nomination, rare for its appointment of a woman, was already in motion in the Senate. Louisa Block Jonas held that position from June 28, 1864, to March 10, 1865.[32]

In August 1864, Lincoln received yet one more request from a member of the Jonas family, this one from George Jonas, who had served in the Confederate forces and then moved to New York. Recalling "the friend-ship existing between my Father and yourself, for so long a time," George appealed to Lincoln for a brief furlough prior to entering "regular active service" on behalf of the Union. Whether he received that furlough is not recorded, but that he expected a positive response "as a matter of personal friend-ship to my late Father" testifies both to the enduring memory of that friendship and to the hope that the obligations of friendship would carry over to the next generation.[33]

The death of Abraham Jonas deprived Lincoln of a "most valued friend" and one of his most ardent and able strategists and political campaigners—the man who had suggested, prior to the 1860 election, that the Republican Party focus on attracting political outsiders, such as "freethinking Germans" and "Israelites." Jonas's suggestion had partly been motivated, we have seen, by the widely publicized 1858 Mortara Affair, the heartbreaking story of a young Jewish lad, secretly baptized as an infant, who was forcibly removed from his parental home to be raised within the Catholic Church.[34] In early 1864, less than ten months prior to another presidential election, Lincoln revisited the Mortara Affair—this time through the medium of theater. Twice, on January 25 and 28, he and his wife, Mary, attended

you will lay me under great Obligations,
and increase the devotion I have ever
had for you and the Government—
I remain with great respect
Your truly,
A Jonas

Quincy Ill.
October 22. 1863

His Excellency A Lincoln
President of the United States
My dear Sir

I have taken the liberty of
enclosing the written communication to the
Secretary of War, to you, and ask, in consideration
from your old friendship, and my well known
devotion to the cause of the Union and the
Government—that you will be kind, enough, to direct that my request be granted—

My unfortunate Son, had been
living in the South for many years, previous,
to the commencement of the Rebellion and
had been a zealous Union man until after
Louisiana seceded, but like hundreds of
other young men he was carried away, by the
popular vortex, and to avoid conscription into
the ranks, accepted a position of acting assistant Quarter Master in the rebel Army— His
mother & myself desire to see him not only
for the purpose of affording him necessary aid,
but also to induce him, again to seek protection
under the glorious flag of our Country— by granting
me this, not I think unreasonable request,

Allow Charles H. Jonas
now a prisoner of War at
Johnson's Island, a parol
of three weeks to visit
his dying father, Abra-
ham Jonas, at Quincy, Illinois, June 2, 1864   A Lincoln

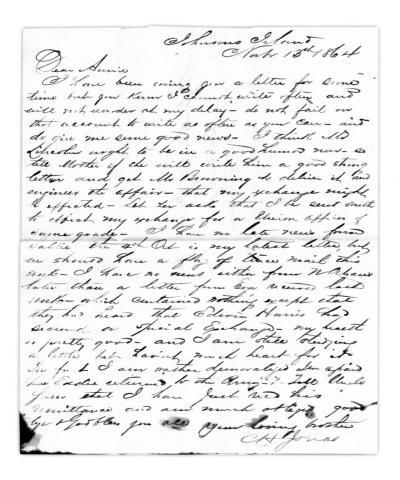

LEFT

CHARLES JONAS TO ANNIE JONAS: AGAIN CALLING UPON "MR. LINCOLN," NOVEMBER 13, 1864

Five months after Lincoln grants Charles Jonas passage to see his dying father in Quincy, Browning is again called upon to intercede on behalf of the prisoner, this time in order to expedite his release. Hoping Lincoln's reelection victory five days earlier might affect his chances, Charles writes to his sister Annie: "I think Mr. Lincoln ought to be in good humor now—so tell Mother if she will write him a good strong letter and get Mr. Browning to deliver it and engineer the affair . . . "

Wells Family

OPPOSITE

JUNE 13, 1864: A FINAL HONOR

Less than a week after the death of Abraham Jonas, Lincoln again lost no time honoring yet another request from Browning, this time to appoint Jonas's widow, Louisa, postmistress at Quincy. This document, signed by Lincoln, also mentions the late Jonas, thus linking the three friends.

U.S. National Archives & Records Administration

productions of *Gamea*, *The Jewish Mother*, an English adaptation of a French play, *La Tireuse de Cartes* (The Fortune-Teller), inspired by the Mortara controversy.[35]

The original text of the play that Lincoln saw was written by Victor Séjour (1817–74).[36] A Creole of New Orleans birth and superior education, he settled in Paris and is today best remembered for producing the earliest known work of fiction by an African American, a short story entitled "The Mulatto," concerning the rejected black son of a white father. In *Gamea*, Séjour returned to questions of identity, but instead of focusing upon blacks and whites, he focused upon Jews and Christians. His Mortara-inspired tale took place in the eighteenth century, and in his telling, the child torn from home and hearth and raised as a Christian was actually a girl. But the central elements of his drama drew upon the real Mortara story—such emotion-laden themes as

child loss (a tragedy all too familiar to the Lincolns), maternal love, nature versus nurture, multiple allegiances, and conflicting loyalties. The "Jewish Mother" in his play, *Gamea*, was a sympathetic character—so much so, that one New York newspaper thought that she illustrated "the vital endurance of Judaism," and a French Catholic paper condemned the playwright for pleading "too eloquently the cause of Jews."[37] The kidnapped daughter—named Silvia in the American version—sought simultaneously to satisfy both sides of a divided house ("You would have me choose to reject my God or to betray my mother! How can I? How?") That theme, echoing Lincoln's famous "House Divided" speech, delivered the same year as the Mortara Affair, surely resonated with Civil War–era audiences.[38]

Séjour's skill as a dramatist and Mary Lincoln's "susceptibility to sentimentality"[39] may suffice to explain

502

To the Senate of the United States.

I nominate *Mrs. Louisa Jonas,*
to be Deputy Postmaster at *Quincy* , in the
county of *Adams* , and State of *Illinois*
in place of *Abraham Jonas, deceased.*

Washington, D. C.,   *Abraham Lincoln*
June 13th, 1864.

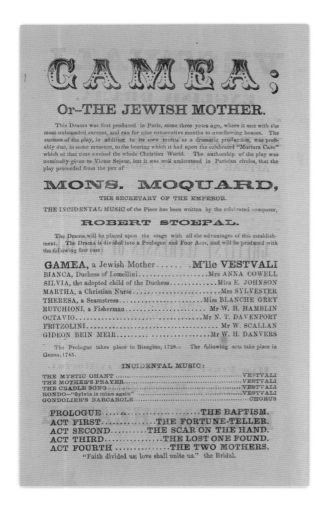

why the Lincolns returned to see *Gamea* just three days after they first saw it. The fact that the play was written by a black writer, drew upon a Jewish historical episode, and reflected on issues deeply relevant to the era suggests that they may have had other motivations for watching it a second time as well.[40]

Although the Mortara Affair would not be an issue in the 1864 election and Abraham Jonas would no longer be offering political advice, Abraham Lincoln

remained interested in the Jewish vote and eager to attract as many Jews as possible into the Republican Party's ranks. In August, just months before the election, the president's prospects seemed grim, and it was widely believed that he would be defeated. "This morning, as for some days past, it seems exceedingly probable that this Administration will not be re-elected," he wrote in a famous memorandum on August 23. His chances of winning New York looked especially bleak.[41] This likely explains Lincoln's renewed association with Issachar Zacharie, who vigorously campaigned for the president's reelection in the summer and fall and worked especially hard to win Jews over to the president's ranks. Jewish stalwarts from Lincoln's 1860 campaign, such as Abram Dittenhoefer and Isidor Bush, likewise campaigned for his reelection.

Zacharie's renewed ardor for Lincoln was, in part, an expression of gratitude for the release of Goodman Mordecai and J. G. Cohen. Indeed, Samuel A. Lewis, the same Jewish communal leader who had worked with Zacharie to free Mordecai, now worked with him again, offering to help fund Jewish political activities on Lincoln's behalf.[42] General Banks, whom Zacharie had once clandestinely supported for president, was no longer a serious contender. The badly bungled Red River campaign, in the spring of 1864, put an end to his presidential hopes.

Zacharie began his efforts on the president's behalf in early August. "Allow me to introduce Dr. Zacharie of New York . . . who has been kind, and, in some instances, useful to me," Lincoln wrote to Treasury Secretary William P. Fessenden.[43] What the particular "kindness" was that Lincoln hoped Fessenden would show Zacharie is not clear, but by mid-September, the president was thanking his chiropodist "for the deep interest you have constantly taken in the Union [Republican] cause."[44] By then, Zacharie was busy electioneering on his behalf. "Work and keep on working," he exhorted, "untill [*sic*] he is Elected."[45] According to historian Bertram W. Korn, Zacharie "conferred with

**DETAIL FROM S. KAUFMANN AND
A. DITTENHOEFER TO LINCOLN, MARCH 2, 1865**

*Two of Lincoln's Jewish presidential electors, one from each
of his campaigns, requested an appointment of a colleague.
Sigismund Kaufmann, who served as elector from New York
in 1860—and Abram Dittenhoefer, also from New York, in
1864—here sign a recommendation to Lincoln of a fellow
New Yorker for a consular appointment; Lincoln respectfully
referred the request to the secretary of state.*

U.S. National Archives & Records Administration

1864 MISSOURI BALLOT

*Electors Abram Dittenhoefer and Isidor Bush helped carry
their states for Lincoln in 1864. New York stayed in the
Republican column, and Missouri, which had gone for
Douglas in 1860, turned.*

Rail Splitter Archives, New York City

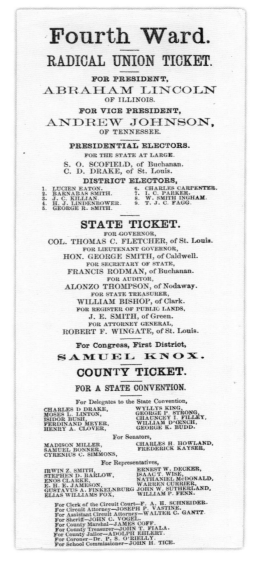

local party officials, took their demands and queries
to the President, and obtained statements from him
designed to quiet the more restless spirits among his
following." He also visited key states on behalf of the
campaign. For Lincoln to succeed, he knew, "We must
carry Pennsylvania & Ohio."[46] In addition, he continued to use his ties to the president to secure favors for
friends. "The personal matter on behalf of your friend,
which you mention," Lincoln cryptically wrote to him

on September 19, "shall be fully and fairly considered
when presented."[47]

Whether Zacharie ever did present the matter is
unclear, but three days later, a young chiropodist and
former business partner of Zacharie's named Samuel M. Barnett, whom he had once described to General Banks as "a student of mine," shot Zacharie in the
face following an argument. "The matter is . . . much
involved in mystery," the *New York Times* reported,

LINCOLN TO ISSACHAR ZACHARIE, SEPTEMBER 19, 1864

"Thank you again for the deep interest you have constantly taken in the Union Cause," Lincoln writes to Zacharie, a message loaded with political innuendo in light of Zacharie's activism in Lincoln's reelection. Notably, Lincoln saved a handwritten draft of the letter for his own papers.

Brown University

adding yet another mysterious layer to a life that was plenty overlaid in mystery already. The wound was initially described as "serious and probably fatal," but in fact Zacharie returned to the campaign trail within weeks. The titillating story of the "affray in Broadway" was quickly submerged.[48]

In the meanwhile, Lincoln was reported to be "tired and downcast," for he expected to lose such critical states as New York, Pennsylvania, New Jersey, and Illinois to his Democratic opponent, George B. McClellan, on November 8. Anticipating a close election, he knew that every vote would count.[49] That probably explains why, on October 23, he met with "certain gentlemen of

the Hebrew faith" to discuss the Jewish vote—possibly the first time that any president had ever formally discussed that subject in the Executive Mansion. Rumors circulated, abetted by the voluble Zacharie, that the "gentlemen" pledged to deliver New York's Jewish vote in return for suitable "contributions." John Hay, writing for the president, issued a categorical denial of that claim: "No pledge of the Jewish vote was made by these gentlemen and no inducements or promises were extended to them by the President." Behind the scenes, however, the wealthy Samuel A. Lewis advised Lincoln to direct any "Jewish committees" seeking political funds straight to him: "I will furnish them such

ISSACHAR ZACHARIE TO LINCOLN, NOVEMBER 3, 1864: ZACHARIE ROUNDS UP HIS FELLOW ISRAELITES

Five days before the election, Zacharie promises Lincoln good news.

Courtesy of the Library of Congress

amounts as we see can be used to advantage." He promised that "nothing shall be wanting on the part of your friends here towards carrying the Union [Republican] Cause."[50] Myer Isaacs, the editor of the *Jewish Messenger* and secretary of the Board of Delegates of American Israelites, likewise wrote to the president concerning the Jewish vote. "The Israelites are not, as a body, distinctively Union or democratic in their politics," he piously insisted; "the Jews, as a body, have no politics." He nevertheless assured Lincoln that there were many Jews—himself included—who warmly supported the Republican Party. What he and other Jewish leaders of the day really feared was public discussion of the Jewish vote, lest that foment suspicion and hatred. So long as discussions were conducted discreetly, behind closed doors, they were fine.[51]

Zacharie, as an ex-spy, had lots of experience working behind closed doors. On November 3, just five days before the election, he felt confident enough to reassure the president that the Jewish vote would swing his way: "As regards the Isr[a]elites—with but few Exceptions, they will vote for you. I understand them well, and have taken the precaution to see that they do as they have promised. I have secured good and trustworthy men to attend on them on Election Day. My men have been all the week seeing that their masses are properly Registered so that all will go right on the 8."[52] Whether the Israelites actually voted en masse for Lincoln on November 8 cannot be known, but a string of much-needed Union victories on the battlefield, divisions within the Democratic Party, and an effective Republican slogan ("Don't change horses in the middle of a stream") turned the tide decisively in Lincoln's favor. He won by more than 400,000 votes and carried all but three states.[53]

Zacharie had anticipated Lincoln's victory and even told the president how to thank him—by saying "Well done my good and faithfull [sic] servant."[54] But as Lincoln knew, he also wanted a favor that the president had promised to grant: a pass to visit his father and family in Savannah as soon as that city was recaptured. No sooner had General Sherman presented Savannah to Lincoln as a "Christmas present" than Zacharie reminded him of that promise in a cleverly worded telegram: "Allow me to congratulate you on the fall of Savannah my family are crazy with joy."[55] Lincoln responded within twenty-four hours, precisely as Zacharie had hoped: with a travel pass and a note addressed to Sherman, introducing "Dr. I. Zacharie, of New York who visits his Father and friends at Savannah, where the Dr. is well acquainted, and where very likely he could be of aid to you in some matters. He is entirely loyal and devoted to the Union cause."[56] On the same day, Lincoln also provided a pass for Zacharie's nephew, Jacob G. Cohen, whom he had freed from prison nine months earlier but who had not previously been able to return home to his wife and four-year-old son in Savannah.[57] Zacharie, overjoyed that the two could travel together, sent Lincoln a gift of bananas and a fervent "God Bless You." He then booked passage to Savannah.[58]

But Zacharie only got as far as Hilton Head, South Carolina, before he was detained. According to an eyewitness, Major John Chipman Gray, judge advocate for the Department of the South, Zacharie, when he arrived in Hilton Head, noticed the boat of Secretary of War Edwin Stanton, who was himself on his way to Savannah to meet with General Sherman. He "very foolishly went on Stanton's boat and spoke to him; whereupon the Secretary ordered him into close confinement where he still is."[59] Zacharie had known Stanton in Washington and, we have seen, had won his support back when he sought to head up a "chiropody corps" for the army. Why the secretary of war now turned and placed him under house arrest, notwithstanding the pass he had received from Lincoln and the introduction he held to General Sherman, is yet another Zacharie-related mystery. Gray, who would later serve as professor of law at Harvard, described the confinement as "rather an arbitrary proceeding," and explained it on the basis of Zacharie's religion, which he personally disdained ("this man . . . is in appearance the lowest and vulgarest of Jew pedlars . . . an odious creature"). He also confided that Stanton, who was ill, had been "very bearish and boorish, as his nature."[60] Did the imperious secretary of war, known for making arbitrary arrests, consider Zacharie's friendship with Lincoln a threat to his authority and mission?[61] Did he worry, based on earlier reports from New Orleans, that Zacharie was dishonest and corrupt?[62] Whatever the case, it required renewed intervention from the president to get Zacharie to Savannah.

So, on January 25, Lincoln sent Stanton a message that began with the eye-catching words, "About Jews."[63] Concerning Zacharie, Lincoln delivered a one sentence order crafted in precise legal language that left no doubt as to his intentions: "I wish you would give Dr. Zacharie a pass to go to Savannah, remain a week and return, bringing with him, if he wishes, his father and sisters or any of them." Then, as if to mollify Stanton, he appended two sentences in highly personal terms, justifying his order: "This will spare me trouble and oblige me. I promised him long ago that he should be allowed this whenever Savannah should fall into our hands."[64] That very day, Stanton delivered a pass made out in Zacharie's name to Lincoln's secretary, John G. Nicolay ("presuming that you know where to send it").[65] Zacharie traveled to Savannah with that pass and returned to New York, accompanied by his nephew, on February 22.[66] Lincoln would not hear from him again.

Continuing his memo "about Jews," Lincoln proceeded to the case of Leopold Blumenberg, whom the War Department had dismissed as provost marshal for the 3rd District of Maryland.[67] A native of Frankfurt-on-the-Oder, Blumenberg fought and was decorated in the Danish-Prussian War of 1848 and immigrated to the United States in 1854. Settling in Baltimore, he opposed slavery, came under the influence of Rabbi David Einhorn, and joined the Republican Party. Curiously, his brother, Rudolph Blumenberg, served as a bondsman for illegal slave traders, and was imprisoned for perjury. Lincoln would pardon him, in 1863, after he provided valuable information concerning the slave trade to federal officials.[68] Following the attack on Fort Sumter, Leopold Blumenberg helped to organize a regiment of volunteers, was appointed major, and served as a commanding officer.

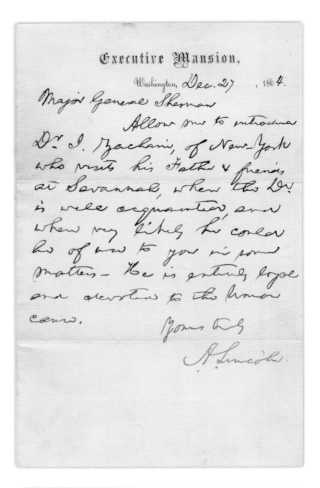

TOP RIGHT

LINCOLN TO WILLIAM T. SHERMAN: ZACHARIE IS "ENTIRELY LOYAL AND DEVOTED TO THE CAUSE," DECEMBER 27, 1864

Whether Lincoln knew of Zacharie's true intentions in his travel to Savannah with nephew J. G. Cohen is not known. We know, however, that Zacharie was not just visiting his father; in fact, he was mysteriously arrested after trespassing onto Stanton's boat, for reasons unclear.

John Hay Library, Brown University Library

CENTER RIGHT

DECEMBER 27, 1864, PASS FOR J. G. COHEN

This pass to Savannah, Georgia was written by Lincoln on behalf of Zacharie's nephew, who would accompany his uncle on a mysterious trip to the South.

Shapell Manuscript Collection

BOTTOM RIGHT

DECEMBER 27, 1864, PASS FOR ISSACHAR ZACHARIE

Lincoln's pass for Zacharie to travel to Savannah, dated the same day as that for his nephew.

John Hay Library, Brown University Library

Executive Mansion
Washington Jan, 25. 1865

Hon. Secretary of War.
      My dear Sir.

      About Jews, I wish you would
give Dr. Zacharie a pass to go to Savannah, remain a
week and return, bringing with him, if he wishes,
his father and sisters or any of them. This will
spare me trouble and oblige me. I promised him
long ago that he should be allowed this whenever
Savannah should fall into our hands.

Blumenberg, at Baltimore, I think he should
have a hearing. He has suffered for us & served
us well. had the rope around his neck for
being our friend. raised troops. fought, and been
wounded. He should not be dismissed in a
way that disgraces and ruins him without a
hearing.

                              Yours truly,
                              A Lincoln

*"About Jews. I wish you would give
Dr. Zacharie a pass to go to Savannah…"*

He distinguished himself for heroism in the 1862 Battle of Antietam, the bloodiest single-day battle in American history, and sustained a severe wound. In recognition of what he had done, Lincoln, in May 1863, appointed him provost marshal (head of the military police) in Maryland's 3rd District, headquartered in Baltimore. There, according to one biographer, "the stringency with which he executed the conscription laws . . . incurred him the animosity of many citizens."[69] That explains his dismissal on January 17, 1865. Among other things, he was charged with torture: "gag[g]ing men to make them confess they were deserters."[70] Lincoln, in his memo, nevertheless proved sympathetic. "I think he should have a hearing," he wrote. "He has suffered for us & served us well. . . . He should not be dismissed in a way that disgraces and ruins him without a hearing."[71] Though Stanton demurred ("he was removed for cause of which a statement will be furnished you"[72]), Lincoln appointed Blumenberg to a new patronage position, superintendent of the warehouses at the Baltimore customhouse.[73]

Why Lincoln titled his memo concerning Zacharie and Blumenberg "About Jews" remains a riddle. Maybe, as some suggest, Lincoln was responding to a document, now lost, that was similarly titled. Maybe, as others insist, this was his shorthand way of dismissing the anti-Jewish prejudice that he knew to exist even at high levels of government. Or maybe, with his exquisite sense of language and irony, he marveled at the fact that on a single day and in a single memo, he was dealing with two personnel matters involving Jews, though Jews formed but a tiny minority at that time (perhaps one-half of one percent of the entire U.S. population). Whatever the case, the significance of the memo lies less in the phrase "About Jews" than in Lincoln's double display of generosity toward Jews. In an era when anti-Semitism was commonplace, he openly sided with Zacharie and Blumenberg, against the advice of his secretary of war.[74]

As Lincoln's first term wound down, three Jews found themselves guests at a reception held on Saturday afternoon, February 11, 1865, in the drawing room

LEFT

LEOPOLD BLUMENBERG

Born in Prussia, Leopold immigrated to the United States in 1854. At the outbreak of the Civil War, he enlisted in the Union army and rose to lead a regiment as a colonel at Antietam. Though ruling with stringency, Leopold continued to rise in the ranks and, following Lincoln's involvement in his case, was later brevetted brigadier general by President Andrew Johnson.

The Jewish Museum of Maryland

BELOW

THE PARDON OF RUDOLPH BLUMENBERG, JULY 25, 1863

Rudolph Blumenberg, in contrast to his brother Leopold, was an unsavory bondsman involved in the slave trade. However, after he provided valuable information concerning the slave trade to federal officials, the district attorney petitioned for Blumenberg's pardon, which Lincoln granted on July 24, 1863: "Make out and send a pardon in this case."

Shapell Manuscript Collection

I hereby authorize and direct the Secretary of State to affix the seal of the United States to a Warrant for the pardon of ⸺ Rudolf Blumenberg, ⸺ ⸺ dated this day, and signed by me: and for so doing this shall be his warrant

Abraham Lincoln

Washington, 25th July, 1863.

of the Executive Mansion, hosted by the first lady, with the president assisting.[75] One guest was the Washington printer and bookstore owner Adolphus S. Solomons, who had served as one of the "managers" of Lincoln's inaugural ball four years earlier and had business dealings with the government. Mrs. Lincoln made occasional purchases from him. The second guest was Solomons' young daughter, Zillah. The president, who loved children, held a brief conversation with her. The third guest was Myer S. Isaacs, editor of the *Jewish Messenger* and secretary of the Board of Delegates of American Israelites, who just a few weeks earlier had written to Lincoln concerning the Jewish vote. The fact that these three committed and strongly identifying Jews were "presented and cordially greeted" by the Lincolns was no small matter. Just a few weeks earlier, the wife of General John G. Foster, who commanded the Department of the South, had "absolutely refused to sit at the same table" as Issachar Zacharie, because he was a Jew.[76] By contrast, Mrs. Lincoln was "kindly and gracious in her welcome, having a pleasant word and a pleasant smile," according to Isaacs. Given the president's "regard for the Jews," his family had long treated them as equals.

At the reception, Isaacs, like Edward Rosewater at the Lincolns' New Year's gathering back in 1863, paid particular attention to how the president looked. The war's progress, he and others believed, could be tracked upon the countenance of Lincoln's face. "His countenance [is] strongly expressive of good nature as well as of resolution," Isaacs wrote, "an index of his heart." In fact, Lincoln knew by then that the war was approaching its end. Charleston, South Carolina, surrendered to Union forces on the very day that the reception took place.

What concerned Isaacs as he looked at the president's face was the place of Jews in post–Civil War America. Indeed, he had traveled to Washington expressly to oppose "the submission to Congress of proposed amendments to the Constitution of the United States recognizing Christianity as the religion of the land." He believed that Jews needed to "watch with extreme jealousy and

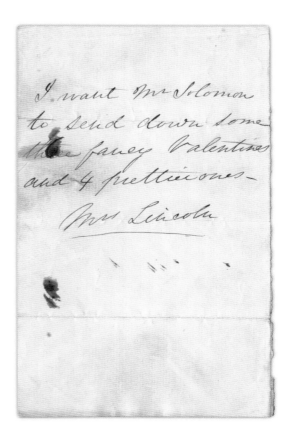

MARY'S JEWISH VALENTINE

On her way to amassing a personal debt of, in today's money, a quarter of a million dollars—spent on carpets, upholstery, drapes, furniture, wallpaper, china, silver, glassware, gowns, hats, shawls, jewelry, and books—Mary Lincoln paused to order some valentines from the local Jewish-owned stationery, printing, and publishing firm of Philp & Solomons.

Shapell Manuscript Collection

anxiety any attempt to abridge their liberties." Evangelical attempts to write Christianity into the Constitution evoked his darkest fears.[77]

Lincoln had so far proved a steadfast defender of Jewish rights, befriending some Jews, appointing others to significant posts, and tailoring his vocabulary ("this nation, under God") so as to exclude none of them. Standing with Adolphus S. Solomons and Zillah in the presidential drawing room must have given Isaacs hope that the president's second term would see more of the same.

CHAPTER SEVEN

TO SEE JERUSALEM
BEFORE HE DIED

1865

Two months prior to the start of his second term, on January 7, 1865, Lincoln, Mary, and their son, Tad, went to the theater. The Lincolns were frequent theatergoers. This was the seventeenth time in two years that they were attending a performance at Grover's Theater, also known as the New National Theater. Most often, they attended performances of Shakespeare, and on at least three occasions the performances were of Jewish-themed plays. For example, one month following their multiple viewings of *Gamea, or The Jewish Mother*, the Lincolns, on February 26, 1864, watched *The Merchant of Venice*, starring Edwin Booth as Shylock. This time, however, they attended a new play featuring the tall, black-eyed

actress Avonia Jones.[1] Entitled *Leah, the Forsaken*, the play was an adaptation by a young American playwright named Augustin Daly of the German-Jewish writer Salomon Hermann Mosenthal's play *Deborah*. Its subject was the persecution of Jews in an eighteenth-century Austrian village.

As the Lincolns watched, the play's protagonist, Leah, the daughter of a rabbi, fell in love with Rudolf, the son of the village's old Christian magistrate. Peasants, their passions whipped up by a Jewish apostate named Nathan, shouted vile accusations at the Jews: they "poison our wells and fountains"; they "devour little children as a sacrifice" on Passover; they haunt Austria's villages "to beg, to steal, or to wheedle money from the unsuspecting—it is part of their faith"; they are a "soulless and a grasping race, who value more the chink of gold than all the virtues of humanity strung together."[2] Notwithstanding these prejudices, Leah and Rudolf pledged themselves to one another and made plans "to leave this old Mizriam [Egypt] and wander through the desert into the promised land" of America, "to plough the soil and on it rear the altar of a new religion that

OPPOSITE

A CALCULATED SHOT

Halfway into the third act and timing his actions with the play's punch line so that the audience's laughter would mute the sound of the shot, John Wilkes Booth stepped out from behind a peephole, with gun drawn.

George Eastman House

SCENE FROM THE DRAMA OF "LEAH," AT THE NEW ADELPHI THEATRE; LEAH CURSING THE LORRENZ FAMILY.—(LEAH.—*Miss Bateman married Dr. Crowe.*

LEAH, THE FORSAKEN

Containing many offensive lines of dialogue, Leah, The Forsaken *may have reminded Lincoln of the anti-Semitic remarks of Benjamin Butler and other Civil War generals.*
National Portrait Gallery, London

shall teach love and brotherhood to all men."[3] Through a cruel ruse, Nathan thwarted these happy plans, misleading Rudolf into believing that Leah valued money more than his love. So, breaking off with Leah, Rudolf married a Christian named Madalena. But on the very eve of that marriage he realized his error and begged forgiveness. Leah refused and cursed him, but Rudolf, in contrition, became an advocate for the Jews and named his own daughter Leah. He even visited the emperor to plead for the right of Jews to remain in the village. The emperor in the play must have seemed familiar to Lincoln: he was "a plainly-dressed mild-looking man" whose doors were "wide open, everybody goes to him, and everybody finds place in his turn."[4] The fanciful emperor, indeed, smilingly hearkened to Rudolf's plea, declaring, "Let them stay; the laws of exile are of ancient date; I will make a new law, I myself am anxious that all my subjects should be equal, for, Jew or Christian, they all belong to me."[5] So, in the end, Rudolf and Leah reconciled, Nathan was unmasked as a scheming apostate, and Leah resolved to leave with her people for America, "the far-off—the promised land."[6]

Leah, the Forsaken, like Harriet Beecher Stowe's great novel, *Uncle Tom's Cabin,* appealed to emotion and sentiment to combat prejudice. It depicted raw anti-Semitism

and hatred in the hope that viewers would sympathize with Leah and recoil from her oppressors. "It is a true picture—every line and point of it limned to the life," the *Jewish Messenger*'s theater critic cheered. He hoped that the play would help to dispel "unfounded prejudice" and lead theatergoers "to cherish kindlier sentiments towards a people who, for no fault of theirs, have been driven about from post to pillar, scarcely anywhere befriended, only recently permitted to enjoy an equal footing with other men."[7]

George William Curtis, the antislavery editor of *Harper's Weekly,* insisted that *Leah* also carried a more universal message, applicable to the Civil War. This, indeed, may have been what inspired the Lincolns to see the play with Tad. To Curtis, who was the son-in-law of abolitionist Francis Shaw, the anti-Jewish rabble-rousers of Austria had their counterparts in the Union and the Confederacy: those who "appeal to the popular prejudice against an outcast race." If in Europe the question was whether a Jew might be equal to a Christian, in America it was "is a negro equal to a white man?" *Leah* thus served as an object lesson for Americans: "Upon this hatred of race," according to Curtis, reactionaries sought to gain power "in order to abase, divide, and destroy this nation." "Go and see Leah," he

"Both parties deprecated war; but one of them would _make_ war rather than let the nation survive; and the other would _accept_ war, rather than let it perish. And the war came."

Abraham Lincoln.

ABOVE

"AND THE WAR CAME," MARCH 1865

In this exceedingly rare handwritten quotation from Lincoln's second inaugural, Lincoln declares: "Both parties deprecated war but one of them would make war, rather than let the nation survive, and the other would accept war rather than let it perish. And the war came."

Shapell Legacy Partnership

RIGHT

ADMISSION TICKET TO LINCOLN'S SECOND INAUGURAL

With this card, the family of Joseph A. Wright, then the American ambassador to Prussia, is invited to Lincoln's second inaugural. There he would hear one of the greatest addresses in presidential history.

Shapell Manuscript Collection

1865.

Inauguration Day,

MARCH 4.

Admit _family of Hon. Mr. Wright_

Serg't-at-arms, U. S. S.

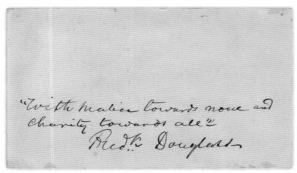

"With Malice towards none and Charity towards all"
Fredk Douglass

charged his readers, "and have the lesson [it teaches] burned in upon your mind, which may help to save the national life and honor."[8]

On March 4, at his second inaugural, Lincoln offered his own lesson concerning the Civil War and its meaning. The date that year happened to coincide with the sixth of the Hebrew month of Adar, the day, according to ancient Jewish tradition, when Moses completed his farewell address to the Jewish people and learned that his own death was imminent.[9] The weather in Washington on Inauguration Day was awful: it had, seemingly, been raining for weeks. Riding down Pennsylvania Avenue to the Capitol,

BOOTH STALKS LINCOLN

Gazing down on Lincoln during the second inaugural, unmoved, was the actor John Wilkes Booth. Six weeks later, he would kill the president.
Courtesy of the Library of Congress

FREDERICK DOUGLASS ON LINCOLN'S FAMOUS INAUGURAL CONCLUSION

Also listening in the crowd at Lincoln's second inaugural was Frederick Douglass, born into slavery but now the most famous free black man in America. Later, at the White House inaugural reception, policemen refused to admit a person of color. Lincoln got word of the outrage and not only ordered Douglass admitted but greeted him warmly and asked in a loud voice about his inaugural address. "There is no man in the country," Lincoln added, "whose opinion I value more."
Shapell Manuscript Collection

LINCOLN'S HISTORIC UTTERANCE FROM THE CONCLUSION OF HIS SECOND INAUGURAL ADDRESS, MARCH 4, 1865

These seventy-five words from the famous conclusion of Lincoln's second inaugural address, written out by Lincoln in an album for a friend, are, in American memory, indelible, and clearly have their roots in the Old Testament's espousal of charity and compassion for the suffering of those swept up in the plague of war.
Shapell Legacy Partnership

"With malice toward none; with
charity for all; with firmness in
the right, as God gives us to see
the right, let us strive on to fin=
ish the work we are in; to bind
up the nations wounds; to care
for him who shall have borne
the battle, and for his widow
and his orphan — to do all
which may achieve and cherish
a just, and a lasting peace am=
ong ourselves, and with all na.
tions"

Abraham Lincoln.

Lincoln's carriage churned through some ten inches of mud and standing water. A crowd, waiting for hours at the Capitol, now stood sodden, deep in sludge.[10] Above the inaugural platform, dark clouds scudded across the horizon. At noontime, Andrew Johnson, visibly intoxicated, was sworn in as vice president of the United States, ranting somewhat incoherently about his plebian origins. But as President Lincoln stood to take the oath of office, the sun suddenly burst through the clouds and flooded the scene. Lincoln considered the sunshine at his second inaugural a "happy omen," recalling the words on the eve of the 1860 election: "Just now, the skies look bright." Sadly, the "clouds" would rise again and plunge the nation into mourning the following month.

Lincoln's second inaugural address, delivered from a makeshift platform at the east front of the Capitol, was, as Frederick Douglass understood at the time, "a sacred effort." According to one scholar's calculations, it "mentioned God fourteen times, quoted the Bible four times, and invoked prayer three times"—this in a mere 700 words.[11] No previous inaugural address had ever been so overtly religious. Nevertheless, the second inaugural, unlike Lincoln's first, made no direct reference to Christianity. Instead, Lincoln posed timeless religious questions concerning God's actions and ultimate purposes. He explored the meaning of war, the wages of sin, the mystery of fraternal hatred ("both read the same Bible and pray to the same God, and each invokes His aid against the other"), and, invoking Psalm 19 ("the judgments of the Lord are true and righteous altogether"), the inscrutability of Divine judgment. His peroration—"With malice toward none, with charity for all, with firmness in the right as God gives us to see the right, let us strive on to finish the work we are in" and, borrowing from Exodus 22, from Deuteronomy 14 and 16, from Jeremiah 7, and from Isaiah 1, calling for the nation "to care for him who shall have borne the battle, and for his widow and his orphan"—set the stage for postwar reconstruction and appealed to values cherished by Jews and Christians alike: hope, charity, reconciliation, and peace.[12]

Lincoln emphasized in his second inaugural that slavery, and not secession, was the principal cause of the Civil War. To his mind, the war's terrible toll represented divine punishment upon both sides for the crime of slavery. Much as he prayed for the war to end, he was prepared for it to continue "until all the wealth piled by the bond-man's two hundred and fifty years of unrequited toil shall be sunk, and until every drop of blood drawn with the lash, shall be paid by another drawn with the sword."[13] This sharp focus upon slavery as the cause of the war distinguished Lincoln from members of the National Reform Association and other Christians who blamed the war on the omission of God and of Christianity from the text of the Constitution. Their goal was "to secure such an amendment of the Constitution of the United States as will declare the nation's allegiance to Jesus Christ and its acceptance of the moral laws of the Christian religion, and to indicate that this is a Christian nation, and place all the Christian laws, institutions and usages of our government on an undeniable legal basis in the fundamental law of the land." Lincoln was polite to the National Reform Association's leaders when he met with them, but much to the relief of Jews like Myer Isaacs, he did nothing to advance their goals.[14] Instead, as his inaugural address

OPPOSITE

LINCOLN TO AMANDA H. HALL: "FONDLY DO WE HOPE, FERVENTLY DO WE PRAY . . . ," MARCH 20, 1865

In the most overtly religious portion of the second inaugural address, here from a letter written at the request of a supporter, Lincoln ruminates upon the divine will—and concludes, in an attempt to come to grips with four years of the terrible slaughter with a verse from Psalm 19: "The judgments of the Lord are true, and righteous altogether." In evidence of his wide grasp of the Bible, Lincoln here takes an obscure half verse from Psalms and makes it the lead-in to one of his greatest utterances: "With malice toward none, with charity for all . . . "

Abraham Lincoln Presidential Library & Museum

Executive Mansion,

Washington, March 20. , 1865.

Mrs Amanda H. Hall

Madam

Induced by a letter of yours to your brother, and shown me by him, I send you what follows below.

Respectfully

A. Lincoln

"Fondly do we hope— fervently do we pray— that this mighty scourge of war may speedily pass away. Yet, if God wills, that it continue until all the wealth piled by the bondman's two hundred and fifty years of unrequited toil shall be sunk, and until every drop of blood drawn with the lash shall be paid by another drawn with the sword, as was said three thousand years ago, so still it must be said; "The judgments of the Lord are true, and righteous altogether".

Abraham Lincoln

"The judgments of the Lord are
true, and righteous altogether"
Psalm 19

THE PURPOSES OF THE ALMIGHTY

LINCOLN'S OWN COMMENTARY on his second inaugural was contained in a letter to Thurlow Weed of New York, a journalist and political advisor. Weed had been critical of the Emancipation Proclamation. Still, he supported Lincoln's reelection and had written to compliment him on his address.

"Every one likes a compliment," Lincoln wrote in his response, dated March 15, 1865, ten days after his inauguration. "Thank you for yours . . . on the recent Inaugural Address. . . . Men are not flattered by being shown that there has been a difference of purpose between the Almighty and them. To deny it, however, in this case, is to deny that there is a God governing the world. It is a truth which I thought needed to be told."

THE LAST PAGE OF LINCOLN'S LETTER TO ALBERT HODGES, APRIL 4, 1864

Courtesy of the Library of Congress

Lincoln, who had hoped for a quick and victorious end to the war that the South had started, and who consistently believed that the South was morally wrong to have so long sustained an economy supported by the enslavement of human beings, nonetheless struggled with the question of why God was hesitating for years in bringing victory to the Union.

By 1864, the answer began to dawn on him. Writing to publisher Albert Hodges on April 4, he declared: "I claim not to have controlled events, but confess plainly that events have controlled me." God now willed, he wrote, the removal of a great wrong—slavery—"and wills also that we of the North as well as you of the South, shall pay fairly for our complicity in that wrong . . ."

With the North fighting the battle against slavery and secession so fervently, how, the question arises, could Lincoln have dared to suggest its complicity? Both sides, he believed, were accountable to God for their actions and guilty of the cruel offense that caused the war—slavery. But what "difference of purpose" could there possibly be between the Almighty and the North? Had not the North chosen to ignore the slave markets in Washington in the years prior to the war? Or Congress's 1854 endorsement of the extension of slavery with the passage of the Kansas-Nebraska Act? The North was further implicated in its role in the Dred Scott decision of 1857, when the Supreme Court ruled that blacks were so inferior that they had no rights that the white man was bound to respect (before the Civil War, killing a slave was not considered murder but rather destruction of property). The Fugitive Slave Law, the New York draft riots, and the Constitution itself, in which slavery was legally protected and untouchable until Lincoln alone changed its essence, were all evidence to him of the North's undeniable collusion in the sins against humanity.

Toward the end of the war, both the North and the South, each praying to God to invoke his wrath upon the other, were not able to understand what Lincoln had come to believe: That the purpose of the war was, in essence, retribution. "The Almighty has his own purposes," Lincoln wrote toward

Executive Mansion,

Washington, March 15, 1865

Thurlow Weed, Esq,

My dear Sir.

Every one likes a compliment, Thank you for yours on my little notification speech, and on the recent Inaugeral Address, I expect the latter to wear as well as— perhaps better than— anything I have produced; but I believe it is not immediately popular. Men are not flattered by being shown that there has been a difference of purpose between the Almighty and them, To deny it, however, in this case, is to deny that there is a God governing the world, It is a truth which I thought needed to be told; and, as whatever of humiliation there is in it, falls most directly on myself, I thought others might afford for one to tell it,

Yours truly
A. Lincoln.

LINCOLN TO THURLOW WEED, MARCH 15, 1865

Shapell Legacy Partnership

the end of his speech. Mentioning God no fewer than fourteen times, he goes on to say: "If God wills that it [the war] continue, until all the wealth piled by the bondman's two hundred and fifty years of unrequited toil shall be sunk, and until every drop of blood drawn with the lash, shall be paid by another drawn with the sword. . . ."

Lincoln then goes on to declare that God has his own reasons—and the final word—for allowing the slaughter of more than 600,000, summarized in ten simple, and perhaps cleansing, words, taken from an obscure half verse in Psalms: "The judgments of the Lord are true and righteous altogether."

THE FALL OF RICHMOND

On April 2, 1865, Richmond was on fire, falling into Union hands. On the very next day, Lincoln would tell Stanton of his intention to visit the fallen city.

Shapell Manuscript Collection

made clear, he focused on slavery and reconstruction, and looked ahead to "a just and a lasting peace."

The Jewish lawyer and B'nai B'rith leader Simon Wolf thought that Lincoln's inaugural address "evinced more of the priest than the statesman."[15] Overall, responses to the second inaugural were decidedly mixed. Lincoln himself, however, was pleased with his performance. He correctly foretold that the address would "wear as well as—perhaps better than—anything I have produced." While he recognized that his words were "not immediately popular," he attributed this to the fact that "men are not flattered by being shown that there has been a difference of purpose between the Almighty and them." "It is a truth," he explained, "which I thought needed to be told."[16]

Lincoln visited the front soon after his inauguration and reassured General Grant that "never for a moment" had he doubted the final success of the Union's cause. On April 3, at Grant's invitation and over the objections of Secretary of War Stanton ("Consider whether you ought to expose the nation to the Consequence of any disaster to yourself"), he came to inspect the just-fallen city of Petersburg, Virginia. He urged, as he had several times before, that vanquished rebels be treated leniently. On his return, he thanked Stanton

for worrying about him. "I will take care of myself," he promised.[17]

The very next day, Union troops entered Richmond. "Thank God that I have lived to see this!" Lincoln declared upon hearing the exciting news.[18] Along with his son, Tad, a bodyguard, and some military men, he set sail for Richmond that morning. Crowds of newly freed blacks and poor whites surrounded Lincoln, shouting, singing, dancing; some even knelt before him. "Don't kneel to me," he gently upbraided them. "That is not right. You must kneel to God only, and thank him for the liberty you will hereafter enjoy." When "an old negro" blessed Lincoln with a paraphrase of the priestly blessing "May the good Lord bless and keep you safe," (Numbers 6:24),

OPPOSITE

LINCOLN TO EDWIN STANTON: ". . . NOW THAT RICHMOND IS IN OUR HANDS," APRIL 3, 1865

By April 3, 1865, the carnage was almost over, and Lincoln, barely able to contain himself, hurried to the front, waiting for Richmond, the Confederate capital, to fall. Stanton, appalled at the danger, warned Lincoln not to "expose the nation to the Consequence of any disaster" that could easily befall him. Lincoln replied here, reassuringly, with what in little more than a week would become sad irony: "I will take care of myself."

Shapell Legacy Partnership

City Point, April 3. 5. P.m. 1865

Hon. Sec. of War
        Washington. D.C.

        Yours received. Thanks for your
caution; but I have already been to Petersburg, stained
with Gen. Grant an hour & a half and returned
here. It is certain now that Richmond is in our
hands, and I think I will go there to-morrow.
I will take care of myself.

                                A Lincoln

*"It is certain now that Richmond is in
our hands . . . I will take care of myself."*

LINCOLN AND SON AT THE FALL OF RICHMOND

Lincoln arrives in Richmond and tours the fallen city.

Gilder Lehrman Institute

the president raised his hat in gratitude and bowed. In so doing, one observer recounted, he "upset the forms, laws, customs and ceremonies of centuries."[19] Many old-time white residents, of course, were heartbroken at what they saw going on around them. Emma Mordecai, scion of a large slave-holding Jewish family, saw black Union troops guarding the roads and declared that they were "all as ill-bred as old Lincoln himself."[20]

The general in charge of those black troops and now of all of Richmond, Godfrey Weitzel, soon dispatched cavalry to accompany Lincoln to the executive residence of Jefferson Davis. Along the way, he passed the city's first synagogue, Kahal Kadosh Beth Shalome, established in 1790. Arriving at the "Confederate White House," the president sat in Jefferson Davis's chair and asked for a glass of water. Later, he toured the city, reassuring blacks that they were free. That evening, on the USS *Malvern*, Lincoln met with the only high-ranking Confederate to remain in the capital: John A. Campbell, assistant secretary of war for the Confederacy and a former U.S. Supreme Court associate justice. Lincoln's goal was to pacify the city and return Virginia to the Union. He therefore proposed

to Campbell that the two of them sit down with other moderate state leaders the next morning to consider how best to proceed.

Only one Southern leader joined Campbell for that meeting: Gustavus Adolphus Myers (1801–69), the city's most prominent Jew and a noted attorney and businessman. A third-generation American and a descendant of one of the city's oldest and wealthiest Jewish families, Myers was a close friend of the Jewish Confederate statesman and secretary of state, Judah P. Benjamin; a former president of the city council; a founder of the Virginia Historical Society; a prominent Mason; a leader in his synagogue; and the proud husband of Anne, the Episcopalian daughter of Virginia's former governor William Branch Giles.[21] Although he did not know it, Myers had also played a symbolic role in the entry of Union troops into Richmond. His mulatto grandson, William Gill Forrester, scion of Myers's youthful relationship with a free woman of color named Nelly Forrester, had raised the American flag at the Virginia capitol when Union soldiers recaptured it; Forrester had secretly saved and hidden that flag four years earlier when Virginia seceded.[22]

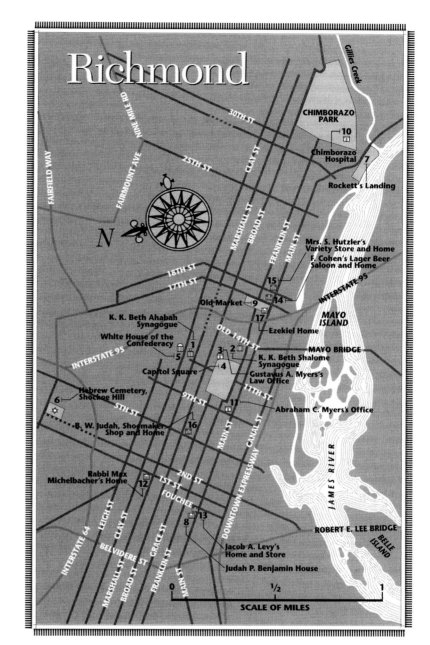

WALKING PAST THE SYNAGOGUE

From the Richmond harbor, Lincoln left the
USS Malvern *and walked through the center*
of the city, passing the the 14th Street Kahal
Kadosh Beth Shalome synagogue, the center
of Richmond's prominent Jewish community,
as well as other Jewish sites, on his way to
Davis's wartime residence—the Confederate
White House—a short distance away.

Courtesy of Tim Belshaw

Myers, Campbell, and General Weitzel met with
Lincoln on the *Malvern*, docked in the Richmond harbor, on the morning of April 5. "Our interview with
the President commenced," Myers reported in a memorandum of the conversation, "by his stating that he
understood we came in no official capacity and that
we were unauthorized to act on any matter that might
be the subject of our conversation, which we of course

confirmed. He then told us that he had written a paper
which he would read to us, accompanied by a verbal
running commentary of his own when he considered explanation was necessary." Lincoln, according to
Myers, called for the restoration of national authority,
made clear that "he could not retract from anything"
that he had announced concerning the emancipation
of slaves, promised to exercise "sincere liberality" when

GUSTAVUS MYERS

On April 5, Lincoln met with Confederate assistant secretary of war John A. Campbell, and was joined by Gustavus Adolphus Myers, one of Richmond's most prominent Jewish citizens and a well-respected attorney.

Virginia Historical Society

USS *MALVERN*

Lincoln met with Campbell, Myers, and Union General Weitzel aboard the gunboat USS Malvern, *lying on the James River in the Richmond harbor, where he had also spent the previous night.*

Courtesy of the Library of Congress

it came to confiscating property (though in his written paper Lincoln added the threat that "if the war be now further persisted in" he would insist on confiscating property "to bear the additional cost"), and, finally, "professed himself really desirous to see an end of the struggle," trusting "in the Providence of God that there never would be another." In subsequent conversation—conducted in a spirit of "entire civility and good humor"—he talked about convening the Virginia legislature in hopes of restoring Virginia to the Union and discussed the question of loyalty oaths. (Myers believed that they would "be productive of irritation and conducive to no good result.")

Most significantly, the president set forth the philosophy that he expected to guide his postwar reconstruction policies: a "disposition to be lenient towards all persons, however prominent, who had taken part in the struggle" without "any feeling of vindictiveness or of exultation."[23] Ten years earlier, incensed at the repeal of the Missouri Compromise, he had expressed the contrary view, that "like Haman," those responsible "should hang upon the gallows of their own building."[24] Many advocated applying just such a policy to the leaders of the Confederacy. Yet Lincoln refused. Instead, in a private conversation with General Weitzel, he expressed in the homespun language that he preferred the conciliatory philosophy that he had now come to champion: "If I were in your place," he said, "I'd let 'em up easy, let 'em up easy."[25]

Just four days after this meeting, on April 9, Lincoln's philosophy was placed on public display when Robert E. Lee surrendered his army to Ulysses S. Grant at the brick home of Wilmer McLean in the village of Appomattox Court House, Virginia. Grant, in keeping with Lincoln's orders, was magnanimous. Confederate officers and men would be allowed to return home, "not to be disturbed by U.S. authority so long as they observe their paroles and the laws in force where they may reside." They were thus immune from prosecution for treason. Grant let the defeated soldiers take their

As to peace I have said before, and now repeat, that three things are indispensable.
1 The restoration of the national authority throughout all the States.
2. No receding by the Executive of the United States on the slavery question from the position assumed thereon in the late Annual Message to Congress, and in preceding documents.
3. No cessation of hostilities short of an end of the war, and the disbanding of all forces hostile to the government.
That all propositions coming from those now in hostility to the government, and not inconsistent with the foregoing, will be respectfully considered, and passed upon in a spirit of sincere liberality;
I now add that it seems useless for me to be more specific with those who will not say they are ready for the indispensable terms, even on conditions to be named by themselves. If there be any who are ready for those indispensable

...y conditions whatever, let them say *such conditions* ... to their conditions, so that ~~they~~ can ...y known, and considered.
...her added that, the remission of ... being within the executive pow: ...ar be now further persisted in, by those opposing the government, the making of confiscated property at the least to bear the additional cost, will be insisted on; but that confiscations (except in cases of thero party intervening interests) will be remitted to the people of any state which shall now promptly, and in good faith, withdraw its troops and other support from further resistance to the government.
What is now said as to remission of confiscation has no reference to supposed property in slaves.

> "*As to peace . . . these things are indispensable.*"

LINCOLN'S NOTES REGARDING CONDITIONS FOR PEACE, APRIL 5, 1865

In a handwritten memorandum that he read at the meeting aboard the Malvern *with Judge Campbell and Gustavus Myer, Lincoln laid out his conditions for peace with the South, demanding the surrender of all Confederate armies, the restoration of the Union, and the end of slavery. "The President was prepared for the visit and spoke with freedom," Campbell recalled. Lincoln addressed inquiries to Myers relative to the composition of the legislature, the character of its members, and the advisability of the oath of allegiance. The meeting, however, led nowhere: four days later Lee surrendered to Grant at Appomattox Court House.*

Abraham Lincoln Presidential Library & Museum

Memoranda.

On Sunday evening (April 4/65) I was requested by Judge J. A. Campbell to consent to accompany him (and as it was suggested, other Gentlemen of the city) the next morning at 9 o'clock, to see the President of the U.S., who as I understood from Judge C. had sent for him, or on the President's arrival in Richmond, and had made the appointment referred to for the next morning. Having heard during Monday that much uneasiness was felt by the citizens of Richmond about an enforced oath of allegiance to the U.S. and desiring if I could in any manner remove that uneasiness, and wishing also to ascertain the tone and temper existing on the part of the Federal authorities towards the citizens, I felt no hesitation in acceding to Judge C's request, independently of my high esteem for that Gentleman and my confidence in his sage city, wisdom and prudence.

On Wednesday morning accordingly we repaired together, no other Gentleman having appeared, to Genl. Weitzel's Head quarters, (late the residence of Mr. Davis,) and were accompanied by Genl. Weitzel to Rocketts, where the Gun boat of Admiral Porter was lying, and on board of which was the President of the U.S.

During our drive to Rocketts we had a conversation with Genl. W. in which he mentioned several interesting matters, but in reference to an enforced oath of allegiance expressed his own decided opinion adversely to requiring it, considering the course as unadvisable and to use his own language as "opening the door to perjury." For said he, "when men take an oath reluctantly, they are not apt to respect it, and I regard it as wrong to place them in" which we of course confirmed. He then told he had written a paper which he would accompanied by some reassuring comment or other he considered explanation was necessary there end to us the paper which he after ... to Judge Campbell and which is in ... of that Gentleman. The President regarding authority of the U.S. ... he recognized ... in all parts of the country, and declared would not retract from any thing he had announced as his opinion in his public ... gress, and said that ... in ... his own opinions about the question of ... Slaves, he could not without a violation of ... change any of his sentiments in that ... one to confiscation of property, the Presd. ... was in his power, and he showed a disposition that power in the spirit of sincere liberality ... stated that it had not gone to any great ... that, except in the cases of the rights of the ... persons by purchase, a question he meant ... to the courts to decide, he did not think any insurmountable or ... obstacle in ... matter. He professed himself really ...

of the struggles, and said he hoped in the ... that their own would be as there. He ... that he was thinking over a plea by which ... Legislature might be brought to hold their ... the capitol in Richmond — for the mere ... whether they desired to take any action ... the State in view of the existing state of ... informed Genl. Weitzel that he would ... finitely point on that subject in a day or ... ence of his plan being, that if he could not ... to the members to come hither, and ... reasonable time were allowed them to delib ... they arrive at no conclusion, they would ... appeared to them to leave Richmond. ... take of the oath of allegiance being again ... served the President that the conciliatory ... by the Federal forces since their arri ... , had had a powerful effect in allay ... and producing kindly feelings in the ... zens, and expressed the opinion that the ... any other town or the part of the Federal ... would be productive of irritation and ... The President answered ... not feel disposed to do it here.

Other conversation occurred, in which the Presi ... declared his disposition to be lenient towards ... persons, however prominent, who had taken ... part in the struggle, and actually so exhibit ... by him of any feeling or ... of exultation.

Judge Campbell handed to the President a paper a copy of which he retained, containing proposed Articles for a Military convention to be held by Genl. Grant and Lee, having an armis- tice for its basis, for a time to be agreed upon between those Officers during which negotiations might be opened and conducted. The President after hear- ing it read, requested that he might take it which was done accordingly, and our interview ended.

Throughout, it was conducted with entire civility and good humor.

G. A. Myers
Richmond April 4, 1865.

GUSTAVUS MYERS REPORTS ON HIS MEETING WITH LINCOLN

Though misdated for a day earlier, Myers's report details the meeting with Lincoln, which took several hours and ended "with mutual goodwill," but with no results.

Virginia Historical Society

LINCOLN TO JOSHUA SPEED, "IF LIKE HAMAN THEY SHOULD HANG UPON THE GALLOWS . . ."

Where once, ten years before, Lincoln had declared his satisfaction at the thought that those who wished to protect slavery might, like Haman, "hang upon the gallows of their own building," now, in Richmond, he urged that Confederate leaders instead be, he said, "let up easy." Having for four terrible years presided over a conflict that had already taken the lives of 600,000 of his countrymen, he would, it seems, do anything to prevent one more drop of blood being shed.

Courtesy of the Massachusetts Historical Society

horses along with them, so that they could plant crops; he provided them with three days of rations; and he muted Union celebrations. "The war is over," he told his troops; "the rebels are our countrymen again, and the best sign of rejoicing after the victory will be to abstain from all demonstrations."[26]

The surrender at Appomattox occurred fortuitously just one day before Jews across the country sat down to observe the Passover seder, commemorating their own ancestors' passage from slavery to freedom, the exodus of the ancient Israelites from Egyptian bondage. The coincidence won notice from contemporaries. "As the forefathers of the Jews passed over the Red Sea at the time

of which this festival is the anniversary," the *New York Herald* reported, "so also the American people seemed to have passed over and beyond the red sea of blood which has been spilt so freely during the last four years." The *Boston Daily Advertiser* explicitly pointed to the "coincidence that the modern people of bondage [Southern slaves] have seen their deliverance confirmed and nearly consummated, about the same season of the year [as Passover]; and from what we have seen of their bearing and understanding of the event they are not unlikely to regard its anniversary with equal reverence."[27]

The events of April 11 continued that same pattern. Just as many Jews were sitting down to a second seder, Lincoln delivered what would be his last public address, on reconstruction, including his most explicit statement yet on black suffrage. After acknowledging "He, from Whom all blessings flow"—an epithet for the divine that once again bespoke his sensitivity to non-Christians—he turned to the long-simmering problem of how to readmit Louisiana into the Union. More than a year earlier, Lincoln had thrown his support to the state's governor—the Jewish-born but not Jewish identifying Michael Hahn—who was elected by a minority of voters that excluded both former rebels and all blacks. After congratulating Hahn for "having fixed your name in history as the first free-state Governor of Louisiana," the president had quietly suggested that he consider widening the franchise to include "some of the colored people . . . as, for instance, the very intelligent, and especially those who have fought gallantly in our ranks." Enfranchising those men, he argued in a striking metaphor, "would probably help, in some trying time to come, to keep the jewel of liberty within the family of freedom."[28]

While Louisiana's new state constitution did not go as far in preserving that "jewel" as Lincoln had hoped, it did provide for the education of all children without regard to race, guaranteed equal rights to all in court, and permitted blacks to serve in the militia.[29] Lincoln, in his public address on April 11, declared for the first time that those concessions might not suffice: "It is also unsatisfactory to some that the elective franchise is not given to the colored man. I would myself prefer that it were now conferred on the very intelligent, and on those who serve our cause as soldiers." Still, he advocated that Louisiana be welcomed back into the Union "as it is, and help to improve it." He disagreed with those who sought to reject and disperse the state's new government. His approach to reconstruction, he indicated, would be to remain flexible and build up gradually and incrementally, until the early buds of freedom "ripened to a complete success."[30]

The popular but deranged young actor John Wilkes Booth, who heard Lincoln's address on that second night of Passover, understood exactly what the president meant by his timely discussion of freedom. "That means nigger citizenship," he exclaimed to a friend. Forgoing his previous plot to kidnap Lincoln in order to end the war, he now resolved upon another course of action: "Now by God, I'll put him through. That is the last speech he will ever make."[31]

Booth belonged to a celebrated family of actors frequently described as being of Jewish "extraction" or "descent."[32] They traced their ancestors back to Spain. Booth's father, the tragic actor and unstable alcoholic Junius Brutus Booth, was characterized by his daughter as a man who "worshipped at many shrines." "In the synagogue," she recalled, "he was known as a Jew, because he conversed with rabbis and learned doctors, and joined their worship in the Hebraic tongue. He read the Talmud, also, and strictly adhered to many of its laws."[33] Booth's brother, the eminent actor Edwin Booth, was a favorite of the Jewish community and, according to Isaac Mayer Wise, personally confessed to him "that he was the son of a Jew."[34] As for John Wilkes Booth, he is not known ever to have identified as Jewish or have been so identified. In the 1850s, he had played on the amateur stage in Cleveland with various Jews, including Simon Wolf, whom some said

Executive Mansion,

Washington, March 13. 1864.

Hon. Michael Hahn

    My dear Sir:

        I congratulate you on having fixed your name in history as the first. free-state Governor of Louisiana. Now you are about to have a Convention which, among other things, will probably define the elective franchise. I barely suggest for your private consideration, whether some of the colored people may not be let in— as, for instance, the very intelligent, and especially those who have fought gallantly in our ranks. They would probably help, in some trying time to come, to keep the jewel of liberty within the family of freedom. But this is only a suggestion, not to the public, but to you alone.

            Yours truly

            A. Lincoln.

". . . to keep the jewel of liberty
within the family of freedom."

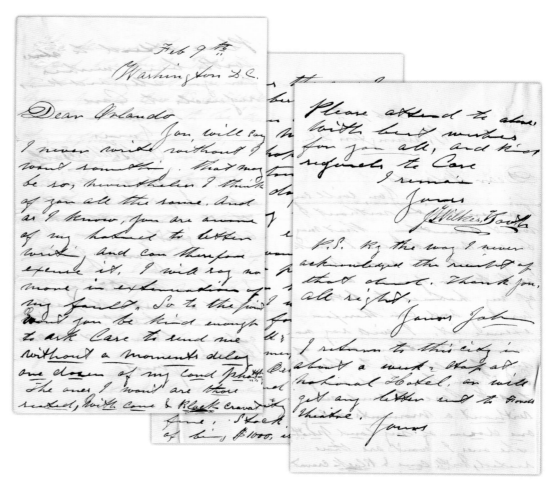

"I return to this city in about a week, stop at National Hotel, and will get any letter sent to Fords Theatre."

ABOVE

JOHN WILKES BOOTH, FEBRUARY 9, 1865

Whether, when John Wilkes Booth wrote this long and intriguing letter, he was just planning to abduct President Lincoln or to kill him instead, is impossible to determine. Writing to a longtime friend, he makes an urgent request: "Would you be kind enough to ask Case to send me without a moments delay one dozen of my card photghs . . ." It is thought that Booth wanted the photos for identification purposes connected to the Lincoln conspiracy, adding "I return to this city in about a week, stop at National Hotel, and will get any letter sent to Fords Theatre." On April 14, 1865, picking up his mail at Ford's, Booth heard that Lincoln would be attending Our American Cousin *there that evening and decided to use that opportunity to kill Lincoln. His favorite photograph, "seated, with cane & black cravat," would soon adorn the wanted poster for the assassination of the president.*

Shapell Manuscript Collection

LEFT

ACTOR AND ASSASSIN JOHN WILKES BOOTH, 1865

Courtesy of the Library of Congress

**A PAGE FROM THE DIARY OF
SIMON WOLF, APRIL 14–15, 1865**

*In this page from Simon Wolf's diary, he describes
the "tumult . . . and consternation" in the immediate
aftermath of Lincoln's assassination, the conspiracy,
and Lincoln's last hours. Wolf was one of the few
people who had personal relationships over a
number of years with both Lincoln and Booth.*

Simon Wolf, *Presidents I Have Known*

REPRODUCTION OF PAGES FROM MY DIARY OF 1865

resembled him. He also, as we have seen, played the part
of Shylock at Grover's Theater. On the Friday morning of April 14, 1865, according to Wolf, remarkably,
he and Booth met in front of the Metropolitan Hotel
in Washington and shared a drink.[35]

While Wolf and Booth were drinking, Lincoln was
meeting with his cabinet. The discussion that Friday covered numerous issues: regulations concerning trade, the
reassertion of federal authority, plans for reconstruction,
and more. Everybody's mind, however, was on North
Carolina, for Confederate forces there were holding
out in Raleigh, and word was awaited imminently from
General Sherman, whose job it was to subdue those
holdouts and bring the war formally to an end. Secretary of the Navy Gideon Welles recorded in his diary
that Lincoln was optimistic, "for he had last night the
usual dream which he had preceding nearly every great
and important event of the War." In the dream, Lincoln
recounted, "he seemed to be in some singular, indescribable vessel, and that he was moving with great rapidity
towards an indefinite shore." "Generally the news had

been favorable which succeeded this dream," he declared
hopefully, "and the dream itself was always the same. . . .
We shall, judging from the past, have great news very
soon." As Welles noted gloomily when he recorded this
remarkable scene, "Great events did, indeed, follow."[36]

Meanwhile, in Cincinnati, Rabbi Max Lilienthal
was already celebrating the "national victory." In a public
lecture delivered at his synagogue on April 14, he spoke
of how far he and his congregants had advanced "intel-
lectually, morally and politically" during the course of
the war. "Four years ago," he confessed, "how many of us
were Abolitionists? How many of us dreamt of the possibility that this sacred soil of liberty should be cleansed
from the scourge of slavery? How many of us had the
moral courage enough to think that this great stain could
be or should be removed from the brilliant escutcheon of
the American people?" He recalled the contempt shown
toward Abraham Lincoln ("the scorned railsplitter")
upon his election and first inauguration. He doubtless
remembered that he had himself opposed Lincoln at
that time and that his friend Rabbi Isaac Mayer Wise

Allow the bearers, Mrs Dr. Stone, Mrs Gittings, and a gentleman, escort, to pass to Richmond, Va. visit their friends there, and return.

April 14, 1865. A. Lincoln

Department of State
Washington, Apr 14 1865

Sir:

The President desires a meeting of the Heads of Departments at the Executive Mansion, at eleven o'clock this morning

To the Honorable
Secretary of the Navy

ABOVE

ONE OF LINCOLN'S LAST NOTES, APRIL 14, 1865

In a subtle twist of irony, Lincoln interacts with both Dr. and Mrs. Stone on the last day of his life. Here the president issues a pass for "Mrs. Dr. Stone" to travel to Richmond; by that night, her husband, the Lincoln family physician, would be attending at Lincoln's deathbed.

Shapell Manuscript Collection

LEFT

TOWARD AN INDEFINITE SHORE

On this, one of the happiest days of his life, and his last, Lincoln called a cabinet meeting with this summons. "Secretary of the Navy Gideon Welles is desired to attend at the Executive Mansion, at eleven o'clock in the morning, April 14th, 1865." Welles's diary entry for that day recorded that Lincoln related to the cabinet a curious dream he had the night before. "It related to your element, the water," he told Welles. "I seemed to be in some singular, indescribable vessel," he said, "moving with great rapidity toward an indefinite shore." It presaged, he was sure, that they should have "important news" very soon, as he had had that dream previously. And they did: within hours, Lincoln was dead, assassinated.

Shapell Manuscript Collection

had mocked Lincoln repeatedly. Now, four years later, it was time to repent, for "the same man, re-elected to the same office" was "respected and revered . . . as a man of manifest destiny and heroic immortality." "May the Lord forgive those who slandered our good President," Lilienthal exclaimed, as if seeking absolution for himself and his friends. "We had rather complain of the goodness and mercy of his heart than the severity of his administration." Echoing Lincoln, he then called for "no hatred, no vengeance to the South" and urged his listeners to show "that we can be as magnanimous in peace as terrible in war."[37]

That night, the evening of Good Friday on the Christian calendar, was, for Jews, the commencement of the Sabbath and the start of the fifth day of Passover. While many Jews settled down to a special holiday dinner, Abraham Lincoln and his wife, accompanied by their guests, Clara Harris and Major Henry R. Rathbone, traveled to Ford's Theatre, arriving late at a performance of *Our American Cousin*, by Tom Taylor. Jacob H. Rosewald, a Jewish musical prodigy who normally played with the orchestra, was away from the theater that evening, probably on account of the holiday.[38] The orchestra struck up "Hail to the Chief" as the Lincoln party entered the presidential box, and the audience greeted them with a standing ovation.

John Wilkes Booth lurked in the anteroom of the presidential box. Peering through the tiny peephole he had prepared earlier, he watched Lincoln and with his

A TICKET TO TRAGEDY, FORD'S THEATRE, STAMPED APRIL 14, 1865

On the evening of April 14, 1865, Lincoln attended a play at Ford's Theatre in Washington, D.C. Sometime around ten, John Wilkes Booth slipped unnoticed into the presidential box and, standing four feet away from the president, discharged a single bullet from a derringer into the back of Lincoln's head. "There will never be anything like it on earth," one witness said of the pandemonium following the shot. Lincoln never regained consciousness, and when he died the next morning, he became the first president to be assassinated.

Shapell Manuscript Collection

knowledge of the script waited for the perfect moment when one actor stood alone on the stage and an enormous laugh would muffle sounds from the box. When that moment came, he opened the inner door, stepped toward the back of the president's rocking chair, and fired a shot that went into the back of Lincoln's head. He then struggled briefly with Major Rathbone, leaped down upon the almost empty stage, screamed, "Sic semper tyrannis" (Thus always to tyrants), and made his escape out the back door.[39]

Lincoln, unconscious and bleeding, was soon carried across the street to a boardinghouse and laid diagonally across a bed. Around him gathered family, friends, cabinet members, generals, and, of course, doctors. One of the latter was Charles H. [Carl Heinrich] Liebermann (1813–86), a Russian-born Jewish surgeon who was "for over twenty years the leading oculist in Washington,"

"Armory Square"

U.S.A Gen. Hospital
Washington D.C.
May 28th 1865

Dear Friend Dudley

Your last
You will please exc[use]
for not answering
as I have been ve[ry]
As you noticed I al[so]
volunteer service
no vacancies in the
army, and after
examined for se[rvice]
By three old army
I was accepted. an[d]
been on duty sin[ce]
this hospital. Whe[n]
Came I had char[ge]
the sick and wou[nded]
which duty I fulf[illed]
about two weeks a[go]

The former was holding his head
and crying bitterly for a
Surgeon While the others there
were standing crying for Stimulant
Water etc not one going for
anything. While going towards
him I sent one for Brandy
and another for Water, then
told Mrs. L. that I was a
Surgeon, when she asked
me to do what I could
He was then in a profound
Coma, pulse could not be
felt: eyes closed. stertorous
breathing. I immediately with
assistance placed him
in a recumbent position
on the floor. While doing this
I put my hand on a
part of his coat near the
left shoulder Saturated
with Blood supposing him
to have been stabbed I asked

"... in a profound Coma, pulse could not be felt,
eyes closed.... It is impossible for him to recover."

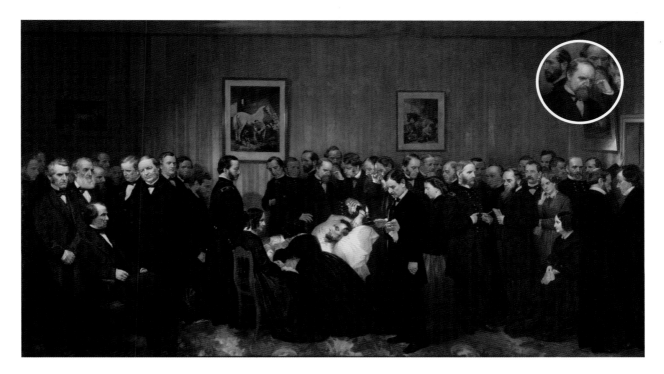

ABOVE

THE LAST HOURS

Alonzo Chappel's famous 1867 painting, The Last Hours of Lincoln, *depicts the ten-by-fifteen-foot room in which Lincoln lay dying as large enough to be filled with almost as many doctors who later claimed to be there. Of the nine actually in attendance, Dr. Liebermann is prominently featured here, gazing intently at the president. Liebermann was misidentified in the key that accompanies the painting; research has now correctly determined the likeness of the Jewish doctor.*

Chicago History Museum

OPPOSITE

CHARLES AUGUSTUS LEALE
TO DWIGHT DUDLEY, MAY 28, 1865

Charles Augustus Leale—age twenty-three and six weeks out of medical school—went to Ford's Theatre especially to see Lincoln on April 14, sat as close as he could to the presidential box, and witnessed Booth enter the box and then jump to the stage with his dagger drawn. Leale immediately hurried to Lincoln and was the first doctor to attend the stricken president. Recalling the event in graphic detail six weeks later, Leale writes that he found Lincoln "in a profound Coma, pulse could not be felt, eyes closed. . . . It is impossible for him to recover."

Shapell Manuscript Collection

ABOVE

CHARLES H. LIEBERMANN

The Russian-born Jewish ophthalmologist Dr. Charles H. Liebermann was a leading Washington physician, and while attending Lincoln's deathbed vigil cut a lock of hair away from the president's wound and, in a desperate attempt at resuscitation, poured brandy down his throat.

Georgetown University Archives

and also, in 1865, president of the Medical Society of the District of Columbia. Liebermann had been imprisoned in Siberia for promoting Polish independence, trained in Germany, and subsequently immigrated to the United States, bringing with him a superior European medical training. He was a pioneer of strabismus surgery to cure misalignment of the eyes, helped to create Georgetown University's medical school, and, in the face of prejudice, had come to be esteemed by his colleagues, who knew him as a Jew even though he did not otherwise identify with the Jewish community. Upon arriving at Lincoln's bedside, Liebermann poured brandy down the president's throat, removed hair from the area surrounding his wound, and diagnosed the gunshot as fatal.[40] Alonzo Chappel's famous painting, *The Last Hours of Lincoln*, depicts Liebermann as one of the bearded, bald, grave-looking physicians staring down intensely to the left of Lincoln's bed. He remained at that bedside until the president was pronounced dead at 7:22 on the morning of April 15. "It is all over," he and the other physicians gravely reported to the first lady, who was in the front room. "The President is no more!"[41] In his death vigil, Lincoln's family doctor, Robert K. Stone, counting the president's final breaths, recorded: "Death closed the scene."[42]

News of the president's death spread quickly that Saturday morning. In Washington, Simon Wolf recalled, "the bells of the churches tolled the death knell of the Great Martyr"[43] very soon after he was pronounced dead. In New York, the news hit just as Jews were "proceeding to their places of worship for the services of the Sabbath of Passover."[44] In Philadelphia, Isaac Leeser heard the news from his synagogue president, "during the pause in the morning service, when the Sepher [Torah scroll] was taken out."[45] In San Francisco, Elkan Cohn of Congregation Emanu-El was handed a note with the news just as he was "ascending his pulpit, on Saturday, to deliver the usual sermon . . . he was so overcome that, bursting in tears, he sank almost senseless."[46] Fittingly, the prophetic portion read in synagogues on the Sabbath when Lincoln was pronounced dead was Ezekiel's vision of the Valley of Dry Bones, a chapter that Lincoln himself had quoted in one of his earliest known addresses.[47] "Behold. . . . Our bones are dried, and our hope is lost. . . . Thus saith the Lord God; Behold, O my people, I will open your graves, and cause you to come up out of your graves, and bring you into the land of Israel."[48] The prophet's message of comfort and hope, uttered against the background of death and destruction, was appropriate to the national mood in the wake of the war's end, and even more so in the face of the assassination. For Jews, the prophecy also reinforced the age-old yearning proclaimed at the conclusion of the seder just days before, "Next Year in Jerusalem!"

Lincoln, Mary Todd Lincoln later recalled, shared a similar yearning. Writing from Chicago on December 17, 1866, she described a carriage ride they had taken that last afternoon on April 14. With the war over, she said, Lincoln had told her that they needed to make an effort to be happier—they had both been so miserable. "At the expiration of his second term, we would visit Europe, and," she wrote, "he appeared to anticipate much pleasure, from a visit to Palestine."[49] In fact, she told her friends, he wanted to see Jerusalem before he died.

OPPOSITE

DEATH CLOSED THE SCENE, APRIL 15, 1865

Considered the dean of the mid-nineteenth-century Washington medical establishment, Dr. Robert K. Stone was the Lincoln family physician and attended, along with Dr. Liebermann, whom he calls in the report "my old friend," the president's deathbed and autopsy. His seven-page narrative details his dramatic rush to the stricken president's side, and, some eight hours later, Lincoln's final minutes, decline, death, and autopsy. This page, notably, is stained with human blood; it is, very likely, Lincoln's.

Shapell Manuscript Collection

On the evening of Friday, April 14th /65, I was summoned in haste to the late Presdt of the U.S— to whom I had the honor to be family physician— I was called for, at, or very near, a quarter past ten oclock P.M. the carriage which was sent for me, having been driven at top speed, in coming for me & returning, to the scene of blood— The least possible time was spent in the passage to the house— I then found, that the president had been carried to the residence of Mr Peterson, who resided on 10th St. off the scene of the deplored slaughter—

The Presdt body had been conveyed to a small room in the back building of the house as the easiest of access & most convenient— a plain but comfortable apartment The Presdt was laid upon the occupant's bed & so great was his stature, that his body had to be placed obliquely across it & while his head reached the left hand top of the bed— his feet nearly extended to the Right hand bottom of the Couch I found him surrounded by sympathizing fellow citizens— when overpowered, seen crying with woe— but who, in spite of the exasperating influence of the act— still controlled the surging of their aroused passions & maintained a decorous silence around his humble Couch— I found my friend Assistant Surgn Taft supporting the sufferer's head— Dr Leal, also of the army, & _____ very near— my old friend Dr Liebermann Chief with Dr Ford Surgeon of the old Capitol Prison, making every attempt to render the President aid & afford him every comfort, in the power of man & best ___ As soon as I was recognized by my friends, the Case was surrendered to my care & I proceeded to the exploration of the wound

The President, then lay, perfectly passive on his back as if quietly asleep, without any disturbing symptoms— tho' at times, his respiration was somewhat stertorous Examination showed that he had recd a gun shot wound on the posterior aspect of the head— not far from the median line & about 3 inches from the left auditory ___ greatest in an oblique line— a clean, well defined orifice the wound the bone being remarkably clean cut as if punched like a gun wad ___ It was remarked that the Presdt Left Eye was discolored— the periphery— or orbital surface was ecchymosed presenting the ordinary appearance of "blackeye"— This, the gentlemen around, he said, had been produced by the fall— Having by this time seen the wound in the cranium, I begged leave to differ & expressed the opinion that it was the result of the direct violence of the ball— that I had repeatedly seen such an altered condition following a wound in the back of the head (all respects) in which, fracture of the base of the Cranium, near the main ___ ___ It was also noticed, that the pupil of the Right eye was

EPILOGUE

As a result of the fact that so many Jews happened to be in synagogue or on their way there when word of Lincoln's death became known, many of the first prayers memorializing the slain president were Jewish ones. Adolphus S. Solomons noted this at the time: "It is a singular fact," he wrote, "that it was the Israelites' privilege here, as well as elsewhere, to be the first to offer in their places of worship, prayers for the repose of the soul of Mr. Lincoln."[1] Newspapers preserved accounts of those prayers. At Temple Emanu-El, according to *The New York Times*, the congregation rose and "as if by a simultaneous impulse, repeated the Kadisch, a prayer for the nearest deceased relative. After which they were dismissed."[2] Elsewhere, the prayer for the government and the nation was recited, and also prayers for peace. At Shearith Israel, "a highly impressive prayer was . . . offered up to the throne of Grace by the minister for the repose of the soul of the late President." This was followed, according to the *Jewish Messenger*, by the Sephardic prayer for the dead, "being the first time in the history of Judaism in America that these prayers have been said in a Jewish house of worship for other than one professing the Jewish religion."[3]

Jewish leaders had the opportunity to deliver polished eulogies for Lincoln during the ensuing days, when funeral services were held across the country and Lincoln's coffin made its more than 1,600-mile trip from Washington, D.C. to New York to Springfield, Illinois. Practically every Jewish religious leader in America eulogized Lincoln, many of them at noon on April 19, when the president's official memorial service took place in the East Room of the Executive Mansion in Washington, and "the various religious denominations throughout the country [were] invited to meet in their respective places of worship at that hour for the purpose of solemnizing the occasion with appropriate ceremonies."[4] Rabbis spoke of Lincoln's character, his values, his leadership abilities, and his faith. They compared him to the greatest of human heroes, particularly to Abraham, his biblical namesake ("Mr. Lincoln had not only the name of our glorious patriarch Abraham, but like him he was a self-made man. Like him he had

OPPOSITE

PRESIDENT LINCOLN'S FUNERAL

After a journey of 1,600 miles from Washington, D.C.,
Lincoln was buried at Oak Ridge Cemetery
in Springfield, Illinois on May 4, 1865.
Sketched by W. Waud for *Harper's Weekly*

PASS TO LINCOLN'S FUNERAL IN THE EXECUTIVE MANSION, APRIL 19, 1865

Lincoln's official memorial service took place in the East Room of the Executive Mansion. Many Jewish congregations around the country also conducted memorial services at that date and hour.

Shapell Manuscript Collection

ABRAHAM LINCOLN, THE TRIBUTE OF THE SYNAGOGUE, EDITED BY EMANUEL HERTZ

This collection of Jewish eulogies of Abraham Lincoln was published in 1927.

Shapell Manuscript Collection

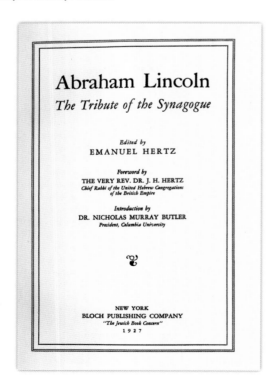

a high mission from God."[5]); to Moses ("like our own law-giver, Moses, brought a nation to the verge of the haven of peace, and, like him, not allowed to participate in its consummation"[6]); and to George Washington ("Washington's name is identified with our liberty and independence. The name of Lincoln will be identified with our nationality and greatness"[7]). Lewis Dembitz, who, as a delegate from Kentucky, had voted for Lincoln at the Republican convention of 1860, claimed that Lincoln was sometimes known as "Rabbi Abraham, as if he was one of our nation—of the seed of Israel."[8] Isaac Mayer Wise, who had criticized Lincoln repeatedly while he lived and then characterized him in death as "the greatest man that ever sprung from mortal loins," insisted that Lincoln was fully a Jew, "bone from our bone and flesh from our flesh. He supposed himself to be a descendant of Hebrew parentage. He said so in my presence."[9]

What distinguished these Jewish eulogies from their Christian counterparts was, of course, the absence of Jesus. Pious Christians, noting that Lincoln was shot on Good Friday, inevitably drew parallels between his death and that of "the son of God," implying that Lincoln died to expiate the nation's sins. The *Chicago Tribune*, for example, characterized the assassination as "the most horrid crime ever committed on this globe, since the wicked Jews crucified the Savior."[10] Jews, eager to participate as equals in the national rites of mourning, found such allusions insensitive and disturbing. Their neighbors, they feared, viewed them through a New Testament prism, rather than as fellow citizens the way Lincoln had.[11]

In New York, at least, Jews did participate as equals when Lincoln's remains were accompanied through the streets. More than twenty different synagogues and Jewish organizations joined in the solemn procession. The *Jewish Messenger* calculated that "there were Jewish members sufficient to bring the aggregate of Israelites in the procession to about seven thousand."[12]

In the eleven other major cities where the funeral

LINCOLN'S FUNERAL PROCESSION

Jewish photographer Samuel Alschuler, who had twice photographed Lincoln in Illinois, captured Lincoln's funeral procession in Chicago on May 1, 1865, three days before his interment. This later etching is based on Alschuler's photograph.

Courtesy of the Library of Congress

train paused, Jews participated to a lesser degree. In some, no Jewish participation at all was recorded. In Cleveland, "Solomon and Montefiore Lodges I. O. B. B. [International Order B'nai B'rith], under the marshalship of B. F. Peixotto, Grand Master of the Order in the United States," marched in the funeral procession that accompanied Lincoln's coffin. In Chicago, "the reverend clergy . . . merged in the one great sorrow— Protestant and Catholic and Hebrew—all moving side by side." The city's Hebrew Benevolent Association, the B'nai B'rith Ramah Lodge, and at least one synagogue participated in the funeral procession.

Finally, in Springfield, where Lincoln was laid to rest on May 4, 1865, the clothing store of the Hammerslough Brothers displayed a portrait of Lincoln with the motto "Millions bless thy name," and Julius Hammerslough was among those who met the body, while his firm provided the black plumes that ornamented the cortege on the last leg of its journey. The funeral oration in Springfield went out of its way to mention Jewish participation in the obsequies in New York ("The Archbishop of the Roman Catholic Church in New York and a Protestant minister walked side by side in the sad procession, and a Jewish Rabbi performed a part of the solemn services").[13] While no Jew participated in the burial ceremony itself, the larger aim of the Jewish community—"to join our fellow citizens in paying a national tribute to a nation's lost chief"—was amply fulfilled.[14]

Jews had much more trouble joining with their fellow citizens on June 1, the day set aside by President Andrew Johnson "for special humiliation and prayer in consequence of the assassination of Abraham Lincoln."[15] Johnson had originally set aside the day of May 25 for the commemoration. Following protests, however, he canceled that date, explaining that it was Ascension Day, "sacred to large numbers of Christians as one of rejoicing for the ascension of the Savior." Without checking with other religious groups, he proclaimed "that the religious services recommended as aforesaid should be postponed until Thursday, the 1st day of June next."[16] That conflicted with the second day of Shavuot, the Jewish Feast of Weeks, commemorating the giving of the Torah on Mt. Sinai. "It is not to be expected that President Johnson shall, amid the trying and important duties that devolve upon him at the outset of his administration, keep in memory every festival, fastday, and ceremonial," the *Jewish Messenger* explained apologetically to its readers. But the lack of regard for Jewish sensibilities stung nevertheless. The paper wondered how broadly Ascension Day was really observed in America and noted that the new date placed Jews in "a position of . . . delicacy," since Shavuot was usually celebrated with "flowers and evergreens" and betokened

LINCOLN ON MOURNING

IN 1844, LINCOLN PAID HIS RESPECTS at the graves of his mother and sister in Indiana, following a fifteen-year absence. The visit had a profound impact on him, and during a period in which he was practicing his prose, Lincoln wrote a long poem grappling with their deaths. "And feel (companion of the dead) / I am living in the tombs," Lincoln completed the poem, so strong was his connection with his mother and sister upon the visit. Nearly twenty years after penning this poem, and, with having written the greatest speeches in American history, President Lincoln joined his mother and sister in the tombs. Just as Lincoln wrote about his mother and his sister with a great sense of loss, generations of poets and writers, would join him in step to write about another great loss, this time of their "lost Chief" Lincoln.

BELOW

LINCOLN TO ANDREW JOHNSTON, APRIL 18, 1846

Lincoln shares this poem on mourning with Illinois friend and colleague, Andrew Johnston.

Shapell Manuscript Collection

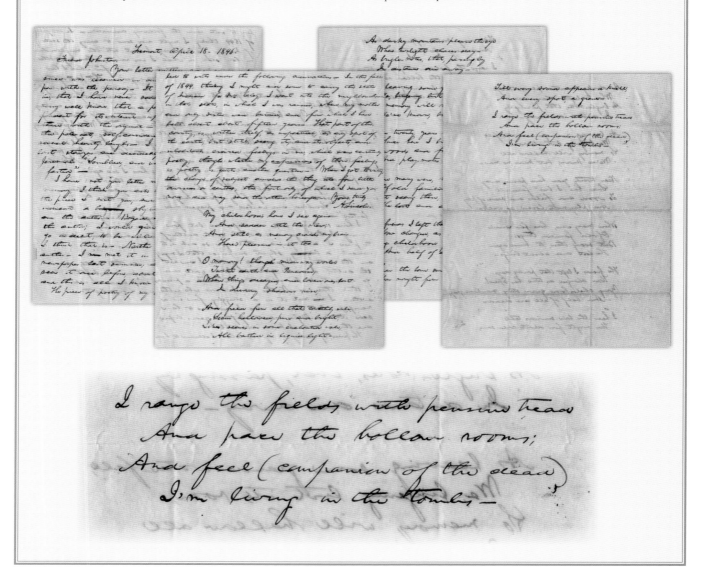

"joy and happiness." Still, it pledged obedience: "There will not be a more faithful compliance with the spirit of President Johnson's Proclamation than in the Synagogues." "The Israelites of America," it patriotically promised, "will yet join in a sincere and earnest prayer to God for the repose of the soul of the late President Lincoln, whose memory all revere [and] for whose loss there is universal mourning."[17]

Johnson's dismissal of Jewish needs was emblematic of his broader anti-Semitism. Charles Francis Adams, son of John Quincy Adams, remarked that "toward Jews, [Johnson] evidently felt a strong aversion."[18] Even in death Lincoln stood out against his predecessors and successors in his inclusiveness towards Jews.

Sabato Morais of Congregation Mikve Israel in Philadelphia, one of Lincoln's foremost rabbinic admirers, led the way on June 1 in memorializing the much-lamented slain president. "In this land of equal right, where the religious tenets of a majority can claim no higher privileges than those revered by a minority, there should not have been found protestants against the first summons of the authorities," he declared, lamenting that the original May 25 date had been changed. "But who among us will this day, let any motives sever him from the community?"[19] Some seven other Shavuot sermons memorializing the assassinated president survive, testimony to the "general attendance at synagogue," noted by the *Messenger*, as well as to the public's growing obsession with all things Lincoln ("we do not get weary of speaking of his life and his calamitous end," one rabbi admitted), and to the Jewish community's prudent decision to comply with Johnson's executive order.[20] "Jews, Catholics, and Protestants Equally Observe the Day," *The New York Times* headlined, doubtless to the Jewish community's satisfaction.[21] Several synagogues included Lincoln in the Jewish memorial prayer (Yizkor) traditionally recited on the second day of Shavuot "for the repose of the souls of departed relatives, friends and prominent men of Israel."[22]

Jews abroad commemorated Lincoln as well. Great

ANDREW JOHNSON, A CONTRAST IN TRUST

Andrew Johnson behaved in a way that was the antithesis of Lincoln's admiration and respect for Jews. Of Senator David Levy Yulee, Johnson once remarked, " . . . a miserable little cuss—a contemptible Jew . . . despicable little beggar . . . " About Judah P. Benjamin, Johnson said in a speech on the floor of the Senate, that "he belongs to that tribe that parted the garments of our Savior."
Courtesy of the Library of Congress

Britain's chief rabbi, Nathan Marcus Adler, pronounced what was described as a "magnificent funeral oration" for Lincoln. Speaking on the same platform, the world's best-known Jew and human rights advocate, Sir Moses Montefiore of England, linked Lincoln's efforts to liberate slaves to his own efforts to liberate Jews. "The Negroes are free and will remain so," he was quoted as saying. "Oh that I could say so much for my brothers of all the other lands."[23]

Not all Jews, however, agreed that Lincoln's passing was to be mourned. "God grant so may all our foes perish!" twenty-six-year-old Eleanor H. Cohen of Columbia, South Carolina, wrote in her diary, echoing the biblical Deborah's words in the Book of Judges (5:31). She described the news that "our worst enemy is laid low" as "glorious tidings."[24] David Naar, a pro-slavery Democrat from St. Thomas, who edited the Trenton,

ISAAC GOLDSTEIN'S HEBREW ACROSTIC OF ABRAHAM LINCOLN'S NAME

The key lines of Goldstein's acrostic honoring Lincoln, translated into English, read as follows:

> *The Black people thou hast redeemed unto Freedom:*
> *Forever they will praise and bless thy name.*
> *Who among princes is like Lincoln? And who can be praised like him?*

Courtesy of The University of Pennsylvania Library

New Jersey, *Daily True American* and in 1843 served as appointive mayor of Elizabeth and a judge in Essex County, was more circumspect. Though he had long been critical of Lincoln, whom he labeled a "weak and unfortunate President," he publicly expressed the "sincerest sorrow at his death." Privately, however, he evinced "disgust at the various instances of fulsome adulation exhibited by our people." In an anonymous letter to the *Occident* under the name "Israelite," he attacked those who considered the president "deserving of any of the religious services appertaining to Jewish worship" and lambasted Jews who made "any comparison between the late President and their great law-giver [Moses], 'whom the Lord knew face-to-face.'"[25]

Most Jews, though, eagerly participated in the national memorialization of Abraham Lincoln. The

different ways that they did so bespoke their growing position in the nation's cultural life. A poet-businessman from Poland named Isaac Goldstein even published in the *Jewish Messenger* an unusual Hebrew acrostic in Lincoln's memory.[26]

The renowned Jewish artist Solomon Nunes Carvalho (1815–97), born in South Carolina, produced a magnificent allegorical painting of Lincoln in 1865, the only known painting of him by a contemporary Jew. Lincoln is shown holding a scroll with words from his second inaugural clearly visible—"with malice toward none, with charity for all." A statue of George Washington, standing behind him, looks on with approval, while to his right, the ancient Greek Cynic philosopher Diogenes, remembered for carrying a lamp in daylight in search of a truly honest man, has dropped his lamp in shocked amazement—he has finally found one! The painting anticipated themes that would prove central to Lincoln iconography through the years and bespoke the terrible sense of loss that Carvalho felt upon Lincoln's death.[27]

Even the so-called last or "cracked-plate" photograph of Lincoln by the pioneering photographer Alexander Gardner, an image central to the memorialization of the slain president, had a Jewish angle to it. Adolphus S. Solomons, whose firm did substantial business with the government, recalled at the end of his life that Gardner was in charge of the photography branch of his company, Philp & Solomons. Solomons took credit for persuading Lincoln to give Gardner "another sitting" at his establishment, shortly before the assassination, and described how several initial snaps by the photographer failed to elicit an appropriate presidential expression. "Solomons, tell me one of your funny stories, and we will see if I can't do better," he quoted Lincoln as saying. The result was the photograph now considered to be "one of the great works of art in American history," an image that conveys both the likeness of Lincoln in his final days and the torments of his inner soul.[28]

Other Jews, even if they did not themselves help to

TOP RIGHT

A PORTRAIT OF LINCOLN BY SOLOMON NUNES CARVALHO

The renowned Jewish artist Solomon Nunes Carvalho produced a magnificent allegorical painting of Lincoln in 1865, the only known painting of him by a contemporary Jew.
Rose Art Museum, Brandeis University

BOTTOM RIGHT

THE "CRACKED PLATE" PORTRAIT

Even the so-called last, or "cracked plate" image by photographer Alexander Gardner, involved a Jewish associate: Gardner worked for longtime Lincoln acquaintance Adolphus S. Solomons, who was also present at the photography shoot. The sitting produced at least five different Lincoln images and were the last of Lincoln taken while he was alive.
National Portrait Gallery, Smithsonian Institution / Art Resource NY

create memorial art, responded generously when asked to contribute to public art in the president's memory. Sabato Morais proudly sent a check for $300 (about $4,400 in today's money) to Philadelphia's mayor, as "the voluntary contribution of my constituents towards rearing a monument to the memory of the deeply and universally lamented Abraham Lincoln." The synagogue's contribution, amounting to 1 percent of the total cost of the $30,000 bronze statue sculpted by Randolph Rogers, publicly evidenced the Jewish community's desire to be included among the religiously benevolent.[29]

In Springfield, Illinois, the National Lincoln Monument Association, which looked to erect a $250,000 ($3.7 million in today's money) monument to the slain president at the site of his tomb at Oak Ridge cemetery, directly solicited the country's Jews. Clothier Julius

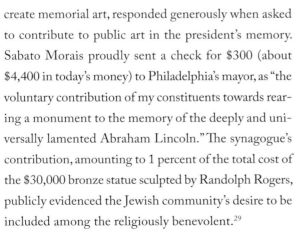

Hammerslough, who served as the association's "special agent" to the Jewish community, called upon "Hebrews" throughout the country to show "how highly we, as a race, appreciate freedom and the martyrs of liberty." "By contributing to this holy national work," he intimated, Jews would help "to meet prejudices still existing in the minds of many" and prove themselves "foes of all oppression and wrong."[30] Cincinnati's Jews responded warmly to this plea, appointing a five-man "Central Committee with power to collect funds for the purpose."[31] Nationwide, however, the campaign fizzled. By early 1867, the *Jewish Messenger* complained that the nation had become "strangely forgetful . . . of the good President who lived and died for his country" and it wondered what had "become of the subscriptions that were collected . . . for the national and local monuments?"[32]

Thanks to an infusion of state funds, the Springfield monument at Lincoln's Tomb was finally dedicated in 1874. A young Springfield Jew named Julius Rosenwald, later president of Sears Roebuck, recalled selling commemorative pamphlets to the crowd gathered at the event.[33] But by then, Hammerslough's efforts to solicit Jews had been forgotten, and no leading Jews participated in the dedication, which went unnoticed in the contemporary Jewish press. Only in 1886, when, in a break with precedent, a rabbi named Charles Austrian was invited to offer the closing prayer and benediction at the National Lincoln Monument on the twenty-first anniversary of Lincoln's death, did any hint of what had transpired earlier appear. "There has been a great deal of prejudice against the Jehudim [Jews] here formerly," the Springfield correspondent of the *American Israelite*

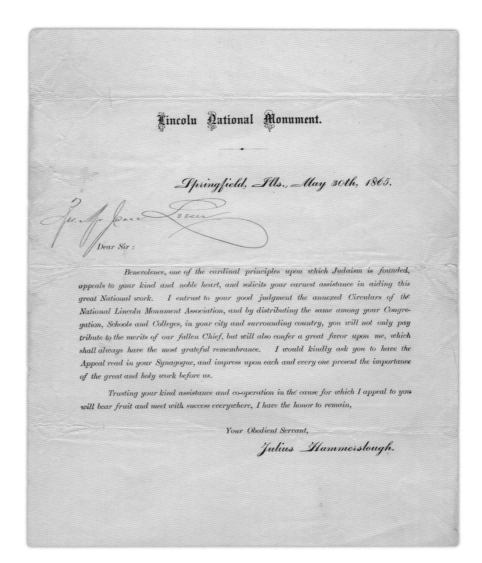

JULIUS HAMMERSLOUGH ENLISTS THE JEWS FOR LINCOLN, MAY 30, 1865

Addressed to Rev. Isaac Leeser, Hammerslough, who befriended Lincoln in Springfield as a young man, and who served as the association's "special agent" to the Jewish community, called upon "Hebrews" throughout the country to show "how highly we, as a race, appreciate freedom and the martyrs of liberty" and to support the efforts of the National Lincoln Monument Association.

Shapell Manuscript Collection

revealed, an indication that Hammerslough's earlier comments about "prejudices still existing" was based upon personal experience. The correspondent therefore took special pleasure in noticing that "the community at large" spoke "very favorably" of the rabbi's prayer "and were very much pleased."[34]

By the time Rabbi Austrian delivered his closing prayer and benediction, the majority of Americans and the great majority of American Jews held no conscious memories of Abraham Lincoln. They were immigrants or young people, and all that they really knew of America's sixteenth president was what they had read and heard about him. In the years that followed, books,

articles, sermons, speeches, films, and eventually Web sites filled out the Lincoln story. They portrayed Lincoln as the savior of the Union, the Great Emancipator, a peerless leader, a consummate politician, a man of the people, a self-made man, a student of the Bible, a prophet, a storyteller, a wit—and, above all, as the personification of all of the noblest qualities that Americans and Jews held dear. He became a never-ending source of inspiration and wisdom.[35]

Jews played a very significant role in shaping this portrayal of Abraham Lincoln. They studied Lincoln, collected Lincoln, chronicled Lincoln, quoted Lincoln, fictionalized Lincoln, dramatized Lincoln, painted Lincoln, sculpted Lincoln, wrote about Lincoln, preached about Lincoln, sang about Lincoln, and even, in the case of an east European Jewish immigrant named Victor David Brenner, designed the Lincoln image for the penny in 1909, on the occasion of the centennial of Lincoln's birth.

This Jewish love affair with all things Lincoln harks back, one suspects, to Lincoln's own remarkable regard for the Jews. Over the course of his tragically foreshortened life, he interacted with Jews, represented Jews, befriended Jews, admired Jews, commissioned Jews, trusted Jews, defended Jews, pardoned Jews, took advice from Jews, gave jobs to Jews, extended rights to Jews, revoked an expulsion of Jews, and even chose a Jew as his confidential agent. His connections to Jews went further and deeper than those of any previous American president.

This happened, we have seen, even though Abraham Lincoln was not raised among Jews. Growing up, the only Jews he knew were those he read about in the Bible. It was only in the second half of his life, when he was already a grown man, that he encountered almost all the Jews that he personally became familiar with. Others who similarly watched the Jewish presence in America expand, including members of Lincoln's own inner circle, displayed overt prejudice, sometimes generalizing about Jews as a class. Lincoln never did. Instead, influenced by the Jews whom he befriended, he took account of Jewish sensitivities. His rhetoric and actions exemplified for Americans what it meant to embrace Jews as trusted insiders.

TOP

LINCOLN AND LITHOGRAPHER MAX ROSENTHAL

On October 3, 1861, Lincoln asked Secretary of State William H. Seward to see Jewish lithographer, Max Rosenthal.
Shapell Manuscript Collection

ABOVE

In 1908, Max Rosenthal created this signed image of Lincoln, based on the June 3, 1860 photograph by Alexander Hesler.
Shapell Manuscript Collection

OPPOSITE

THE LINCOLN PROFILE AND 1909 PENNY

The Lincoln image that would go on to grace the one-cent coin was taken by Mathew Brady on February 9, 1864. The original Lincoln penny, designed in 1909 by Victor David Brenner, a Jewish engraver, was, for a short time, engraved with Brenner's initials on the back.
Shapell Manuscript Collection, Stack's Bowers Galleries

LINCOLN AND THE JEWS CHRONOLOGY

Highlighting Connections with Abraham Jonas (Blue) and Issachar Zacharie (Red)

1843

February 22: Washington's birthday is celebrated in Springfield. Abraham Jonas gives the address with Abraham Lincoln in attendance.

1848

Abraham Lincoln represents Elias Salzenstein in court.

1854

September 16: Earliest known letter from Abraham Jonas to Lincoln; it regards political affairs.

October 31: Lincoln meets with Abraham Jonas after arriving in Quincy, Illinois.

November 1: Following a political speech, Lincoln accompanies Jonas to an "oyster saloon" in Quincy.

December 2: In a letter, Abraham Jonas offers Lincoln his support for a Senate run in 1855.

1855

January 1: Lincoln meets Henry Greenebaum for the first time.

Lincoln meets Julius Hammerslough for the first time, in Springfield, Illinois.

1856

October 21: In a sign of their closeness, Lincoln writes Abraham Jonas of being "hobbled" by a case.

November 4: Lincoln and Jonas are electors in the 1856 presidential election, listed together in numerous poll books.

Lincoln is a judge on a case involving Gerhard Foreman, the brother-in-law of Henry Greenebaum.

1857

June 4: Abraham Jonas's son Benjamin works with Lincoln on freeing John Shelby, a black man held unjustly in a New Orleans jail.

Henry Rice serves as a witness in a court case of Lincoln's.

1858

April 3: Jackson Grimshaw writes to Lincoln about politics and mentions the role of Abraham Jonas in local events.

April 25: Lincoln sits for photographer Samuel Alschuler in Urbana, Illinois.

July 30: Abraham Jonas invites Lincoln to visit him in Augusta, Illinois, the next month.

August 2: Lincoln writes to Jonas that he will be with him in Augusta on August 25th.

August 5: Jonas writes to Lincoln that he has announced the visit of August 25th, and expects a large crowd for Lincoln's speech.

August 25: Between the first and second Lincoln-Douglas debates, Lincoln gives a speech with Abraham Jonas in Augusta.

August 25: Lincoln teases Abraham Jonas's son Edward during the assembly in Augusta.

December 26: At a meeting in the law offices of Jonas and Asbury, Lincoln is suggested as a potential presidential candidate.

1859

December 4–5: On the campaign trail, Lincoln visits the Wollman family in Leavenworth, Kansas.

1860

February 3: Jonas writes to Lincoln to request a copy of the Lincoln-Douglas debate book.

February 4: Lincoln writes to Abraham Jonas, noting that Jonas is one of his "most valued friends."

May 16: Mortiz Pinner attends the 1860 Republican National Convention as an unofficial delegate in support of Lincoln.

May 16: Lewis Dembitz attends the 1860 Republication National Convention as a delegate from Kentucky in support of Lincoln.

July 20: Jonas warns Lincoln of the rumors of Lincoln's presence at a Know-Nothing Lodge.

July 21: Lincoln responds to Jonas's warning regarding his rumored association with the Know-Nothings.

November 6: Sigismund Kaufmann serves as a Republican elector for Lincoln in the 1860 presidential election.

November 25: Lincoln sits for photographer Samuel Alschuler in Chicago.

November 26: Lincoln writes that he gave photographer Samuel Alschuler a sitting.

December 9: Orville Hickman Browning writes to Lincoln to request the appointment of Jonas as postmaster of Quincy, Illinois.

December 30: Jonas reports to Lincoln of a plot to assassinate the president-elect prior to Inauguration Day.

Lincoln inscribes a copy of the Lincoln-Douglas debate book to Abraham Jonas.

1861

January 1: Abraham Jonas signs a petition to Lincoln recommending a consular post.

February 11: Henry Greenebaum is part of the crowd that bids president-elect Lincoln goodbye at Springfield, Illinois.

February 19: Lincoln meets Sigismund Kaufmann, likely for the first time, at a reception for members of the Electoral College in New York.

March 4: Adolphus Solomons attends Lincoln's 1861 Inaugural Ball.

April 29: Lincoln nominates Abraham Jonas as postmaster of Quincy.

May 20: Lincoln endorses Julian Allen's proposal for a regiment of Polish-American volunteers.

May 26: Lincoln writes to Secretary of War Simon Cameron that he is "very much inclined to accept Col. [Max] Einsteins Regiment and wish you would have it mustered into service as soon as possible."

June 1: Lincoln appoints Charles Bernays as consul to Zurich.

July 10: Lincoln writes to the Senate to nominate Abraham Jonas.

July 21: Lincoln signs another appointment of Abraham Jonas as deputy postmaster.

August 10: Lincoln appoints Alfred Mordecai Jr. as second lieutenant.

September 3: Lincoln endorses Moritz Pinner as quartermaster.

September 10: Lincoln endorses the promotion of Isaac Moses to paymaster of New York.

September 25: Lincoln appoints Isaac Moses as assistant adjutant general with rank of captain.

October 3: Lincoln asks Secretary of State William Seward to see lithographer Max Rosenthal.

November 13: Lincoln appoints Max Einstein consul at Nuremberg.

November 23: Magicians Alexander and Carl Hermann perform at the White House.

December 6: Lincoln endorses clothier Henry Rice as military storekeeper.

December 11: Amid the chaplaincy affair, Lincoln receives Arnold Fischel at the White House.

December 14: Lincoln addresses the chaplaincy affair, on behalf of the "Israelites," in a letter to Arnold Fischel.

December 24: As a favor, Lincoln sends an autograph for Republican elector Sigismund Kaufmann.

1862

January 6: Lincoln nominates Charles Bernays as consul at Elsinore.

January 25: Lincoln recommends that Henry Moses Judah be appointed brigadier general.

February 17: Lincoln writes to Stanton to "renew" his endorsement of Henry Moses Judah.

March 13: Lincoln thanks Abraham Hart for his sermon.

May 27: Joshua Speed appeals to Lincoln to free Simon and Emanuel Bamberger, noting they are Jews.

July 31: Lincoln writes to financier—and Rothschild emissary—August Belmont that "broken eggs can not be mended."

August 21: William Cullen Bryant writes to Lincoln to introduce Issachar Zacharie and attest to his skills.

August 21: Isaac Leeser writes to Lincoln with a request; John Hay replies that Lincoln wants "it done."

September 11: Lincoln writes to Stanton regarding two long letters he has received from August Belmont.

September 13: Issachar Zacharie treats Lincoln for wrist sprains.

September 18: Lincoln appoints Jacob Frankel as the first Jewish chaplain in the Union army.

September 20: Lincoln writes his first testimonial for Zacharie.

September 22: Lincoln signs his second testimonial for Zacharie, on the day the Emancipation Proclamation is announced.

September 23: Lincoln writes his third testimonial for Zacharie.

November 4: Lincoln writes "We have not yet appointed a Hebrew," and recommends C.M. Levy as assistant quartermaster with rank of captain.

November 25: Lincoln writes to General Nathanial Banks to recommend Zacharie and his potential usefulness to the Union among his "countrymen" in the South.

December 2: Lincoln queries Stanton about Congressman Leonard Myers's recommendation for a chaplaincy appointment.

December 4: Lincoln appoints Charles Bernays as paymaster.

December 13: Lincoln directs Abraham Jonas, his "Loyal and Sensible" friend, to review a legal case.

December 29: Cesar Kaskel telegrams Lincoln to alert him to Grant's General Orders No. 11 expelling Jews from the area under Grant's control.

1863

January 4: Lincoln meets with Cesar Kaskel in Washington, D.C. about Grant's Orders No. 11.

January 5: Lincoln rescinds Grant's General Orders No. 11.

January 7: Lincoln meets with a delegation of Jews regarding General Orders No. 11.

January 14: Zacharie writes to Lincoln to seek permission to visit General Banks.

January 22: Lincoln considers the appeal of Confederate clothier Herman Koppel.

February 19: Zacharie reports to Lincoln with information from his mission to Louisiana

February 27: Lincoln pardons Simon and Emanuel Bamberger.

March: Lincoln speaks of his regard for the Jews with Henry Wentworth Monk.

March 6: Nathaniel Banks writes to Lincoln about Zacharie in Louisiana, noting that Zacharie has "been very active and among the People, especially among his own countrymen, who are numerous and powerful."

March 17: Zacharie telegrams Lincoln reporting his arrival in New York.

March 25: Lincoln writes to Benjamin Gratz to grant permission for a cross-border house guest.

March 25: Lincoln writes to Zacharie that he is "running your matter down as fast as I can."

March 27: Zacharie writes to Lincoln that he hopes Lincoln will follow his advice.

April 10: Lincoln appoints Ferdinand Sarner as Jewish chaplain in the Union army.

April 22: Lincoln reappoints Jacob Frankel as Jewish chaplain in the Union army.

April 25: Zacharie writes to Lincoln regarding the political and military situation in New Orleans.

May 6: Lincoln appoints Bernhard Gotthelf as Jewish hospital chaplain.

May 9: Zacharie writes to Lincoln with an update on the situation in New Orleans.

July 20: Zacharie writes to Lincoln to seek permission to visit General Banks.

July 24: Lincoln endorses a pardon for Rudolph Blumenberg.

July 25: Lincoln signs the pardon for Rudolph Blumenberg.

August 26: George Kuhne is among five convicted deserters to write to Lincoln requesting a stay of execution.

August 27: General George Meade writes to Lincoln regarding the execution of deserters, including George Kuhne.

August 27: Lincoln responds to George Meade regarding the execution of five soldiers, including Kuhne.

August 28: Lincoln writes to Major General John G. Foster to introduce Zacharie.

August 28: Lincoln writes that William Mayer "was the most efficient officer in suppressing the late New-York riots."

August 29: Benjamin Szold meets Lincoln at the White House to appeal the execution of George Kuhne.

September 29: Zacharie sends Lincoln a telegram saying that he will meet with him the following day.

September 30: Zacharie visits Lincoln at the White House.

October 3: Lincoln appoints Charles Weil as a 2nd Lieutenant in the U.S. Signal Corps.

October 22: Zacharie assures Lincoln in a letter that he has not told anyone about their recent meeting.

October 22: Abraham Jonas requests that Lincoln grant him a permit to visit his son Charles in a Union prison.

November 14: Lincoln considers the promotion of William Mayer to brigadier general.

November 14: Lincoln writes to Stanton about William Mayer's request to raise new troops.

1864

January 9: Rachel Rosalie Phillips meets Lincoln at a White House event with her uncle Adolphus Solomons.

January 9: On Lincoln's behalf, John Hay thanks Alexander Hart for sending a sermon by Sabato Morais.

January 12: Lincoln appoints Nehemiah Miller as Justice of the Peace in Washington, DC.

January 16: Lincoln renominates C.M. Levy as assistant quartermaster with the rank of captain.

January 25: Lincoln attends a performance of *Gamea, or the Jewish Mother*, in Washington, DC.

January 28: Lincoln attends *Gamea* for the second time in one week.

February 4: Zacharie visits Lincoln at the White House with Goodman Mordecai, a confederate POW freed by Lincoln.

February 13: Zacharie writes to Lincoln and encloses a barrel of hominy.

February 24: Lincoln interviews Joseph Merrifield, a soldier who has filed a complaint of anti-Semitism against General Butler.

March 1: Lincoln promotes Ephraim Joel to the rank of Captain.

March 2: Lincoln reappoints Jacob Frankel as Jewish chaplain in the Union army.

March 13: Lincoln asks Michael Hahn, the governor of Louisiana, how might full citizenship, the "jewel of liberty," be extended to African Americans in a postbellum state.

March 16: Lincoln frees Confederate POW Jacob G. Cohen, at the request of Zacharie, Cohen's uncle.

March 24: Famed pianist Louis Gottschalk plays for Lincoln in a concert at Willard's Hotel.

April 26: Lincoln endorses the court-martial of Ferdinand Levy, removing Levy's disability.

April 30: Lincoln endorses what Senator Conness says about Julius Silversmith.

April 30: Lincoln "cheerfully" endorses what Governor Nye says about Julius Silversmith.

May 4: Lincoln purchases a pair of eyeglasses from Jewish optometrist Isaac Heilprin, with a personal check.

May 13: Zacharie writes again to Lincoln, and sends his regards to Mrs. Lincoln.

June 2: Lincoln allows Charles Jonas, a Confederate POW, to visit his dying father, Abraham Jonas, in Illinois.

June 10: Orville Browning visits Lincoln to request the nomination of Louisa Jonas as postmistress of Quincy, Illinois.

June 13: Lincoln nominates Louisa Jonas as postmistress in place of her deceased husband, Abraham Jonas.

June 28: Lincoln signs the appointment of Louisa Jonas as postmistress of Quincy.

July 15: Lincoln thanks Philadelphia civic leader Lazarus Lieberman for the gift of a suit of clothes.

August 2: Lincoln writes to Treasury secretary William Fessenden to introduce Issachar Zacharie.

August 18: Lincoln appoints Ephraim Joel to serve on General Blair's staff.

September 9: Responding to a request by congressman Leonard Myers, Lincoln responds that "I really wish this done."

September 15: Lincoln orders Moses Waldauer, convicted on a spurious charge of aiding deserters, released from prison.

September 19: Lincoln thanks Zacharie for his commitment to the Union cause and mentions that the matter of his friend will be considered.

September 21: Zacharie writes to Lincoln that his note of the 19th has had the "desired effect."

September 24: Mary Lincoln writes to General Patrick requesting that Herman Grau be able to set up a business in City Point, Virginia.

September 24: Lincoln requests that Treasury secretary Fessenden "see and hear" Sigmund Griff.

September 26: Lincoln requests Secretary of War Stanton to receive Sigmund Griff.

September 27: Lincoln tells Griff that he will meet with Secretary of War Stanton on Griff's behalf.

October 8: Lincoln overturns the conviction of Moses Waldauer for assisting deserters.

October 26: Lincoln meets with Jews in the White House to discuss the Jewish vote in the upcoming presidential election.

November 1: At Lincoln's request, John Hay writes Myer Isaacs regarding issues of the Jewish vote.

November 3: Zacharie writes to Lincoln about political affairs.

November 8: Abram Dittenhoefer serves as Republican presidential elector for New York, upon Lincoln's reelection.

December 2: Lincoln directs Secretary of the Treasury Fessenden to "see and hear" Major Joseph H. Stiner.

December 9: Lincoln asks Attorney General James Speed to reappoint Nehemiah Miller as Justice of the Peace.

December 10: Lincoln frees prisoner Abraham B. Samuels, held by the notoriously anti-Semitic General Benjamin Butler.

December 26: Zacharie telegrams Lincoln to congratulate him on the fall of Savannah.

December 27: Lincoln grants Jacob G. Cohen, Zacharie's nephew, a pass to travel to Savannah.

December 27: Lincoln grants Zacharie a pass for travel to Savannah.

December 27: Lincoln writes to General William Sherman to introduce Issachar Zacharie.

1865

January 7: Lincoln goes to a performance of *Leah, the Forsaken* at Grover's Theater in Washington, DC.

January 8: Lincoln orders the protection of Philip and Meyer Wallach while they are held in prison.

January 11: Lincoln endorses the appointment of Abram Dittenhoefer.

January 12: Lincoln requests a review of the case of Philip and Meyer Wallach.

January 13: Lincoln writes of a request from congressman Leonard Myers: "I will do it, because Mr. Myers requests it."

January 25: Lincoln writes to Secretary of War Stanton, "About Jews," regarding Zacharie and, separately, Leopold Blumenberg.

January 25: Stanton responds to Lincoln's note "About Jews" that the requests have been addressed.

January 28: Lincoln endorses petition by Abram Dittenhoefer for the pardon of Morris and Abraham Leon.

February 6: Lincoln arranges for the release of Leopold Markbreit, a Union POW held and tortured by the Confederacy.

February 11: Myer S. Isaacs, Adolphus S. Solomons, and Zillah Solomons attend a reception at the Executive Mansion hosted by the first lady, with the President assisting.

February 17: Lincoln, in his third intervention in the Wallach brothers' case, allows them a "jubilee."

March 6: Lincoln grants Lion and Frank Silverman a pass to move their products across blockade lines.

March 11: Lincoln nominates Benjamin Levy to the volunteer force.

April 5: Gustavus Myers meets with Lincoln aboard the USS *Malvern* to discuss the conditions of peace.

April 14: C.H. Liebermann attends Lincoln's deathbed, pouring brandy down his throat.

NOTES

List of Abbreviations:

AJA – American Jewish Archives, Cincinnati, OH

AJA – American Jewish Archives (Journal)

AJHS – American Jewish Historical Society, New York, NY

AL – Abraham Lincoln

ALPLM – Abraham Lincoln Presidential Library and Museum, Springfield, IL

CW – The Collected Works of Abraham Lincoln. Abraham Lincoln and Roy P. Basler, 8 vols. New Brunswick, N.J: Rutgers University Press, 1953.

PAJHS – Publications of the American Jewish Historical Society

LOC – The Library of Congress, Washington, D.C.

AGO - *The Adjutant General's Office.* Washington: Dept. of Defense, Dept. of the Army, Adjutant General's Office, 1979.

NARA – U. S. National Archives and Records Administration

OR – *The War of the Rebellion: A Compilation of the Official Records of the Union and Confederate Armies.* Washington, D.C.: Government Printing Office, 1880-1901.

PUSG – *The Papers of Ulysses S. Grant,* ed. John Y. Simon, 31 vols. Carbondale: Southern Illinois University Press, 1967-2009.

INTRODUCTION

1. Robert D. Putnam, *American Grace: How Religion Divides and Unites Us* (New York: Simon & Schuster, 2010), 526-27.

2. *Israelite* (January 16, 1863), 218; see below, chapter 4, 112-18.

3. Jonathan D. Sarna, *American Judaism: A History* (New Haven: Yale University Press, 2004), 375; Jacob R. Marcus, *To Count a People: American Jewish Population Data, 1585-1984* (Lanham: University Press of America, 1990).

4. AL to Edwin M. Stanton (November 4, 1862); see below, chapter 4, 92

5. *CW* 5, 497-98; see below, chapter 4, 92.

6. Richard S. Lambert, *For the Time Is at Hand* (London: Andrew Melrose, Ltd., [1947]), 82, see below, chapter 5, 138–41.

7. Lester I Vogel, *To See a Promised Land: Americans and the Holy Land in the Nineteenth Century* (University Park: Pennsylvania University Press, 1993); Hilton Obenzinger, *American Palestine: Melville, Twain, and the Holy Land Mania* (Princeton: Princeton University Press, 1999).

CHAPTER ONE: THE PROMISED LAND . . . WHOSE STONES ARE IRON AND OUT OF WHOSE HILLS THOU MAYEST DIG BRASS

1. Jonathan D. Sarna, *American Judaism: A History* (New Haven: Yale University Press, 2004), 375.

2. Joseph Rauch, "Kentucky," *Universal Jewish Encyclopedia* (1942), 6: 362-63; William Vincent Byars, *B. and M. Gratz: Merchants in Philadelphia* (Jefferson City, MO: Hugh Stephens Printing Co, 1916), 258. 262, 278;

Morris Feuerlicht, "Indiana," *Universal Jewish Encyclopedia* (1942) 5:557-8; Ralph D. Gray, "Judah, Samuel," http://www.anb.org/articles/11/11-00481.html, American National Biography Online Feb. 2000, (accessed February 11, 2013); Ruth Marcus Patt, *The Jewish Experience at Rutgers* (East Brunswick, NJ, 1987), 4-14.

3. Ronald C. White, Jr., *A. Lincoln: A Biography* (New York: Random House, 2009), 13.

4. http://quod.lib.umich.edu/l/lincoln/lincoln7/1:1184?rgn=div1;singlegenre=All;sort=occur;subview=detail;type=simple;view=fulltext;q1=best+gift+God

5. Rufus Rockwell Wilson, *What Lincoln Read* (Washington DC, 1932), 13; Michael Hoberman, *New Israel/New England: Jews and Puritans in Early America* (Amherst, MA: University of Massachusetts Press, 2011), 26; Philip L. Ostergard, *The Inspired Wisdom of Abraham Lincoln* (Carol Stream, ILL: Tyndale House Publishers, 2008), 245-52; quote is from CW 7:542.

6. See Minute Book of Little Pigeon Creek Baptist Church Spencer County, Indiana 1816–1840, 2–3; online at http://www.bakerscreekbaptistchurch.com/history/history/bakerscreekbaptistchurchlinkswithabrahamlincoln.html; spelling modernized.

7. Mark A. Noll, *America's God* (New York: Oxford, 2002), 370-85.

8. Perry Miller, *Nature's Nation* (Cambridge: Harvard University Press, 1967), 209.

9. Ronald White, *A. Lincoln: A Biography* (New York: Random House, 2009), 8-9; Ida Tarbell, *In the Footsteps of Lincoln* (New York: Harper, 1924), 1-16; William E. Barton, *The Lineage of Lincoln* (Indianapolis: Bobbs Merrill, 1929), 20-40; Robert D. Linder, "Protestant Traditions in Western Europe on the Eve of North American Colonization," *The Cambridge History of Religions in America*, ed. Stephen J. Stein (New York: Cambridge University Press, 2012), 70-71; for the Lincolns in Hingham, see Solomon Lincoln, *History of the Town of Hingham, Plymouth County, Massachusetts* (Hingham, 1827), esp. 180-181. A Lincoln to Solomon Lincoln, March 24, 1848, Rosenbach Company, Philadelphia.

10. Clarence E. Macartney, *Lincoln and the Bible* (New York: Abingdon-Cokesbury, 1949), 10-12; Don E. Fehrenbacher and Virginia Fehrenbacher (eds.), *Recollected Words of Abraham Lincoln* (Stanford: Stanford University Press, 1996), 372-74.

11. Robert Bray, *Reading with Lincoln* (Carbondale: Southern Illinois University Press, 2010), 4.

12. Lindley Murray, *The English Reader* (Stockbridge: Charles Webster, 1822; orig. ed. 1799), 19-21.

13. Ibid, quotations (in order) from pp. 79, 96, 223, 36. Contrast, William H. McGuffey, *The Eclectic Third Reader* (Cincinnati: Truman and Smith, 1837; reprint Mott Media, 1982), 69, 75.

14. Minute Book of Little Pigeon Creek Baptist Church Spencer County, Indiana 1816-1840, 2-3; online at http://www.bakerscreekbaptistchurch.com/history/history/bakerscreekbaptistchurchlinkswithabrahamlincoln.html (accessed 12 February 2013); spelling modernized.

15. Allen C. Guelzo, *Abraham Lincoln: Redeemer President* (Grand Rapids, MI: Eerdmans, 1999), 36.

16. *Religious Intelligencer* 1 (1817), 555-558; Jonathan D. Sarna, *American Judaism: A History* (New Haven: Yale University Press, 2004), 74; Jonathan D. Sarna, "The American Jewish Response to Nineteenth-Century Christian Missions," *Journal of American History* 68 (June 1981), 35-51.

17. *The Reformer* 4 (1823), 60-62; Jonathan D. Sarna, "American Christian Opposition to Mission to the Jews, 1816-1900," *Journal of Ecumenical Studies*, 23:2 (Spring 1986), 225-38; Guelzo, *Abraham Lincoln*, 36-38; see the discussion of missions on http://www.bakerscreekbaptistchurch.com/history/history/bakerscreekbaptistchurchlinkswithabrahamlincoln.html (accessed 12 February 2013).

18. William H. Herndon and Jesse W. Weik, *Herndon's Lincoln,* eds. Douglas L. Wilson and Rodney O. Davis (Urbana: University of Illinois Press, 2006), 264.

19. Guelzo, *Abraham Lincoln*, 119; quotes are from Lincoln's second inaugural address.

20. George Washington to the Hebrew Congregation in Newport, Rhode Island (n.d, August 1790); for a discussion and commentary see *To Bigotry No Sanction: George Washington and Religious Freedom* (Philadelphia: National Museum of American Jewish History, 2012).

21. *The German Correspondent* 1 (1820), 6.

22. Jonathan D. Sarna, "The 'Mythical Jew' and the 'Jew Next Door' in Nineteenth-Century America," *Antisemitism in American History,* ed. David A. Gerber (Urbana: University of Illinois Press, 1986), 57-78.

23. Frederic Cople Jaher, *A Scapegoat in the Wilderness: The Origins and Rise of Anti-Semitism in America* (Cambridge: Harvard University Press, 1994), 114-69; Leonard Dinnerstein, *Antisemitism in America* (New York: Oxford, 1994), 13-34; Jonathan D. Sarna, "American Antisemitism," in David Berger (ed.), *History and Hate* (Philadelphia: Jewish Publication Society, 1986), 115-28.

24. Joseph L. Blau and Salo W. Baron, *Jews of the United States 1790-1840: A Documentary History* (New York: Columbia U Press, 1963), I, 28-32; Jacob R. Marcus, *United States Jewry 1776-1985* (Detroit: Wayne State University Press, 1989), I, 506-9.

25. Thomas Jefferson to Benjamin Rush (April 21, 1803) in *The Writings of Thomas Jefferson,* ed. Andrew A. Lipscomb (Washington, DC, 1904), 10:382; Thomas Jefferson to John Adams (October 12, 1813) in *The Adams-Jefferson Letters,* ed. Lester J. Capon (Chapel Hill, NC: University of North Carolina Press, 1959), 2:383; Thomas Jefferson to Mordecai M. Noah (May 28, 1818) in *Publications of the American Jewish Historical Society* 3 (1895), 94-95; Robert M. Healey, "Jefferson, Judaism and the Jews: Divided We Stand, United We Fall!" *American Jewish History* 73 (June 1984), 359-374.

26. Constitutional guarantees of no "religious test" for public office, as well as no "establishment of religion" and the "free exercise" of religion only applied, at that time, to congressional legislation, not to state legislation.

27. Blau and Baron, *Jews in the United States: A Documentary History* I, 15-16, 33-55; Edward Eitches, "Maryland's 'Jew Bill,'" *American Jewish Historical Quarterly* 60 (March 1971), 258-80.

CHAPTER TWO: AND THIS TOO SHALL PASS AWAY—NEVER FEAR

1. *Johnson v. M'Intosh,* 21 U.S. 543, 5 L.Ed. 681, 8 Wheat. 543 (1823); for an explanation of this famous case, see Eric Kades, "History and Interpretation of the Great Case of *Johnson v. M'Intosh*," *Law and History Review* 19:1 (Spring 2001), 67-116.

2. Douglas L. Wilson and Rodney O. Davis, eds. *Herndon's Informants: Letters, Interview, and Statements about Abraham Lincoln* (Urbana: University of Illinois Press, 1998), 201.

3. Herman E. Snyder, "A Brief History of the Jews in Springfield, Illinois and of Temple Brith Sholom," p.2, copy in Snyder Papers, American Jewish Archives, Cincinnati, OH; George W. Hawes, *Illinois State Gazetteer and Business Directory for 1858 and 1859* (Chicago, 1858), 205-7; Curtis Mann, "North Side of Public Square," *For the People: A Newsletter of the Abraham Lincoln Association* 12 (Spring 2010), 1-2, online at http://www.abrahamlincolnassociation.org/Newsletters/12-1.pdf; M. R. Werner, *Julius Rosenwald* (New York: Harper, 1939), 7 dates the store to 1856.

4. Snyder, "Brief History," 2; "Julius Hammerslough, "*Men's Wear* 25 (1908), 54-55, online at Google books; "Julius Hammerslough, 1832-1908," http://www.frf.com/family/individual.php?pid=I200&ged=FRF_GED_ONLINE.ged (accessed 25 April 2013); George W. Hawes, Illinois State Gazetteer and Business Directory for 1858 and 1859 (Chicago, 1858), 205-7; *New York Times,* June 20, 1908; David Herbert Donald, *"We Are Lincoln Men": Abraham Lincoln and His Friends* (New York: Simon & Schuster, 2003), xiv-xvi; Markens, *Abraham Lincoln and the Jews,* 22–23.

5. Werner, *Julius Rosenwald,* 8; "Julius Hammerslough, "*Men's Wear* 25 (1908), 54-55.

6. [Baltimore] Sun, Feb 16, 1856, Local Matters, pg. 1; Snyder, "Brief History," 2; *Israelite,* June 9, 1865, 397.

7. Selma Stern, *The Court Jew* (Philadelphia: Jewish Publication Society, 1950, esp. 59, 254; Yehezkel Kotik, *Journey to a Nineteenth-Century Shtetl: The Memoirs of Yehezkel Kotik,* ed. David Assaf (Detroit: Wayne State University Press, 2002), 114-15.

8. "Salzenstein's Store: Abraham Lincoln Shopped Here," *Chicago Jewish History* 26 (Winter 2002), 7.

9. For the court cases, see *The Law Practice of Abraham Lincoln,* University of Illinois Press, Champaign, IL, 2000.

10. "Salzenstein's Store: Abraham Lincoln Shopped Here," *Chicago Jewish History* 26:1 (Winter 2002), 6-7; http://www.abrahamlincolnlongninemuseum.com/map.php; Howard M. Sachar, *A History of the Jews in America* (New York: Alfred Knopf, 1992), 3-7. James E. Myers, a son of Albert Myers, helped to preserve and restore the Springfield office where Lincoln and William Herndon practiced law, today known as the Lincoln-Herndon Museum, and also authored *The Astonishing Saber Duel of Abraham Lincoln* (1968).

11. On Jonas, see Bertram W. Korn, *American Jewry and the Civil War* (Philadelphia: Jewish Publication Society, 1951), 189-94; Ira L. Harris, "Abraham Jonas: Lincoln's Valued Friend," *Lincoln Herald* 92:4 (1990), 118-23; Mike Mehlman, "One of Lincoln's Most Valued Friends," *Lincoln Herald* 103:3 (2001), 145-55; Wayne C. Temple, "Abraham Jonas: One of Lincoln's 'Most Valued [Masonic] Friends,'" *The Illinois Lodge of Research Transactions* 14 (September 2005), 15-24 (online at http://www.illor.org/2005.pdf).

12. CW 3, 516, cf. CW4, 495.

13. Joseph Jonas, "The Jews in Ohio," reprinted in *A Documentary History of the Jews in the United States 1654-1875,* ed. Morris U. Schappes (3rd Edition, New York: Schocken, 1971), 224; Jonathan D. Sarna and Nancy H. Klein, *The Jews of Cincinnati* (Cincinnati: Center for the Study of the American Jewish Experience, 1989), 2, 25-29; *London Jewish Chronicle,* May 14, 1880, 5.

14. Jonas, "The Jews in Ohio," 225; Sarna & Klein, 27-29.

15. David Philipson, *The Oldest Jewish Congregation in the West, Bene Israel* Cincinnati (Cincinnati, 1924), 16-17. Lucia Orah's death is frequently misdated, but the tombstone clearly states "1st of Tammuz 5585." Rachel, the wife of Joseph Jonas, passed away less than two years later on February 19, 1827. Abraham Jonas married Louisa Block on October 11, 1829; see Malcolm Stern, *First American Jewish Families* (New York: Ottenheimer,

1981), 136 and Ira Rosenwaike, "Eleazar Block—His Family and Career," *American Jewish Archives* 31 (November 1979), 143-44.

16. On Jews and Freemasonry, see especially Jacob Katz, *Jews and Freemasons in Europe 1723-1939* (Cambridge: Harvard University Press, 1971); Samuel Oppenheim, "The Jews and Masonry in the United States before 1810," *Publications of the American Jewish Historical Society* 19 (1910), 1-94; and for a Jewish Mason who was contemporary with Jonas, Joseph L. Blau and Salo W. Baron, *The Jews of the United States 1790-1840* (New York: Columbia University Press, 1963), 3, 697-700. Jonas's Freemasonry career is explored in Wayne C. Temple, "Abraham Jonas: One of Lincoln's 'Most Valued [Masonic] Friends,'" *The Illinois Lodge of Research Transactions* 14 (September 2005), 15-24, online at illor.org/2005.

17. According to legislative records, he was elected in 1828, 1829, 1831, and 1833.

18. CW 3, 29; see also Shearer Davis Bowman, "Comparing Henry Clay and Abraham Lincoln," *The Register of the Kentucky Historical Society* 106 (Summer/Autumn 2008), 495-512.

19. Robert V. Remini, *Henry Clay Statesman for the Union* (New York: Norton, 1993), 745.

20. Henry Clay to Abraham Jonas (May 3, 1838), Wells Family Collection; I am grateful to Cynthia Gensheimer for providing me with a transcript of this letter.

21. Henry Clay to Abraham Jonas (16 September 1842), *The Papers of Henry Clay: The Whig Leader,* ed. Robert Seager II (Lexington: University of Kentucky Press, 1988), IX, 768.

22. Wayne C. Temple, "Abraham Jonas: One of Lincoln's 'Most Valued [Masonic] Friends," *The Illinois Lodge of Research* 14 (September 2005), 17.

23. John C. Reynolds, *History of the M.W. Grand Lodge of Illinois Ancient, Free and Accepted Masons: From the Organization of the First Lodge Within the Present Limits of the State Up to and Including 1850* (Springfield, 1860).

24. *Times and Seasons* 3 (1842), 749-50 as quoted in Rudolf Glanz, *Jew and Mormon* (New York: Waldon Press, 1963), 159.

25. Gary Vitale, "Abraham Lincoln and the Mormons: Another Legacy of Limited Freedom," *Journal of the Illinois State Historical Society* 101 (Fall–Winter 2008), 260-71.

26. Vitale, "Abraham Lincoln and the Mormons: Another Legacy of Limited Freedom," 262. *The Latter-Day Saints Millennial Star* 24 (London: 1862), 583, 663-65, 775.

27. Earl Schenck Miers, *Lincoln Day by Day: A Chronology 1809-1865* (Dayton: Morningside Press, 1991), 202; Charles M. Segal, "Abraham Jonas' Role in Lincoln's First Presidential Nomination," *PAJHS* 4 (December 1954), 98-99.

28. Brian J. Kenny. "Browning, Orville Hickman"; http://www.anb.org/articles/04/04-00164.html; American National Biography Online Feb. 2000; Access Date: Thu May 23 2013; see Maurice Baxter, *Orville H. Browning, Lincoln's Friend and Critic* (Bloomington: Indiana University Press, 1957).

29. *The Diary of Orville Hickman Browning,* ed. Theodore Calvin Pease and James G. Randall (Springfield: Illinois State Historical Library, 1927), 185 (May 31, 1855). Claims that they were partners from 1843 are unfounded.

30. Donald, *We Are Lincoln Men,* 103.

31. See the references to Jonas in *The Diary of Orville Hickman Browning* and Miers, *Lincoln Day by Day,* 271 (April 23, 1846).

32. Gustav Philipp Körner, *Memoirs of Gustave Koerner, 1809-1896: life-sketches written at the suggestion of his children* (Cedar Rapids, OH: Torch Press, 1909), vol. 1, 479-80.

33. David Frolick, "From Strangers to Neighbors: The Children of Abraham in Quincy, Illinois," *Journal of Illinois History* 7 (2004) 17.; http://www.bnaisholomquincy.com/history.php.

34. *Diary of Orville Hickman Browning,* 425 (August 25, 1860) et passim; AL to Abraham Jonas (July 21, 1860), CW 4, 86.

35. Harrison Dills to Abraham Lincoln (February 19, 1849, April 10, 1849), Abraham Lincoln Papers, LOC, online at memory.loc.gov; on Dills see http://djdills.blogspot.com/2013/05/harrison-dills-bits1.html.

36. *Diary of Orville Hickman Browning,* 100 (April 15, 1853); 158 (October 18, 1854); Abraham Jonas to Abraham Lincoln (September 16 1854), Abraham Lincoln Papers, LOC.

37. CW 2, 282.

38. CW 4, 67.

39. Burlingame, *Abraham Lincoln,* I, 363-76.

40. Abraham Jonas to Abraham Lincoln (September 16, 1854), Abraham Lincoln Papers, LOC.

41. CW 2, 240-283; Douglas, as quoted in David H. Donald, *Lincoln* (New York: Simon & Schuster, 1995), 178.

42. Abraham Lincoln to Abraham Jonas (July 21, 1860), CW 4, 85-86 recounted the visit, which is also described in *Diary of Orville Hickman Browning,* 160 (November 1, 1854).

43. Abraham Lincoln to Richard Yates (October 30, 1854), CW 2, 284.

44. Abraham Jonas to Abraham Lincoln (December 2, 1854), Abraham Lincoln Papers, LOC.

45. David Osborn, "Trumbull, Lyman"; http://www.anb.org/articles/04/04-00998.html.

46. American National Biography Online Feb. 2000. Access Date: Mon May 27 2013: Ronald C. White, *A. Lincoln* (New York: Random House, 2009), 208.

47. Abraham Lincoln to Abraham Jonas (October 21, 1856), CW II, 380. Shapell Manuscript Collection.

48. Henry Clay Whitney, *Life on the Circuit with Lincoln...* (Boston: Estes and Lauriat Publishers, 1892), 475-77.

49. Ibid, 475-77; *People v. Johnson,* http://www.lawpracticeofabrahamlincoln.org/Details.aspx?case=136604.

50. http://www.historycentral.com/elections/1856Pop.html.

51. Charles M. Segal, "Lincoln, Benjamin Jonas and the Black Code," *Journal of the Illinois State Historical Society* 46 (Autumn 1953), 277-282; Eric Foner, *The Fiery Trial: Abraham Lincoln and American Slavery* (New York: Norton, 2010), 121.

52. Benjamin Franklin Jonas (1834-1911) subsequently fought for the Confederacy and, in 1879, was elected senator from Louisiana. During his term of office (1879–85), he was the Senate's only Jew; see Kurt F. Stone, *The Jews of Capitol Hill: A Compendium of Jewish Congressional Members* (Lanham:Scarecrow Press, 2011), 35-37.

53. B. F. Jonas to Abraham Lincoln (June 4, 1857), Abraham Lincoln Papers, LOC; Annie Jonas to Wm H. Herndon (October 28, 1866) in *Herndon's Informants: Letters, Interviews, and Statements About Abraham Lincoln,* eds. Douglas L. Wilson and Rodney O. Davis (Urbana: University of Illinois Press, 1998.), online at http://lincoln.lib.niu.edu/file.php?file=herndon379.html; William H. Herndon and Jesse W. Weik, *Herndon's Lincoln,* eds. Douglas L. Wilson and Rodney O. Davis (Urbana: University of Illinois Press, 2006), 232-33.

54. *Dred Scott v. Sandford,* 60 U.S. 393, at 16; see Justice Curtis's pointed dissent at 181.

55. CW 2, 398-410.

56. Gale v Morgan County Bank, file ID: L02145, The Law Practice of Abraham Lincoln, http://www.lawpracticeofabrahamlincoln.org/Details.aspx?case=137526. On Rice, see the *New York Times* obituary, June 8, 1914.

57. Isaac Markens, *Abraham Lincoln and the Jews,* 23-24; Shapell Manuscript Collection.

58. Markens, *Abraham Lincoln and the Jews,* 27-28; H. L.Meites, *History of the Jews of Chicago* (Chicago: Jewish Historical Society of Illinois, 1924), 47-48; Tobias Brinkmann, *Sundays at Sinai* (Chicago: University of Chicago Press, 2012), 60-62.

59. Matthew 12:25, Mark 3:25.

60. CW 2, 461-69. Douglas, upon the death of his wife, became an owner of Mississippi slaves, which he held in trust for his children; see Martin H. Quitt, *Stephen A. Douglas and Antebellum Democracy* (Cambridge: Cambridge University Press, 2012), 186-94.

61. Henry Asbury to Abraham Lincoln (July 28, 1858), Lincoln Papers, LOC.

62. CW 2, 533.

63. Abraham Jonas to AL (July 30, 1858), Abraham Lincoln Papers, LOC; CW 2, 533-34; 3, 37-38; John E. Boos, *Rare Personal Accounts of Abraham Lincoln,* William R. Feeheley and Bill Snack, eds. (Cadillac, Mich: Rail Splitter Publishing, 2005), 40-42.

64. *Quincy Daily Whig* (September 30, 1858), 2.

65. William A. Richardson Jr., "Pen Pictures of the Central Part of the City of Quincy as It Was when Douglas and Lincoln Met in Debate," *Journal of the Illinois State Historical Society* 18 (July 1925), 401-2.

66. *Quincy Daily Whig,* October 7, 1858, 2:1 as quoted in Mike Mehlman, "One of Lincoln's Most Valued Friends," *Lincoln Herald* 103:3 (2001), 148.

67. Maurice G. Baxter, *Orville H. Browning: Lincoln's Friend and Critic* (Bloomington: Indiana University Press, 1957), 94; http://www.thelincolnlog.org/Calendar.aspx?year=1858&month=10 (accessed June 4, 2013).

68. CW 3, 245-83; Michael Burlingame, *Abraham Lincoln: A Life* (Baltimore: Johns Hopkins University Press, 2008), 534-37, provides a summary and contrasting contemporary views on whether Lincoln or Douglas won the debate.

69. *Reminiscences of Abraham Lincoln by Distinguished Men of His Time,* ed. Allen Thorndike Rice (New York: North American Publishing Company, 1886), 537; Burlingame, *Abraham Lincoln,* 545-54; Lincoln to Norman B. Judd (October 20, 1858), CW 3, 329-30.

70. Henry Asbury to Abraham Lincoln (November 13, 1858), Abraham Lincoln Papers; LOC; Lincoln to Asbury (November 19, 1858), CW 3, 339.

71. AL to Norman B. Judd (November 15, 1858), AL Papers, LOC; AL to Norman B. Judd (November 16, 1858) Shapell Manuscript Collection. For Lincoln's discussion of the phrase "And this too shall pass away," see

his address before the Wisconsin State Agricultural Society, Milwaukee, Wisconsin (September 30, 1859), CW 3, 482. See also Shnayer Z. Leiman, "Judith Ish-Kishor: This Too Shall Pass," *Tradition* 41: 1 (2008): 71-77; and Zola, *We Called Him Rabbi Abraham*, 374–376.

72.   Harry E. Pratt, *The Personal Finances of Abraham Lincoln* (Springfield: Abraham Lincoln Association, 1943), 54, 77-79, 105. By the time the investment was repaid, Lincoln was no longer alive.

73.   AL to Alexander Sympson (December 12, 1858), CW 3, 346; Burlingame, *Abraham Lincoln: A Life,* I, 549-51.

74.   Henry Asbury to K. K. Jones (October 2, 1882), copy in SC5836, AJA; *Diary of Orville Hickman Browning,* 345 (December 26, 1858); Charles M. Segal, "Abraham Jonas' Role in Lincoln's First Presidential Nomination," *PAJHS* 44 (December 1954), 100.

CHAPTER THREE: ONE OF
MY MOST VALUED FRIENDS

1.   Abraham Jonas to Lyman Trumbull (December 26, 1858), Trumbull Papers, LOC.

2.   *Occident* 16 (February 1, 1859), 536-42; David I. Kertzer, *The Kidnapping of Edgardo Mortara* (New York: Knopf, 1997), esp. 127; Bertram W. Korn, *The American Reaction to the Mortara Case* (Cincinnati: American Jewish Archives, 1957).

3.   Jonas to Trumbull (December 26, 1858), Trumbull Papers.

4.   AL to Nathan B. Dodson (July 29, 1859) in CW 3, 396; AL to Hawkins Taylor (September 6, 1859) in CW 3, 400.

5.   AL to Lyman Trumbull (January 29, 1859) in CW 3, 351.

6.   CW 3, 369.

7.   AL to Samuel Galloway (July 28, 1859), CW 3, 395; AL to Thomas J. Pickett (April 16, 1859), CW 3, 377-78.

8.   AL to Schuyler Colfax (July 6, 1859), CW 3, 390. Shapell Manuscript Collection item.

9.   Schurz's lecture (April 18, 1859) can be read at http://www.angelfire.com/ma3/bobwb/schurz/speech/americanism1859.html. On Schurz and his relationship with Jews, see Hans L. Trefousse, "German-American liberalism against Bigotry: Carl Schurz and the Jews," in *Germans in America: Aspects of German-American Relations in the Nineteenth Century,* ed. Edward A. McCormick (New York: Brooklyn College Press, 1983), 31-44.

10.   AL to Theodore Canisius (May 17, 1859), CW 3, 380.

11.   *Daily State Journal* (May 17, 1859) as reprinted in F. I.Herriott, *The Premises and Significance of Abraham Lincoln's Letter to Theodore Canisius (1915)*, online at http://libsysdigi.library.uiuc.edu/OCA/Books2009-06/premisessignific00herr/premisessignific00herr.pdf, 35-37.

12.   CW 3, 383.

13.   Gary Ecelbarger, "Before Cooper Union: Abraham Lincoln's 1859 Cincinnati Speech and Its Impact on his Nomination," *Journal of the Abraham Lincoln Association* 30 (Winter 2009), online at http://quod.lib.umich.edu/j/jala/2629860.0030.103/--before-cooper-union-abraham-lincolns-1859-cincinnati-speech?rgn=main;view=fulltext#link_note_12 (accessed July 12, 2013).

14.   http://www.census.gov/population/www/documentation/twps0027/tab09.txt; Jacob R. Marcus, *To Count a People: American Jewish Population Data, 1585-1984* (Lanham: University Press of America, 1990), 172-73. There were only about 1,500 Jews in Chicago at that time and 5,000 in San Francisco (Ibid, 28, 57).

15.   http://library.cincymuseum.org/lincoln/items/litho1859.htm. Meyer Rosenbaum had a tin shop around 1860, and in 1861 he was selling stoves at 191 West 5th Street. According to the Cincinnati City Directory, it was not until 1866 that a "Rosenbaum & Bros. - Stoves" appears at No. 24, the address depicted in the lithograph, which reads: "Hanging Rock Stove - Foundry - Rosenbaum & (Bros.) - Stoves…"

16.   Ecelbarger, "Before Cooper Union."

17.   CW 3, 462; see Luke 11:23.

18. Quoted in Michael Burlingame, *Abraham Lincoln: A Life* (Baltimore: Johns Hopkins University Press, 2008), I, 568.

19. Ecelbarger, "Before Cooper Union."

20. Mark W. Delahay and 53 others to AL (November 15, 1859), AL Papers, LOC.

21. http://lincolninkansas.org/LincolnInKSFront-Info%20copy%201.pdf; a pitcher from that dinner is preserved in the city's Frontier Army Museum. An advertisement for J.Wollman & Co is found in the *Kansas Herald of Freedom* (March 14, 1857) and Betty Wollman's memories are preserved in the *New York Times* (March 27, 1927 and December 26, 1927). On Wollman and Abeles, see Joan Ferris Curran, *Jonas and Betty (Kohn) Wollman and Their Descendants* (Kansas City: J. F.Curran, distributed by H.W.B. Glock, 1986); Joan Ferris Curran, *Descendants of Salomon Bloch of Janowitz, Bohemia, and Baruch Wollman of Kempen-in-Posen, Prussia* (Baltimore: Gateway Press, 1996), 112-22, 192 (quote from p. 118); and Julia Wood Kramer, *The House on the Hill: The Story of the Abeles Family of Leavenworth, Kansas* (Chicago: 1990), 13-56. Kramer (p. 21) questions whether Abeles "was stirred by the slavery question or was an ideologue."

22. S. M. Pettingill to William H. Bailhache (October 12, 1859), as quoted in Burlingame, *Abraham Lincoln: A Life,* I, 582.

23. Burlingame, *Abraham Lincoln: A Life,* I, 582-83.

24. Harold Holzer, *Lincoln at Cooper Union: The Speech that Made Abraham Lincoln President* (New York: Simon & Schuster, 2004).

25. Jacques J. Lyons and Abraham de Sola, *A Jewish Calendar for Fifty Years* (New York: Bloch, 1854), 160-167; Howard B. Rock, "Upheaval, Innovation and Transformation: New York City Jews and the Civil War," *American Jewish Archives Journal* 64 (2012), 2-3.

26. Holzer, Harold. *Lincoln at Cooper Union* (2005)

27. Abram J. Dittenhoefer, *How We Elected Lincoln: Personal Recollections* (Philadelphia: University of Pennsylvania, 2005 [1916]), 16.

28. Ibid, 4-5.

29. Ibid, 18-19; CW 3, 522-550.

30. Dittenhoefer, *How We Elected Lincoln,* 20; Harold Holzer, "The Speech That Made the Man," *American Heritage* 59:4 (2009), online at http://www.americanheritage.com/content/speech-made-man (accessed July 14, 2013).

31. AL to W. H. Wells (Jan 8, 1859), CW 3, 349; AL to W. H. Ross (March 26, 1859), CW 3, 372-73; AL to George Parsons et al. (December 19, 1859), CW 3, 510; Abraham Jonas to AL (February 3, 1860), http://memory.loc.gov/cgi-bin/query/r?ammem/mal:@field(DOCID+@lit(d0232800)) (accessed July 15, 2013); AL to Abraham Jonas (February 4, 1860), CW 3, 516; Jay Monaghan, "The Lincoln-Douglas Debates, The Follett, Foster Edition of a Great Political Document," *Lincoln Herald* 45 (June 1943), online at http://archive.org/stream/thelincoln-dougla00mona#page/12/mode/2up (accessed July 15, 2013); David Henry Leroy, *Mr. Lincoln's Book: Publishing the Lincoln-Douglas Debates* (New Castle, DE: Oak Knoll Press; Chicago: Abraham Lincoln Book Shop, Inc., 2009), esp. 64-66, 145-49, 160.

32. Walter Stahr, *Seward: Lincoln's Indispensable Man* (New York: Simon & Schuster, 2012), 174-81.

33. AL to Samuel Galloway (March 24, 1860), CW 4, 34.

34. K. K.Jones, "Abraham Lincoln: How He Was Nominated," *Indianapolis Sentinel* (29 Sept. 1882), p. 7. Jonas's former law partner, Henry Asbury, confirmed hearing this story from Jonas; see his letter to Jones (October 2, 1882), SC5386, American Jewish Archives, Cincinnati OH [available online at http://americanjewisharchives.org/exhibits/aje/details.php?id=677]. See also *Proceedings of the Republican National Convention* Held at Chicago, May 16, 17 and 18, 1860 (Albany: Weed, Parsons, 1860), 108; Charles M. Segal, "Abraham Jonas' Role in Lincoln's First Presidential Nomination," *Publications of the American Jewish Historical Society* 44 (1954), 98-105; and for an account that credits Alexander Conner, Republican state chairman of Indiana, with rounding up the supporters, Burlingame, *Abraham Lincoln: A Life,* I, 620.

35. Philippa Strum. "Dembitz, Lewis Naphtali"; http://www.anb.org/articles/11/11-00958.html; American National Biography Online Feb. 2000 (accessed Jul 16,

2013); Nelson I. Dawson, "Dembitz, Lewis Naphtali," *The Encyclopedia of Louisville*, ed. John Kieber (Louisville: University Press of Kentucky, 2001), 241-42; *Proceedings of the Republican National Convention*, 11, 35; Markens, *Abraham Lincoln and the Jews*, 36.

36. Charles L. Bernays, the delegate from Missouri, descended from a prominent Jewish family and was known to be of Jewish extraction. A freethinker, he and his siblings had been Christened and confirmed as Lutherans by their Jewish parents in Germany. Bernays was a staunch opponent of slavery and editor of the German-American newspaper *Anzeiger des Westens*. See *PAJHS* 9 (1901), 52; 11 (1903), 50; Bertram W. Korn, *Eventful Years and Experiences* (Cincinnati: American Jewish Archives, 1954), 8, 17; Carol S. Porter, *Meeting Louis at the Fair* (St. Louis: Virginia Publishing, 2004), 4-12; and, for the family background, Thekla Bernays, *Augustus Charles Bernays: A Memoir* (St. Louis: Mosby, 1912), 11-33.

37. *Daily Missouri Republican* (March 11, 1860); Moritz Pinner to Wendell Phillips (June 1, 1860), Blagden Collection of Wendell Phillips Papers, Houghton Library, Cambridge, MA, online at http://www.math.rutgers.edu/~zeilberg/family/wp2.html (accessed July 16, 2013); Markens, *Abraham Lincoln and the Jews*, 34-36. A great deal of additional material on Pinner is available on the Web site established by his descendants: http://www.math.rutgers.edu/~zeilberg/family/moritz.html (accessed July 16, 2013). On the *Missouri Post*, see http://chroniclingamerica.loc.gov/lccn/sn87052125/.

38. Moritz Pinner to Wendell Phillips (September 2, 1860), Blagden Collection of Wendell Phillips Papers, Houghton Library, Cambridge, MA, online at http://www.math.rutgers.edu/~zeilberg/family/wp3.html (accessed July 16, 2013).

39. Dittenhoefer, *How We Elected Lincoln*, 38-40.

40. Segal, "Abraham Jonas' Role in Lincoln's First Presidential Nomination," 103-4; *Quincy Whig Reoublican* (May 26, 1860, June 9, 1860); Iris A. Nelson and Walter S. Waggoner, "Sick, Sore and Sorry: The Stone's Prairie Riot of 1860," *Journal of Illinois History* 5:1 (2002), esp. 28.

41. Abraham Jonas to AL (July 20, 1860), LOC, online at http://memory.loc.gov/cgi-bin/query/P?mal:1:./temp/~ammem_e.

42. AL to Abraham Jonas (July 21, 1860), CW 4, 85-86.

43. AL to Joshua F. Speed (August 24, 1855) CW 2, 323.

44. AL to Abraham Jonas (July 21, 1860), CW 4, 86. Many Know-Nothings and members of the American Party ultimately supported Lincoln, preferring him to Douglas (who had a Catholic wife) and to the Southern candidates; see Burlingame, *Abraham Lincoln: A Life*, I, 659-62, 682-83.

45. AL to Joshua F. Speed (May 22, 1860), CW 10, 53-54.

46. Markens, *Abraham Lincoln and the Jews*, 35-36.

47. Theodore Calvin Pease and James G. Randall, eds., *The Diary of Orville Hickman Browning*, 2 vols., Collections of the Illinois State Historical Library (Springfield: Illinois State Historical Library, 1925-1933), 2:415.

48. AL to Cassius M. Clay (May 26, 1860), Shapell Legacy Partnership.

49. CW 3, 395.

50. AL to William D. Kelley (October 13, 1860), Shapell Legacy Partnership.

51. AL to David L. Phillips (July 2, 1860), Shapell Manuscript Collection; CW 4, 81; on Phillips see John Y. Simon, "Union County in 1858 and the Lincoln-Douglas Debate," *Journal of the Illinois State Historical Society* 62 (1969) 267-92, esp. 281.

52. AL to Hannibal Hamlin (July 18, 1860), CW 4, 84.

53. AL to William Seward (October 12, 1860), Shapell Legacy Partnership.

54. Burlingame, *Abraham Lincoln: A Life*, I, 680.

55. Howard B. Rock, "Upheaval, Innovation and Transformation: New York Jews and the Civil War," *American Jewish Archives Journal* 64 (2012), 11.

56. Edward H. Mazur, "Chicago's Jews and Abraham Lincoln: The Politics of the Civil War Era," *Chicago Jewish History* 33 (Winter 2009), 6.

57. "Translation of Selected Minutes of the New York Turn Verein,", July 20, 1850, p.15, http://www2.ku.edu/~maxkade/finding_aid_nytv.pdf; see also Frank Baron, "Abraham Lincoln and the German Immigrants: Turners and Forty-Eighters." *Yearbook of German-American Studies Supplemental Issue 4* (Lawrence, KS: Society for German-American Studies, 2012).

58. *New York Daily Tribune* (February 10, 1861), 8, col. 4. Markens, *Abraham Lincoln and the Jews,* 32, embellished the quote and misdated it.

59. Markens, *Abraham Lincoln and the Jews*, 32; see also Jacob R. Marcus, *United States Jewry 1776-1985* (Detroit: Wayne State University Press, 1993), III, 211.

60. Lincoln to Weed, December 17, 1860. Shapell Legacy Partnership.

61. *Charleston Mercury* (December 21, 1860).

62. Judah P. Benjamin, Speech of Hon. J. P. Benjamin of Louisiana on the Right of Secession (December 31, 1860), 16, online at http://ia700303.us.archive.org/23/items/speechofhonjpben00benj/speechofhonjpben-00benj.pdf.

63. Abraham Jonas to AL (December 30, 1860), AL Papers, LOC.

64. William H. Seward to AL (December 29, 1860) as quoted in CW 4, 170.

65. AL to Salmon P. Chase (December 31, 1860), Shapell Manuscript Collection.

66. The proclamation may be found at http://www.wallbuilders.com/libissuesarticles.asp?id=3587.

67. *Israelite* (November 30, 1860), 172; (December 28, 1860), 205.

68. *Jewish Messenger* (January 11, 1861), 10.

69. Morris J. Raphall, "The Bible View of Slavery" (1861), http://www.jewish-history.com/civilwar/raphall.html (accessed July 21, 2013); Adam Goodheart, "The Rabbi and the Rebellion," *New York Times* (March 7, 2011), http://opinionator.blogs.nytimes.com/2011/03/07/the-rabbi-and-the-rebellion/; Bertram W. Korn, *American Jewry and the Civil War* (New York: Atheneum, 1970), 15-31.

70. *Jewish Messenger* (January 11, 1861), 10.

71. R.S.H., "Rabbi Raphall," *The Independent* (February 21, 1861), 8.

72. "David Einhorn's response to 'A Biblical View of Slavery,'" http://www.jewish-history.com/civilwar/einhorn.html.

73. http://www.jewish-history.com/civilwar/heilprin.html; for his brother, Isaac, and Lincoln's spectacles, see Roland T. Carr and Hugh Morrow, "We Found Lincoln's Lost Bank Account," *Saturday Evening Post* (February 14, 1953).

74. Rev. Hugh Brown, Review of Rev. Dr. Raphael's [*sic*] disco'rse on "American slavery as being consistent with the Hebrew Servitude of the Old Testament," a sermon preached (by request) in the Baptist church, Shushan, on Wednesday, March 27th, 1861; http://archive.org/stream/reviewofrevdrrap00brow/reviewofrevdrrap00brow_djvu.txt (accessed July 21, 2013).

75. Illowy's speech is available in full at http://www.jewish-history.com/Illoway/sermon.html (accessed July 21, 2013).

76. *Speech of Hon. Joseph Jonas of Hamilton County in the House of Representatives, February 25, 26, 1861*, SC 5829, American Jewish Archives, Cincinnati, OH.

77. Hyman L. Meites, *History of the Jews of Chicago* (Chicago: Chicago Jewish Historical Society and Wellington Publishing, 1924), 45; Markens, *Abraham Lincoln and the Jews,* 25-26; Abram Vossen Goodman, "A Jewish Peddler's Diary 1842-1843," *American Jewish Archives* 3 (June 1951), 81-110.

78. Abraham Kohn to AL (February 6, 1861), RG 59, Entry 760, Records of the State Department, Appointment Records, Applications and Recommendations for Office, Applications and Recommendations for Public Office, 1797-1901, National Archives College Park. On Waughop, see *The Bench and Bar of Chicago: Biographical Sketches* (Chicago: H. C.Cooper, 1883), 395-96.

79. *New Hampshire Statesman* (February 23, 1861) col. D; *The Daily Cleveland Herald* (February 25, 1861), col. B; *Lowell Daily Citizen and News* (February 16, 1861), *Col. B; Highland Weekly News* (February 28, 1861), 1. Note that Markens, *Abraham Lincoln and the Jews,* 25, and later sources consistently describe the gift as a "silk flag," but the contemporary newspapers all describe it as a "picture." The acknowledgment found in the archival collection of Congregation KAM from Chicago businessman J. Scammon Young [wrongly identified as a presidential aide], who apparently made the actual presentation of the gift to Lincoln, similarly refers to "your beautiful painting of an American flag," see *Chicago Jewish History* 33 (Winter 2009), 4, and Korn, *American Jewry and Civil War,* 205, 301 n. 64. Harold Holzer, *Lincoln President-Elect: Abraham Lincoln and the Great Secession Winter 1860-1861* (New York: Simon & Schuster, 2009), 187, provides context but misidentifies the biblical verse.

CHAPTER FOUR: WE HAVE NOT YET APPOINTED A HEBREW

1. CW 4, 190; Markens, *Abraham Lincoln and the Jews,* 27-28; for the Provisional Constitution of the Confederacy, see http://avalon.law.yale.edu/19th_century/csa_csapro.asp.

2. CW 4, 218; *Israelite* (February 15, 1861), p.262.

3. Abram J. Dittenhoefer, *How We Elected Lincoln: Personal Recollections* (Philadelphia: University of Pennsylvania, 2005 [1916]), 43; CW 4, 233.

4. CW 4, 239.

5. David H. Donald, *Lincoln* (New York: Simon & Schuster, 1995), 273; Isaac M. Fein, "Baltimore Jews During the Civil War," *American Jewish Historical Quarterly* 51 (December 1961), 67-96.

6. CW 4, 262-71.

7. CW 4, 271.

8. *Israelite* (March 15, 1861), 294.

9. Ibid.

10. See, generally, Catherine A. Brekus and W. Clark Gilpin (eds.), *American Christianities: A History of Dominance and Diversity* (Chapel Hill: University of North Carolina Press, 2011), esp.1-24.

11. Don E. Fehrenbacher and Virginia Fehrenbacher (eds.), *Recollected Words of Abraham Lincoln* (Stanford: Stanford University Press, 1996), 25; Allen Guelzo, *Abraham Lincoln: Redeemer President* (Grand Rapids: Eerdmans, 1999), 313.

12. Jonathan D. Sarna, "Christians and Non-Christians in the Marketplace of American Religion," *American Christianities,* ed. Brekus & Gilpin, 119-32.

13. *Jewish Messenger* (February 18, 1861), online at http://www.jewish-history.com/civilwar/semi02.htm.

14. Ari Hoogenboom, *Outlawing the Spoils: A History of the Civil Service Reform Movement* 1865-1883 (New York: Praeger, 1982); Michael Burlingame, *Abraham Lincoln: A Life* (Baltimore: John Hopkins University Press, 2008), II, 69-97.

15. *Israelite* (April 5, 1861), 317.

16. *Israelite* (May 24, 1861), 374.

17. *Quincy Daily Herald* (November 30, 1860), 3; *Orville Browning to Abraham Lincoln* (December 9, 1860), AL Papers, LOC; *Quincy Whig Republican* (May 25, 1861), 3.

18. CW 4, 386

19. AL to Simon Cameron (May 26, 1861) in CW 4, 386; Shalom E. Lamm, "Colonel Max Einstein," http://www.jewish-history.com/civilwar/einstein.html, which also quotes Geiss's letter to William Seward (February 24, 1862); Henry S. Morais, *The Jews of Philadelphia* (Philadelphia: Levytype, 1894), 480-82; George B. McClellan to Irvin McDowell (August 16, 1861); Max Einstein to Simon Cameron (August 18, 1861), Simon Cameron Papers, LOC; George B. McClellan to Simon Cameron as quoted in Roger D. Hunt, *Union Army Colonels of the Civil War* (Mechanicsburg, PA: Stackpole books, 2007), 61, and in Letters Received, Volunteer Service Branch, Adjutant General's Office, File P17(VS)1861, National Archives; for a history of the 27th Regiment, see http://www.pa-roots.com/pacw/infantry/27th/27thorg.html.

20. Burlingame, *Abraham Lincoln*, II, 93-94; *Israelite* (November 6, 1861), 76; Sol Stroock, "Switzerland and American Jews," *PAJHS* 11 (1903), 50; Richmond Dispatch (June 8, 1861), *Journal of the Executive Proceedings of the Senate of the United States of America (1861-1862)*, First Session: 375 (July 10, 1861), 484 (July 26, 1861); Second session: 70 (January 6, 1862), 96 (January 22, 1862); on Bernays, see above chapter 3, n. 36.

21. Francis B. Cutting to AL (May 28, 1861), AL Papers, LOC.

22. Sigmund Diamond (ed.), *A Casual View of America: The Home Letters of Salomon de Rothschild 1859-1861* (Stanford: Stanford University Press, 1961), 123-24 [Salomon's letter, written from New Orleans, was dated 28 April 1861].

23. David Black, *The King of Fifth Avenue: The Fortunes of August Belmont* (New York: Dial, 1981)

24. August Belmont to Lionel de Rothschild (May 21, 1861); Francis B. Cutting to AL (May 28, 1861), AL Papers, LOC.

25. David Black, *The King of Fifth Avenue: The Fortunes of August Belmont* (New York: Dial Press, 1981), 207.

26. August Belmont to AL (May 9, 1862), AL Papers, LOC; Black, *King of Fifth Avenue*, 209-11.

27. August Belmont to Thurlow Weed (July 20, 1862), AL Papers, LOC; AL to August Belmont (July 31, 1862) in CW 5, 350-51; Black, *King of Fifth Avenue*, 216-18, 241-60.

28. John Bassett Moore (ed.), *The Works of James Buchanan* (Philadelphia: Lippincott, 1911), XI: 353 (online at http://archives.dickinson.edu/digitized-resources/works-james-buchanan-comprising-his-speeches-state-papers-and-private); *New York Times* (November 9, 1864), 2; Black, *King of Fifth Avenue*, 242, 257-58.

29. Appointment of Alfred Mordecai Jr. (August 10, 1861), Shapell Manuscript Collection.

30. Varina Davis, *Jefferson Davis: Ex-President of the Confederate States of America* (New York: Belford, 1890), I, 535-36; Emily Bingham, *Mordecai: An Early American Family (New York: Hi*ll & Wang, 2003), 235-37; Stanley

Falk, "Alfred Mordecai, American Jew," *American Jewish Archives* 10 (1958), 125-32.

31. Bingham, *Mordecai*, 245-51; Stanley L. Falk, "Divided Loyalties in 1861: The Decision of Major Alfred Mordecai," in Sarna & Mendelsohn, *Jews and the Civil War: A Reader*, 201-25; Jean E. Friedman, "The Moral Imagination of Confederate Family Politics," in *Inside the Confederate Nation: Essay in Honor of Emory M. Thomas*, eds. Lesley J. Gordon and John C. Inscoe (Baton Rouge: Louisiana State University Press, 2005), 167-87.

32. Bingham, *Mordecai*, 237, 250, 261. Mordecai concluded his career, in 1895, as superintendent and commandant of the Springfield Armory.

33. John Fitch, *Annals of the Army of the Cumberland* (Philadelphia: Lippincott, 1864), 264, 270.

34. Philip Kearny to AL; AL to Kearny (September 3, 1861), Abraham Lincoln Collection, Clements Library, University of Michigan (see http://quod.lib.umich.edu/c/clementsmss/umich-wcl-M-816lin?view=text); CW, Supplement I, 95 ,; http://www.math.rutgers.edu/~zeilberg/family/moritz.html.

35. The Shapell Roster of Jews in the service of the Union and Confederate Armies and Navies during the American Civil War period of 1861–1865.

36. Robert N. Rosen, *The Jewish Confederates* (Columbia: University of South Carolina Press, 2000), 118-26.

37. On Alfred Raphall, see House of Representatives, 53rd Congress, 2nd Session, "Alfred M. Raphall: Report to Accompany H.R. 954."

38. AL to Edwin M. Stanton (November 4, 1862), CW Supplement, p.162; original in Shapell Manuscript Collection; for evidence of Levy's Orthodoxy and stature, see Hyman B. Grinstein, *The Rise of the Jewish Community of New York 1654-1860* (Philadelphia: Jewish Publication Society, 1945), 577 n. 64.

39. Korn, *American Jewry and the Civil War*, 108.

40. AGO, General Orders No. 332, Shapell Manuscript Collection; "Proceedings of a General Court Martial, August 10, 1863, Trial of Captain Cherrie [*sic*] M. Levy," NARA; AL to Samuel C. Pomeroy (November 8, 1863), CW 7, 4.

41. Richard Busteed to AL (November 18, 1863) and other letters appended to "Proceedings of a General Court Martial, August 10, 1863, Trial of Captain Cherrie [*sic*] M. Levy," NARA (Busteed was appointed judge on November 17, 1863.) In his letter, Busteed noted that Levy's "father-in-law is the well-known Jewish prelate Dr. Raphael [*sic*], and a large circle of his countrymen are much interested in the case." "I have heard his story," he concluded, "and I believe his narration of the affair." In his eulogy for Lincoln, Raphall reported in the third person that he had seen Lincoln but once, "but on that single occasion, he had shown himself friendly to him— he [Raphall] had asked him but one favor, but that time he had granted it freely—he had granted it lovingly, because he knew the speaker was a Jew—because he knew him to be a true servant of the Lord"; Emanuel Hertz, *Abraham Lincoln: The Tribute of the Synagogue* (New York: Bloch Publishing, 1927), 169.

42. M. J. Raphall to AL (March 1, 1864), AL Papers LOC; for the renomination, see *Senate Executive Journal* (January 18, 1864), 380.

43. *Senate Executive Journal* (March 25, 1864), 458; Samuel F. Chalfin to Cheme M. Levy (July 16, 1864), AL Papers, LOC; "Proceedings of a General Court Martial, August 10, 1863, Trial of Captain Cherrie [sic] M. Levy," NARA; Samuel C. Pomeroy to AL (July 22, 1864), AL Papers, LOC; *Report of Committees of the Senate of the United States for the First Session of the Forty-Fourth Congress 1875-1876* (Washington DC: Government Printing Office, 1876), Report #370.

44. Shakespeare Henry V, ii. i. 106.

45. On sutlers see Sarna, *When General Grant Expelled the Jews, 19*; Korn, *American Jewry and the Civil War, 90.*

46. AL to Simon Cameron (September 5, 1861), Shapell Manuscript Collection.

47. AL seemingly to Simon Cameron (December 6, 1861), Shapell Manuscript Collection. On sutlers, see Francis A. Lord, *Civil War Sutlers and Their Wares* (New York: Thomas Yoselof, 1969); David Michael Delo, *Peddlers and Post Traders: The Army Sutler on the Frontier* (Salt Lake City, 1992).

48. The Shapell Manuscript Collection has compiled a preliminary list of Jewish sutlers. For the March 19, 1862 Act "to provide for the appointment of sutlers . . . and to define their duties," see OR, Series 3, Vol. 1, 938-40.

49. CW 5, 447.

50. Herman A. Norton, *Struggling for Recognition: The United States Army Chaplaincy* (Washington DC: Office of the Chief of Chaplains, 1977); Warren B, Armstong, *For Courageous Fighting and Confident Dying: Union Chaplains in the Civil War* (Lawrence: University Press of Kansas, 1998); Steven Woodworth, *While God Is Marching On: The Religious World of Civil War Soldiers* (Lawrence: University Press of Kansas, 2001), 145-74; Gardiner H. Shattuck Jir, *A Shield and Hiding Place: The Religious Life of the Civil War Armies* (Macon, GA: Mercer University Press, 1987), 51-72.

51. OR, Series 3, volume 1, 380-82; for the chaplaincy, see section 9.

52. *Congressional Globe* (July 12 [13], 1861), 100.

53. OR Series 3, volume 1, 154,157.

54. *Congressional Globe* (July 12 [13], 1861), 100.

55. *Israelite* (September 6, 1861), 76 (quoted); (July 19, 1861), 23.

56. Korn, *American Jewry and the Civil War,* 58-60; David de Sola Pool, "The Diary of Chaplain Michael M. Allen, September 1861," *PAJHS* 39 (December 1949), 177-82; http://www.jewish-history.com/civilwar/mmallen.htm (accessed 1 September 2013).

57. For documents, see Myer S. Isaacs, "A Jewish Army Chaplain," *PAJHS* 12 (1904), 127-37; and Gary P. Zola, *They Called Him Rabbi Abraham* (Carbondale: Southern Illinois University Press, 2014). The standard account of this episode is Korn, *American Jewry and the Civil War,* 56-97. For the "sizable number of undesirables," among early Civil War chaplains, including illiterates and irreligious laymen, see Norton, *Struggling for Recognition,* 85. On Fischel, see Jonathan Waxman, "Arnold Fischel: 'Unsung Hero' in American Israel," *American Jewish Historical Quarterly* 60 (June 1971), 325-43. Note that Fischel's term at Shearith Israel was ending, and he may well have been looking for another job.

58. Steven E. Woodworth, *While God Is Marching On: The Religious World of Civil War Soldiers* (Lawrence: University Press of Kansas, 2001), 145.

59. *Israelite* (November 15, 1861), 157; (December 6, 1861), 177.

60. For an analysis of these petitions, see Korn, *American Jewry and the Civil War*, 66 and 258, nn.37-42.

61. AL to John J. Hughes (October 21, 1861), CW 4, 559-60.

62. Arnold Fischel to Henry I. Hart (December 11, 1861), Board of Delegates Papers, AJHS, NY reprinted in *PAJHS* 12 (1904), 131-32.

63. United States Christian Commission, *Facts, Principles and Progress* (Philadelphia: Sherman, 1863), 7-8; AL to George H. Stuart (December 12, 1861), CW 5, 67.

64. AL to Arnold Fischel (December 14, 1861), CW 5, 69.

65. *PAJHS* 12 (1904), 134.

66. *The Presbyter* as quoted in Korn, *American Jewry and the Civil War*, 64.

67. Statutes at Large, 37th Congress, Second Session (1862), 595; Norton, *Struggling for Recognition*, 87-93; Korn, *American Jewry and the Civil War*, 71-72.

68. Isaac Leeser to AL (August 21, 1862), endorsed by John Hay and Joseph R. Smith, AL Papers, LOC; Korn, *American Jewry and the Civil War*, 77; in 1864, Frankel was appointed visiting chaplain with specific responsibility for Jewish soldiers, see Armstrong, *For Courageous Fighting and Confident Dying*, 39.

69. Henry I. Hart and Myer J. Isaacs to AL (October 6, 1862), Thomas F. Perley to William H. Hammond (October 27, 1862), AL Papers, LOC; Fischel had estimated that there were "thirty to forty" Jews in Washington-area hospitals, but that would not have justified a chaplain either, *PAJHS* 12 (1904), 136; Waxman, "Arnold Fischel," 341-42.

70. Korn, *American Jewry and the Civil War*, 84-87.

71. Ibid, xv-xvi, 82-83; *Israelite* (May 15, 1863), 357. On Gotthelf, see Iuliu Herscovici, *The Jews of Vicksburg, Mississippi* (2007), 322-34.

72. James Shrigley in Osborn H. Oldroyd, *Lincoln Memorial: Album Immortelles* (New York: Carleton, 1883), 336-37; P. M. Zall (ed.) *Abe Lincoln Laughing* (Berkeley: University of California Press, 1982), 82-83. Philadelphia Congressman Leonard Myers, of Jewish descent, was among those who recommended Shrigley to Lincoln. See Myers to AL (November 19, 1862), Shapell Manuscript Collection.

73. CW 8, 102-3; on Gibson, see Ann Braude, *Radical Spirits: Spiritualism and Womens Rights in Nineteenth-Century America* (Boston: Beacon, 1989), 92, 127.

74. CW 5, 497-98; the order was dated November 15, 1862. Washington's earlier order was dated July 9, 1776.

75. *Occident* (January 1, 1863), 25.

76. Bernhard Behrend to AL (December 4, 1862) in *Occident* (January 1, 1863), 25; online with additional information on Behrend at http://www.jewish-history.com/civilwar/shabbat.htm; see also *Jewish Life in Mr. Lincoln's City*, eds. Laura Cohen Apelbaum and Claire Uziel (Washington, DC: Jewish Historical Society of Greater Washington, 2009), 39, 138.

77. *Israelite* (January 16, 1863), 218; Jonathan D. Sarna, *When General Grant Expelled the Jews* (New York: Schocken, 2012), 23.

78. On this episode, see Sarna, *When General Grant Expelled the Jews*.

79. *PUSG* 6:238, 283, 393-94; Sarna, *When General Grant Expelled the Jews*, 44-45.

80. *PUSG* 7: 8-9; Sarna, *When General Grant Expelled the Jews*, 45,170 n.34.

81. Sarna, *When General Grant Expelled the Jews*, 47.

82. Sylvanus Cadwallader, "Forty Years With Grant," 47-49 in Abraham Lincoln Presidential Library, Springfield Illinois; Sarna, *When General Grant Expelled the Jews*, 47-48, 171.

83. PUSG 7: 53; see John Y. Simon, "That Obnoxious Order," *Jews and the Civil War,* eds. Jonathan D. Sarna & Adam Mendelsohn (New York: NYU Press, 2010), 358.

84. U. S. Grant to Jesse Grant, August 14, 1868, Shapell Manuscript Collection.

85. OR, series I, vol. 17 (part 2), 463, 471; Sarna, *When General Grant Expelled the Jews,* 8.

86. *Israelite* (January 2, 1863), 202; *Jewish Record* (January 13, 1863); Sarna, *When General Grant Expelled the Jews,* 17-18.

87. Korn, *American Jewry and the Civil War,* 123; John E. L. Robertson, *Paducah: Frontier to the Atomic Age* (Charleston, SC: Arcadia Books, 2002), 44; Sarna, *When General Grant Expelled the Jews,* 6-7.

88. OR, series I, vol. 17 (part 2), 506; PUSG 7: 54; Sarna, *When General Grant Expelled the Jews,* 11.

89. *Memphis Daily Bulletin* (January 6,1863) as cited in Korn, *American Jewry and the Civil War,* 272 n.16; Sarna, *When General Grant Expelled the Jews,* 11, 35-37.

90. SC-4218, AJA; Sarna, *When General Grant Expelled the Jews,* 12-13.

91. Korn, *American Jewry and the Civil War,* 125; Markens, *Lincoln and the Jews,* 118.

92. *Israelite* (January 16, 1863); PUSG 7: 53-54; OR, series I, vol. 17 (part 2), 544; Sarna, *When General Grant Expelled the Jews,* 21-22.

93. St. Louis B'nai B'rith to Abraham Lincoln (January 5, 1863), AL Papers, LOC; Isidor Bush to Edward Bates (January 6, 1863), endorsed by Edward Bates (January 12, 1863), AL Papers, LOC.

94. *Israelite* (January 16, 1863), 218; the article was reprinted as far away as San Francisco: *San Francisco Evening Bulletin* (February 10, 1863).

CHAPTER FIVE: I MYSELF HAVE A REGARD FOR THE JEWS

1. Diary of Edward Rosewater, January 1, 1863, American Jewish Archives, Cincinnati, OH, online at http://americanjewisharchives.org/exhibits/aje/_pdfs/X_58.pdf.

2. Edward Rosewater to Leah Colman, September 18, 1862, Colman-Schwarzenberg family album, private collection, as quoted in Kathryn Hellerstein, "A Letter from Lincoln's Jewish Telegrapher," *Jewish Quarterly Review* 94:4 (Fall 2004), 629-30.

3. Diary of Edward Rosewater, January 1, 1863, American Jewish Archives, Cincinnati, OH, online at http://americanjewisharchives.org/exhibits/aje/_pdfs/X_58.pdf.

4. Don E. Fehrenbacher and Virginia Fehrenbacher, *Recollected Words of Abraham Lincoln* (Stanford: Stanford University Press, 1996), 397; Michael Burlingame, *Abraham Lincoln: A Life* (Baltimore: Johns Hopkins University Press, 2008), II, 469.

5. CW 6, 28-20; John Hope Franklin, "The Emancipation Proclamation: An Act of Justice." *Prologue Magazine* 25 (Summer 1993), online at http://www.archives.gov/publications/prologue/1993/summer/emancipation-proclamation.html; Hellerstein, "A Letter from Lincoln's Jewish Telegrapher," 625-36; see also Isaac Markens, *Abraham Lincoln and the Jews* (New York, 1909), 56.

6. *Jewish Record* 1 (January 23, 1863) as quoted in Bertram W. Korn, *American Jewry and the Civil War* (Philadelphia: Jewish Publication Society, 1951), 27.

7. *Israelite* (February 27, 1863), 268.

8. *Occident* (February 1, 1863), 16.

9. Simon Wolf, *The Presidents I Have Known from 1860-1918* (Washington, DC, 1918), 8.

10. *Hamagid* 7 (January 29,1863), 34. Earlier, Vidaver was more sympathetic to the South; see Harvey A. Richman, "The Image of America in the European Hebrew Periodicals of the Nineteenth Century (Until 1880)" (Ph.D., University of Texas, Austin, 1971), 206-15, esp. 211.

11. Esther 8:8.

12. AL to John Alexander McClernand (January 8, 1863), Shapell Legacy Partnership.

13. *New York World* (September 24, 1864) as quoted in Korn, *American Jewry and the Civil War,* 194.

14. Korn, *American Jewry and the Civil War,* 194; Gary P. Zola, *We Called Him Rabbi Abraham: Lincoln and American Jewry—A Documentary History* (Carbondale: Southern Illinois University Press, 2014), 44.

15. While later sources list his birth as 1827, he was listed on the ship's manifest upon the arrival of the Zacharias in 1832 as being seven years old, and the 1850 U.S. Census lists him as being aged twenty-five. His marriage in 1844 likewise points to the earlier birth year.

16. Elizabeth P. Bentley, *Passenger Arrivals at the Port of New York, 1830-1832, From Customs Passenger Lists* (Baltimore: Genealogical Publishing Co., 2000), 1102.

17. I. Zacharie to N. P. Banks (December 28, 1863), reprinted in Charles M. Segal, "Isachar Zacharie: Lincoln's Chiropodist," *Publications of the American Jewish Historical Society* 43 (December 1953), 115 (for Charles Johnson, his letter writer, see p. 94); he likewise admitted to his lack of education in a talk reprinted in *Jewish Messenger* (May 13, 1864), 141.

18. Charles E. Krausz, "Issachar Zacharie, 1827-1900," *A Fast Pace Forward: Chronicles of American Podiatry* (Philadelphia: Pennsylvania College of Podiatric Medicine, 1987), 19.

19. The 1850 U.S. Census lists him as living with his wife's family (see below, n. 29); for quote see *Jewish Messenger* (May 13, 1864), 141 and for Lincoln, see below and CW 8, 238.

20. Cameron Kippen, "A Potted History of Podiatry," http://foottalk.blogspot.com/2008/12/potted-history-of-podiatry.html; D. R. Tollafield & J. C. Cagnall, "Introduction: an historical perspective," in D. R. Tollafield & L. M. Merriman (eds.) *Clinical Skills in Treating the Foot* (Edinburgh: Churchill Livingstone, 1997), 1-6 ; James E. Bates (ed.) *A Fast Pace Forward: Chronicles of American Podiatry* (Philadelphia: Pennsylvania College of Pediatric Medicine, 1987), 5; Collin Dagnall, "The Origin of 'Chiropodist'" *Podiatry Now* 12 (April 2009), 48.

21. "Lewis Durlacher," *The Palgrave Dictionary of Anglo-Jewish History,* ed. William D. Rubinstein et al. (New York: Palgrave Macmillan, 2011), 235; W. Seelig, "Durlacher: Four Generations of a Family in English Chiropody," *The Chiropodist* 11 (1956), 76-83.

22. *British and Foreign Medical Review* 20 (1845), 521.

23. *The Medico-chirurgical Review, and Journal of Practical Medicine,* new series, 2 (1845), 546.

24. J. C. Dagnall, "Who Wrote 'Eisenberg on the Diseases of the Human Foot'?" *The ClioPedic* Items 1 (1985), 7-12 suggests that Eisenberg was the nom de plume of George Gabriel Sigmond. Many thanks to Dr Anthony S. Travis for valuable research that is partially incorporated here.

25. I. Zacharie, *Corns, Operations on the Feet* (New York: [I. Zacharie, 186?]) as quoted in Charles M. Segal, "Isachar Zacharie: Lincoln's Chiropodist," *Publications of the American Jewish Historical Society* 43 (December 1953), 72-73, 78.

26. I. Zacharie, *Surgical and Practical Observations on the Diseases of the Human Foot* (Rev. ed, London: Adams Brothers, 1876), ii; the dedication is practically word-for-word identical to John Eisenberg's dedication of his book to the great British physician and physiologist Marshall Hall; see John Eisenberg, *Surgical and Practical Observations on the Diseases of the Human Foot* (London: Henry Renshaw, 1845), iii. Zacharie presumably backdated his dedication to 1844 so as to pretend that Eisenberg plagiarized him. A "certificate," purportedly from Valentine Mott and dated August 1858 testifying to Zacharie's skills, appears in *Corns, Operations on the Feet.* For the original, see Shapell Manuscript Collection.

27. Bates, *A Fast Pace Forward,* 12 includes an ad for Davidson's establishment; for his Jewish connections, see *Jewish Exponent* 1 (July 22, 1887), 8.

28. *The Freemason,* 29 September 1900; on Mutter see E. S. Harris and R. F. Morgan, "Thomas Dent Mutter, MD: Early Reparative Surgeon," *Annals of Plastic Surgery* 33 (September 1994):333-38.

29. The Census listed him as "Isicca Zackriah" and misidentified him as female but correctly listed the first names of his wife and children and listed the head of the household as Jacob Lawson, his father-in-law.

30. Charles M. Segal, "Isachar Zacharie: Lincoln's Chiropodist," *Publications of the American Jewish Historical Society* 43 (December 1953), 74-79, quoting documents now in the possession of the Shapell Manuscript Collection.

31. Ibid, 76, Shapell Manuscript Collection.

32. Ibid, 77, Shapell Manuscript Collection.

33. Krausz, "Issachar Zacharie, 1827-1900," 19.

34. *Freemason's Chronicle* 51 (29 September 1900), 147-148; http://www.orderofthesecretmonitorlondon.org.uk/history.html (accessed 25 December 2013).

35. *New York Atlas* (August 29, 1858) as reprinted in Segal, "Isachar Zacharie," 77-78; see also Zacharie's brochure *Corns: Operations on the Feet* (n.p., n.d. [1862?])

36. Gilbert Muller, *William Cullen Bryant: Author of America* (Albany: SUNY, 2008), 74.

37. *New-York Evening Post* (February 19, 1859), as quoted in Segal, "Isachar Zacharie,"78-79. For his "personal experience" as a patient, see Willliam Cullen Bryant to Edwin M. Stanton (August 21, 1862), Shapell Manuscript Collection.

38. *New York Times* (December 12, 1862); Frank R. Freemon, "Lincoln Finds a Surgeon-General: William A. Hammond and the Transformation of the Union Army Medical Bureau," *Civil War History* 33 (1987), 5-21; Bonnie E. Blustein, *Preserve Your Love for Science: Life of William A Hammond, American Neurologist* (New York: Cambridge, 2002), 62, 82.

39. Bryant to Stanton (August 21, 1862), Shapell Manuscript Collection.

40. W. C. Bryant to AL (August 21, 1862), Shapell Manuscript Collection. Zacharie, of course, was not a "regularly educated surgeon," but he performed like one.

41. George Opdyke to AL (August 28, 1862), Shapell Manuscript Collection.

42. Rufus F. Andrews to AL (August 29, 1862), Shapell Manuscript Collection.

43. Segal, "Isachar Zacharie," 80-81.

44. *New York Herald* (October 3, 1862), 4.

45. I. Zacharie to E. M.Stanton (August 26, 1862), Letters Received Files, August 27, 1862, Records of the War Department, Office of the Surgeon General, National Archives, Washington, DC in Segal, "Isachar Zacharie," 80.

46. *New York Herald* (October 3, 1862), as reprinted in Zola, *We Called Him Rabbi Abraham*, 54.

47. Lincoln's signed, handwritten testimonial (September 20, 1862) is in the Shapell Manuscript Collection.

48. Lincoln's signed, handwritten card, dated September 22, 1862, is in the Shapell Manuscript Collection.

49. *New York Herald* (September 26, 1862) as quoted in http://www.thelincolnlog.org/Calendar.aspx?date=1862-09-25. Lincoln had sprained his wrist on September 13th trying to restrain his runaway horse during a morning ride.

50. The testimonial signed by Lincoln and Seward (September 23, 1862) is in the Shapell Manuscript Collection; see also CW Supplement I, 152-153.

51. The order is reprinted in *PAJHS* 43 (1953), 123. The pass was subsequently continued for sixty days more.

52. "Ode to Dr. Zacharie," *Vanity Fair* 6 (October 18, 1862), 190.

53. Bryant was president of the New York Homeopathic Society; see http://homeoint.org/photo/b2/bryantwc.htm.

54. Blustein, *Preserve Your Love for Science: Life of William A Hammond, American Neurologist*, 81-83; see also p. 59: "Hammond was more than a little arrogant."

55. CW 5, 444-445.

56. William A. Hammond, *A Statement of the Causes Which Led to the Dismissal of the Surgeon-General William A. Hammond from the Army with a Review of the Evidence Adduced Before the Court* (New York: 1864), 52. https://archive.org/details/statementofcause01hamm.

57. Maine Historical Society; Zola, *We Called Him Rabbi Abraham*, 58.

58. N. P. Banks to J. A. Dix (October 6, 1862), Shapell Manuscript Collection; Segal, "Isachar Zacharie," 83, 124.

59. I. Zacharie to William H. Seward (November 24, 1862) reprinted in Charles M. Segal, "Isachar Zacharie: Lincoln's Chiropodist—Addendum," *PAJHS* 44 (1954), 107.

60. AL to Banks (November 25, 1862), CW Supplement 1, 165; Brown University Library Center for Digital Scholarship, Call no. LA2260 (online: http://library.brown.edu/cds/catalog/catalog.php?verb=render&id=1212770838390625&view=pageturner&pageno=1).

61. James G. Hollandsworth Jr., *Pretense of Glory: The Life of General Nathaniel P. Banks* (Baton Rouge: Louisiana State University Press, 1998), 83-88.

62. Bertram W. Korn, *The Early Jews of New Orleans* (Waltham: American Jewish Historical Society, 1969), 227.

63. Benjamin F. Butler to Myer S. Isaacs (February 13, 1864), in *PAJHS* 29 (1925), 121; on Butler's anti-Semitism, see also Korn, *American Jewry and the Civil War,* 164-66 and Robert N. Rosen, *The Jewish Confederates* (Columbia: University of South Carolina Press, 2000), 275.

64. Benjamin F. Butler to U.S. Attorney General, October 23, 1862, Shapell Manuscript Collection.

65. Numbers of Zacharies and Zacharias are listed in the 1840 census from New Orleans, and Zacharie later reported that he had hired "men I have known from my infancy" to assist him in his mission; see Segal, "Isachar Zacharie," 86.

66. Jonathan D. Sarna, *When General Grant Expelled the Jews* (New York: Schocken, 2012), 44-45. Actually, Grant's order only applied to the area under his command, which did not include New Orleans.

67. N. P. Banks to I. Zacharie (January 1, 1863) in Segal, "Isachar Zacharie," 85.

68. I. Zacharie to AL (January 14, 1863, February 19, 1863), AL Papers, LOC.

69. I. Zacharie to AL (May 9, 1863) reprinted in Segal, "Isachar Zacharie-Addendum," 112-13. Zacharie sent practically the same words to Banks (Segal, "Isachar Zacharie," 98). For Gutheim's view of Lincoln, see Korn, *American Jewry and the Civil War,* 48. While Gutheim was an immigrant, his wife was a native of Mobile, Alabama.. Gutheim was banished and moved to Montgomery; he did not return to New Orleans until July 1865. See William Warren Rogers, "In Defense of Our Sacred Cause: Rabbi James K. Gutheim in Confederate Montgomery," *Journal of Confederate History* 7 (1991): 113-122; Gary P. Zola,"Gutheim, James Koppel"; http://www.anb.org/articles/08/08-01796.html; American National Biography Online (accessed July 9, 2012); and Scott Langston, "James K. Gutheim as Southern Reform Rabbi, Community Leader and Symbol," *Southern Jewish History* 5 (2002), 69-102.

70. *New York Herald* (June 13, 1863), 8; see also Korn, *American Jewry and the Civil War,* 196.

71. I. Zacharie to AL (January 14, 1863, February 19, 1863), AL Papers, LOC.

72. Raymond H. Banks, *King of Louisiana, 1862-1865 and Other Government Work: A Biography of Major General Nathaniel Prentice Banks* (Las Vegas: R. H. Banks, 2005), 588-89; see Zacharie to Banks (May 3, 1863): "I write by every Steamer to the President & Mr. Seward" in Segal, "Isachar Zacharie," 98.

73. I. Zacharie to N. P. Banks (January 11, 1863) in ibid, 86-87.

74. James Marten, "The Making of a Carpetbagger: George S. Denison and the South, 1854-1866," *Louisiana History* 34:2 (Spring 1993), 141.

75. Salmon P. Chase, "Diary and Correspondence of Salmon P. Chase," in *Annual Report of the American Historical Association, the Year 1902* (Washington: U.S. Government Printing Office, 1903), 355, 359; cf. 353.

76. G. F. Shepley to B. F. Butler (February 20, 1863) in *Private and Official Correspondence of General Benjamin F. Butler* (Norwood: Plimpton Press, 1917), 3:14.

77. Michael Hahn to AL (June 6, 1863), AL Papers, LOC.

78. See Segal, "Isachar Zacharie," 90-95; and Segal "Isachar Zacharie-Addendum," 110-12 for key evidence. In a letter to Lincoln (Zacharie to AL (February 19,

1863), AL Papers, LOC, Zacharie blamed his enemies for accusations that he was speculating. A secret March 7, 1863 business agreement between Zacharie and rebel sympathizer W. G. Betterton suggests that Zacharie did indeed stand to benefit personally from a deal he advanced to exchange Southern cotton for Northern goods, but Banks may have had knowledge of the matter. See the letter from Zacharie's secretary, Charles Johnson, to Banks (September 24, 1863): "the doctor [Zacharie] just before leaving recd a very scurrilous letter from Mr. Betterton, & intended writing you on the subject, but did not have time" [Typescript in SC 13335, American Jewish Archives, Cincinnati, OH; original at the University of Rochester].

79.   N. P. Banks to W. H. Seward (July 2, 1863) reprinted in Fred H. Harrington, "A Peace Mission of 1863," *American Historical Review* 46 (October 1940), 77.

80.   I. Zacharie to AL (March 17, 1863), AL Papers LOC.

81.   Segal, "Isachar Zacharie," 92-95; Banks, *King of Louisiana,* 760-62; 1209.

82.   I. Zacharie to AL (March 27, 1863), AL Papers, LOC.

83.   Richard S. Lambert, *For the Time Is at Hand: An Account of the Prophecies of HENRY WENTWORTH MONK of Ottawa, Friend of the Jews, and Pioneer of World Peace* (London: Andrew Melrose, Ltd., [1947]); Peter A. Russell, "Monk, Henry Wentworth," in *Dictionary of Canadian Biography,* vol. 12, University of Toronto/Université Laval, 2003–, accessed December 31, 2013, http://www.biographi.ca/en/bio/monk_henry_wentworth_12E.html. On Artas, which was also the home of Clorinda Minor's short-lived colony of former supporters of the American end-of-days prophet William Miller and is misnamed and mischaracterized both by Lambert and by Russell, see Lester I. Vogel, *To See a Promised Land: Americans and the Holy Land in the Nineteenth Century* (University Park: Pennsylvania State University Press, 1993), 128-32.

84.   Lambert, *For the Time Is at Hand,* 81-82. Lambert quotes this from a contemporaneous letter sent by Monk to his friend the Canadian publisher and businessman,

William Cameron Chewett. We have been unable to locate the original letter, which Lambert reported to be in private hands, but we take the letter to be genuine, for it includes language and allusions that are characteristic to Lincoln and that neither Monk nor Lambert could have invented.

85.   Joel 2:27/3:1

86.   Edward Yates to Abraham Lincoln (February 16, 1863), AL Papers, LOC; see Yates's *A Letter to the Women of England, on Slavery in the Southern States of America* (London, 1863).

87.   W. T. Sherman to Philemon B. Ewing (November 2, 1862); Shapell Manuscript Collection. See above Chapter 4

88.   *Lincoln Day by Day: A Chronology 1809-1865,* eds. E. S. Miers and C. P. Powell (Dayton: Morningside, 1991) lists just four personal visits of Zacharie to the White House, two of them after Monk was there; cf. n. 13 above, where the *New York World* described Zacharie as the "favored family visitor at the White House."

89.   On the peace mission, see Harrington, "A Peace Mission of 1863," 79-86; Fred Harvey Harrington, *Fighting Politician: Major General N. P. Banks* (Westport: Greenwood Press, 1970 [orig. ed. 1948]), 126; James G. Hollandsworth Jr. *Pretense of Glory: The Life of General Nathaniel P. Banks* (Baton Rouge: Louisiana State University Press, 1998), 154-57; and Banks, *King of Louisiana,* 763-65; the quoted phrase was used by Zacharie in his letter to Banks (December 28, 1863), in Harrington, "A Peace Mission of 1863," 86.

90.   I. Zacharie to N. P. Banks (July 30, 1863) in Harrington, "A Peace Mission of 1863," 79.

91.   Both Gordon and Jefferson Davis were related to the Confederate general Richard Taylor, the son of former President Zachary Taylor; see Banks, *King of Louisiana,* 765 n.30.

92.   N. P. Banks to AL (September 11, 1863) in Harrington, "A Peace Mission of 1863," 82-83.

93.   I. Zacharie to N. P. Banks (September 8, 1863); AL to J. G. Foster (August 28, 1863), John A. Dix to J. G. Foster (September 7, 1863), Lincoln Manuscripts,

Brown University Library, https://repository.library.brown.edu/studio/item/bdr:71965/ and CW Supplement I, 199-200.

94.   Eli N. Evans, *Judah P. Benjamin: The Jewish Confederate* (New York: Free Press, 1988), 232.

95.   I. Zacharie to J. P. Benjamin (September 28, 1863) in Zola, *We Called Him Rabbi Abraham,* 59-60; for a possible interpretation of what they may have been doing that night, see Daniel Brook, "The Forgotten Confederate Jew," *Tablet* (July 17, 2012), http://www.tabletmag.com/jewish-arts-and-culture/books/106227/the-forgotten-confederate-jew.

96.   Zacharie to AL (September 29, 1863), AL Papers, LOC.

97.   I. Zacharie to N. P.Banks (October 9, 1863) in Harrington, "A Peace Mission of 1863," 83-84.

98.   Ibid; Zola, *We Called Him Rabbi Abraham,* 55-56, 61 reprints both that letter and the *New York Herald* report (October 21, 1863) on his peace plan. For the request to "lay quiet" see I. Zacharie to N. P. Banks (December 28, 1863), in Harrington, "A Peace Mission of 1863," 86. Blair's plan was likewise discussed at the Hampton Roads Peace Conference of 1865, see James P. Conroy, *Our One Common Country: Abraham Lincoln and the Hampton Roads Peace Conference of 1865* (Guilford, CT: Lyons Press, 2014).

99.   I. Zacharie to N. P. Banks (October 9, 1863) in Harrington, "A Peace Mission of 1863," 84.

100.   I. Zacharie to N. P. Banks (October 16, 1863) in Harrington, "A Peace Mission of 1863," 85.

101.   I. Zacharie to N. P. Banks (December 28, 1863) in Harrington, "A Peace Mission of 1863," 86.

102.   *New York Daily Tribune* (June 24, 1864), 5.

103.   G. L. Mordecai, *A Tribute to Lincoln: "Happy to Serve an Enemy"* [New York: Lownsbury, n.d. [1910]), available on the Internet Archive; reprinted from *New York Daily Tribune* (February 13, 1901); see also Markens, *Abraham Lincoln and the Jews,* 50-51; Korn, *American Jewry and Civil War,* 199; Rosen, *The Jewish Confederates,* 41, 434 n.184; and on Lewis, Howard S. Stein, "Samuel A. Lewis: Nineteenth-Century Jewish

American Leader," SC-15490, American Jewish Archives, Cincinnati, OH.

104.   J. G. Cohen to I. Zacharie (March 5, 1864), RG 45, entry 36, miscellaneous letters received, NARA, online at http://lincolnpapers2.dataformat.com/images/1864/03/291966.pdf. For evidence that Cohen was actually captured while running the blockade in the sloop *Annie Thompson,* see *Official Records of the War of the Rebellion* (Washington DC, 1902), Series I, vol. 15, 245.

105.   I. Zacharie to AL (February 13, 1864); I. Zacharie to AL (May 13, 1864) AL Papers, LOC.

106.   *Jewish Messenger* 15 (May 13, 1864), 141; Korn, *American Jewry and the Civil War,* 199.

107.   OR, Series 1, vol. 24, part 1, 9.

108.   Eric Benjaminson, "A Regiment of Immigrants: The 82nd Illinois Volunteer Infantry and the Letters of Captain Rudolph Mueller," *Journal of the Illinois State Historical Society* 94:2 (Summer 2001), 137-80; Joseph R. Reinhart, *Yankee Dutchmen Under Fire; Civil War Letters from the 82nd Illinois Infantry* (Kent: Kent State University Press, 2013), 23-26, 37-44. For Lincoln's knowledge of Hecker's military activities, see CW 4, 390.

109.   H. L. Meites, *History of the Jews of Chicago* (Chicago: Jewish Historical Society of Illinois, 1924 [1990 Facsimile edition]), 93; Reinhart, *Yankee Dutchmen Under Fire,* 84-98.

110.   *Jewish Messenger,* July 10, 1863, online from Morais's ledger at http://sceti.library.upenn.edu/pages/index.cfm?so_id=1661&PagePosition=40&level=1; see Marc Saperstein, *Jewish Preaching in Times of War 1800-2001* (Oxford: Littman Library of Jewish Civilization, 2008), vii-viii.

111.   Others claim that he borrowed it from Speaker of the House Galusha Grow, who used the phrase "Fourscore years ago" back on July 4, 1861; see Burlingame, *Abraham Lincoln: A Life,* II, 570.

112.   Abraham Hart to AL (April 23, 1862) AL Papers, LOC. Lincoln responded to Hart on May 13, 1862, AL Papers LOC: "My dear Sir Permit me to acknowledge the receipt of your communication of April 23d

containing a copy of a Prayer recently delivered at your Synagogue, and to thank you heartily for your expressions of kindness and confidence. I have the honor to be Your Obt. Servt. A. LINCOLN."

113. Korn, *American Jewry and the Civil War,* 36; Arthur Kiron, " 'Dust and Ashes,' The Funeral and Forgetting of Sabato Morais," *American Jewish History* 84:3 (1996), 164; John Hay to A. Hart (January 9, 1864), Shapell Manuscript Collection.

114. Edward Everett, "Gettysburg Oration" (1863) online at http://en.wikisource.org/wiki/Gettysburg_Oration.

115. *History of the 118th Regt. P.V. Corn Exchange* (Philadelphia: JL Smith, 1905), 296—online at http://freepages.military.rootsweb.ancestry.com/~pa91/cc382902.html; see also Alexandra Lee Levin, *The Szolds of Lombard Street* (Philadelphia: Jewish Publication Society, 1960), 37.

116. Joan E. Cashin "Deserters, Civilians and Draft Resistance in the North," in *The War Was You and Me,* ed. Joan Cashin (Princeton: Princeton University Press, 2002), 264. Proportionately, even more soldiers deserted from the Confederacy: see Ella Lonn, *Desertion During the Civil War* (Gloucester: Peter Smith, 1966 [orig. ed.1928]); cf. Robert Fantina, *Desertion and the American Soldier 1776-2006* (New York: Algora, 2006).

117. Quoted in Michael Burlingame, *Abraham Lincoln: A Life* (Baltimore: Johns Hopkins University Press, 2008), II, 493.

118. Simon Wolf, *The Presidents I Have Known From 1860 to 1918* (Washington: 1918), 5-7. Original research from the Shapell Roster suggests that the soldier about whom Corwin and Wolf are referencing is actually a combined account of the lives of Private Michael Wolf(e), Company C, 20th Regiment Massachusetts Infantry (Shapell Roster ID #1193) and Private Adam Wolf(e), Company H, 13th Regiment Massachusetts Infantry.

119. Burlingame, *Abraham Lincoln: A Life,* II, 492-94; Thomas P. Lowry, *Don't Shoot That Boy: Abraham Lincoln and Military Justice* (Mason City: Savas, 1999). According to Cashin (p. 270), 80,000 deserters were arrested, but only 141 were executed.

120. Charles Walter et al. to George Meade (August 25, 1863)

121. Meade to AL (August 27, 1863), AL Papers, LOC.

122. Walter, Rainese, Faline, Lae. and Kuhn to AL (August 26, 1863), AL Papers, LOC.

123. Abraham Lincoln to George G. Meade, Autograph telegram signed, August 27, 1863, ALPLM, copied onto a telegram. Thomas T. Eckert Papers, Series 1: Telegrams Sent, vol. 16: p. 281, Huntington Library.

124. George Meade to AL, August 27, 1863 Abraham Lincoln Papers at the Library of Congress.

125. Korn, *American Jewry and the Civil War,* 109; Gregory Acken (ed.) *Inside the Army of the Potomac: The Civil War Experience of Captain Francis Adams Donaldson* (Mechanicsburg, PA: Stackpole, 1998), 332–36; Levin, *Szolds of Lombard Street,* 37; Markens, *Lincoln and the Jews,* 47–48; *Jewish Messenger* (September 4, 1863), 69. Korn's account relies on contemporary sources including the *Jewish Record,* and is preferable to some later retrospective accounts.

126. *History of the 118th Regt. P.V. Corn Exchange* (Philadelphia: JL Smith, 1905), 296 – online at http://freepages.military.rootsweb.ancestry.com/~pa91/cc382902.html; James H. Clossen to Mother (September 3, 1863), Shapell Manuscript Collection.

127. Jessie L. Pryer (?) to Sallie (September 11, 1863), Shapell Manuscript Collection.

128. The Survivors' Association. *History of the 118th Regt. P.V. Corn Exchange.* Philadelphia: JL Smith, 1905.

129. George Levy, "President Lincoln Rejects an Appeal for Mercy," *The Lincoln Newsletter,* 13:3 (Fall 1994): 1, 4–7.

CHAPTER SIX: ABOUT JEWS

1. *Israelite* (January 16, 1863), 218.

2. Korn, *American Jewry and the Civil War,* 156-88.

3. AL to Edwin M. Stanton and Henry W. Halleck (Nov 14, 1863), Shapell Manuscript Collection; for an August 28, 1863, letter on the same subject, see CW 6, 419-20 and Milton Shutes, "The Case of Colonel William Mayer," *Lincoln Herald* 63 (1961), 24-26; an additional letter on Nov 14, 1863 AL to Stanton about Mayer raising troops, CW 10, 210. On Mayer, see the *New York Times* (April 18, 1906), 11; Korn, *American Jewry and the Civil War,* 117; Howard Rock, *Haven of Liberty: New York Jews in the New World 1654-1865* (New York: NYU Press, 2012), 248-49; Simon Wolf, *The American Jew as Patriot, Soldier and Citizen* (New York: Gregg Press, 1972 [orig. 1895]), 284.

4. War Department. The Office of the Judge Advocate General. Court Martial File No. NN-2345 (Moses Waldauer) in Court Martial Case Files 1809–1894. Record Group 153: Records of the Office the Judge Advocate General- Army. National Archives and Records Administration, National Archives Building, Washington, DC.

5. AL to Officer in Charge of Caroll Prison (January 8, 1865), Shapell Manuscript Collection; War Department, General Court Martial Orders #398 (December 30, 1864); Mark E. Neely, *The Fate of Liberty: Abraham Lincoln and Civil Liberties* (New York: Oxford, 1991), 99-103; AL to Joseph Holt (February 17, 1865), CW 8, 303-4; for the pardon, see War Department, General Court Martial, Orders No. 99 (February 18, 1865), Case Files of Investigations by Levi C. Turner and Lafayette C. Baker, compiled 1862-1865. NARA microfilm publication M797. Record Group 94, Records of the Adjutant General's Office. National Archives and Records Administration, National Archives Building, Washington, DC.

6. *Journal of the Executive Proceedings of the Senate of the United States of America* 13 (January 11-12, 1864), 369.

7. "Local News," *Evening Star,* Washington, DC (November 21, 1864).

8. National Archives online: Letter from Chief Justice D. K. Cartter and Andrew Wylie, Justice of the Supreme Court of D.C., 12/05/1864. http://research.archives.gov/description/6783000.

9. David Hirsch to AL (December 23, 1863), AL Papers, LOC; David Hirsch to Ulysses S. Grant (January 28, 1864), *The Papers of Ulysses S. Grant: January 1 - May 31, 1864,* Vol. 10 (Carbondale, IL: Southern Illinois University Press, 1982), 519-20; Jeffrey N. Lash, *A Politician Turned General: The Civil War Career of Stephen Augustus Hurlbut* (Kent, OH: Kent State University Press, 2003), 107-47, esp. 127-28.

10. J. W. Calvert et al to AL (September 9, 1864) AL Papers, LOC; AL notes (September 24, 26, 27, 1864), in the David Benjamin Family Collection.

11. AL to Hon. Sec of Navy (September 9, 1864), Shapell Manuscript Collection.

12. AL to Myers, January 13, 1865, CW 8

13. AL to Joseph H. Stiner (December 2, 1864), Shapell Manuscript Collection.

14. Mary Lincoln to General Patrick (September 24 [1864], Shapell Manuscript Collection.

15. David Rankin Barbee, "The Musical Mr. Lincoln," *Abraham Lincoln Quarterly* 5 (December 1949), 449-50, 452.

16. Mary Lincoln to General Patrick (September 24 [1864], Shapell Manuscript Collection; "City Point During the Civil War," *Encyclopedia Virginia,* http://www.encyclopediavirginia.org/City_Point_During_the_Civil_War (accessed April 7, 2014).

17. AL to L. J. Lieberman (July 15, 1864) Shapell Manuscript Collection. On Lieberman [Leberman], see Herbert S. Morais, *The Jews of Philadelphia* (Philadelphia: 1894), 58, 268, and on Rockhill and Wilson, see Mark R. Wilson, *The Business of Civil War* (Baltimore: Johns Hopkins University Press, 2006), 124.

18. Carr, Roland T. and Hugh Morrow, "We Found Lincoln's Lost Bank Account," *Saturday Evening Post,* February 14, 1953.

19. Robert Putnam, *American Grace: How Religion Divides and Unites Us* (New York: Simon & Schuster, 2010), 526-34.

20. Shapell Manuscript Collection, CW 6, 1-2; Leslie J. Perry, "Appeals to Lincoln's Clemency," *The Century*

Magazine 51 (December 1895), 252. On Thoroughman, see Howard L. Conard, *Encyclopedia of the History of Missouri* (New York: Haldeman, Conard, & Co., 1901), VI, 190.

21. *The Diary of Orville Hickman Browning,* Volume I, 1850-1863, eds. Theodore C. Pease and James G. Randall (Springfield: Illinois State Historical Society, 1927), 627 [April 16, 1863].

22. Amy E. Murrell, "Union Father, Rebel Son: Families and the Question of Civil War Loyalty," *The War Was You and Me: Civilians in the American Civil War,* ed. Joan E. Cashin (Princeton: Princeton University Press, 2002), 358-91; Sarna, *American Judaism,* 114.

23. "Postmaster Jonas and the Herald," *Quincy Daily Whig,* July 26, 1862. We are greatly indebted to Cynthia Gensheimer for this and other material concerning Abraham Jonas.

24. *Quincy in the Civil War: A View of the Great Conflict.* Charles A, Landrum, Quincy and Adams Historical Society, 1965; *Quincy Daily Whig,* October 21, 1862.

25. Robert Rosen, *The Jewish Confederates* (Columbia: University of South Carolina Press, 2000), 151.

26. *The Diary of Orville Hickman Browning,* Volume I, 1850-1863, eds. Theodore C. Pease and James G. Randall (Springfield: Illinois State Historical Society, 1927), 639.

27. Abraham Jonas to Abraham Lincoln (October 22, 1863), AL Papers, Library of Congress, online at lincolnpapers2.dataformat.com/images/1863/10/280384.pdf. We are indebted to Cynthia Gensheimer for bringing this letter to our attention. O. H. Hickman to W. Stanton (October 22, 1863), Records of the Commissary General of Prisoners, Letters Received, Box 17 (1863), RG 249, NARA.

28. W. Hoffman to Abraham Jonas (October 30, 1863), Records of the Commissary General of Prisoners, Letters & Telegrams Sent, vol. 5, R.G. 249, NARA.

29. O. H. Browning to Annie Jonas (June 2, 1864), Abraham Lincoln Presidential Library, Browning, O. H. SC 195 and in Charles M. Segal, "New Light on Lincoln's Parole of Charles H. Jonas," *Publications of the*

American Jewish Historical Society 42 (June 1953), 407-12; cf. *Diary of Orville Hickman Browning,* 671-672.

30. Order for Parole of Charles H. Jonas, Shapell Manuscript Collection (June 2, 1864).

31. Segal, "New Light on Lincoln's Parole," 412; Markens, *Lincoln and the Jews,* 20-21.

32. *Diary of Orville Hickman Browning,* 672; Cynthia Gensheimer, "Annie Jonas Wells: Jewish Daughter, Episcopal Wife, Independent Intellectual," *American Jewish History* 98 (July 2014), 102 n. 98.

33. George B. Jonas to Abraham Lincoln (August 31, 1864), AL Papers, LOC.

34. See above, chapter 3, nn. 1-3.

35. David H. Donald, *Lincoln* (New York: Simon & Schuster, 1995), 569-70; Thomas Bogar, *American Presidents Attend the Theatre* (Jefferson, NC: McFarland, 2006), 103; cf. David I. Kertzer, *The Kidnapping of Edgardo Mortara* (New York: Knopf, 1997), 252.

36. Some sources credit the play (partly or wholly) to Jean-François Mocquard; see, for example, Olive Logan, "Mocquard," *Harper's New Monthly Magazine* 36 (December 1867-May 1868), 114. Modern scholarship credits Séjour.

37. "Albion, 1863," *Bulletin of the New York Public Library* 44 (New York: New York Public Library,1940); *L'Ami de la Religion* as quoted in Victor Séjour, *The Fortune Teller,* translated from the French by Norman Shapiro. Introduction by M. Lynn Weiss (Urbana: University of Illinois Press, 2002), xxi.

38. Séjour, *The Fortune Teller,* translated from the French by Norman Shapiro. Introduction by M. Lynn Weiss, makes available the original French play in translation, with an illuminating introduction; for quote, see p. 162. While I have not located the text of the nineteenth-century English adaptation, which included music for Vestvali to sing, a synopsis of the play survives in *Vestvali in English Drama: "Monday, March 28th, 1864, at the Boston Theatre in the New and Powerful Drama . . . Called Gamea; Or—the Jewish Mother"* (Boston 1864).

39. Thomas A. Bogar, *American Presidents Attend the Theatre* (Detroit:McFarland, 2006), 103

40. Sejour, *The Fortune-Teller,* xxii-xxiii.

41. CW 7, 514; Burlingame, *Abraham Lincoln,* II, 704-10.

42. Samuel A. Lewis to Abraham Lincoln (October 26, 1864), AL Papers, LOC.

43. AL to W. P. Fessenden (August 2, 1864), Brown University Library, https://repository.library.brown.edu/studio/item/bdr%3A72310/ and in CW Supplement I, 253-54.

44. AL to Isachar Zacharie (September 19, 1864), CW 8, 12.

45. I. Zacharie to W. H.Seward (September 21, 1864) reprinted in Segal, "Isachar Zacharie," 116.

46. Ibid, and Korn, *American Jewry and the Civil War,* 199-200.

47. AL to Isachar Zacharie (September 19, 1864), CW 8, 12.

48. *New York Times* (September 23, 29, 1864); Segal, "Isachar Zacharie," 114, 116-17.

49. Burlingame, *Abraham Lincoln,* II, 721.

50. Samuel A. Lewis to AL (October 26, 1864), AL Papers, LOC; John Hay to Myer S. Isaacs (November 1, 1864), AL Papers, LOC; *Jewish Messenger* (October 28, 1864), 124.

51. Myer S. Isaacs to AL (October 26, 1864), AL Papers LOC.

52. Isachar Zacharie to AL (November 3, 1864), AL Papers, LOC [English slightly modernized].

53. Burlingame, *Abraham Lincoln,* II, 681-730.

54. Isachar Zacharie to AL (November 3, 1864), AL Papers, LOC.

55. Isachar Zacharie to AL (December 26, 1864), AL Papers LOC.

56. Pass for Isachar Zacharie (December 27, 1864); AL to William T. Sherman (December 27, 1864), Lincoln Collection at Brown University.

57. Pass for J. G. Cohen from New York to Savannah, Shapell Manuscript Collection. See the obituary for Cohen in the *New York Times* (January 21, 1900) and the sketch of his son, Eugene Yancey Cohen, in *Universities and the Sons: History, Influence and Characteristics of American Universities, with Biographical Sketches,* ed. Joshua L. Chamberlain (Boston: Herndon, 1899), 160.

58. I. Zacharie to AL (n.d.[December 28, 1864?])AL Papers, LOC. Roy Basler (CW 8, 238) argues that this undated letter "seems certainly to have been written after January 25, 1865," but the Lincoln Papers cataloged it in December 1864, and that fits the chronology much better.

59. John C. Gray Jr. to Elizabeth Gray (January 14, 1865) in J*ohn Chipman Gray and John Codman Ropes, War Letters 1862-1865* (Cambridge: Riverside Press, 1927), 442.

60. Ibid, 14; Wolf, *Presidents I have Known,* 10-11, speaks favorably of Stanton, who freed him when he was arbitrarily arrested for belonging to B'nai B'rith and thereby "helping the traitors."

61. Benjamin P. Thomas and Harold M. Hyman, *Stanton: The Life and Times of Lincoln's Secretary of War* (New York: Knopf, 1962), 346.

62. In his memoirs, William T. Sherman insinuated that Stanton himself engaged in corrupt practices in Savannah, but Sherman despised the secretary of war, and historians have not given this charge credence; see William Tecumseh Sherman, *Memoirs of William T. Sherman* (New York: Library of America, 1990), 723.

63. AL to Edwin M. Stanton (January 25, 1865), CW8, 238.

64. Ibid.

65. Edwin M. Stanton to AL (January 25, 1865); William G. Moore to John G. Nicolay (January 25, 1865), AL Papers, LOC.

66. *New York Times* (February 22, 1865), 8.

67. On Leopold Blumenberg, see Isaac Markens, *The Hebrews in America* (New York: 1888), 131-32; Wolf, *The American Jew as Patriot, Soldier and Citizen,* 199-200; *Universal Jewish Encyclopedia* (1940), 2: 418; Isaac M. Fein, *The Making of an American Jewish Community* (Philadelphia: Jewish Publication Society, 1971), 99; Jacob R. Marcus, *United States Jewry 1776-1985* (Detroit: Wayne State University Press, 1993), 39-40; and notes to the letters quoted below.

68. AL, Pardon of Rudolph Blumenberg (July 25, 1863), Shapell Manuscript Collection, item 1525; Warren S. Howard, *American Slavers and the Federal Law 1837-1862* (Berkeley and Los Angeles: University of California Press, 1963), 176; *New York Daily Tribune* (July 31, 1863), 5.

69. Markens, *The Hebrews in America,* 132; see also John L. Chapman to AL (November 25, 1864) AL Papers, LOC.

70. Edwin M. Stanton to AL (January 25, 1865), AL Papers, LOC.

71. AL to Edwin M. Stanton (January 25, 1865), CW 8, 238.

72. Edwin M. Stanton to AL (January 25, 1865), AL Papers, LOC.

73. Abraham Lincoln, Memorandum on Maryland Patronage (March 9, 1865), AL Papers, LOC.

74. Bertram W. Korn, "Lincoln and the Jews," *Journal of the Illinois State Historical Society* 48 (Summer 1955), 190.

75. For what follows except where otherwise noted, see *Jewish Messenger* (February 17, 1865), 5, and for background, Markens, *Abraham Lincoln and the Jews,* 57, and Early S. Miers, *Lincoln Day by Day* (Dayton: Morningside, 1991), 3:313.

76. John C. Gray Jr. to Elizabeth Gray (January 14, 1865) in *Gray and Ropes, War Letters 1862-1865,* 442.

77. *Jewish Messenger* (February 17, 1865), 5 and Zola, *We Called Him Rabbi Abraham,* 129-30, 135-37.

CHAPTER SEVEN: TO SEE JERUSALEM BEFORE HE DIED

1. Andrew Morrison, *Theatre Guide of Washington D.C.* (Washington: The Theatre Historical Society, 1972); "Civil War Washington," http://civilwardc.org/data/places/view/316 (accessed March 30, 2014); *The Lincoln Log,* January 7, 1865, http://www.thelincolnlog.org/ (accessed March 30, 2014).

2. Augustin Daly, *Leah, The Forsaken* (New York: Samuel French, n.d.), 8, 9, 20.

3. Ibid, 13-14.

4. Ibid, 41.

5. Ibid, 42.

6. Ibid, 44.

7. *Jewish Messenger* (February 6, 1863), 50.

8. "Leah," *Harper's Weekly* (March 7, 1863), 146; for the attribution to Curtis, see Louis Harap, *The Image of the Jew in American Literature from Early Republic to Mass Immigration* (Philadelphia: Jewish Publication Society, 1974), 218.

9. Chaim Milikowsky, *Seder Olam: Critical Edition, Commentary, and Introduction* (Jerusalem: Yad Ben Zvi Press, 2013), I, 249; II, 180 (in Hebrew).

10. David Herbert Donald, *Lincoln* (New York: Simon & Schuster, 1995), p.56

11. Frederick Douglass, *Life and Times of Frederick Douglass* (Hartford: Park Publishing Company, 1882), 402; Ronald C. White Jr., *A. Lincoln: A Biography* (New York: Random House, 2009), 663, 667.

12. CW8, 332-333.

13. CW 8, 333. At the time, the meaning of "sunk" in this context referred to being repaid.

14. James Mitchell Foster, *Christ Is King* (Boston: James H. Earle, 1894) 26, 37; Gary P. Zola, *We Called Him Rabbi Abraham: Lincoln and American Jewry—A Documentary History* (Carbondale: Southern Illinois University Press, 2014), 117-137. Lance Sussman, *Isaac*

Leeser and the Making of American Judaism (Detroit: Wayne State University Press, 1995), 226-27.

15.   *Jewish Messenger* (March 17,1865), 96.

16.   AL to Thurlow Weed (March 15, 1865), Shapell Legacy Partnership, CW 8, 356. For other responses, see Burlingame, *Abraham Lincoln,* II, 770-772.

17.   Edwin M. Stanton to AL (April 3, 1865), CW 8, 384-85; AL to Stanton (April 3, 1865, 5:00 P.M.), Shapell Legacy Partnership , CW8, 385; Burlingame, *Abraham Lincoln* II, 780, 787-88.

18.   As quoted in Burlingame, *Abraham Lincoln,* II, 788.

19.   Ibid, II, 790.

20.   Jacob R. Marcus, *Memoirs of American Jews 1775-1865* (Philadelphia: Jewish Publication Society, 1955), III, 333; Emily Bingham, *Mordecai: An Early American Family* (New York: Hill & Wang, 2003), 258.

21.   On Myers, see Herbert T. Ezekiel and Gaston Lichtenstein, *The History of the Jews of Richmond from 1769 to 1917* (Richmond: Ezekiel, 1917), 60-62; Myron Berman, *Richmond's Jewry 1769-1976* (Charlottesville: University Press of Virginia, 1979), 127-29; Eli Evans, *Judah P. Benjamin: The Jewish Confederate* (New York: Free Press, 1988), 198-200.

22.   Theresa M. Guzman-Stokes, "A Flag and a Family: Richard Gill Forrester, 1847-1906," *Virginia Cavalcade* 47:2 (Spring 1998), 52-63.

23.   "Abraham Lincoln in Richmond," *Virginia Magazine of History and Biography* 41 (October 1933), 318-22; AL Memorandum on Conditions for Peace [April 5, 1865], AL Papers, LOC; CW 8, 386-87; Burlingame, *Abraham Lincoln* II, 792-793.

24.   AL to Joshua F. Speed, August 24, 1855; CW 2, 321.

25.   Don E. Fehrenbacher and Virginia Fehrenbacher, *Recollected Words of Abraham Lincoln* (Stanford: Stanford University Press, 1996), 182.

26.   James McPherson, *Battle Cry of Freedom: The Civil War Era* (New York: Oxford, 1988), 849-50.

27.   *New York Herald* as quoted in the *Jewish Messenger* (April 21, 1865), 124; *Boston Daily Advertiser* (April 13, 1865), col. B.

28.   AL to Michael Hahn (March 13, 1864), Shapell Legacy Partnership.

29.   Burlingame, *Abraham Lincoln,* II, 608.

30.   CW 8, 399-405.

31.   Burlingame, *Abraham Lincoln,* II, 803; McPherson, *Battle Cry of Freedom,* 852.

32.   *American Hebrew* (February 6, 1885), 202; *Washington Post* (November 9, 1902), 26; *American Israelite* (June 29, 1893), 4; Arthur Hornblow, *A History of the Theatre in America* (Philadelphia: Lippincott, 1919), I, 320. Stephen M. Arthur, *Junius Brutus Booth: Theatrical Prometheus* (Carbondale: Southern Illinois University Press, 1992), 4, considers the family legend "untrustworthy."

33.   Asia Booth Clarke, *The Elder and the Younger Booth* (Boston: Osgood, 1882), 114, cf. 49.

34.   *American Israelite* (June 29, 1893), 4; *Jewish Messenger* (November 7, 1862), 139; (November 14, 1862), 147.

35.   Simon Wolf, *The Presidents I have Known from 1860-1918* (Washington: Byron Adams, 1918), 12; Isaac Markens, "Jews Mourned for Lincoln," *American Hebrew* (April 9, 1915), 671.

36.   Gideon Welles, *Diary of Gideon Welles* (Boston: Houghton Mifflin Company, 1911), II, 280-83.

37.   Max Lilienthal, "The Flag and the Union," in David Philipson, *Max Lilienthal: American Rabbi* (New York: Bloch, 1915), 398-414 [the volume misdates the lecture, which was actually delivered on April 14, 1865], cf. *Israelite* (April 28, 1865), 348; Bruce l. Ruben, *Max Lilienthal: The Making of the American Rabbinate* (Detroit: Wayne State University Press, 2011), 179-83.

38.   *Jewish Messenger* (November 1, 1895), 2.

39.   Burlingame, *Abraham Lincoln,* II, 816-17; Thomas A. Bogart, *Backstage at the Lincoln Assassination: The Untold Story of the Actors and Stagehands at Ford's Theatre* (Washington, DC: Regnery History, 2013), 84.

40. "Necrology: Dr. Charles H. Liebermann," *Journal of the American Medical Association* 7 (1886), 222-23; "The Romance of Liebermann," *Journal of the American Medical Association* 22 (1894), 291-92; Edward W. Markens, *Lincoln and His Relations to Doctors* (Newark: 1922), 8; Samuel H. Holland, "Charles H. Liebermann, M.D.: An Early Russian-born Physician of Washington DC," *Medical Annals of the District of Columbia* 38 (September 1969), 499-504; http://www.medicalmuseum.mil/index.cfm?p=exhibits.lincoln.page_03 (accessed 2/23/2014); Robert Emmett Curran, *The Bicentennial History of Georgetown University: From Academy to University 1789-1889* (Washington: Georgetown University Press, 1993), 146-47; for Liebermann's effort to be compensated for emancipating his slave, see http://civilwardc.org/texts/petitions/cww.00782.html.

41. As quoted in Donald, *Lincoln,* 598.

42. Shapell Manuscript Collection

43. Wolf, *The Presidents I Have Known,* 13.

44. *Jewish Messenger* (April 21, 1865), 124.

45. *Occident* (May 1, 1865), 36.

46. *The Hebrew,* San Francisco (April 21, 1865) as quoted in William M. Kramer, "They Have Killed Our Man But Not Our Cause: The California Jewish Mourners of Abraham Lincoln," *Western States Jewish Historical Quarterly* 2 (July 1970), 194.

47. "An Address Delivered before the Springfield Washington Temperance Society, on the 22d February, 1842," CW 1, 278.

48. Ezekiel 37:11-12.

49. Justin G. Turner and Linda Levitt Turner, *Mary Todd Lincoln: Her Life and Letters* (New York: Alfred A. Knopf, 1972), 218, cf. 400.

EPILOGUE

1. *Jewish Messenger* (May 5, 1865), 139. "Semi-Occasional" was the nom de plume of Adolphus Solomons; see Isaac Markens, *The Hebrews in America* (New York: 1888), 248.

2. *The New York Times* (April 16, 1865), 9.

3. *Jewish Messenger* (April 21, 1865), 124: Kramer, "They Have Killed Our Man but Not Our Cause," 195.

4. W. Hunter, Acting Secretary of State to the People of the United States (April 17, 1865) in William T. Coggeshall, *Lincoln Memorial: The Journeys of Abraham Lincoln: from Springfield to Washington, 1861, as President Elect; and from Washington to Springfield, 1865, as President Martyred; Comprising an Account of Public Ceremonies on the Entire Route, and Full Details of Both Journeys* (Columbus: Ohio State Journal, 1865), 112.

5. A. Guinzberg (April 25, 1865), as quoted in *Israelite* (May 26, 1865), 181; see also Samuel M. Isaacs at Broadway Synagogue in Hertz, *Abraham Lincoln: The Tribute of the Synagogue,* 71-77.

6. Congregation Mikveh Israel in *Occident* (May 1, 1865), 36.

7. Hertz, *Abraham Lincoln: The Tribute of the Synagogue,* 183; see Michael H. Mehlman, " 'There Is a Prince and a Great Man Fallen This Day in Israel': The Response of the Rabbis in America to the Assassination of Abraham Lincoln, April-June 1865," *Lincoln Herald* 111 (2009), 213-14.

8. Zola, *We Called Him Rabbi Abraham,* 165-67.

9. *Israelite* (April 21, 1865), 339; Hertz, *Abraham Lincoln: The Tribute of the Synagogue,* 98. Rabbi Benjamin Szold, as if in answer to Wise, declared that "if he was not as it is said, flesh of our flesh or bone of our bone, he was mind of our mind and soul of our soul" [Alexandra Lee Levin, *The Szolds of Lombard Street* (Philadelphia: Jewish Publication Society, 1960), 42].

10. *Chicago Tribune* (April 17, 1865); see Liebmann Adler's angry response in *Abraham Lincoln: The Tribute of the Synagogue,*143; cf. *The Jeffersonian* (May 11, 1865), http://chroniclingamerica.loc.gov/lccn/sn84026399/1865-05-11/ed-1/seq-2/.

11. Zola, *We Called Him Rabbi Abraham,* 140; and for Protestant sermons, David B. Chesebrough, "No Sorrow Like Our Sorrow" in *Northern Protestant Ministers and the Assassination of Lincoln* (Kent: Kent State University Press, 1994).

12. *Jewish Messenger* (April 28, 1865), 4; the *Jewish Record*'s calculation was somewhat more conservative; see its description of the pageant in Korn, *American Jewry and the Civil War,* 239-43.

13. Coggeshall, *Lincoln Memorial,* 221-22, 274, 294, 307; Morris A. Gutstein, *A Priceless Heritage: The Epic Growth of Nineteenth Century Chicago Jewry* (New York: Bloch, 1953), 333; Korn, *American Jewry and the Civil War,* 214; Markens, *Abraham Lincoln and the Jews,* 22.

14. *Jewish Messenger* (April 28, 1865) 4.

15. Andrew Johnson Executive Order (May 31, 1865), http://www.presidency.ucsb.edu/ws/index.php?pid=72168.

16. Andrew Johnson, "Proclamation 130—Postponing the Day of Mourning for the Death of President Lincoln Until June 1" (April 29, 1865), http://www.presidency.ucsb.edu/ws/index.php?pid=72245.

17. *Jewish Messenger* (May 5, 1865), 140.

18. Charles F. Adams, *Charles Francis Adams 1835-1915: An Autobiography* (Cambridge: Riverside, 1916), 94

19. Hertz, *Abraham Lincoln: The Tribute of the Synagogue,* 9-10.

20. *Jewish Messenger* (June 9, 1865), 180; Israelite (June 16, 1865), 404.

21. *The New York Times* (June 2, 1865), 1.

22. Hertz, *Abraham Lincoln: The Tribute of the Synagogue,* 176, cf. 20. 39, 63, 145, 151, 164; Zola, *We Called Him Rabbi Abraham,* 178-90.

23. All of these are reported by Isaac Markens in "Jews Mourned for Lincoln," *American Hebrew* (April 9, 1915), 665, 671; see also *Universe Israelite* (July 1865), 506.

24. Jacob R. Marcus, *Memoirs of American Jews* (Philadelphia: Jewish Publication Society, 1955), III, 367.

25. S. Joshua Kohn, "David Naar of Trenton, New Jersey," *American Jewish Historical Quarterly* 53 (June 1964), 373-95; David Naar to Isaac Leeser (May 24, 1865), Shapell Manuscript Collection; *Occident* (July 1, 1865), 172-74.

26. *Jewish Messenger* (May 26, 1865), 165; Zola, *We Called Him Rabbi Abraham,* 220 includes a translation, which we have slightly altered. On Goldstein, see Jacob Kabakoff, "Isaac Goldstein—Pioneer Merchant-Author," *Seekers and Stalwarts: Essays and Studies on American Hebrew Literature and Culture* (Jerusalem: Rubin Mass, 1978), 11-19. Goldstein's poem was likely written in the wake of the Emancipation Proclamation but was only published following the assassination.

27. Justin G. Turner, *A Note on Solomon Nunes Carvalho and His Portrait of Abraham Lincoln* (Los Angeles: Plantin Press, 1960); Agnes Halsey, "A 'New' Lincoln Portrait by Solomon Nunes Carvalho" *Old Printshop Portfolio* 11:6 (February 1952), 122-127, 129; Joan Sturhahn *Carvalho, Artist-Photographer-Adventurer-Patriot: Portrait of a Forgotten American* (New York: Richwood, 1976), 162-65 (Sturhahn believes that that the 1865 painting was completed just prior to the assassination).

28. Markens, *Abraham Lincoln and the Jews,* 29–31; David Ward, "Photographic Imagery," in *Abraham Lincoln: Great American Historians on Our Sixteenth President,* eds. Brian Lamb and Susan Swain (New York: Public Affairs, 2008), 162.

29. Sabato Morais to Alexander Henry (June 21, 1865), Shapell Manuscript Collection; Hertz, *Abraham Lincoln: The Tribute of the Synagogue,* 11; *New York Times* (March 8, 1868), 6. Rev. Jacques Judah Lyons of Shearith Israel and the *Jewish Messenger* briefly collected contributions toward a monument for Lincoln in New York; see *Jewish Messenger* (May 12, 1865), 145.

30. *Israelite* (June 9, 1865), 397.

31. *Israelite* (July 7, 1865), 5.

32. *Jewish Messenger* (January 11, 1867), 4; Zola, *We Called Him Rabbi Abraham,* 239-41.

33. Merrill D. Peterson, *Lincoln in American Memory* (New York: Oxford, 1994), 53-55; *New York Times* (January 7, 1932), 18.

34. *American Israelite* (May 7, 1886), 6.

35. Peterson, *Lincoln in American Memory,* passim. For details, see Zola, *We Called Him Rabbi Abraham.*

ACKNOWLEDGMENTS

Soon after I completed the first draft of this book, I suffered cardiac arrest on the streets of New Haven. The miraculous work of Dr. Grant Bailey, who jumped out of his car and expertly performed CPR, saved my life. An army of other dedicated doctors and nurses at Yale-New Haven Hospital and Brigham and Women's Hospital in Boston facilitated my recovery. Thanks to them, I was able to see *Lincoln and the Jews: A History* through to its final stages.

My collaborator, Benjamin Shapell, conceived this project and placed his remarkable team of researchers and writers at my disposal. Without the efforts of Menachem Grossman, Ariane Weisel Margalit, Sara Willen, Dina Grossman, Janice Parente, and Michal Gorlin Becker, this book would never have come into being. It was a great privilege to be able to access Ben's remarkable private collection of Lincolniana. This book also makes abundant use of the 20,000 documents in the Abraham Lincoln Papers of the Library of Congress, many of them now online; Roy P. Basler's *The Collected Works of Abraham Lincoln;* the collection of the Abraham Lincoln Presidential Library & Museum; and an array of Jewish and general newspapers, many of them now also available online.

Everyone who writes about Abraham Lincoln knows that they stand on the shoulders of giants: generations of formidable Lincoln scholars who produced majestic works. This book makes abundant use of previous secondary scholarship, both well known and obscure, even as it breaks new ground in exploring Lincoln's relationship with Jews. I extend special thanks to the interlibrary loan office at Brandeis University for tracking down rare Lincoln-related publications for me, mystified as its librarians doubtless were by my unlikely interest in the history of chiropody!

Numerous friends and colleagues assisted with this book in different ways. Cynthia Gensheimer alerted me to the existence of invaluable private correspondence in the possession of the Wells family. Gary Zola sent me an advanced copy of his own *We Called Him Rabbi Abraham: Lincoln and American Jewry* and placed the remarkable holdings of the American Jewish Archives at my disposal. He and Adam Mendelsohn read and commented on the entire manuscript, offering invaluable suggestions. Carolyn Hessel offered friendship, guidance, support, and criticism—always in the right proportions and at the right time. Sylvia Barack Fishman, my department chair during this project, championed the project and left me time to complete it. I also learned much from discussions with T. Forcht Dagi, David Dalin, Menachem Genack, Shalom Lamm, David Saperstein, and John Stauffer. In addition, I thank the late Dr. Bernard G. Sarnat and Rhoda G. Sarnat, who established the Bernard G. and Rhoda G. Sarnat Center for the Study of Anti-Jewishness, which I direct, and Lawrence E. and Nancy S. Glick, who made the Joseph H. & Belle R. Braun Chair in American Jewish history at Brandeis possible.

Finally, I thank my amazing family. While they may sometimes have tired of hearing about Lincoln, they never flagged in their love and devotion—not even when that meant sitting at my bedside for hours at a time while I battled to live. My children, Aaron and Leah; Aaron's wonderful wife, Talya; and her parents, Robert and Sue Housman; my brother, David, and his family; my in-laws, Elinor & James Langer; and above all, my wondrous wife, Ruth Langer, are the unsung heroes of this book. Their encouragement and fortitude recall one of Abraham Lincoln's most telling aphorisms: "Your own resolution to succeed is more important than any other one thing."

—*Dr. Jonathan D. Sarna*

Over many years it has been my dream to one day publish a book on Lincoln and the Jews as seen literally in his own hand, through letters in my own collection, as well as those in other archives. I feel very fortunate now in having been privileged to work with so many people who shared this vision, and who worked so passionately to give it a voice.

I wish to thank, first and foremost, my co-author, Jonathan Sarna, with whom it has been for me a great honor to collaborate on this work, which began in 2011 with brainstorming sessions in his Boston office. Without his scholarship and expertise this book would have remained just a dream. I am thankful that Jonathan is on the road to recovery and wish him continued strength.

Though mentioned previously by Jonathan but well worth repeating, I am particularly indebted to the tireless efforts of Menachem Grossman, Ariane Weisel Margalit, and Sara Willen, as well as Dina Grossman and Michal Gorlin Becker. Working with them has been a great privilege for me, and I appreciate more than they know their devotion to this work.

The images in this book bring Lincoln's association with Jews to a new and intimate understanding never before seen, and I am eternally grateful to my longtime and trusted friend Joseph Maddalena for his keen eye,

guidance, and selfless devotion in helping me build the collection to what it is today.

The Shapell Manuscript Foundation has been fortunate to have on its staff wonderful researchers and consultants who have contributed to this book in invaluable ways: Dr. John Sellers, with whom I worked on a joint exhibition with the Library of Congress on the occasion of Lincoln's Bicentennial in 2009; Adrienne Usher, Sharon Hannon, Adam Geibel, Janice Parente, Caitlin Eichner, fellow Lincoln (and Twain) enthusiast Tony Travis, Jamie Levavi, Clark Hall, Brian Chanes, and Dyon Maki. In particular I'd like to thank my good friend and fellow collector Bob Marcus, with whom I have shared many fascinating conversations on Lincoln and Jewish Civil War soldiers.

I also want to thank Carolyn Hessel and Marcia Markland: their indefatigable stewardship of this project has been instrumental in bringing the book to life.

My sincere thanks to Eileen Mackevich and Carla Knorowski at the Papers of Abraham Lincoln in Springfield for all their wonderful assistance and professionalism, and especially Daniel Stowell, whose generous sharing of images and original research has so consistently advanced Lincoln scholarship.

Of course to my family, I owe everything, and offer, finally, this book to them in tribute to their patience, understanding, and inspiration. My parents, David and Fela Shapell, who recently celebrated their sixty-fifth wedding anniversary and whose philanthropy and generosity know no bounds; my wife, Susan, and our four wonderful children, Jennifer, Adam, Andy, and Rachel; Jennifer's husband, Mark Smith, and their two daughters, Kaitlin and Alexandra; and Adam's wife, Elisheva, who have all patiently endured what has been my lifetime obsession with Lincoln.

—*Benjamin Shapell*

INDEX

Page locators in *italic* refer to illustrations and accompanying captions. **Bold** entries indicate titles of boxes.